The Internal Colony

The Internal Colony

Race and the American Politics of Global Decolonization

SAM KLUG

The University of Chicago Press
Chicago and London

Publication of this book has been aided by the Meijer Foundation Publication Fund, which supports books of enduring interest in the disciplines of American political history, political science, and related areas.

The University of Chicago Press, Chicago 60637
The University of Chicago Press, Ltd., London
© 2025 by The University of Chicago
Published 2025
Printed in the United States of America

34 33 32 31 30 29 28 27 26 25   2 3 4 5

ISBN-13: 978-0-226-82051-4 (cloth)
ISBN-13: 978-0-226-82052-1 (e-book)
DOI: https://doi.org/10.7208/chicago/9780226820521.001.0001

Library of Congress Cataloging-in-Publication Data

Names: Klug, Sam, author.
Title: The internal colony : race and the American politics of global decolonization / Sam Klug.
Other titles: Race and the American politics of global decolonization
Description: Chicago ; London : The University of Chicago Press, 2025. | Includes bibliographical references and index.
Identifiers: LCCN 2024023286 | ISBN 9780226820514 (cloth) | ISBN 9780226820521 (ebook)
Subjects: LCSH: African Americans—Political activity—History—20th century. | African Americans—Intellectual life—20th century. | Internationalism. | Black nationalism—United States—History—20th century. | Black power—United States. | Colonies. | Decolonization. | World politics—1945–1989. | United States—Politics and government—1945–1989. | United States—Social policy.
Classification: LCC E185.61 .K565 2025 | DDC 320.54089/96—dc23/eng/20240712
LC record available at https://lccn.loc.gov/2024023286

♾ This paper meets the requirements of ANSI/NISO Z39.48-1992 (Permanence of Paper).

For my parents, and Maddy

A vocabulary to use, to find our own ways in, to change as we find it necessary to change it, as we go on making our own language and history.

RAYMOND WILLIAMS

Contents

Introduction

On the afternoon of April 25, 1969, James Boggs rose to deliver a speech to a crowded auditorium at Wayne State University in Detroit. An African American autoworker, activist, and writer, Boggs had left his job at a Chrysler plant the previous year to focus his time and attention on the Black Power movement. His remarks, which were part of the opening day of the National Black Economic Development Conference (NBEDC), skewered President Richard Nixon's promotion of "Black capitalism" as an antipoverty strategy. Nixon's policy platform emphasized private enterprise, rather than the government programs of the Lyndon Johnson administration's War on Poverty, as the solution to Black poverty. This agenda had attracted support from some civil rights leaders and Black politicians. But Boggs saw it as a misdiagnosis at best and at worst an intentional effort to subject Black Americans to continuing economic hardship.[1]

Boggs elaborated his criticisms of Nixon's programs through a sustained comparison between the economic predicament of Black America and that of the colonial and postcolonial world. "Black America is underdeveloped today because of capitalist semi-colonialism," he proclaimed, "just as Africa, Asia and Latin America are underdeveloped today because of capitalist colonialism." This comparison was not an assertion of equivalence. In fact, Boggs argued, the distinctions between the colonial underdevelopment of much of the world and the underdevelopment of Black America made it necessary to consider this relation closely. Whereas European colonial powers turned their colonies into "one-crop countries to supply raw materials or agricultural produce to the Western imperialists," the underdevelopment of Black communities in the United States was "the direct result of industrial development, which has turned these communities into wastelands, abandoned by an

industry that has undergone technological revolutions." The five hundred attendees of the NBEDC, which included civil rights luminaries such as Fannie
Lou Hamer and Julian Bond, and even former football star Jim Brown, would
not have been surprised by Boggs's language. By 1969, colonial comparisons
like this one had become part of the lingua franca of Black Americans' analyses of domestic social policy.[2]

One year earlier, such comparisons had drawn the attention of two of the
country's foremost experts on national security. Albert and Roberta Wohlstetter, formerly strategists at the RAND Corporation who had recently moved to
the University of Chicago, were among the most influential and sought-after
authorities on nuclear strategy and military intelligence. Throughout the
1950s and 1960s, their writings focused on what Albert Wohlstetter described
as the "delicate balance of terror" that the US maintained in its conflict with
the Soviet Union in the thermonuclear age. After the unprecedented spate
of urban uprisings that followed the assassination of Martin Luther King Jr.,
these experts in the science of apocalypse identified a new threat. Unexpected
danger, they argued, lurked in the vocabulary Americans used to describe
racial and class conflict in their own country.[3]

The widespread use of analogies between the global system of colonialism and racial inequality within American society alarmed the Wohlstetters.
"'Colonialism,' they wrote in a RAND Corporation working paper in August
1968, "is a rich source of varied metaphor." They took note of a proliferation of such metaphors over the preceding years, from depictions of urban
violence as "guerrilla war" to analyses of the political economy of American
racism. The language of colonialism was increasingly in vogue, they noted,
to refer to the "large handicaps placed on the Negro in America in acquir-
ing and using his skills productively to earn income, in choosing a place to
live, and in taking part in the political process." Yet to view the political and
economic position of Black Americans as akin to that of colonial subjects, in
their view, only "evoke[d] a cloud of ideologies of economic development"
that could "confuse analysis of the actual problem of improving the status of
the Negro in the United States."[4]

Most important, in the Wohlstetters' estimation, was just how widely
these colonial comparisons had spread across the American scene. It was not
only Black Power advocates such as James Boggs who employed this "evocative" language. In fact, they noted, it had equally seduced many "civil rights
moderates" and "some able social scientists." Even Nixon himself sometimes
relied on a colonial analogy to promote the very program of "Black capitalism" that Boggs excoriated. Talk of colonialism, it seemed, was everywhere.[5]

Discussions of politics and economics in the midcentury United States referred often to the history of European and American colonial rule in Africa, Asia, Latin America, and the Caribbean, and to the ongoing process of decolonization. Colonial comparisons were marshaled in struggles over how to define the US system of government, its racial order, and its political economy. These definitional contests, waged by state actors and by movement activists such as Boggs, reached a peak of intensity in the 1960s. Paul Potter, cofounder of Students for a Democratic Society (SDS), captured the perceived urgency of projects of definition when he famously declared, at an anti–Vietnam War march in 1965, "We must name [the] system."[6] The Wohlstetters' panicked proclamations represented a project of definition of their own. By attempting to rule out references to colonialism in discussions of race and economics in the United States, these thinkers only testified to their importance.

Naming the system is always a relational activity. Every effort to promulgate new terms of social analysis implies, or states outright, a rejection of competing terminologies and modes of description. Prominent labels given to American society in the decades following the Second World War often contrasted the prosperity of the postwar years with the years of the Great Depression or drew distinctions among the global hegemon of the United States, the crumbling European empires, and the Soviet Union. This bundle of semantic innovations construed the United States as a land of material security and a polity defined by consensus: an "affluent society," which bred a politics that had reached the "end of ideology." Yet the "politics of nominalization" in the postwar United States were also deeply entangled with global decolonization.[7]

African American internationalists—Black thinkers and activists who viewed the American racial order in global terms—were especially important to the story of these entanglements. The idea that African Americans constituted an *internal colony* represented the most prominent attempt to rethink race and political economy in the United States in terms of colonialism and decolonization. This idea both constituted an important part of the political thought of the Black Power movement and had an influence well beyond it. The concept of the internal colony provides a skeleton key for understanding the influence of colonial comparisons on US politics in the postwar era.[8]

Between the Second World War and the middle of the 1970s, conflicts over how to define colonialism and how to understand its relation to American racial and class inequality pervaded both internal debates within the Black freedom movement and struggles between Black activists and state policymakers. These conflicts first surfaced in foreign policy, as Black activists advocated for anticolonial priorities in debates about the creation of the United Nations and the formation of US international development policy. But ideas formed in relation to what are often considered foreign affairs soon migrated to domestic politics. The question of how colonialism should be defined became a fault line of American political debate in the 1960s. Leading liberal thinkers promoted an image of the United States as the first postcolonial state, and antipoverty policymakers sought to apply domestically the lessons of international development policy. At the same time, many Black activists and writers began to envisage the African American population as an internal colony, employing in domestic policy debates a language of colonialism and decolonization drawn from the longer history of Black internationalism. The end of empire transformed the terms of debate over race and class in the twentieth-century United States.

Since well before the middle of the twentieth century, African American thinkers had understood the United States' particular forms of racial hierarchy, both during slavery and after Emancipation, in relation to the global system of colonial rule. Nineteenth-century abolitionist Martin Delany's vision of Black Americans—both enslaved and free—as constituting a "nation within a nation" relied on an explicit linkage to European empires. As Delany put it in 1852, "We are a nation within a nation, as the Poles in Russia, the Hungarians in Austria, the Welsh, Irish and Scotch in the British dominions." Delany's references illuminate the exemplarity of intra-European imperialisms before the establishment of the British Raj in India in 1858 and the assertions of political sovereignty by European powers over much of Africa in the period surrounding the Berlin Conference of 1884. His comparisons further suggest that he saw relations of political-economic inequality and cultural domination that were not explicitly racialized as directly relevant to the struggle for African American freedom. Delany envisioned American slavery, and racial inequality more broadly, as linked to European imperial domination through their shared suppression of the collective, national identities of subordinate groups. At the same time, both for Delany and for the broader tradition of Black nationalism he helped to inaugurate, claims to nationhood did not always entail demands for territorial sovereignty and political separatism.[9]

The notion that African Americans constituted a "nation within a nation" was an ideologically flexible one. It held a place in several distinct political formations in the early twentieth century. Marcus Garvey's Universal Negro Improvement Association (UNIA) cultivated a sense of nationhood among its members, tied to a vision of the "Universal Negro" as a new kind of political subject. Cyril Briggs of the African Blood Brotherhood (ABB), writing in response to Woodrow Wilson's declaration of support for national self-determination in Europe during the First World War, identified African Americans as an "oppressed nationality as worthy of . . . a separate political existence as any of the oppressed peoples of Europe." And, thanks largely to the efforts of Black Communist Harry Haywood, in 1928 the Sixth World Congress of the Communist International (Comintern) adopted a resolution calling for "national self-determination in the southern states where the Negroes form a majority of the population." In 1934, W. E. B. Du Bois argued that, with integration only a distant prospect, African Americans should form economic cooperatives and separate political institutions to develop "an economic nation within a nation." In the early twentieth century, Delany's formulation helped authorize an expansive range of political projects.[10]

Beginning in the 1940s, colonial comparisons took on a new significance in American politics. The material and ideological effects of the Second World War radically altered Americans' expectations of the continued viability of European empires. Decolonization slowly began to appear as an inevitability among European and American elites, though its timeline and form were the subjects of sustained and vigorous debate. The acceleration of the Great Migration in the same period saw millions of African Americans move from the South to the cities of the North, Midwest, and West, reducing the demographic concentration of the African American population in the areas that had formed the imagined land bases for the Communist Party's vision of national self-determination. Mass migration and the formation of an urban Black working class facilitated the decoupling of the politics of Black self-determination from efforts to assert control over southern land and the means of agrarian production. While questions of territorial control were often implicated in invocations of the "internal colony" between the 1940s and 1970s, the conditions that produced the "Black Belt thesis" in its classical form no longer held true. The progress of decolonization and the ongoing reconstitution of Black politics during and after the Great Migration inspired more widespread and more flexible uses of colonial comparison in Black political debate—and beyond.[11]

During the Second World War, efforts to remake international institutions generated new discussions about the nature of colonialism and its connections to American racial hierarchy. For US postwar planners, especially those working to design a new system of trusteeship to replace the mandates system of the League of Nations, the definition of colonialism mattered a great deal. As these policymakers sought to balance their hopes for US global primacy in the postwar world with the interests of their wartime allies, especially the British Empire, they confronted thorny questions about whether control over distant territories constituted a version of empire distinct from the internal forms of unequal governance exerted by the United States over Indigenous nations, African Americans, and other racialized minorities, or by the Soviet Union over its various national communities. African American thinkers and activists who were well practiced in thinking about these relationships, including Ralph Bunche, W. E. B. Du Bois, Rayford Logan, and Merze Tate, came into direct conversation with these policymaking elites seeking to design new international institutions for the postwar world. In their disputes with other scholars, philanthropists, and policymakers about the future of colonial rule in Africa and the structure of the United Nations, this group of thinkers articulated a definition of colonialism as a problem of *racialized economic exploitation*, one that the mere granting of political sovereignty would not be enough to solve.

The vision of colonialism as a problem of racialized economic exploitation developed during the Second World War deeply influenced African American internationalists' interventions in the sphere of international development politics in the early years of the Cold War. As development grew in importance both for US foreign policymakers and for anticolonial movements in Africa, a transnational cohort of Black thinkers and activists shaped the politics of development from multiple vantage points. In the United States, advocacy organizations such as the NAACP lobbied the State Department and Congress, seeking to influence both the size and the shape of US foreign aid programs. Other African American thinkers, tied to a transnational network of Black activists spanning Europe, Africa, and the Caribbean, engaged in debates over British colonial development policy and the development strategies of both the Gold Coast independence movement and the postcolonial state of Ghana. Across these arenas, an anticipatory critique of neocolonialism—the persistence of economic dependency after political independence—loomed large in African Americans' interventions in development politics.

Debates about the structure of the United Nations and the politics of international development produced new ways of thinking about the definition of colonialism—a question that took on new importance in domestic political discourse in the 1960s. Social scientists, State Department officials, and liberal politicians, including John F. Kennedy, began to depict the United States as the "first new nation" to emerge from colonial rule. Meanwhile, leading philanthropists and War on Poverty policymakers, drawing on their experiences in international development work, increasingly saw domestic poverty as analogous to underdevelopment in the decolonizing world. At the Ford Foundation and in the administration of Lyndon B. Johnson, these figures developed a new policy instrument, known as community action, to address this underdevelopment. Inspired partly by their narrow vision of decolonization as a transfer of power to politically moderate leaders, US policymakers worked to elevate and empower appropriate versions of what they referred to as "indigenous leaders" in poor communities throughout the United States.

Black thinkers and activists largely rejected both the image of the US as the "first new nation" and the emphasis on elevating suitable "indigenous leaders" in antipoverty policy. Instead, drawing on the definition of colonialism as racialized economic exploitation forged through Black internationalist activism in prior decades, many African Americans began to portray American racism as a form of internal colonialism. The widespread embrace of this language reflected the crisis of vocabulary faced by the Black freedom movement after the passage of the Civil Rights Act in 1964 and the Voting Rights Act in 1965. Activists from across the movement, including leaders of the Southern Christian Leadership Conference (SCLC) and the Student Nonviolent Coordinating Committee (SNCC), turned to the concept of internal colonialism to theorize the forms of racial inequality that persisted after these legislative victories.

Advocates who organized under the protean sign of Black Power, in particular, adopted the concept of internal colonialism in their efforts to transform metropolitan political economies in the latter half of the 1960s. On the battlegrounds of metropolitan politics, activists informed by the colonial analogy clashed with social policymakers who understood African American poverty very differently, but still in terms dependent on a reading of decolonization and postcolonial development. Even among writers and activists who embraced Black Power, varied interpretations of what a program of internal decolonization entailed indexed a growing divide between radical and conservative strands of the movement. As conflicts in American cities came to occupy more and more national attention at the end of the 1960s and the beginning of the 1970s, these struggles were mediated by the colonial comparisons that actors on all sides embraced.

The colony was not the only evocative term of comparison to gain currency in Black politics in the 1960s and 1970s. Descriptions of the Black "ghetto"— itself a term drawn from a different historical context, that of medieval European Jewish communities—as prison, as urban plantation, and even as concentration camp proliferated, sometimes emanating from the same thinkers who employed the colonial analogy.[12] The adoption of all of these metaphors signaled a rejection of the "creedal narrative" of American society, according to which African Americans were gradually attaining the liberal freedoms that had always been immanent in the country's founding documents and ideals.[13] Highlighting continuities or similarities between the condition of the formally free populations of Black ghettos and that of people subjected to forced confinement, forced labor, or genocidal violence buttressed the insistence of many Black activists that the end of de jure segregation and disfranchisement represented only one of the goals of the Black freedom movement. At the same time, each of these metaphors had more specific resonances. The image of ghettos as prisons, for example (in the striking words of Malcolm X, the proclamation that "that's what America means: prison") formed a crucial part of Black nationalist and Black radical organizing against the burgeoning carceral state in the 1960s, linking structures of urban inequality with the state's repressive apparatus.[14]

Each of these metaphors deserves careful consideration, and several receive sustained attention in other studies.[15] Within this semantic field, though, the colonial analogy was distinctive for several reasons. More than other metaphors of confinement and oppression, the colonial analogy emerged out of contestations over the meaning of ongoing international events, contestations that included not only Black Power activists but figures much closer to the centers of state power. The colonial analogy also uniquely stimulated debate about what, exactly, rendered the comparison valid or politically useful. Whereas predictable fault lines emerged around the question of *whether* the Black ghettos of American cities *really were* commensurable to prisons, concentration camps, or colonies, the colonial analogy prompted deeper discussions of its analytic purchase and strategic utility. Among those who employed the internal colony thesis, there were substantial disagreements over *what* features of American racial hierarchy made it comparable to colonialism, and what political strategies followed from such comparisons. The uses to which the colonial analogy was put and the range of settings in which it was deployed were especially dynamic, as developments in both the decolonizing world and the Black freedom struggle within the US brought new issues to the fore. The rich debates the analogy engendered open a window onto the broader historical question of how Americans conceived of their relationship to the world-historical transformation of decolonization.[16]

The political valences of colonial comparison shifted between the 1940s and the 1970s, both for insurgent Black thinkers and for US state actors. The normative delegitimation of colonial rule in the decades after the Second World War prompted a shift in outlook among some American policymakers. An earlier willingness to consider the United States as a successful model of quasi-imperial governance, which influenced postwar planning debates, was transformed into a desire to label the country a postcolonial state amid the accelerating process of decolonization in Africa and Asia. Whereas State

Department planners during the early 1940s may have been happy to identify the US as a composite state consisting of both democratic governing structures and colonial arrangements, by the early 1960s it was much more common for policymakers and politicians to emphasize the nation's origins in anti-imperial revolt.

The meaning and purpose of colonial comparisons shifted in this period for Black thinkers and activists as well. One critical shift occurred in the way African Americans perceived the vanguard of African liberation. Prior to the 1940s, for the organizers of the early Pan-African Congress movement and the leaders of the UNIA alike, African Americans represented the natural leaders of movements for African freedom. This claim reflected the intertwining of Pan-Africanist thought with the dominant discourses of civilization that were increasingly put under strain by the world wars in Europe. But after the Second World War, many African Americans began to understand the Black freedom struggle within the United States as lagging behind African liberation movements. Following the Fifth Pan-African Congress in Manchester in 1945, which was led and organized not by African Americans but by leaders of independence movements in Africa and the Caribbean, the perception of African American vanguardism in the global Black freedom struggle faded.[17] This trend only accelerated as African nations won their independence in the 1950s and 1960s. A frequently related anecdote from the independence celebrations in Ghana in 1957 encapsulates the eastward migration of the perceived leading edge of Pan-African liberation. Vice President Richard Nixon, as the possibly apocryphal story goes, turned to a group of bystanders attending the festivities and asked, "How does it feel to be free?" to which they responded, "We wouldn't know. We're from Alabama."[18]

As this story suggests, changing perceptions of who was in the vanguard in the march toward global Black freedom influenced African American thinkers to look to decolonization not as a process they might shape but as a guide to follow. This shift in the polarities of diasporic politics happened quickly—much more quickly than most African American intellectuals, even as late as 1945, expected. Further, as more and more African Americans migrated north, the system of legal segregation maintained through racial terror in the Jim Crow South lost its place as the primary target of many Black thinkers who deployed colonial comparisons in political argument. By the middle of the 1960s, as international debates about the definition of colonialism shifted toward an emphasis on relations of economic dependency, the Black politics of colonial comparison in the US developed a distinctly urbanized character. The insistence by Black Power activists James and Grace Lee Boggs that "the city is the Black man's land" was intertwined with their own visions of the internal colony, as invocations of colonialism became tied to the Black Power politics of community control and metropolitan restructuring. Such applications of terms drawn from international politics to the dynamics of urban politics represented an innovative example of what Musab Younis calls the "underground scalar thought" of the Black anticolonial tradition.[19]

The Boggses' vision of the American metropolis as a colonial economy of racialized exploitation grew increasingly popular among Black Power activists in the late 1960s. This image stood in stark contrast to the views of both the city and the world held by policymakers involved in designing the War on Poverty. Liberal social policy in the Great Society was itself deeply influenced by American officials' understandings about international development and decolonization. Policymakers' narrow vision of decolonization as a transfer of power to appropriate leaders clashed with Black activists' attempts to apply the lessons of decolonization to remake the racialized economic order of American cities. Decolonization haunted the politics of the urban crisis.

Most of the Black thinkers and activists who adopted the language of the internal colony held European colonial rule in Africa, the Caribbean, and Asia as the models of colonialism to which American racial inequality should be compared. The settler colonial nature of the American project and the history of Indigenous genocide and dispossession were relatively infrequent points of comparison for African American internationalist thinkers, at least before the 1960s. As scholars such as Tiffany Lethabo King demonstrate, American settler society and the US state have both connected Black and Indigenous peoples through regimes of violence and expropriation and created divisions between these peoples' struggles for freedom and self-determination. The absence of a sustained discussion of US settler colonialism among many African American internationalists in the mid-twentieth century speaks to the immense power of the variegated system of American racial hierarchy to divide those it subjugates.[20]

At the same time, important points of commonality exist between Black theorizations of internal colonialism and Indigenous critiques of settler colonial sovereignty and violence. Both vocabularies challenged the politics of civic inclusion that pervaded American racial liberalism, as political theorist David Myer Temin explains. The call for self-determination in the Black Power movement, for example, was embraced as a critical resource in the struggle for tribal sovereignty and Indigenous self-determination by key figures within the emergent Red Power movement. The efforts of Black and Indigenous intellectuals and activists who forged explicit organizational connections in the 1960s and 1970s built upon the commonalities in these two modes of thought, despite the difficulties of coalition-building they faced.

Black internationalists who debated the meaning and implications of an American politics of decolonization, then, could be seen as participating in an unacknowledged conversation with Indigenous thinkers who considered the variegated forms of American colonialism from a distinctive vantage point.[21]

Seeing this history at all requires viewing the midcentury United States from outside the prism of Cold War America.[22] In most histories of American politics between the 1940s and 1970s, the US-Soviet conflict appears as the only international dynamic that matters. The transition from the Second World War to the Cold War did indeed reconfigure American political rhetoric around a redefined keyword of "freedom," giving rise to defenses of capitalism as a system of "free enterprise" that was counterposed to the "totalitarianism" of Communism. Defense spending geared toward Cold War aims, moreover, provided stimulus to important sectors of industrial production and helped underwrite a period of economic growth on which labor peace and corporatist coordination depended. And Cold War anticommunism placed hard limits on socialist and social democratic political discourse and reform movements.[23]

To the extent that global decolonization plays any role in most studies of these topics, though, it serves simply as a complicating factor in the Cold War, which continues to supply the master key to global politics. Even historians of the "global Cold War" subordinate the autonomous issues and dynamics at the heart of decolonization to a world-spanning conflict between the United States and the Soviet Union, despite their insistence that this conflict's most consequential battles took place in the decolonizing world.[24]

Yet decolonization consisted of a combination of locally embedded logics and widely shared dynamics that could not be attributed to or contained by the Cold War conflict—as many American thinkers at the time recognized. Just as the hardening of the Cold War prompted reconsiderations of "free enterprise" that proved important for the ideological justification of American capitalism, the global transformation wrought by decolonization provided equally important keywords to struggles over racial and class inequality in the United States. These keywords may have had shorter lifespans in American politics than that of "free enterprise," but that does not diminish their importance. From the widespread image of the United States as the "first new nation" in John F. Kennedy's foreign policy, through War on Poverty policymakers' emphasis on "indigenous leadership," to Black Power activists' analysis of "internal colonialism," global decolonization shaped some of the most controversial spheres of American political argument. As Raymond Williams has argued, political vocabularies are both products of social struggle and active forces that define and delimit the scope of political possibility. Divergent languages of colonial comparison developed out of the conflicting ways Black activists and state officials sought to influence the process of decolonization abroad. Once formed, these vocabularies intensified ideological conflict at home—by framing debates over a range of policy issues as reflections on the nature of American society itself.[25]

Global decolonization was not, as many Western observers at the time insisted, simply the repeated transfer of power from a distant European sovereign to a local elite or the modular diffusion of the European nation-state form throughout the rest of the world. Contemporary scholars of decolonization, rejecting this older view, have called attention to the contingent outcomes of processes of imperial withdrawal, the anxiety and anticipation that the prospect of independence occasioned, and the expansive political imaginaries of colonial subjects. A crucial insight of this work has been a recognition of the *conceptual labor* involved in the process of decolonization. As anticolonial movements began to capture state power, and as empire—the world's oldest variety of formal state governance—came to be seen as internationally illegitimate, people struggled to define the parameters and purpose of a new world order. Did decolonization mean the transfer of political sovereignty? Did it necessitate a redrawing of borders? Did it entail a cultural campaign against ideologies of European superiority? Did it require a restructuring of the world economy? The work of posing and answering these questions generated new fields of political and social contestation on the world stage.[26]

These contestations played out within the United States as well. Decolonization has figured in most histories of the United States in three ways: first, as an arena of Cold War conflict in which the fate of US global hegemony would be decided; second, as a moment that included the end of formal US sovereignty over much of its own territorial empire; or, third, as a goal of discrete anticolonial movements abroad, to which some Americans provided material and ideological support. *The Internal Colony* suggests a different way of analyzing the relation between the history of global decolonization and the history of the United States. The end of empire forced Americans to ask new questions about racial and economic inequality in their own country.

Seen in this light, Black internationalism appears at the center of one of the most important stories of twentieth-century American politics. Global concerns did not fade from African American politics with the onset of the Cold War, even as anticommunism shattered a promising left-liberal alliance of the 1930s and early 1940s. Tensions about the institutional forms that decolonization should take, the scale on which political-economic decision-making should take place, and the relationship between economic development and political self-determination coursed through Black internationalist politics in the 1940s and 1950s. As historians Glenda Sluga and Patricia Clavin have written, histories of internationalism must attend to the question of "what historical difference internationalisms made." Black internationalism in the midcentury United States was not simply a global supplement to a primarily domestic civil rights movement. Rather, it provided the language in which fundamental conflicts over racial and class inequality in the United States were contested. Competing interpretations of the meaning of colonialism, the political economy of the decolonizing world, and the relation between colonial rule and the political order of the United States deepened the rift between postwar liberalism and the Black freedom movement.[27]

Presidents and diplomats, established social scientists and independent social critics, NAACP leaders and Black Power revolutionaries all populate these pages. Though these figures did not always take part in a single conversation, examining them in the same frame of analysis can enrich our understanding of African American, US, and international history. It is necessary to examine the politics of colonial comparison from multiple angles to gain a fuller understanding of how global decolonization influenced the politics of race and class in America. This book, then, follows what historian N. D. B. Connolly calls a "desegregated method," by illustrating the concatenation of differently racialized spheres of debate. Rather than an example of comparative method, this study engages in what political theorist Juliet Hooker calls "juxtaposition": it "stage[s] as proximate" texts and events that are often "viewed as disparate," and, in doing so, treats the comparisons that historical actors *made* in the heat of political contestations as proper subjects of historical analysis.[28]

The purpose of comparison in Black political thought has recently come to the forefront of debates in Black Studies. Leading Afropessimist theorists, most of all Frank B. Wilderson III, insist that the "ruse of analogy" represents a central discursive tactic of antiblackness. In this account, any comparison that links the condition of Black people to that of other oppressed groups serves as a "mystification, and often erasure, of Blackness's grammar of suffering." The range of colonial comparisons employed by Black thinkers and activists in the midcentury United States suggests, by contrast, that some forms of analogy might serve to enrich the grammars both of suffering and of struggle.[29]

From W. E. B. Du Bois and Merze Tate to James and Grace Lee Boggs, writers and organizers involved in battles against colonialism and for Black freedom engaged in the politics of comparison precisely because they did not assume the terms of these grammars in advance. Analyzing what was shared

and what was distinctive between the external and internal colonial situations of Africans and African Americans served in the very making of a Black
world—a transnational Black community engaged in contemporaneous, if
not always conjoined, movements for civil rights, Black Power, and decolonization. Dissensus over whether a particular comparison was apt or useful,
and for what purposes, only indicated the degree to which Black intellectuals
and activists, and their erstwhile coalitional allies, took such comparisons seriously as *options* for both analysis and prescription. The creativity and depth
with which Black thinkers in the midcentury United States engaged in the
politics of comparison indicates that more interesting questions can be asked
of the place of analogy in liberatory politics than the question of whether it
is permissible at all. Either to dismiss this history outright, or to celebrate it
uncritically, would be to neglect the story of political struggle it discloses.

A many-sided story of the politics of colonial comparison unfolds in the
following ten chapters. The imagination of US policymakers, thinkers, and
activists in this period was relentlessly comparative; telling a comprehensive
story of every effort to draw parallels between the decolonizing world and US
politics would be both unwieldy and tedious. Instead, following anthropologist and feminist theorist Ann Laura Stoler's insistence that "to compare is a
situated political act of discernment," the narrative that follows traces lines of
comparison between the United States and the decolonizing world through
discrete political contestations over several decades, on issues ranging from
the founding of the United Nations, to the Johnson administration's War on
Poverty, to the National Black Economic Development Conference of 1969.
Each of these conjunctures sheds light on how the political economy of the
decolonizing world became fertile ground for Americans of varying political
persuasions to develop new ways of thinking about racial and class inequality domestically. Both by examining specific moments of interaction among
activists, intellectuals, and policymakers, and by staging an overarching conversation involving these various actors, this book uncovers the connected
contestations over the meaning of decolonization in different domains of
American political and intellectual life.[30]

Chapters 1 and 2 examine debates among leading African American activists, philanthropists, and state officials over the institutional design of the
international order during the Second World War. The Committee on Africa,
the War, and Peace Aims, established by the philanthropic organization the
Phelps-Stokes Fund in 1941 to make recommendations about US policy toward Africa in the aftermath of the war, formed one important setting of these
debates. Several prominent Black internationalist thinkers, including Rayford
Logan, W. E. B. Du Bois, and Ralph Bunche, participated in the deliberations

of this committee. Through this committee, the press, and direct engagement with State Department officials, leading Black internationalists advocated not for immediate independence but for an internationalized trusteeship system to replace mandatory and colonial rule in Africa. Several factors undergirded this advocacy: a view of African Americans as the vanguard of African liberation rooted in older discourses of civilization; a deep-seated realism about the US policymaking process; and, perhaps most importantly, a distinctive understanding of colonialism itself.

Through these debates, Logan and Du Bois, in particular, put forth a vision of colonialism as a system of racialized economic exploitation that would not be ended with the granting of political sovereignty. As US officials coalesced around a narrower vision of trusteeship that left European empires largely intact, Logan and Du Bois diminished their hopes that international institutions might serve as the midwife of decolonization. Throughout these discussions, African American internationalists, State Department bureaucrats, and European officials all forged their positions on the shape of the postwar order through comparative reflections about the nature of colonialism and its relationship to racial inequality in the United States.

Chapter 3 shows how Black activists translated the concept of colonialism as a system of racialized economic exploitation into the sphere of international development politics in the early postwar years. Rayford Logan served as the leader of the NAACP's advocacy related to the Point Four program, President Truman's signature development initiative in the non-European world. Although anticommunism inflected debates about Point Four, so too did ideas about whether political economy should be governed at the national or the international scale, as Logan and some of his interlocutors embraced visions of development that required political-economic planning above the scale of the nation. Further, Black activists' fear of what would later come to be called neocolonialism—the persistence of economic dependency after political independence—loomed large in their attempts to influence US foreign aid policymaking.

Chapter 4 demonstrates how African American internationalists also intervened in the politics of international development on the other side of the Atlantic. The fear of neocolonial domination after political independence also pervaded the thinking of a transnational circle of Black activists who sought to intervene in development politics from different vantage points, from British colonial development policy to the development strategies of the independence movement in Ghana. A shared anticipation of neocolonialism defined the varied perspectives of these figures, including the social scientist St. Clair Drake and the novelist Richard Wright, on the primary initiative in Kwame Nkrumah's developmental agenda, the building of the Akosombo Dam over the Volta River. By examining Black internationalist development politics in both donor and recipient nations, then, this chapter illustrates how African American internationalists on both sides of Cold War divisions perceived the threat of continuing relations of colonial economic domination after the end of formal empire.

Taken together, the first four chapters trace debates about the international order that generated new reflections on how colonialism should be understood. The definition of colonialism, and the question of its relation to the history, governing structure, and racial hierarchy of the United States, took on new importance in political discourse about purportedly domestic topics in the 1960s, as the following six chapters demonstrate.

Chapter 5 bridges the international and domestic spheres. Amid the rising fortunes of independence movements in Asia and Africa and a growing recognition of the strategic significance of these "new nations" to US foreign policy, policymakers and elite thinkers began to portray the United States as the "first new nation." The image of the United States as the first postcolonial state was coproduced by politicians and diplomats seeking to win the allegiance of the decolonizing world in the Cold War and by leading social scientists engaged in a reconsideration of American history and politics from the perspective of development and modernization. Central to the political language of first new nationhood was the deployment of a particular interpretation of the significance of American federalism in discussions of postcolonial politics. In response to postcolonial attempts to form federations for the purpose of securing economic independence—attempts that often drew on the example of the early United States—US diplomats and social scientists argued that the American federal system spoke instead to issues of internal pluralism. Even more, promoters of the image of the United States as the "first new nation" intervened in ongoing arguments about the definition of colonialism itself. Advancing a narrow definition of colonialism as political rule by a foreign power, diplomats and modernization theorists alike contested the contemporaneous effort by decolonizing states to promulgate a broader definition of "colonialism in all its manifestations" that included economic and cultural dominance. This global debate about the scope of colonialism influenced African American intellectual life as well, providing a crucial context for the turn by some writers, especially the social critic Harold Cruse, to an analysis of American racial hierarchy as a form of internal colonialism.

If the political language of first new nationhood employed a particular reading of American history in efforts to shape postcolonial politics in the early 1960s, a particular reading of postcolonial politics came to exercise significant influence in American debates about antipoverty policy around the same time. Chapter 6 charts a transformation in how US policymakers, foundation officials, and social scientists envisioned American poverty as underdevelopment. As a cultural view of US underdevelopment, undergirded by the concept of a transnational "culture of poverty," replaced a territorial understanding, exemplified by the focus on area redevelopment in the Eisenhower and Kennedy years, the concepts and practices of community development programs overseas seeped into US antipoverty policy. The primary innovation, a new policy apparatus known as community action, began in the Ford Foundation's Gray Areas program before the Johnson administration made it the centerpiece of its War on Poverty. Although community action is often remembered for its empowerment of grassroots organizations, the policymakers who designed it were staunch in their belief that community action depended on the cultivation of so-called indigenous leadership that would guide and temper the desires of poor people. This belief in the power of "indigenous leadership" stemmed from the engagements of the Gray Areas program's director, Paul Ylvisaker, with the urban politics of postcolonial Calcutta. When the Johnson administration looked to Ylvisaker for help in designing the Community Action Program at the heart of the War on Poverty, his emphasis on indigenous leadership came to define federal antipoverty policy as well.

As African American activists across the political spectrum formed community action agencies, the Ford Foundation and the Office of Economic Opportunity channeled philanthropic and federal dollars to those helmed by "indigenous leaders" that fit the model Ylvisaker had first devised in India. Chapter 7 shows how the discourse on indigenous leadership in antipoverty policy resonated in Black politics, where thinkers and activists were engaged in a contemporaneous reconsideration of urban politics in terms of colonialism. Rising criticism of "social welfare colonialism" called for greater reliance on local organizations and experts, recapitulating a central element of policymakers' emphasis on "indigenous leadership." Kenneth Clark, the famed Black psychologist, was a founder of a community action agency in Harlem and an early adopter of the language of "social welfare colonialism." As he grew more disillusioned with the prospects of community action and liberal antipoverty policy, however, Clark devised a more thoroughgoing critique of urban political economy in anticolonial terms. Clark's conception of the "ghetto-as-colony" marked a transitional moment in the Black politics of colonial comparison. The view of colonialism as a form of racialized economic exploitation, forged through engagements in the international arena, here came to be applied to the structure of urban political economy.

Chapter 8 traces the winding path of the language of internal colonialism through the Black freedom movement in the middle of the 1960s. The Black freedom movement faced a crisis of vocabulary after the legislative victories of 1964 and 1965. From its origins on the Black left, the colonial analogy was taken up by a wider range of thinkers and activists who sought to develop a new conceptual account of American racial inequality amid frustrations about the slowing pace of reform after the passage of the Civil and Voting Rights Acts. The translation and publication of the writings of Frantz Fanon was an important impetus for the proliferation of the idea of internal colonialism in the language of movement politics. Leading civil rights and Black Power activists, such as Jack O'Dell, James Forman, and James and Grace Lee Boggs, proposed a variety of meanings for the concept of the internal colony that sought to apply the language to grassroots organizing.

The advent of the rallying cry of "Black Power" accelerated the adoption of a colonial lens in intellectual and activist circles. Chapters 9 and 10 demonstrate how the varied uses of the idea of internal colonialism indexed growing divisions within the Black Power movement. Stokely Carmichael and Charles V. Hamilton's book *Black Power*, published in 1967, attempted to bring conceptual clarity to the meaning of Black Power and to define a political agenda beneath its sign. Carmichael and Hamilton brought the concept of the internal colony into conversation with social-scientific theories of ethnic group pluralism, ultimately promoting an ambiguous agenda for those seeking to apply the language of decolonization to the political economy of American urban development. As the urban uprisings of the 1960s reached their peak of intensity in 1967 and 1968, national political conversation focused on the causes and consequences of the political economy of racism in the American metropolis. Conversative elements of the movement and even some conservative figures in national politics seized upon the linkage between the vocabulary of internal colonialism and the social-scientific language of interest-group pluralism to promote an agenda of Black elite empowerment.

Yet conservative appropriations did not have complete success. Other writers and activists, drawing on longstanding concerns in Black internationalist thought about the incomplete nature of political sovereignty without economic independence, saw parallels between the failure of postcolonial independence to bring broad-based economic gains and the situation in American cities, as Black political leaders won power amid worsening economic conditions for many Black Americans. Attempts to formulate a bold policy agenda around the analysis of internal colonialism reached their peak with the National Black Economic Development Conference in 1969. At the same time, the analysis of internal colonization authorized serious attempts to build solidarity between African American activists and American Indian and Puerto Rican liberation movements.

Over the course of the 1970s, even as the idea of internal colonialism gained more adherents in academic circles, colonial comparisons lost purchase in the broader realm of American political vocabulary, for two reasons. First, the increasing fragmentation of the Black freedom movement made the development of a cohesive political program around the language of internal colonialism difficult. Second, as numerous postcolonial states failed to live up to their egalitarian aspirations and as forms of international hierarchy persisted in the wake of postcolonial self-determination, the allure of decolonization as a source of meaning and inspiration weakened.

By the middle of the 1970s, the normative foundations of postcolonial self-determination came under sustained attack, while the hopes decolonization once inspired of a permanent shift in global power relations diminished. US policymakers continued to treat internal and external borders as part of a continuum of racialized global space, and Black activists continued to pursue international aims. But the contest among divergent visions of the relation between colonialism and American racial and economic inequality largely faded from view.

The Crucible of Postwar Planning

As the Second World War spread across Europe and Asia and came to America's shores, many Black Americans saw the war through the prism of racial equality. James G. Thompson, a cafeteria worker in Wichita, Kansas, described this vision in an especially influential way. In a letter to the largest-circulation Black newspaper in the country, the *Pittsburgh Courier*, Thompson recommended that Black Americans "adopt the double VV for a double victory," with "the first V for victory over our enemies from without," and "the second V for victory over our enemies from within." The editors of the *Courier* turned this slogan into a campaign, calling upon their hundreds of thousands of readers, and Black Americans more broadly, to work for a "double victory" against fascism abroad and Jim Crow at home. Globally minded activists and writers saw a natural third plank to add to this campaign—victory over European colonial rule—and lent their support to anticolonial causes from South Africa to India.[1]

Grassroots Black internationalist protest had been growing since Benito Mussolini's plans to invade Ethiopia became clear in the summer of 1935. Americans' involvement in the global "Hands Off Ethiopia" movement—which included a multiracial march of over twenty thousand people in Harlem—drew both from a burgeoning antifascist consciousness and from a longstanding strand of Ethiopianism in Black nationalist thought. Existing Black nationalist organizations, such as Mittie Maude Lena Gordon's Peace Movement of Ethiopia, grew after the invasion, extending their Pan-Africanist messages of global Black unity and racial pride to a broader American community. New organizations were founded in the wake of the Hands Off Ethiopia movement as well, including the International Council of African Affairs (later the Council of African Affairs, or CAA). Founded by Paul

Robeson and Max Yergan, and later led by Alphaeus Hunton Jr., the CAA grew to become a leading voice of anticolonialism on the Black left, providing political education on global issues, especially in South Africa, through its publications and grassroots campaigns. The conditions of the war years were particularly ripe for the formation of a broad coalition of African American anticolonial activists. Moderate liberals in the NAACP worked alongside the organized left, including Communist Party members, to advocate the end of European colonial rule in Africa and elsewhere as a concomitant goal with the end of Jim Crow and the defeat of fascism.[2]

African American activism on colonial issues intensified during the war in part because the conflict seemed to call the future of colonial rule into question. The militaries of Europe's leading imperial states were overstretched, their budgets strained, and their populations devastated. The genocidal racism of Nazi ideology, meanwhile, contributed to a widespread discrediting of biological theories of race. The numerous proclamations of the antiracist and democratic purpose behind the Allied war effort gave rise, in turn, to new pressures on other forms of racial hierarchy within and among states. As the future of the colonial system came under scrutiny, how to *define* colonialism emerged as an important question. What constituted a colonial relationship? How far did the colonial system extend? Which sorts of colonial arrangements needed to change, and how fast?

Postwar planning debates served as the forum in which these questions were taken up. State actors, elite thinkers with ties to the state, and grassroots activists alike took part in the intellectual labor of imagining a postwar world. For all these groups, postwar planning debates sparked reflection on the relationship between the United States' role in the world, the global colonial system, and the problems of racial hierarchy and racial discord within American borders.

Examining Black internationalists' involvement in postwar planning debates reveals the centrality of questions of international institutional design in their anticolonial imaginary. The institutional design of the postwar international order emerged as a "problem-space," in anthropologist David Scott's terms—"an ensemble of questions and answers around which a horizon of identifiable stakes (conceptual as well as ideological-political) hangs"—for Black internationalism in the early 1940s. Questions of institutional design became "questions worth having answers to" because the war's devastating effects on colonial powers in Europe, along with the collapse of the League of Nations, presented an opportunity to push colonial reform and eventual decolonization to the center of discussions about the postwar order.[3]

In unofficial planning spaces and in conversations with state actors, a cohort of influential thinkers and advocates—led by W. E. B. Du Bois, Ralph Bunche, and Rayford Logan—envisioned novel institutional forms that would replace both outright colonial control in Africa and the system of national administration of League of Nations mandates. Although the importance of anticolonial concerns to Black politics during the war is well established, scholars have largely overlooked the substance of African Americans' ideas about what political theorist Adom Getachew calls the "institutional forms of a postimperial world." African American internationalists not only worked as transnational activists and critics of US foreign policy—as they appear in most accounts—but as prospective architects of the postwar international order. Casting African American thinkers in this role both provides a fuller picture of Black internationalism during the Second World War and advances what scholar Christy Thornton labels an "'outside-in' reading of the history of international institutions."[4]

Through debates about the institutional structure of the postwar international order, Black thinkers brought previously marginal arguments about the parallels between the conditions of African Americans and colonial subjects into discussions that reached the very centers of state power. For US policymakers, the defeated Axis powers needed not only to be disarmed or to embrace new leadership but also to embark on a sustained path of internal reconstruction before they could be welcomed as members in good standing of the new international order. At times during the postwar planning process, US policymakers urged programs of internal reconstruction even on their wartime allies, identifying British colonialism as a potential obstacle to postwar peace and stability. Official American criticisms of European colonialism during the war and in postwar peace negotiations, muted and contradictory as they were, made an impression on many Black activists. Presenting American racism as a parallel system to these relic imperial orders began to appear as an effective way to portray Jim Crow as an equal affront to policymakers' imagined postwar democratic order. If colonialism presented a problem for the ideal postwar order, as some policymakers thought, then portraying the American racial order as a version of colonialism might raise African Americans' supposedly domestic issues to the same level of global concern. In the crucible of postwar planning, then, new concepts of colonialism—both external and internal—began to be molded.

The Colonial South

In the American political discourse of the 1930s, comparisons between domestic inequalities and the global colonial system were regionalized. Writers and activists who made such comparisons typically fixated on the South and the peculiarities of both its political economy and its entrenched racial hierarchy.

In 1928, the Sixth Congress of the Third Communist International (Comintern) adopted a new resolution on the "Negro Question" in the United States. The resolution declared the "right of the Negroes to national self-determination in the southern states, where the Negroes form a majority of the population." Following from an analysis that linked the American "Negro Question" with anticolonial struggles around the world, the declaration of this right to "self-determination" announced the Comintern's intention to make Black Americans an explicit focus of their political organizing in the United States.[5]

The adoption of this resolution was due in part to the work of the Nebraska-born son of former slaves, Harry Haywood. After serving in a Black regiment of the US army in the First World War, Haywood was radicalized by the violence of the "Red Summer" of 1919 and joined the secretive, Communist-aligned African Blood Brotherhood at the invitation of his brother Otto Hall in 1921. Haywood went on to study at the Communist University of the Toilers of the East and the International Lenin School in Moscow, where he encountered anticolonial revolutionaries including Ho Chi Minh. Appointed (along with his brother) to the special subcommittee on the "Negro Question" at the Sixth Congress, Haywood argued that the Comintern needed to recognize and counter the appeal of Marcus Garvey's Universal Negro Improvement Association, which he construed as a reactionary form of Black nationalism. "To the slogan of 'Back to Africa,'" Haywood argued, as he later put it in his autobiography *Black Bolshevik*, "we must counterpose the slogan of 'right to self-determination here in the Deep South.'" When the Comintern adopted this slogan, it applied a shared conceptual rubric to the status and struggle of African Americans in the Deep South and other peoples struggling for national liberation against colonial rule.[6]

The decision to apply the label of "national minority" to African Americans in the South did not gain immediate approval at the Congress. But whatever its status among theoreticians in Moscow, the adoption of the so-called Black Belt thesis undeniably had an enabling effect on the organizing efforts of the Communist Party in the US South. As leading African American Communist James Ford had observed in his speech at the Sixth Congress, "We have no more than 50 Negroes in our Party, out of the 12 million Negroes in America." By insisting that rural Black southerners held the potential to lead movements for broad social transformation, the 1928 resolution began to change that. Amid a worsening agricultural depression, and helped by

the fact that the leading organs of non-Communist "New Negro" radicalism largely ignored the rural South, Communist organizers found a receptive
audience among Black sharecroppers and tenant farmers, who turned to the
party in greater numbers than ever before in the 1930s. As the party grew, its
conception of African Americans as an "oppressed nationality" with a "right
to self-determination" became a key part of the region's political vocabulary.[7]

The young scholar Ralph Bunche penned an essay on "Marxism and
the 'Negro Question'" shortly after the Sixth Congress. Bunche, who was at the
beginning of a decade-long engagement with Marxism, dissented from the
new slogan of self-determination in the Black Belt. Of the factors that make
up a nation—"a community (and distinctness) of language, of territory, of
economic life (a national economy), of psychic structure (culture) and
tradition"—Bunche insisted, "not a single one . . . is characteristic of the Negroes in the United States." Further, when political and economic elites were
united in upholding segregation as the principal means of racial domination
and working-class division, the "slogan of self-determination" would merely
provide unwitting support to "jim-crowism." A more promising approach
would treat Black Americans as a "depressed caste," Bunche wrote, exemplified by the "semi-servile condition" of Black workers in agriculture and their
"inferior position" in industrial occupations. The superexploited position of
African Americans in the labor force, rather than their putative territorial or
national unity, should serve as the starting point for a Marxist analysis of the
"Negro Question."[8]

Even as Bunche denied the "national minority" theory, he held that this
form of superexploitation provided grounds on which African Americans
might be considered an internal colony within the United States. "The deliverance of the Negro people from their caste existence is in its content essentially a democratic task," Bunche wrote, and "in that respect it is similar to the
liberation of subject nations of colonies." The abolition of "semi-feudal forms
of exploitation, of peonage, tenancy, sharecropping, furnishing," along with
the "elimination of all elements of inferiority of the Negro's status in industry,"
represented analogous tasks to the removal of a colonial overlord. In both
cases, these tasks represented "merely the demands of consistent democracy;" in Bunche's mind, "not a single one is a specifically socialist demand."
Bunche insisted, though, that the "democratic character of the task of the
Negro liberation from caste status by no means implies that the Negro question today can be solved within the framework of the capitalist democracy."
Rather, in an echo of earlier Communist doctrine, he wrote that the "racial
emancipation of the American Negro" would only be possible "as an integral
aspect and an inevitable consequence of the revolutionary overthrow of the

capitalist system." Like the national liberation of colonies, Bunche concluded, the end of African Americans' social subjection and economic superexploitation would occur only as a consequence of, rather than as a first step toward, broader social transformation.[9]

This moment would not be the last time Bunche weighed in on the politics of colonial comparison. But in this early phase in his career, his thinking on fundamental questions of race, nation, labor, and revolution was intertwined with the relationship between the predicament of African Americans and the global colonial system. While Bunche's perspective on this relationship would change as he moved from radical scholar to liberal diplomat, it would remain a core concern in his thought. His comments further previewed the growing importance of colonial analogies in American political debate—in spheres that extended well beyond the Communist Party.

In this same period, two groups of white southern intellectuals argued, along lines completely opposed to the ideas of both Bunche and Haywood, that the largely agrarian South operated as a "colonial economy" vis-à-vis the more industrial North. A group of writers and poets known as the Southern Agrarians, best known for their racist and revanchist defense of the "agrarian tradition" of the Old South, endorsed the view that relations of dependency persisted between the rural South and the increasingly industrial national economy. The writer John Crowe Ransom, in one of the group's most thorough attempts to articulate a perspective on political economy, argued in 1932 that the paradigmatic rural southern town had "scarcely any control over its own economic life" and resembled nothing so much as an "outpost of empire." The only alternative he conceived was to "reestablish self-sufficiency as the proper economy for the American farm."[10]

A parallel view of the South as a "colonial economy" emerged from a group of liberal sociologists, including Howard Odum and Rupert Vance, at the Institute for Research in Social Science at the University of North Carolina at Chapel Hill. These thinkers differed from the Southern Agrarians in both the genre of their writing and their political outlook, but they put forward an analysis of the South's political-economic situation in similar language. In their minds, the South had always occupied a dependent place in the economy of the nation, defined by its reliance on northern capital, its low-wage labor market, and its production of raw materials for export (both to other regions of the United States and abroad). Rupert Vance elaborated on the colonial frame for analyzing southern economics in his 1932 tome *Human Geography of the South*. Emphasizing the region's reliance on natural resource exploitation since the seventeenth century, and especially the dominant position of cotton since the nineteenth, Vance reached the same conclusion as the agrarians that "the South remains a colonial economy." Unlike the Agrarians, however, Vance turned this analysis not toward nostalgia for the Old South but toward support for the New Deal's program of regional development to counter the legacy of "colonial" exploitation—a program that, as historian David Ekbladh has shown, later formed an important model for US development policies abroad. To the Chapel Hill sociologists, this form of colonial-style development was, in Howard Odum's terms, a brand of "regionalism," as distinct from the destructive "sectionalism" of the Agrarians, that could uplift the benighted South and promote its full reintegration into the national body.[11]

Both conservatives and liberals who promoted an image of the South as a colonial economy diminished the significance of race and racism in their analyses of the economic challenges facing the South. To these white writers, the Jim Crow racial order appeared not as the primary feature of a colonial-style racial hierarchy, but as an ancillary feature of a primarily regional form of economic exploitation. Their refusal to confront Jim Crow directly—or, for many of the Agrarians, their outward support for the Jim Crow system—marked an unbridgeable divide between their understandings of the "colonial South" and those articulated by Black thinkers in the same period. Despite these immense and significant differences, there existed a shared focus on the rural South as the distinctive site of colonial dynamics within the United States.

This regional emphasis receded in the 1940s. The social and demographic changes wrought by the Great Migration, the growth of new forms of Black internationalist politics, and the crucible of the Second World War created the conditions for a more widespread and wide-ranging political conversation about colonialism and its relation to domestic inequalities. Between 1940 and 1950, over 1.6 million Black southerners migrated north and west, with 1.5 million more to follow in the next decade. The migration went hand in hand with the creation of a large industrial proletariat among African Americans in cities from St. Louis to Chicago to Oakland, with many migrants finding work in burgeoning defense industries. Black migrants formed a new pool of voters in Northern cities, as most were gaining the right to vote for the first time due to the systematic disfranchisement of Black people in the Jim Crow South. These new voters put new forms of pressure on political establishments, and white politicians often believed them to hold the balance of power in municipal—and sometimes even national—elections.[12]

One cultural effect of this migration was a growing association of Black life with urbanity. This shift was marked by the beginning of a sustained conversation about the "Black ghetto," which would come to the forefront of national debate in the 1960s and 1970s. First used in the sixteenth century to name the segregated and enclosed neighborhood of Venice's Jewish population, the term "ghetto" remained primarily associated with Jewish communities through the early twentieth century. The term "ghetto" came to encompass both immigrant Jewish neighborhoods in the cities of North America and the horrors of Nazi-occupied Europe. In the early 1940s, two young Black scholars in Chicago, St. Clair Drake and Horace Cayton, adopted the term "ghetto" to characterize the regime of spatial segregation and economic exploitation that delimited Black life in the city. Drawing from their interlocutors in Chicago's Bronzeville neighborhood, they argued in their 1945 book *Black Metropolis: A Study of Negro Life in a Northern City* that the "Black ghetto" had developed through a combination of employment discrimination, racially restrictive housing covenants, and white mob violence. As Drake and Cayton further observed, the resident of Bronzeville "found the problems of the Chinese, the Indians, and the Burmese strangely analogous to his own," while the "problem of all the common peoples of the earth . . . came to include the problem of the American Negro" during the Second World War. The distinct predicament of Black Americans in the "ghettos" of the urban North, their analysis suggested, provided new grounds for comparison with the subjects of European colonial rule.[13]

It was the coming of the Second World War, as Drake and Cayton suggested, that ultimately transformed Black Americans' discussions of global colonialism and its domestic entanglements. As the war accelerated the growth of grassroots Black internationalist activism, it also provided a unique opportunity for a set of African American thinkers and activists to seek to influence policymaking more directly—in the elite circles of postwar planning.

The Committee on Africa, the War, and Peace Aims

A group called the Committee on Africa, the War, and Peace Aims (CAWPA) served as the most important link between Black internationalist activism and the world of state policymaking during the war. This committee was convened by Anson Phelps Stokes, the founding director of the Phelps-Stokes Fund, a philanthropic organization focused on African American and African education. Stokes wanted the United States to play a major role in shaping the politics of the African continent once the Second World War ended. Further, he believed his fund—with its experience in missionary education, close ties to leaders of the National Association for the Advancement of Colored People (NAACP), and connections to the State Department—was the ideal body to sway policymakers and "influenc[e] public opinion on wise lines" regarding an eventual postwar settlement in Africa. Between the summer of 1941 and the summer of 1942, he brought together a committee of scholars, policy experts, and missionaries at the Phelps-Stokes Fund's headquarters at 101 Park Avenue in New York City to discuss US policy toward the European colonies and League of Nations mandates in Africa.[14]

Stokes's committee operated in a crucial space of unofficial policy planning during the Second World War. The war strengthened ties between the US government's understaffed diplomatic apparatus and a variety of external agencies—what historian Stephen Wertheim has called a "proto-national security state, furnishing officials with knowledge and personnel." The State Department, for example, outsourced much of its postwar planning to experts at the Council on Foreign Relations early in the war. Stokes hoped that CAWPA might play a similar role on the topic of African affairs, which he saw as an overlooked, even neglected, element in US foreign policy. Within this arena of unofficial policymaking, the Phelps-Stokes Fund's committee was distinctive, both for its emphasis on European colonialism in Africa as a sticking point in a postwar peace settlement and for its inclusion of African Americans in postwar planning discussions.[15]

A number of prominent Black thinkers, including W. E. B. Du Bois, Ralph Bunche, Howard University historian Rayford Logan, Fisk University sociologist Charles Johnson, and NAACP board member Channing Tobias, played a part in the committee. Though notable for its integrated membership, the group was characterized by sharp disagreements between two white officials at the fund, Anson Phelps Stokes and Thomas Jesse Jones, and several of its Black members, most of all Du Bois and Logan. Stokes and Jones were the Phelps-Stokes Fund's two most powerful officials, and both upheld the fund's founding belief that Black uplift required white leadership. Du Bois, at the age of seventy-three, was the doyen of the Pan-African movement. His politics were in the midst of a decade-long shift from a reformist social-democratic perspective to the socialist internationalism that would define the last phase of his career. Logan, the author of respected studies on the US occupation of Haiti and the workings of the league's mandates system, gained prominence over the course of 1940 and 1941 as a leading advocate for a Fair Employment Practices Commission and an end to discrimination in war-related industries, and he would become the NAACP's leading foreign affairs consultant after the end of the war. Together, they represented the two poles of left-liberal collaboration that characterized much of the dynamic Black internationalist activism of the period.[16]

The temporary collaboration between these Black thinkers and leading white philanthropists Jones and Stokes—with whom several of them, especially Du Bois, had previously been in conflict—points to a commonality between the dynamics of CAWPA and the wider realm of Black internationalism during the war. Because of their marginality in most discussions of international affairs, Black activists of varying political persuasions pursued alliances with people holding divergent, and sometimes deeply racist, views in order to have their voices heard. As historian Keisha N. Blain has shown, Black nationalist activist Mittie Maude Lena Gordon worked to cultivate the support of white supremacist Senator Theodore Bilbo for the cause of Black emigration during the 1930s and 1940s. The decision of Du Bois, Logan, Bunche, and others to work with Thomas Jesse Jones in particular—whom Carter G. Woodson argued should be "execrated and abhorred by Negroes who suffered from his career in Negro Life"—reveals the importance of strategic flexibility in their approach to institutional change. It also reflects, as historian Maribel Morey has pointed out in her study of the Carnegie Corporation, the deeply unequal power relations between white philanthropists who engaged with the issue of racial inequality and their Black interlocutors, whose work they both relied on and often misrepresented.[17]

The composition of the committee sparked debate from the beginning, especially concerning the nationalities and political views of its members. Stokes felt strongly that the committee ought to be racially integrated but not international, and he persuaded other committee members to "includ[e] only American citizens," although provisions were made for "consult[ing]" Africans directly. Similarly, while several of the committee's African American members held views substantially to the left of the center of US politics, or even of the New Deal coalition, there were limits on the political heterodoxy that the fund's leaders would tolerate. Max Yergan, the cofounder with Paul Robeson of the Council on African Affairs, was considered, but because he had been "a fellow traveler in the days when the youth movement was rife with some of the Marxian theories," Stokes opted not to include him. Anticommunism and a civilizationist attitude about African cultural development that permeated the views of many Americans—both Black and white—thus circumscribed the range of Black voices involved with the project.[18]

Franklin Roosevelt and Winston Churchill issued the Atlantic Charter in the interim between Stokes's initial efforts to bring the group together in August and the committee's first meeting in September. The third point of the charter declared that the United States and United Kingdom "respect the right of all peoples to choose the form of government under which they will live; and they wish to see sovereign rights and self-government restored to those who have been forcibly deprived of them."[19] Whether this principle should apply only to the territories conquered by the Axis powers, or to the entire globe, including the "forcibly deprived" territories held by Allied powers in Africa, quickly became a subject of debate in the African American press, and this question resonated through CAWPA's deliberations.[20] As a smaller editorial committee, consisting of Stokes, Jones, Bunche, Charles Johnson, Channing Tobias, and Emory Ross, began to draft their report, they determined that it should center on "the application of the Roosevelt-Churchill 'Eight Points' to African welfare.'"[21]

The first draft of the report was principally the work of Thomas Jesse Jones, although the rest of the small editorial committee had some input. This draft presented a moderate path toward the reform and eventual dissolution of European colonial rule in Africa. Opening with the comment that "the emergence into political consciousness of the non-white peoples of the world is a recent phenomenon of great significance," Jones argued that the moment was equally "full of promise and full of possibility of danger." The colonial powers' intransigence and the possibility of "premature" independence were, he claimed, equal threats to African development and the creation of a stable global order. While repudiating ideas of biological racial difference, the draft report repeatedly emphasized the supposed incapacity of Africans for immediate self-rule—an emphasis that would be lessened but not eliminated during the revision process. Although the draft criticized forced labor and colonial monopolies over trade, it consistently praised the British system of so-called indirect rule. Jones's draft thus presented a vision of colonialism as a system of political sovereignty first and foremost. More than that, his draft viewed colonialism as a redeemable system of governance, one with better and worse applications, rather than as a form of rule that enabled and perpetuated racialized violence, exploitation, and disfranchisement.[22]

The question of African participation remained a sticking point after the draft was circulated to the wider committee. At a meeting in February 1942, "Native Africans in this country especially qualified to give the Native point of view" were invited to share their opinions of the preliminary draft. Ernest Kalibala, a Ugandan sociologist teaching at Lincoln University in Missouri, dissented from the committee's very framing of their objective—"the focussing of public attention on wise treatment of Africa and Africans"—arguing that it reflected an undemocratic approach. He insisted that "Africa and the Africans must not only be treated wisely but must be included in the Democratic Councils to dictate the policy of treatment." By restricting participation to Americans, Stokes had ensured that "[the] committee will formulate policies agreeing with the Colonial Powers." Kalibala's counsel went unheeded. But his view of a connection between personnel and policy resonated with several members of the committee, especially Rayford Logan, who argued throughout the war and long after its conclusion for African and African American representation in international organizations.[23]

The circulation of the preliminary draft to the forty members of the wider committee incited debates about the nature and severity of colonial rule. Du Bois, in particular, sought to add an analysis of the economic origins of colonialism and a sharper critique of the commercial exploitation of African colonies in the present. He contrasted the movement toward social democracy in Europe and the United States, epitomized by the New Deal, with European policies toward the colonies, which, he argued, "repeat and perpetuate the errors of the worst days of capitalistic exploitation in Europe." Du Bois claimed that the United States and European nations were placing the "strong motive of private profit . . . in the foreground of our interracial relations," rather than "the greater objects of cultural understanding and moral uplift." In an argument reminiscent of his analysis of the First World War in the 1915 essay "The African Roots of War," and resonating with the theories of imperialism of J. A. Hobson and V. I. Lenin articulated in the same era, Du Bois urged the committee to recognize that commercial rapaciousness in the colonies not only harmed Africans but "frustrate[d] and nullifie[d] much of the reform effort within the more progressive lands which own and control colonies." Arguing that "the land and natural resources of Africa should be regarded as belonging primarily to the Native inhabitants, to be administered for their advancement and well being," Du Bois pronounced economic self-determination as his fundamental goal for the postwar order.[24]

As revisions to the report began to circulate in the spring of 1942, Du Bois continued to criticize the document's relative silence on the economic exploitation of African workers and peasants by European powers and US corporations. After one meeting in April 1942, he wrote a long message to Stokes, criticizing the report's discussion of the Atlantic slave trade and its sanguine view of British "indirect rule." On these topics, Du Bois felt that the committee had understated the economic motivation of European powers' involvement in Africa and the severity of imperialism's impact on Africans. "Thorough-going reform" could not be effective, he argued, "unless we frankly recognize the profit motive in the white invasion of Africa." The British, in particular, were given too much credit for their system of colonial governance, which "was an expedient, not a plan, in its origins," and which in any case always prioritized "trade and investment of capital" for profit over "native development."[25]

Despite Stokes's opposition to all of Du Bois's suggestions, the renowned scholar was successful in convincing the committee to include several of his proposed changes in the final report. In the opening section, which provided a "balance sheet" of European involvement in Africa, the preliminary draft only mentioned the abolition of the slave trade. The final draft, however, emphasized Europeans' establishment of the Atlantic slave trade, as well as slavery's ongoing impact on African economies, on the negative side of the ledger, two changes that Du Bois had demanded. Du Bois further reshaped the section on "indirect rule," which was almost entirely complimentary in the original draft. The final version, reflecting Du Bois's suggestions, included the analysis that this form of colonialism held "significant appeal to the colonial Power" because it was "a cheaper and more expedient method of providing for the control of native groups." The final draft further included several additional "disadvantages" of "indirect rule," in particular the "danger of the native unit of government not being given sufficient independent authority." The influence of Du Bois thus pushed the committee's report toward an understanding of colonialism as a system of exploitation much closer to his own.[26]

The institutional design of a successor organization to the League of Nations, particularly as it pertained to league mandates in Africa, became increasingly central to the committee's debates as it revised the report over the winter and spring of 1942. Under Article 22 of the Covenant of the League of Nations, individual European states held administrative authority over their mandates in Africa, and the Permanent Mandates Commission held the power to inspect conditions and report their findings to the international body. For residents of these territories, the clearest difference between mandatory governance and direct colonial rule was often the ability to bring petitions to the league itself. The right of petition, which extended not only to mandate residents but to "interested outsiders," provided a means to highlight colonial abuses of power and, perhaps more importantly, facilitated the emergence of an international language of public protest against colonial conditions—even as petitions were routinely ignored by the mandatory powers.[27]

Both Rayford Logan and Ralph Bunche had deep expertise in the workings of the mandates system in Africa. Logan had examined the Permanent Mandates Commission of the League of Nations in a long article he wrote for the *Journal of Negro History* in 1928. There, he argued that the "forces of imperialism—surplus capital, need for tropical products, surplus manufactures, desire for prestige"—all conspired against the mandates' stated intention of providing training in self-government. Bunche had written even more extensively about the mandates in his 1934 Harvard dissertation, which compared the administrative practices of the French colony of Dahomey and the neighboring French mandate territory of Togoland. He argued that few practical differences existed in the two territories' systems of governance and labor management. To Bunche, although there existed a "slight difference in the treatment and status of the natives" that favored the mandate, the primary purpose of mandatory status was to give international legitimacy to a fundamentally colonial relationship. Bunche's dissertation further contained a direct attack on Thomas Jesse Jones for his support of industrial education in British and French Africa along the lines of Booker T. Washington's Tuskegee Institute.[28]

In spite of their critiques of the mandates system, neither Logan nor Bunche—who would go on to administer the United Nations trusteeship program—saw all forms of trust administration as inherently exploitative. Bunche, in particular, conceived of the public accountability made possible by the Permanent Mandates Commission's inspections as a progressive feature of the league that should be preserved in any new international institution. Even in his dissertation, as political scientist Pearl T. Robinson notes, Bunche wrote of the mandates in "two registers"—one that took the league's professions of a "sacred trust" seriously, and one that subordinated such pronouncements to an economic analysis of imperialism, which he would expand upon further in his 1936 book *A World View of Race*. This duality in Bunche's perspective reflected what scholar Jeffrey C. Stewart calls the "mask" of "New Negro foreign policy consciousness," in which Black Americans' attempts to bring racism and colonialism into US foreign policy conversations required at least partial genuflection to prevailing elite discourses.[29]

Thomas Jesse Jones's preliminary draft of the CAWPA report did not reflect the critical views of mandatory governance held by several of the committee's Black members. It reflected much more clearly Jones's own endorsement of the racist structure of the league's mandates system. The draft argued that a new world organization should replicate the structure of the league's mandates wholesale, with European powers in control of administration and an international body holding only the powers of inspection and report. The report's initial suggestion was to ensure the continuation and extension of "progressive and efficient mandate control" under "national responsibility" not only for "existing mandated territories" but for "all European-controlled Colonies in Africa." While an international mandate "might well be tried in Libya, or those parts of it lost to Italy," the thrust of the preliminary draft cut against the idea of any international administration of trusteeships.[30]

Dissent from the African American scholars on the committee, especially Rayford Logan, pushed the final report toward a more favorable assessment of international trusteeship administration. In a meeting of the committee held in May 1942, Logan argued for the complete transfer of all colonies and existing league mandates in Africa to an international mandate administration. While the league's mandates system replicated many of the problems of colonial rule, Logan believed that greater internationalization of colonial governance, combined with the representation of both colonial sub-jects and African Americans on an international mandates commission, held genuine promise in smoothing the road to independence. This system repre-sented, in his mind, the best way to ensure that colonial territories would not fall into relations of economic dependency with their former rulers—or even fall back under direct political control—after decolonization.[31]

Du Bois proposed a compromise between the initial draft's replication of the league's structure, which Jones and Stokes supported, and Logan's call for full international trusteeship administration. He argued that interna-tional administration should be reserved only for colonies that would have "changed hands" by the end of the war. Making distinctions between the co-lonial holdings of the victors and the vanquished was a staple of international politics after the First World War, as the League of Nations had placed only the territories of the Ottoman and German empires under mandatory con-trol. Du Bois's proposal recapitulated that logic, although he argued that the locus of sovereignty in the African territories of the Axis powers should rest not with the Allies but with the new international organization. Such a system would ensure that "conquered territory in Africa" not be "considered as spoils of war," and thus would prevent Allied powers from using the war as a pretext to expand their colonial holdings.[32]

This compromise won unanimous support from the committee. The published report incorporated the recommendation that "international ad-ministration should be introduced into those colonies—not including inde-pendent states such as Ethiopia—which have changed hands or which may change hands during the war; and that similarly such administration might well be tried in some other area or areas." Logan's second major institutional proposal—a recommendation for African representation in the putative in-ternational trusteeship administration—also appeared in the final report, marking another key change from Jones's draft. While the report did not go as far as either Du Bois or Logan wanted, it broke with the precedent of the league in important ways and opened the door to a broader application of the international mandate.[33]

The endorsement of international trusteeship administration by influen-tial African American intellectuals on CAWPA points to important tensions in African American anticolonial thought during the war. Given the conti-nuities between trusteeship's promise of preparation for self-government and the civilizing-mission ideology of colonialism, it is perhaps surprising that prominent African American anticolonialists advocated for the transfer of sovereignty of African colonies and mandates to an international governing body over the granting of immediate independence.[34] The appeal of this institutional arrangement becomes clearer in light of three reasons, all of which are evident in the committee's deliberations. First, the advocacy of Du Bois, Bunche, and Logan was influenced by its setting in an elite advisory group that aspired to policy influence; a strain of political realism constrained their institutional proposals. Second, drawing on a longstanding strand of thought in the Pan-African movement, CAWPA's Black members continued to imagine African Americans as the vanguard of African liberation up until, and in some cases beyond, the end of the war. Their critique of the brutality and exploitation produced by colonial rule was linked to a paternalistic view of Africans as politically underdeveloped—not due to any racial or civilizational deficiency, but due to the exploitative nature of colonialism itself.

Third, and crucially, a definition of colonialism as a form of racialized economic exploitation undergirded their analysis. Their account of the problem of colonialism emphasized not only political rule over a territory and its people by a foreign power but exploitation of its inhabitants for the economic benefit of the colonizers.[35] Their conception of colonialism as racialized economic exploitation envisioned the creation and maintenance of a global racial hierarchy as dynamically interrelated with the political subordination and commercial exploitation of peoples in Africa, Asia, and Latin America, beginning with the establishment of the transatlantic slave trade and the wave of colonization after 1492 and continuing through the establishment of a racialized international order in the League of Nations. By emphasizing colonial underdevelopment, this account held that national independence would prove insufficient to reverse the effects of colonialism and would only leave African nations in a position of dependency toward European and American state and corporate power. Like advocates of postimperial federalism, or those who favored equal citizenship within imperial borders for the subjects in French and British colonies in Africa, these African American thinkers believed at this point that a different form of government than national independence was necessary to ensure that political self-determination would not be undermined by continuing forms of racialized economic exploitation.[36]

These Black thinkers thus based their support for a system of internationalized and democratized trusteeship administration on opposite principles from mainstream commentators who also advocated for trusteeship arrangements to replace colonial rule. Publishing magnate Henry Luce, for example, outlined his vision for the "internationalization of Africa" in quite different terms: "Africa is to be treated as a great corporate treasure-house and playground, trusteed for the benefit of all mankind." Although he granted that "the inhabitants of Africa will be the first charges on the common wealth of Africa"—a claim hard to square with the view that Africa's "treasures" would be "the benefit of all mankind"—he was confident to say that "there will be no hurry in working out ideas for self-government." The distance between Luce's vision and those held by the Black members of CAWPA suggests why the institutional details of trusteeship planning mattered so much for Bunche, Du Bois, and Logan. If one form of trusteeship might serve Luce's rapacious aims, they believed a better one, with international administration by a truly representative body, could prevent them.[37]

The Committee on Africa, the War, and Peace Aims also formulated their arguments about the future of European colonial rule in Africa through re-flection on the relationship between American regimes of racial hierarchy and the global colonial system. Americans, the committee declared, had a legitimate special interest in the problems of colonialism in Africa because of both the country's substantial African American population and its re-cent overseas imperial projects. In the final CAWPA report, the histories of continental and overseas imperialism were transmuted into a national "expe-rience" of navigating the problems of interracial governance. The commit-tee acknowledged the United States' mixed record on these questions and included a subsection of the report entitled "Recognition of America's Own Shortcomings, with Evidences of Recent Improvements." Segregation and anti-Black racism appeared in the document as not only a moral and politi-cal but also a strategic problem: the report acknowledged that "the educated African is aware of the discriminations against Negroes which have existed in our democracy," making them skeptical of the possibility of a positive Ameri-can influence. Articulating a similar stance to what Gunnar Myrdal would ar-gue in *An American Dilemma*, CAWPA called for domestic changes in order to secure foreign influence, both by addressing this attitude of the "educated African" and by "stimulat[ing] those working for better African conditions" at home.[38]

If the American record on African American rights appeared as a hin-drance to its ability to shape African realities, the nation's domestic expansion and overseas conquests came out in a more positive light. The expansion of US sovereignty over "people of different races, including some on various stages of civilization differing greatly from our own," and the nation's sup-posed "considerable success in securing coöperation and good feeling be-tween the different racial groups" in Hawaii and the Philippines represented an "experience of some value" for the future governance of Africa. The status of the United States as a member in the club of overseas imperial nations, the committee argued, increased its standing as an arbiter of the future of colonies elsewhere in the world. At the same time, although the history of violence against Native Americans was largely absent from the report, the authors brought it to bear on their reflections of the particular difficulties of African settler colonies, especially South Africa: "We must realize that it is most difficult for any country which has a very large and dominant settler population to be entirely fair to the needs and rights of a primitive native population. Our historic American experience with the Indian—about which we cannot be proud—has shown this clearly." This brief reference is significant for the committee's acknowledgment of Indigenous dispossession and its placement of US settler colonialism on a continuum with other colonial formations. Yet, as in its discussion of US overseas imperialism, the committee's verdict reflected Jones's and Stokes's perspectives over those of its more radical Black members. The committee portrayed the history of American policy toward a racialized subject population as a set of lessons from which European colonial powers might learn, and a reason for Americans' voices to be included in postwar debates.[39]

In the end, the institutional visions and conceptual orientation of Bunche, Du Bois, and Logan had clear effects on the analysis of colonialism and the policy recommendations of the Committee on Africa, the War, and Peace Aims. Rather than a document of growing liberal consensus on African affairs, as historian Brenda Gayle Plummer describes the report, *The Atlantic Charter and Africa from an American Standpoint* was the product of a tense compromise between the conservative dispositions of the committee's philanthropic leaders and the more expansive (if still, in some ways, deeply constrained) visions of several of its Black intellectuals.[40]

The tensions that pervaded the committee's deliberations, moreover, continued to resonate in debates about colonialism and trusteeship throughout the war. As policy elites and the wider public began to debate the committee's report, the issue of international trusteeship in particular provoked conflicts—both between activists and policymakers and among Black internationalists themselves.

The Tragic Joke of Trusteeship

The Committee on Africa, the War, and Peace Aims released *The Atlantic Charter and Africa from an American Standpoint* in June 1942. Journalists and policymakers on both sides of the Atlantic saw the report as a watershed moment in postwar planning debates. Anson Phelps Stokes was especially keen to follow its reception among US policymakers. To that end, Ralph Bunche's growing role in official Washington proved useful. No longer an academic critic of imperialism and mandatory governance, Bunche had joined the Office of the Coordinator of Information (OCI)—precursor to the Office of Strategic Services (OSS)—in the weeks after the first CAWPA meeting. He was granted permission from his OCI superior Conyers Read to continue his involvement with CAWPA alongside his government work—signaling the committee's place in an approved circle of unofficial policymaking from the beginning.[1]

Throughout 1942 and 1943, Bunche kept Stokes up to date on the figures in Washington who took an interest in African affairs. He urged Stokes to contact them and send them copies of the CAWPA report. Bunche was especially eager to get the report into the hands of the newly formed postwar planning division of the State Department, headed by the Russian émigré Leo Pasvolsky. He expressed to Stokes his "concern" that "Africa and other colonial areas . . . be given adequate and constructive attention by this group." This concern, in part, motivated Bunche's decision to push for a transfer from his position at OSS to the State Department, which he received at the end of 1943. Another member of CAWPA, Benjamin Gerig, would go on to lead the State Department's Division of Dependent Affairs, where, with Bunche, he would take a leading role in US trusteeship planning in the final years of the war.[2]

CAWPA's report was also enthusiastically received in diplomatic circles in the United Kingdom. By early 1943, Stokes's contact at Edinburgh House

Press informed him that there was a "run on the Atlantic Charter volume" and requested a hundred additional copies. Reactions in the British press foreshadowed the postwar primacy of the United States and made use of the report's ambivalence about British colonial governance. According to an editorial in the Manchester *Guardian*, the report showed the world that "colonial questions have definitely passed out of the sphere where they are domestic problems to that in which they are international." At the same time, the *Guardian* editorial board imagined that the United States would serve as a vehicle for the continuation of Britain's new colonial development policies. They viewed the report as a "powerful reinforcement of the measures taken or contemplated by the colonial Powers for attacking the acute problem of Africa's poverty."[3]

Stokes himself contributed to the misleading impression that the committee held an entirely favorable opinion of the methods of British rule during his own publicity tour following the report's release. Despite the criticisms of British colonialism that were included in the final report, Stokes continued to speak in uniformly positive language about the British Empire, even suggesting that it continue unchanged after the end of the war. In a radio address in January 1943, he insisted—in far stronger terms than the CAWPA report had used—that "it is manifestly impossible to turn over certain areas in Africa today entirely to the native population." Instead, he claimed, the focus of postwar planners should be on the extension of "so-called 'indirect rule' through Native chiefs," and on "integrating Native Africans into the central administration of every colony." In his numerous press appearances after the report's release, Stokes selectively portrayed its analysis and recommendations in keeping with his own ideological perspective.[4]

In the United States, the report received coverage in most major newspapers, especially in the Black press. Large-circulation Black newspapers such as the *Baltimore Afro-American* and the *Pittsburgh Courier* amplified the report's argument that African issues should take center stage at the postwar peace conference. Some Black papers also called special attention to the racially integrated composition of the committee itself. The coverage of CAWPA in the Black press thus emphasized not only that the views of African Americans should matter for the postwar future of Africa, but that the committee's modeling of cooperation across racial divides was a reason to take its recommendations seriously.[5]

Although the African American press largely celebrated the release of *The Atlantic Charter and Africa from an American Standpoint*, responses in Black scholarly publications and journals of opinion were mixed. Du Bois took the unusual step of publishing his own review in the journal *Phylon*, which he edited from Atlanta University. Rehashing his disagreements with Stokes from committee meetings, he criticized the report's "distinctly pro-British" orientation and claimed it failed to "stress adequately the dangers of the economic exploitation of Africa for the benefit of white nations." Du Bois even published in his review a statement he had originally written during the committee's internal deliberations. There, he condemned the report's timidity on the question of capital investment in Africa, which was subject to few or none of the controls that it faced in Europe and America. Such an omission, Du Bois wrote, left the committee "open to blame either for a lack of knowledge or a lack of courage." Despite this sharp criticism, Du Bois's final assessment was optimistic. The report represented, in his view, "by far the best thing on the African problems which has been published in recent years."[6]

Other Black thinkers saw it in a less favorable light. The most biting rebuke came from Howard University historian Eric Williams. Williams called attention to the report's failure to challenge what he saw as the fundamental issues of colonial rule: racial segregation in the colonies and the denial of the franchise to colonial subjects. The Trinidadian scholar-activist cited his own "by-no-means-negligible acquaintance with the promises of English governments in the past" and "with the realities against which they have been broken," suggesting that the all-American committee might have benefited from the direct participation and insight of those who had lived under the British colonial system. The report's recommendations, couched in the language of trusteeship and reform, failed to meet Williams's standard for the "radical changes [that] must be made in the condition of the colonial peoples," and thus represented "just another in a by now very lengthy list of mild palliatives for a desperate disease." CAWPA's proposals for institutional change, centered on the endorsement of an experiment in international trusteeship administration, struck Williams as merely another attempt to couch a continuation of colonial rule in the language of reform.[7]

Some African nationalists also found the report too circumspect in its proposals. Nigerian nationalist Kingsley Mbadiwe saw the report as a welcome departure from a "world that dares to overlook Africa in the peace resolution," but warned that its recommendations ought not to take precedence over the views of Africans themselves on the postwar order: "Africa must be the captain of its own destiny."[8] Kwame Nkrumah called out CAWPA by name in his essay "Towards Colonial Freedom," where he listed it among several US organizations which "advocate the 'gradual evolution towards self-government' policy for colonial peoples through some sort of international commission." Asking acerbically, "Do these organizations expect [European] monopoly interests and their agents, the colonial governments, to expropriate

themselves?" Nkrumah rendered a similar verdict as Mbadiwe did, conclud-
ing that "they do not . . . express the fundamental aspirations of the masses of
colonial peoples."[9]

Not all criticisms of the report from Black thinkers came from the perspective of anticolonial nationalism. Merze Tate, a scholar of international
relations who was the first African American woman to receive a graduate
degree from Oxford, and who had recently become a colleague of Logan and
Williams on the Howard faculty, instead criticized the report's reliance on
the idealistic language of the Atlantic Charter. Rooted in a realist analysis
of power politics, Tate's response claimed that CAWPA failed to understand
that "World War II, when considered realistically, is not fought for the Four
Freedoms everywhere." Instead, "it is a militarist and imperialist struggle for
freedom and power—power for some at the expense of others." The Atlantic
Charter's primary relevance to Africans, Tate argued, was not found in its
grand promises of self-determination. Instead, what mattered most about the
charter was its fourth point, which sought to extend open-door trade policies
to colonial territories. This plank was both a threat to the colonial monopolies on trade held by European powers and an invitation to American capital.
To Tate, the trade regime that would emerge from the end of the war would
reshape the lives of Africans much more than would the charter's abstract
declarations of support for self-determination. Tate further judged the report's proposal for international trusteeship administration harshly. Such a
proposal, she argued, reflected the "temporizing" attitude of "even the most
liberal" representatives of European and American elite opinion, who fool-
ishly believed that international cooperation would reduce the incentives for
colonial exploitation.[10]

As these reactions indicate, the publication of *The Atlantic Charter and
Africa from an American Standpoint* inspired debate on questions of international institutional design among Black thinkers both within and outside the
ranks of the committee that authored it. The report's specific endorsement
of an international trusteeship arrangement, as well as the broader orientation of Du Bois, Logan, and Bunche toward institutional reform as a key vector of anticolonial activity, came under fire. For skeptics such as Williams,
Mbadiwe, Nkrumah, and Tate—whatever their differences—the fate of colonial and mandatory regimes in Africa would only be resolved through some
combination of great power politics and nationalist struggle. In the final years
of the war, CAWPA's work continued to frame the lobbying and activism of
some of its key members, even as this skepticism about the liberatory potential of a new international institution spread widely across Black anticolonial
circles.

Colonial Comparisons and Wartime Diplomacy

African American internationalists turned to the question of international institutional design at the same time that US state policymakers began to ascribe increasing importance to the same question. CAWPA's recommendations for a limited system of international trusteeship administration aimed to influence a simultaneous policy planning process in the State Department to create a new organization to replace the League of Nations. The United States began devoting resources toward this question in 1941, much earlier than other Allied powers did.[11] And in the early years of the war, US planners entertained several visions of extending and internationalizing the mandates system. Conflicting views emerged within the Roosevelt administration about how far to pressure the British government to loosen its hold on its colonies and admit international oversight. One proposal would have placed all colonies under a strengthened mandate system administered by regional councils, with US representation. Another fell along the lines of Rayford Logan's preferred system of international administration of all existing mandates. While support for international administration of trust territories in policymaking circles was thin, the early years of the war contained some signs of experimentation.[12]

The Department of State offered no formal response to *The Atlantic Charter and Africa from an American Standpoint*. But one CAWPA member, Benjamin Gerig, served as a direct link between the committee's work and the department's ongoing planning process. Author of a well-respected study on the mandates system and the primary expert on trusteeship at State, Gerig chaired the department's Committee on Dependent Areas throughout the war. He was, according to historian Wm. Roger Louis, "the key man behind the scenes on the American side" with respect to trusteeship planning. In the months after the publication of *The Atlantic Charter and Africa from an American Standpoint*, Gerig worked with the department's Subcommittee on International Organization to draft a policy recommendation on trusteeship.[13]

During the drafting process, Rayford Logan met with Gerig several times. Throughout these conversations, Logan argued for a broad application of international trusteeship administration. After one meeting in December 1942, Logan wrote in his diary that "it is not going to be easy for the U.S. to tell Britain to get out of her colonies," and that the State Department was "leaning toward national administration" in order not to jeopardize their wartime alliance with the British.

Logan's attempt to convince Gerig to support international administration of trust territories relied on a set of comparisons between the Jim Crow regime in the American South and colonial governance in Africa. He argued that *national* administration replicated the problems of the federal system of the United States, where "in practically every case in which the States have been given the administration of funds provided by the national government, Negroes in the Southern states have not received equitable benefits." Granting administrative authority to the colonial powers would have a similar effect as granting governing power to the southern states, for "the mandatory will find means of ignoring the ideals of the system and of circumventing the efforts of the supervisory body to assure those ideals." In the same way that subnational federalism enabled Jim Crow, Logan argued, national administration of trust territories would enable a continuation of the most exploitative forms of colonial rule.

Gerig was unconvinced. At the end of 1942, the Subcommittee on International Organization produced a report that argued against direct international administration—with the possible exception of the Italian colony of Libya. The approach of this subcommittee thus aligned more closely with Thomas Jesse Jones's initial draft than with the final CAWPA report that reflected the interventions of Du Bois and Logan.[14]

The report of the Subcommittee on International Organization presaged the path American policy would take as the war progressed. Policymakers ultimately determined that their goals of economic and military access could be achieved without international administration of British and French colonies. The incorporation of the Allies' empires in an American-led world order would suffice. Between 1943 and 1945, American officials' desire to assert the principle of national self-determination in world affairs became decoupled from the actual institutional machinery of trusteeship under the proposed United Nations Organization. Although Roosevelt briefly proposed an international mandate for the French colony of Indochina, by and large he repudiated proposals to place colonies and mandates, whether held by Allied or Axis powers, under international control after the war. Instead, the United States came to support the continuation of mandates only where they already existed, under the new language of trusteeship, combined with a new commitment by Europe's imperial powers to allow an open-door economic policy in their colonies.[15]

Definitional debates about colonialism and its relation to US racial politics pervaded discussions about trusteeship in the later years of the war. In the State Department's Advisory Committee on Post-War Foreign Policy, the geographer and president of Johns Hopkins University Isaiah Bowman raised the question of "internal colonies" in an attempt to weigh the expanse of Soviet territorial control against British imperialism. While Soviet rule went under a "different label" than the British Empire, Bowman insisted, "Russia is actually one of the major colonial powers; its colonies are merely internal rather than external." The fact that the Soviet Union "merely draws a line around its Empire and governs its colonies as part of a single country" made it more difficult for the United States to assert that the principles of trusteeship and the open door should apply. The Soviet Union had no more reason to agree, Bowman argued, "than it would have to ask us to subscribe to certain principles relating to the Osage Indians." As had been the case in the CAWPA deliberations, the history of US dispossession of American Indians sat awkwardly alongside the colonial arrangements the policy planners were working to change. Bowman only acknowledged this dispossession through a form of dismissal. For him, Indigenous self-determination through international law stood as an obviously absurd prospect, and a reason to oppose overly extensive trusteeship arrangements. Still, as State Department officials worked under the pressures of a changing wartime situation to devise the US position on trusteeship, they acknowledged that the governance of "internal colonies" might raise issues they did not wish to confront.[16]

The difficulty of constructing a universal principle of trusteeship that could apply to all colonies—internal or external—made Bowman suspicious that the United States could effectively exert pressure on its allies, especially Great Britain. At the same time, Leo Pasvolsky, the head of the postwar planning staff, was undeterred by the challenge that Bowman's mention of "internal colonies" posed. To Pasvolsky, "the test of colonial status is a test of unequal rights." States like the Soviet Union were "composite" states, with some inhabitants under colonial status and others holding the rights of full citizenship. Such "composite" states—a category which would necessarily include the United States as well—could still participate productively in the construction of norms and institutions of trusteeship for "outside areas." Figures in the State Department more committed to a broad application of some form of trusteeship, such as Pasvolsky and Undersecretary of State Sumner Welles, thus drew a sharp distinction between internal and external forms of colonialism. In their view, the existence of the former, including US governance over American Indians, African Americans, and other racialized minorities, should not prevent a country from attempting to mitigate the latter.[17]

British officials, on the other hand, highlighted US overseas colonies and internal racial divisions to deflect against American efforts to place British colonies under trusteeship. In early 1945, Arthur Creech-Jones, a Labour

Party member and chairman of the Fabian Colonial Bureau, argued in a meeting with Ralph Bunche that proposals for international oversight of British colonies would never win over colonial subjects, because they sensed that such arrangements merely provided a smokescreen for the extension of US power. The establishment of US bases in the Caribbean during the war and the "fear which the West Indian peoples had of the American racial attitude" only exacerbated the problem. More broadly, Creech-Jones questioned the legitimacy of a trusteeship system that did not extend to the United States' own territories. He wondered whether the proposed council "would deal with the American dependencies as well as those of other countries and whether it would concern itself with the problems of the 'fifteen million dependent peoples in the United States proper' [meaning] the American Negro." Creech-Jones's linkages between Jim Crow and colonial rule emphasized American double standards in a strategic attempt to preserve Europeans' colonial prerogatives.[18]

Bunche's response to Creech-Jones exemplified the stark shift in his political perspective that the war had produced. Bunche's move into the state policymaking apparatus both reflected and required an alteration to his views about the nature of colonialism and its relation to the US racial order. In the late 1920s and 1930s, although Bunche had rejected the Communist Party's call for "self-determination in the Black Belt," he had nonetheless theorized American racism as a particular form of a global pattern of imperial rule. In his 1936 book *A World View of Race*, Bunche examined racial conflict as a "device" of economic elites in "world economic and political conflict." He recognized that "the American Negro is an exceptional case in that he has been torn away from his origins and dumped into an entirely new milieu in which he finds himself a minority group." This status set African Americans apart from African colonial subjects, who were members of a majority group struggling against the minority rule of white Europeans. But he further argued that British and French colonial officials too often make the "mistake of assuming that the African and his problems are so essentially different from the problems confronting the peoples of the Western World." The African, the African American, the "peasants and work-men of England and France of a century ago," and the "other workers and peasants today in less advanced countries" encountered the same problems of capitalist development. By 1940, although the language of an overriding, global class conflict had dropped out of Bunche's analysis, he continued to understand colonialism as a structure of antidemocratic rule that paralleled that which faced African Americans. In another essay, he argued that "the African in Africa . . . is much like the Negro in this country with regard to democracy," and that "his future, as ours, depends upon the preservation and extension of the democratic concepts throughout the world."[19]

Bunche largely abandoned this comparative perspective by the end of the war. By the time of his meeting with Arthur Creech-Jones, Bunche saw the arguments of the British official about US colonial rule and Jim Crow simply as a political tactic to deflect the attention of postwar planners away from the question of placing British colonies under trusteeship. Yet his response extended beyond the immediate context to deny altogether a connection between the questions of colonial and African American freedom. In a public address he delivered a month after his meeting with Creech-Jones, Bunche insisted that "there is utterly no connection between the two problems." No longer envisioning imperialism as a global system of class exploitation or anti-democratic rule, Bunche now considered the relationship solely in terms of nationalist aspiration. Here he saw a vast distance between African Americans and Africans. Translating his longstanding disapproval of cultural nationalist and economic separatist currents in US Black politics into a denial of their existence, he insisted that "unlike the colonial peoples, the American Negro, who is culturally American, has no nationalist and no separatist ambitions." Bunche turned to an exceptionalist understanding of American politics as defined by the gradual extension of liberal freedoms.[20]

These debates within the policymaking apparatus about the comparability of European imperial rule and American racial hierarchy occurred as the commitment of US policymakers to a robust trusteeship system was weakening. The watering down of trusteeship proposals between 1943 and 1945 dismayed many African American observers. The Dumbarton Oaks Conference in the spring of 1944 struck a devastating blow to hopes that a new international institution would take meaningful steps toward the ending of colonial exploitation, sparking criticism from Black activists across the left-liberal spectrum, from the labor radical A. Philip Randolph to the National Council of Negro Women's Mary McLeod Bethune. (That one of the few Black organizations to endorse the Dumbarton Oaks proposals was the Communist-led National Negro Congress [NNC], which followed the wartime posture of the CPUSA of subordinating revolutionary ambitions to the attainment of Allied war aims, speaks to the complexity of ideological alignments in Black politics in the crucible of the war.)[21]

The neglect of colonial issues at Dumbarton Oaks particularly exasperated Du Bois and deeply influenced his writing and activism in 1944 and 1945. Du Bois rejoined the NAACP in 1944, ten years after resigning over a conflict with its board, to take the position of director of research. From this vantage point, he assessed the institutional arrangements of the postwar world as they began to take shape in his 1945 book *Color and Democracy: Colonies and Peace*. Written quickly over the summer and fall of 1944, during and after the Dumbarton Oaks Conference, the book represented Du Bois's most thorough assessment of the possibilities for a lasting peace and the spread of democracy after the Second World War. In it, Du Bois exemplified the paradoxical nature of some Black thinkers' embrace of international trusteeship.[22]

The same critique of colonial labor practices that Du Bois had worked to include in *The Atlantic Charter and Africa from an American Standpoint* rested at the center of his analysis in *Color and Democracy*. The imperial system, he further argued, made political life in Europe and the United States dependent on the absence of democracy elsewhere. In the aftermath of the Second World War, Du Bois predicted, the European and American working classes "are going to demand certain costly social improvements from their governments." The "temptation to recoup and balance the financial burden" of these improvements by increasing the exploitation of the colonies "is going to increase decidedly." The "working people of the civilized world may thus be largely induced to put their political power behind imperialism," he argued, and "democracy in Europe and America will continue to impede and nullify democracy in Asia and Africa." One vector of struggle, then, must take place within the polities of Europe and the United States. Only through the achievement of a racially inclusive "industrial democracy" would the economic incentive for the continuing exploitation of the colonial world be diminished.[23]

The other necessary vector of anticolonial struggle, Du Bois maintained, was the remaking of international institutions. The Allied powers' refusal to allow direct representation of the inhabitants of colonies and mandate territories at postwar planning conferences struck Du Bois as a clear breach of the idea that the war was fought to "establish democracy as a way of life." "It is both intolerable in ethics and dangerous in statecraft," he contended, "to allow . . . 8,000,000 Belgians to represent 10,000,000 Congolese in the new internation without giving these black folk any voice even to complain." The absence of any mention of the Permanent Mandates Commission at Dumbarton Oaks further suggested that territory captured from Germany and Italy during the war would become "integral parts of present empires"—the exact scenario Du Bois had warned against in the CAWPA deliberations.[24]

While the ideal of trusteeship had long ago proven bankrupt to Du Bois, the institutional form of a genuinely internationalized trusteeship system remained attractive to him. His proposals in *Color and Democracy* derived directly from the debates he had participated in with CAWPA: representation for "all colonial peoples" at the United Nations alongside "free nations";

a reorganized mandates commission with a broader array of powers; and the right of mandatory subjects to file oral as well as written petitions. Although his assessment of the problem of colonialism focused on its political economy, his proposed solutions still rested on colonial peoples' international representation—along with the possibility of moral suasion based on investigations the new international body might carry out.[25]

Color and Democracy contained some of Du Bois's most explicit reflections on the definition and boundaries of the political category of the colony. "Colonies are the slums of the world," he wrote, "the places of greatest concentration of poverty, disease, and ignorance of what the human mind has come to know." Acknowledging that this analogy was "none too good," as colonies "are for the most part quite separate in race and culture from the peoples who control them," unlike the "municipal slums of the nineteenth century," Du Bois found that "it is difficult to define a colony precisely." In part, this was due to the diverse array of colonial policies enacted by European powers in matters of education, customary law, the extent of local participation in governance, and the prominence of European settlement.[26]

This diversity in colonial policy, however, did not make broad assessments impossible. Du Bois identified three distinguishing features of modern colonial domination. One was the significance of racialization and the centrality of racial ideology in upholding the colonial system. "For the most part, today the colonial peoples are colored of skin," although "this was not true of colonies in other days." Whereas to "most white folk" this fact "proves . . . the logic of the colonial system," to Du Bois it proved that the emergence of "doctrines of race inferiority" was inseparable from the process of European expansion that began in the fifteenth century. Modern colonies were distinct from premodern ones, in part, because they were enmeshed in a new global system of racial hierarchy.[27]

The second defining feature of a modern colony, to Du Bois, was its economic relation to its imperial ruler. While earlier colonial ventures paid for themselves directly through the transfer of "gold, silver, jewels, and luxuries," beginning in the seventeenth century the economic role of the colony shifted. Modern colonies provided the "raw material" that created wealth for their empires by serving as inputs in production, export commodities, or sources of domestic consumption. But this role, too, was "not universally true today," Du Bois noted, as "it has been shown recently that only 3 per cent of the more valuable raw materials of the world are in colonial areas." Whereas defenders of colonialism pointed to such facts to argue that the colonial project was motivated by a sincere desire to uplift the welfare of the world, Du Bois argued that the economic motivation for colonialism remained equally strong, even if it was once again undergoing a shift. In the twentieth century, he contended, drawing on Hobson, Luxemburg, Lenin, and his own analysis dating back to the 1910s, "colonies are today areas for the investment of capital" offering investors rates of profit "far beyond . . . domestic ventures." Investors increasingly looked to colonial regions because they could exercise greater influence over their governments, "secure labor at the lowest wage," and "evade taxation and profit-limiting legislation." The continuing evolution and increasing financialization of the colonial project in no way diminished the economic exploitation at its core.[28]

The third feature that distinguished a modern colony, to Du Bois, was antidemocracy. Colonial governance, regardless of the degree of local autonomy or the existence of legislative councils, was fundamentally antidemocratic, since even these partial systems of representation for colonial subjects were the creations of the colonial powers themselves. Numerical comparisons featured prominently in this portion of Du Bois's argument, as he sought to emphasize that colonial empires, when considered as single political units, were dramatic examples of minority rule. Between the First World War and the Second, the British empire consisted of "495,000,000 persons ruled by 50,000,000 in the United Kingdom." In the French empire, "38,000,000 ruled 71,000,000"; and so on. These figures presented in simple terms how political inequality defined the status of the "disfranchised colonies."[29]

Du Bois painted a similar picture of the internal political structure of the United States. Federalism and the minoritarian character of the US Senate enhanced the power of Jim Crow disfranchisement laws, rendering the entire American political system undemocratic. In an obvious echo of his earlier discussion of the colonial empires, Du Bois counted the votes necessary to elect a person to Congress in each state, illustrating how Congressional representatives from the "Southern former slave states" were elected on the basis of less than a third of the votes as their counterparts in New York or Illinois. The structure of the Senate, with two senators representing each state, only magnified the problem: the will of "28,000,000 voters in New York, New Jersey, Pennsylvania, Illinois, Ohio, California, Indiana, and Michigan" was subject to a veto from "1,250,000 voters in Mississippi, South Carolina, Wyoming, Nevada, Delaware, Vermont, Rhode Island, Arizona, and New Mexico." As Du Bois put it, "the race problem has been deliberately intermixed with state particularism to thwart democracy." Federalism and Jim Crow combined to create a domestic analog to the colonial system.[30]

The structural and political relationship between external and internal colonialism also resonated in philosopher and literary scholar Alain Locke's considerations of the nascent postwar order. Locke, who was a colleague of

Ralph Bunche, Rayford Logan, and Merze Tate at Howard University, questioned whether the American record of segregation and discrimination would undercut the ability of the United States to play a role in dismantling European imperial rule. Locke's formulation of the problem, however, was distinct. Despite self-conceptions of the United States as a progressive force in world affairs, Locke argued in a speech in Los Angeles in 1944, "at the peace table we may be labeled imperialists." Locke suggested that American credibility would be questioned not because of the litany of overseas territories the United States controlled—territories whose numbers grew substantially over the course of the war—but because of its domestic racial frontiers. American advocacy in a world body for the "abolishment of imperialism" had to mount a defense against the accusation that "we have internal colonies, as well as ghettos legal and illegal, and that the empires of the world have only the external, colonial analogue of what we have at home." Locke did not explain what he meant by "internal colonies," or on what criteria he judged American racial dynamics comparable to colonial ones. It is clear that the territory of the southern "Black Belt" was not his referent, however. Locke had never been a supporter of the Communist Party or its call for "self-determination in the Black Belt," and his speech aimed explicitly to correct the impression that American racism was principally a southern problem. Instead, Locke offered the phrase "internal colonies" as a tentative new vocabulary to describe his longstanding preoccupation with the national cultural and economic subordination—and not solely the political disfranchisement—of Black Americans and other racial minorities within the United States.[31]

The UN Charter and the Eclipse of Institutionalism

Postwar planning debates prompted new transnational and comparative analyses of US racial hierarchy that sought to lay the groundwork for new forms of global solidarity. Yet the continuing commitment to international trusteeship administration by leading African American thinkers created divisions between them and their anticolonial counterparts abroad. These disagreements came to a head at a conference of over sixty anticolonial activists from Africa, the Caribbean, Asia, and the United States that Du Bois organized in Harlem in April 1945, on the eve of the United Nations Conference on International Organization in San Francisco, where the UN Charter was signed.[32] There, both Logan and Du Bois rehashed their arguments in support of international trusteeship administration. In one speech, Logan framed his position as parallel to the proposals for federation or equal imperial citizenship circulating at the time, arguing, "as soon as practicable, eventual independence, self-government, autonomy, dominion status, or first-class citizenship, should be granted."[33] Du Bois, meanwhile, advocated for a revitalized and internationalized mandate commission to oversee colonies that changed hands during the war, recapitulating the proposal that had won the day in CAWPA's deliberations.

In this context, however, these plans met with strong opposition. Kwame Nkrumah insisted that any system of trusteeship, even one under international control, "implie[d] sell-out to the colonial powers."[34] Although Nkrumah and others were ultimately persuaded to endorse the conference's proposal for a "colonial commission" consisting of "all permanent members of the UN Security Council, additional representatives elected by the General Assembly, and members who represent directly the several broad groups of colonial peoples" to oversee trust territories, the Harlem Conference marked the end of any sustained effort by anticolonial activists aimed at the internationalization of colonial rule.[35]

The tensions on display in Harlem continued to fester after the signing of the UN Charter. The sense that some African American activists were not fully committed to immediate African liberation influenced their marginalization at the Fifth Pan-African Congress in Manchester in October 1945. Organized primarily by Nkrumah and Trinidadian Marxist George Padmore, Manchester marked a turning point in the history of Pan-Africanism. Unlike previous Pan-African Congresses, which were organized largely by African Americans and oriented toward colonial reform, the Manchester meeting was driven by Africans themselves and articulated a push for outright independence. Labor unions and student groups made up of colonial subjects living in European metropoles were the strongest voices at the conference, and only two African Americans (including Du Bois) attended. The resolutions passed at Manchester, furthermore, served as a partial rebuke to those endorsed in Harlem a few months earlier. Delegates proclaimed that "the struggle for political power by Colonial and subject peoples is the first step towards, and the necessary prerequisite to, complete social, economic and political emancipation," while their resolution on West Africa specifically disowned "the claims of 'partnership,' 'trusteeship,' 'guardianship,' and the 'mandate system,'" which "do not serve the political wishes of the people of West Africa." As the center of gravity of Pan-Africanism shifted east, the waning appeal of international trusteeship was fully eclipsed.[36]

The project of international institutional reform that Logan, Du Bois, and Bunche had pursued throughout the war came to an end once the UN Charter was codified. The charter was partly Bunche's own handiwork. By 1945, Bunche was associate chief of the Division of Dependent Area Affairs in the State Department, where he reported to his former CAWPA colleague Benjamin Gerig. At San Francisco, Bunche played a key role in drafting the Declaration Regarding Non-Self-Governing Territories (chapter XI of the charter) and the chapters on trusteeship (XII and XIII). Although Bunche privately expressed regret that the charter contained no promise to work toward the eventual independence of trust territories, he envisioned the document as a genuine step toward decolonization. Bunche explained his views in an article in the *Department of State Bulletin*, where he labored to highlight differences between the new trusteeship provisions and the mandates system he had long criticized. The "definite advantages" of the new system included its departure from the racist classification system of A, B, and C mandates, its greater emphasis on the "welfare of the inhabitants of the trust territories," and, revealingly, its open-door trade provisions. Yet even Bunche could not avoid the conclusion that, whatever the lofty aims of the charter's provisions on trusteeship, the international body had little means of advancing them directly. Only the "national policies of responsible governments" could "breathe life" into the international institution he had worked to design.[37]

For Logan and Du Bois, on the other hand, found the UN Charter a terrible disappointment. Both believed it would only hinder anticolonial aspirations in the postwar world. Du Bois testified before the Senate Foreign Relations Committee on July 11, 1945, to make his criticisms known. Du Bois highlighted the lack of representation for colonized peoples and the weakness of the charter's provisions on trusteeship, which granted the Trusteeship Council no real authority and, in any event, allowed imperial powers complete control over whether a territory would even enter into trusteeship. Bunche, in response to Du Bois's testimony, argued that the charter's existing provisions for inspection and report were all that was necessary to place the colonial system on the path to extinction, further highlighting the gap that had emerged between their respective positions.[38]

For Logan, the failure to provide any hint of international administration or adequate representation for colonial subjects rendered the entire charter a "tragic joke." As Logan's grand hope that a well-structured international organization could lead the transition to a postcolonial world faded, his anticolonial imagination looked out on new horizons. In his book *The Negro and the Post-War World*, composed just after the end of the war, Logan imagined a very different path to Black sovereignty: "Is it too utterly fantastic to conceive that black men will one day perfect an atomic bomb? No, it is not. I can picture an international conference, not more than twenty-five years from now, in which a black delegate will rise and declare: 'Gentlemen: five hundred years is long enough for any people to be held in bondage, degraded, spit upon, exploited, disfranchised, segregated, lynched. Here is the formula for a home-manufactured atomic bomb. Give us liberty, or we will give you death.'" With the UN Charter condemned as a "tragic joke," the design of international institutions no longer appeared as a question worth having an answer to. New visions centered on colonial freedom being seized from below—even if more violently than Logan would prefer.[39]

The codification of the UN Charter made questions of international institutional design a less salient feature of Black internationalist thought and activism. But the analysis of colonialism as racialized economic exploitation that undergirded African American thinkers' proposals for a regime of international trusteeship outlived the wartime moment. The crucible of postwar planning produced new debates about the definition of colonialism, its relation to US domestic inequalities, and the relative priority of political and economic self-determination. After the war's end, these debates would persist in a new guise—particularly in the arena of international development politics.

Facing the Neocolonial Future

Shortly after the end of the Second World War, Oliver Cromwell Cox made a prediction. Surveying the devastation of the postwar economic landscape, Cox foresaw that the economic impoverishment of the colonies and trust territories of Africa and Asia would quickly become a primary object of strategic concern for the United States. Cox was a sociologist and a socialist. Born in 1901 in Port-of-Spain, Trinidad, he moved to Chicago in 1919, part of a wave of Caribbean migrants that mingled with the first Great Migration of African Americans from the southern United States. After receiving his PhD in sociology from the University of Chicago in 1938, Cox turned his writings in a direction more in keeping with his socialist politics. He believed that the economic devastation of the war would induce the United States to take on a central role in the economic reconstruction not only of Europe but of the whole world. Acknowledging the central role of capital assistance to Europe during the war, he wrote that "the American ruling class, in its own interest, must make lend-lease permanent, even though it is disguised in the form of loans or outright gifts to 'suffering humanity.'" In the postwar period, this assistance must flow "all over the world to strengthen the position of the various national bourgeoisies as the common people gather about them to exact an accounting of the use of their resources." To Cox, these loans and gifts signaled a broader goal: they meant that "the United States is already fighting its own proletarian revolution on foreign battle fields." Before Harry Truman had announced the Point Four program—the United States government's first major aid program for the decolonizing world—Cox presaged the importance of international development for US foreign policy and global politics.[1]

In the years following the Second World War, Black internationalist thinkers increasingly articulated their longstanding concern with the economic deprivation produced by colonialism in terms of the new politics of inter-national development. Although development discourse and practice had its origins in nineteenth-century notions of the "civilizing mission," early twentieth-century American efforts at "race development," and New Deal–era programs of agricultural modernization, the economic development of the nonindustrialized world emerged as a major priority for policymakers, activists, and social scientists alike after the war's conclusion. European colo-nial governments, US foreign policymakers, and the new specialized agencies of the UN all participated in making development a central concern of world politics in the years following 1945.[2]

The turn to development was not simply imposed from above. Develop-ment also emerged as a critical language of claim-making by popular forces across the world. Labor unions and anticolonial activists in British- and French-controlled territories in Africa appealed to the developmental mis-sion of the colonial powers in their attempts to win higher wages, greater political autonomy, and larger shares of the resources of their empires. The Asian-African Conference at Bandung in 1955 contained a developmental agenda alongside its better remembered anticolonial and antiracist agenda, with the Asian states in attendance proposing to take on the role of provid-ers of technical assistance for Africa. This developmental agenda even took highest priority in the Bandung Conference's final communiqué. Beyond the centers of global power, the formulation of demands by anticolonial activists and politicians in terms of development helped form "development politics" as a new sphere of action in the postwar world.[3]

For African American internationalists who defined colonialism as a problem of racialized economic exploitation, the politics of development be-came an important ground of struggle. Though almost completely ignored by historians of development and modernization, prominent African American thinkers and activists, including Rayford Logan, W. E. B. Du Bois, St. Clair Drake, and others, engaged with development politics from a variety of dif-ferent vantage points.[4] Black internationalist activists sought to influence US foreign aid policy in the Truman and Eisenhower administrations, debated British colonial development policy, and worked to shape the development plans of the Gold Coast independence movement and, ultimately, the govern-ment of the independent nation-state of Ghana.

On both sides of the Atlantic, Black internationalist development poli-tics were characterized by an anticipatory critique of neocolonialism. From discussions of US foreign aid policy in the late 1940s to debates about the speed and scope of Ghanaian industrialization in the late 1950s, the prospect that colonized territories—especially those in Africa—would gain political sovereignty while remaining in a state of economic dependency loomed large in Black political thought. This fear that colonial territories would suffer from economic dependency after political independence had influenced many African Americans' support for a regime of international trusteeship during the Second World War. In the context of postwar development politics, the anticipatory critique of neocolonialism could authorize multiple, conflicting positions. On the one hand, the belief that the US and European powers would continue to exploit the decolonizing world in the aftermath of formal independence presented a prime reason for suspicion of development projects that called for an influx of Western capital. On the other hand, recognition of the economic weakness of newly independent states could also point toward a desire for development aid, on the grounds that it would help build the state capacity necessary for newly independent nation-states to wield power in the international system.

This anticipatory critique of neocolonialism was shared across the Cold War divides that plagued the Black freedom movement in the late 1940s and 1950s. Overt anticommunist repression and broader Cold War pressures sowed division among left and liberal African American internationalist thinkers in this period. The Red Scare, as Black Studies scholar Charisse Burden-Stelly demonstrates, was equally a Black Scare, as government officials and many white Americans envisioned radicalism and Blackness as conjoined threats to the social order. State repression targeted Black radicals with particular vehemence, tragically upending the lives of thinkers and activists through imprisonment, deportation, and travel control. Most famously, the US government detained and deported Trinidadian Marxist and Black feminist Claudia Jones in 1955 and denied or revoked the passports of Paul Robeson and W. E. B. Du Bois due to their opposition to US foreign policy. For those not directly targeted by the state's repressive apparatus, the political climate steered conversations about colonial exploitation away from critiques of capitalism itself.[5]

But the Cold War did not extinguish Black internationalists' understanding of colonialism as a form of racialized economic exploitation, nor did it end their attempts to mobilize political forces around such an understanding. The politics of development became a key arena in which globally minded African American activists, on both sides of the Cold War divide, could continue to advance their critique of the economic effects of colonialism—albeit in a different form.

Anticommunism, moreover, was not the only line of division in development debates among Black activists in the United States and abroad. The question of whether political economy should be governed at the national or the international scale also generated controversy. In the late 1940s, many Black internationalists, including Rayford Logan, embraced a vision of development as a means to overcome the limitations that faced postcolonial polities attempting to engage in political-economic planning at the scale of the nation. But other African American internationalists, notably those engaged in development politics overseas, came to a much more positive conclusion about the desirability of the nation-state as the vehicle for postcolonial development. Over the first decade and a half of the Cold War, Black internationalists devised a shifting array of developmental strategies to confront the neocolonial future.

The NAACP and the Point Four Program

The Point Four program made the economic development of countries outside Europe an official priority of the US government for the first time. The origins of US development aid predated Point Four, as the US sent capital and technical assistance abroad in a variety of forms prior to the Second World War. The immediate postwar years, of course, also saw the massive expansion of American economic aid in the form of the Marshall Plan. Yet this assistance was geared toward reconstruction, not development, and it was geographically limited to Europe—which suggested to many in the Global South that the United States, despite its rhetorical commitment to anticolonialism, was placing its unparalleled economic might behind the colonial powers. When Harry Truman announced the Point Four program in his 1949 inaugural address, he began a new phase in the US government's provision of economic assistance abroad.[6]

Truman hoped his inauguration speech, as he told one adviser, would be "a kind of democratic manifesto . . . addressed to the people of the world rather than the American people." He decided early in the drafting process to make three planks of his foreign policy—support for the UN, the Marshall Plan, and the NATO military alliance—central to the speech. The fourth point, though, originated with a junior official in the State Department's Office of Public Affairs named Benjamin Hardy. Hardy had worked in Brazil for the Office of Inter-American Affairs in the mid-1940s and there became enamored of technical assistance projects. As Hardy was drafting his proposal for the expansion of US technical assistance, Council of Economic Advisers member Walter Salant was simultaneously advising the White House that capital investment in underdeveloped areas was necessary if the United States wanted to reap the full benefits of the Marshall Plan. European growth would only recover enough to enable purchases of American exports, Salant argued, in keeping with the emerging paradigm of growth economics, if the rest of the world could stimulate export-driven growth in Europe by purchasing European goods. Truman and his staff embraced Hardy's proposals for technical assistance and Salant's emphasis on capital export, bringing them together in a single vision of development aid. These policies became the fourth point among Truman's foreign policy priorities to be announced in the inaugural address.[7]

Truman announced the United States' new commitment to foreign aid with dramatic language. Although Point Four had minimal support within the State Department, Truman promoted it emphatically, declaring, "we must embark on a bold new program for making the benefits of our scientific advances and industrial progress available for the improvement and growth of underdeveloped areas." Wary of the possibility that encouraging American investments in "underdeveloped" areas would be seen as an imperial imposition, Truman insisted that "the old imperialism—exploitation for foreign profit—has no place in our plans." Instead, US development aid abroad would seek to enact the "concepts of democratic fair-dealing" Truman hoped to instantiate at home.[8]

Despite Point Four's prominent placement in the inaugural address, the program did not jump to the front of the policy agenda. The State Department minimized the significance of the program, and the White House soon signaled that it was a low priority for the administration as well, failing even to make a request for Point Four legislation before Congress adjourned for the year in 1949. Truman eventually requested $45 million for Point Four, which was a paltry sum for "two-thirds of the world," especially in comparison with the $342 million requested for the reconstruction of occupied Germany, or the $2.25 billion provided for the Marshall Plan. Even this request, though, was too much for House Republicans to stomach. Ultimately, the Point Four program was enacted as Title IV of the Foreign Economic Assistance Act of 1950, authorizing $35 million for the technical assistance program, a compromise between the $45 million Truman originally suggested and the $25 million passed in the House version of the bill. Promoting an ideology of self-help in areas newly defined as "underdeveloped," officials emphasized that the program would rely not on government funding but on private investment, philanthropy, and international organizations to finance development projects.[9]

Over the next several years, development aid became increasingly tied to Cold War priorities. While a subset of the early architects of the Marshall Plan and the Point Four program were left internationalists, who envisioned development aid as a means to extend political and economic democracy worldwide, loyalty investigations forced some of these figures out of government and pushed others to embrace more hardline anticommunist positions. The Korean War further intensified these pressures. The Mutual Security Act of 1951, passed in the middle of the Korean War, insisted that US aid both within and beyond Europe should be directed toward helping countries "develop their resources in the interest of their security and independence and the national interest of the United States." Although Dwight Eisenhower opposed Point Four in his 1952 presidential campaign, by the time the Eisenhower administration took office, the place of foreign economic assistance in US foreign policy was secure—in part because of its linkages with Cold War aims.[10]

The ideological impact of Point Four was more significant than its material effects. Amid the legislative and bureaucratic maneuvers to pass Point Four, developmentalist thinking only increased in importance in American debates about the future of colonial and postcolonial societies. As historian Stephen Macekura argues, Point Four "gave institutional expression to a protean ideology of international development" within the federal government. It further generated a potent language of claim-making and opened a new sphere of political advocacy for civil society groups and international activists.[11]

Among many African Americans, the first reactions to the Point Four proposal were surprisingly positive. After the inclusion of a civil rights plank in the Democratic Party's platform in 1948 helped garner a level of Black support for Truman that proved decisive in his election victory, the absence of any mention of civil rights in his inaugural address might have been cause for concern. The Black press, however, largely embraced the speech. They linked Point Four both to the national party's newfound support for civil rights and to the employment prospects of Black Americans amid postwar reconversion. The NAACP, meanwhile, agreed to support the proposal and sought to play an active role in the shaping of a still-unfinished policy. To lead their advocacy efforts on the program, the NAACP turned to Rayford Logan, whom the organization had brought on as its foreign affairs consultant in 1948.[12]

The NAACP's approach to international politics had undergone substantial changes between the end of the Second World War and the announcement of the Point Four program. Du Bois, who returned to the organization in 1944 as director of special research, led its most significant international endeavor in the immediate aftermath of the war. He supervised and edited *An Appeal to the World*, a petition to the United Nations demanding redress for human rights violations committed against African Americans by the government of the United States. Along with chapters by lawyers, a social worker, and an

industrial relations expert, the volume included a final chapter authored by
Rayford Logan. The petition marshaled documentation of legal discrimination and extralegal violence to argue that the treatment of African Americans
posed a threat to the UN's stated goal of safeguarding international peace.[13]

An Appeal to the World represented a new orientation to international
institutions. Du Bois, along with Logan, Ralph Bunche, and others, had spent
the war seeking to shape the architecture of the new United Nations along anticolonial and antiracist lines. When the structure of the UN failed to live up
to their hopes, Du Bois and the NAACP now invested in a politics of petition,
attempting to use the forum the UN provided to bring the concerns of Black
people in the United States to global attention. In this way, *An Appeal to the
World* was animated less by a sense of possibility about the new international
organization than by disappointment in its institutional design.

Though born in disillusionment, the petition displayed immense ambition. Chapters by lawyers Earl B. Dickerson, Milton R. Konvitz, William
Ming Jr., and Leslie S. Perry outlined the legal history of enslavement, discrimination, disfranchisement and segregation from the early Republic to the
present. The petition also emphasized that extralegal violence existed as both
a constant threat to African Americans and a buttress to the unequal legal regime: "The spectacle of the unwillingness of law enforcement officers to seek
out, much less prosecute or punish, members of lynch mobs is a ghastly, but
familiar, demonstration of the failure of the law to protect Negroes." It further
provided statistical data, mostly compiled by Perry from Census Bureau and
Department of Labor records, on disparities in health, education, and a variety of economic factors, from employment to farm tenancy.[14]

The politics of comparison saturated the document. The conceptual
framework of the *Appeal* was an uneasy mix of references to Gunnar Myrdal's
idea of an exceptional "American Creed" with a Black internationalist consciousness of African Americans as part of a world of colonized and formerly
colonized peoples. This latter perspective emerged most clearly from Du
Bois's introduction and Logan's final chapter. On the very first page of the
introduction, Du Bois designated the group position of African Americans
as a "segregated caste" as well as an involuntarily created "nation within a
nation." As he had done in *Color and Democracy*, Du Bois made his case
that the African American "nation" deserved a hearing in the newly established international body through basic numerical comparisons: "We have
more people than Portugal or Peru; twice as many as Greece and nearly as
many as Turkey . . . in sheer numbers then we are a group that has a right to
be heard; and while we rejoice that other smaller nations can stand and make
their wants known in the United Nations, we maintain equally that our voice

should not be suppressed or ignored." Logan further argued in his chapter
that the right to petition at the League of Nations, along with that body's minority rights guarantees, ought to apply in the new United Nations, to give the
NAACP standing before that body. He emphasized the parallels between the
NAACP's petition and the petition by the government of India regarding
the treatment of Indians in South Africa, citing the language of the UN Charter in support of the NAACP's position that "the violation of human or minority rights constitutes a threat to international peace and security."[15]

Du Bois and Logan had, of course, engaged in similar colonial comparisons in their wartime advocacy about the design of the UN's trusteeship program. But their perspective was not shared by top officials in the NAACP, especially Walter White. White, concerned about the petition's reception in the
Truman administration, maneuvered to delay its release until after the President's Committee on Civil Rights released its own report, entitled *To Secure
These Rights*, which shared none of the *Appeal*'s internationalist bent. Even
still, it was notable that the NAACP as an organization endorsed Du Bois's
and Logan's portrayal of the American state as an outgrowth of European
colonialism and an instrument of racial domination in such a public forum.[16]

The NAACP grew less willing to challenge dominant narratives of American nationalism as the US intensified the Cold War. The 1948 Progressive
Party presidential campaign of Henry Wallace, the former vice president to
Franklin D. Roosevelt who had been replaced by Truman on the 1944 Democratic ticket at the behest of southern segregationists, proved a flashpoint for
the NAACP's leadership. The organization's top leaders, especially White and
Roy Wilkins, translated their longstanding anticommunism into unquali-
fied support for both the Truman campaign and the Truman Doctrine. They
sidelined pro-Wallace figures, including Du Bois, who was dismissed by the
NAACP's board at the end of 1948.[17]

Rayford Logan was caught in the middle. He had been outraged by Wal-
lace's removal from the Democratic ticket in 1944, calling it a "tragic blow
to the cause of liberalism and democracy." But he remained faithful to the
NAACP and was impressed by Truman's qualified support for civil rights
causes, particularly his desegregation of the armed forces. At the same time,
Logan remained supportive of Du Bois after the latter's departure from the
NAACP. Intellectually as well as personally, he sought a middle way between
Du Bois's move toward socialist internationalism and White's embrace of
Cold War priorities.[18]

In international development policy, the NAACP's general alignment with
US Cold War aims did not completely determine the organization's posture.
Logan brought many of the concerns that had animated Black internationalist

activism during the Second World War to the NAACP's advocacy related to Point Four. His emphasis on protections for colonial labor and his desire to see representation of both trust territories and formal colonies in decision-making processes represented points of commonality between his wartime advocacy and the NAACP's engagements with development politics in the early Cold War. At the same time, the Cold War climate forced these arguments into narrower channels. In postwar planning debates, Logan's advocacy for colonial labor protections and colonial representation could easily be linked to a sweeping critique of colonial capitalism. In the context of Cold War development politics, this broader framing disappeared, even as many of his specific concerns remained the same.

Logan first articulated his priorities for American development politics at a conference held in March 1949. This gathering, held shortly after Truman's inaugural address, included Secretary of State Dean Acheson, Assistant Secretary of State Willard Thorp, and future secretary of state Dean Rusk, as well as representatives from organized labor, business, and civil society organizations. Questions of personnel remained as central to Logan's vision for development programs as they had been to his unrealized hopes for the UN. He urged that "extreme care should be exercised in the selection of the personnel who would [be] sent out," in order to avoid the program getting "bogged down because of the superior attitude of many Americans toward the people of the country they were supposed to be helping." Even better, in Logan's mind, would be for the United States to train local experts rather than to send in its own technicians. Beyond personnel, Logan stressed the need for specific protections for colonial labor in the formulation of development programs. Envisioning economic development not solely as the more efficient exploitation of resources but as the building of institutions to ensure improved labor practices, Logan argued that union organizers and labor leaders were among the most important groups of people the United States could send as part of its proposed program of technical assistance. Logan proposed that "since the economic improvement of these areas required the creation and development of strong indigenous trade unions, members of organized labor be sent out for the express purpose of achieving this end."[19]

Logan's emphasis on labor ran counter to the policy's trajectory within the Truman administration. Shortly after introducing Point Four, Truman made clear that private capital, not public expenditures, would have to fund the bulk of the program. Business leaders strongly opposed any public funding for development aid, as they feared it would both add to their tax burden and cast the policy as an extension to the international sphere of a New Deal state they already opposed at home. Although some capitalists embraced the prospect of new sources of natural resources and labor that Point Four promised, most were hesitant about placing investment capital toward development projects. Concerns about the nationalization of property, labor legislation in recipient countries, and foreign exchange restrictions pervaded business leaders' conceptions of the investment climate of the "underdeveloped areas," and even investment guarantees by the United States' Export-Import Bank, which were added to the program in 1951, did little to stimulate private capital. The response of American business to Point Four was lukewarm at best, even without labor protections; with them, the support of business would have been out of the question.[20]

Even American unions offered precious little support to Logan's efforts to make labor protections and worker organizing in the developing world central to US development policy. Anticommunism and what historian Charles Maier calls the "politics of productivity" shaped the American labor movement's approach to questions of international development in the 1950s. Even UAW-CIO president Walter Reuther, who articulated a bold vision for American social democracy even amid the rightward turn of the late 1940s and early 1950s, promoted development beyond Europe principally as a weapon in the Cold War. Just after the outbreak of the Korean War, Reuther and the UAW published a plan for a "Total Peace Offensive" that urged the federal government make a $13 billion annual payment to UN development and reconstruction efforts, in order to take on "poverty and human insecurity—the source of communist power." US labor leaders also promoted reconstruction and development projects, from the Marshall Plan to Point Four, on the grounds that they would help boost the productivity of American industry, which, they believed, would ultimately benefit American workers. The CIO's education department was silent on Point Four's possible effects on workers in Africa, Asia, or Latin America—but argued that the program held the potential to be "good business because it creates markets for our products." The postwar diminution of labor internationalism meant that labor protections and organizing assistance for workers in underdeveloped areas were not major considerations for US unions involved in the politics of international development. This position left Logan with few allies in the effort to make colonial labor a focus of the program.[21]

Beyond his emphasis on colonial labor, Logan emphasized the importance of representation for the inhabitants of colonies and trust territories in international institutions. He argued that the divide between formally independent nations and areas still under colonial rule posed a problem for Point Four's stated intention to offer technical assistance across the "underdeveloped" world. Because "independent underdeveloped regions are . . . free to request aid and capital investment," whereas "the dependent underdeveloped areas, obviously, may receive help and private capital only if the possessing countries make the request," the continuation of European sovereignty had the potential to entrench new forms of inequality between colonized and independent nations in the "underdeveloped" world.[22]

Logan was still hesitant about national independence, however. Instead, he argued that the best solution to the division between independent states and "dependent areas" was the granting of associate membership for "dependent areas" in the specialized agencies of the UN—UNESCO, the WHO, and the ILO—which were taking on development projects themselves. For associate membership to have a meaningful effect on the economic fortunes of the colonized, Logan argued, the majority of the delegates must be drawn from these populations. Otherwise, colonial powers would simply be gaining greater power in international bodies through their colonies. For Logan, if true political sovereignty still depended on economic development, greater political representation in international society offered a means of achieving both aims.[23]

A Welfare World or a Cold War Trick?

The positive potential that Logan and his allies in US civil society saw in the Point Four program was closely linked to a vision of the internationalization of political-economic governance in the postwar world. In this understanding, development aid, though provided by wealthier nations to poorer ones, was imagined as the property of the world as a whole. Similar questions about the appropriate scale of governance inflected development politics all over the world. In Africa and the Middle East, nationalist leaders who envisioned development as part of the nation-building project conflicted with UN bureaucrats who devised regional development schemes. Influential neoliberal economists in the Global North, including Friedrich Hayek, sought to place global economic management in the hands of international organizations in order to "encase" the rights of capital within a legal regime insulated from democratic decision-making. Others in US advocacy organizations, however, believed international management of economic affairs—starting with the international administration of development aid—could serve as the beginning of a more social-democratic world order, with redistributive mechanisms and strong protections for the rights of labor.[24]

Proposals for various forms of international economic management for welfarist aims took center stage at a second conference on Point Four in which Logan represented the NAACP in 1949. Held by the Post-War World Council, an advocacy group founded by Socialist Party leader Norman Thomas, this gathering brought together individuals and organizations committed to the "one world" ideal announced by Wendell Willkie during the Second World War. James Warburg, a banker and former adviser to Franklin Roosevelt, articulated one version of this perspective in the conference's opening address, arguing that the continuation of colonialism and the rise of anticolonial nationalism were equivalent problems for international development. If the uneven political status in the "developing" world, ranging from trusteeship arrangements to dependencies to outright colonies, posed bureaucratic challenges to development, anticolonial nationalism posed the potentially greater problem of "making international or regional planning acceptable to the peoples and governments of countries in which newly acquired independence makes nationalism the predominant sentiment."[25]

Harold Isaacs, another attendee of the Post-War World Council gathering, shared this perspective. Then an associate editor of *Newsweek*, Isaacs would later become a member of the MIT's Center for International Studies—an important home of modernization theory—and a controversial white interlocutor for Black Americans' understandings of their relationships with Africa. In his book *Two-Thirds of the World*, published shortly after the conference, Isaacs, too, made an impassioned argument against colonialism while claiming that anticolonial nationalism was an economic dead end. The scope of the problem of underdevelopment, combined with the economic interdependence of the postwar world, made the "old framework of mutually jealous national sovereignties" untenable, just as it rendered laissez-faire economics obsolete. "It is a cruel paradox," Isaacs argued, "for the emergent peoples of Asia and Africa that nationalism is triumphing when nationalism, as such, is bankrupt; each is setting out to build a new national political economy when national political economy, as such, is a major obstacle in the way of human growth." Political economy must be organized at an international scale, with the input of the decolonizing world and the expertise of American technicians. "The colonies becoming nations must become at once more than nations," Isaacs proclaimed, "or else be thrust back upon themselves and be doomed to frustration that will produce monstrosities greater even than the Russian police state." Isaacs, a former Trotskyite and a supporter of the Communists in the Chinese civil war when he lived in China during the 1930s, here revealed not only his turn toward an anticommunist posture amid the pressures of the Cold War, but also his vision of a postnational future. Without an attempt to become "more than nations," Isaacs argued, the decolonizing world would fail to realize the promise development politics held.[26]

To Isaacs, not only were nationalism and laissez-faire capitalism both outdated; they were ideologically entwined. Liberal capitalism arose alongside the nation-state form in the nineteenth century. But in the twentieth, both systems were becoming obsolete. (Raymond Leslie Buell, an editor at *Time* who had written a major study of colonial administration in Africa in the 1920s, offered a similar verdict near the end of the Second World War: "Today we are witnessing the . . . breakup of what I would call the period of Capitalist Nationalism, which reached its height in the nineteenth century.")[27] Both the interdependence of the world and the scope of the problem of underdevelopment—a problem affecting "two-thirds of the world"—demanded the creation of what Gunnar Myrdal would later term a "welfare world."[28] "Our real political affinities abroad," Isaacs wrote, "lie with those who, like most of us, go along with the general idea of the welfare state dedicated to the broadest possible welfare for the largest possible number." This belief influenced Isaacs's identification of more concrete problems with the Point Four program as it stood. Truman's emphasis on private capital as the predominant source of development funding, which only became more pronounced after opposition to the program arose in Congress, would generate suspicions in the countries for which aid was intended—not only because of its Western sources but because of the profit motive. Leaders of newly independent states "want to attract foreign capital and at the same time they want to protect themselves from it," and, Isaacs thought, "they are right on both counts." Isaacs's preferred solution was internationally directed, publicly controlled development aid.[29]

The writer Pearl Buck exhibited a similar combination of malaise with contemporary capitalism and faith in the international administration of development aid in her analysis of Point Four. The daughter of Presbyterian missionaries and a missionary herself, Buck spent most of her early life in China. A novelist, Buck was the first American woman to win the Nobel Prize for Literature in 1938, primarily because of her depiction of Chinese peasant life in the 1931 novel *The Good Earth*. She quickly thereafter became a sought-after commentator on world affairs, especially in Asia. To Buck, the danger of US development aid was that it might empower a rich few in its target nations. In a newly independent state, "technical assistance . . . can result in setting up . . . an industrial and therefore a political tyranny which was worse" than the colonial order that preceded independence. Decolonizing nations should be wary of industrialization, in her view, because postwar industry in the West promoted "the aggrandizement of the few and the subjection of the many." These dangers could be mitigated by "international administration" of programs such as Point Four, "under the command of the United Nations, made up of persons whose humanity is unquestioned." Revealingly, neither Buck nor Isaacs attempted to explain how their putative international administrators would avoid the pressures of cronyism, lobbying, and sheer greed that they acknowledged as unsavory features of capitalist governance on the national scale.[30]

Attendees of the Post-War World Council conference also held the striking hope that the Point Four program could help the United States transcend its Cold War posture. This belief was sharply at odds with the framing of Point Four by policymakers themselves: Benjamin Hardy's original memorandum proposing the program was titled "Use of U.S. Technological Resources as a Weapon in the Struggle with International Communism," and Truman often linked the plan to the growing conflict with the Soviet Union. The Cold War liberals associated with the anticommunist group Americans for Democratic Action (ADA) embraced technical assistance for precisely this reason. Arthur Schlesinger Jr., for example, saw development aid as "a weapon which, if properly employed, might outbid all the social ruthlessness of the Communists for support of the people of Asia."[31]

But other Americans believed that the turn to development might cut against the single-minded focus in the US foreign policy establishment on the emerging conflict with the Soviet Union. James Warburg argued that Point Four could only succeed if it marked a broader shift in American foreign policy away from the "negative aim of stopping Soviet, or Communist, expansion." While nodding to the American state's construction of a Soviet threat, Warburg emphasized that "other factors contribute to the sad state of world affairs—factors which have nothing to do with the nature or intentions of the Soviet Union and which would exist if the Communist Manifesto had never been written." The economic crisis of postwar Europe and the ongoing breakdown of colonial empires were the more important forces in the postwar restructuring of the world order. Isaacs elaborated on this attempt to frame Point Four as both more important than the Cold War and at least potentially untainted by it. "Even if there were no Communist Russia, no Cold War," Isaacs claimed, "we would still have to wrestle with the problems of the underdeveloped countries, of raising the standard of living of two-thirds of the world, of re-shaping the globe out of the ruins of Western empire." The way forward was not to vest the developmental hopes of Point Four in a broader Cold War project. Rather, Isaacs innocently imagined, the way to begin solving the problem of underdevelopment was "to get together with a lot of other people and go to work with them as if there were no Cold War at all."[32]

Rayford Logan joined this chorus of left-liberal voices who viewed development politics as a potential means to overcome the divisions of the Cold War. Here, again, Logan's position diverged from that of NAACP executive secretary Walter White, who urged Truman to fight for greater funding for Point Four on strictly anticommunist grounds. But Logan also had different priorities than many of his white interlocutors who shared the goal of using development to transcend the nation's Cold War footing. While Harold Isaacs and others imagined that promoting international development might signify a first step toward federated world government, Logan's support for US development aid was more closely tied to his fear that colonial territories would not be able to sustain self-government without sufficient economic development. With these concerns, which ran along similar lines as the ideas Logan had emphasized during the Second World War, Logan emphasized the dangers that would face new states with weak economies in the international system. In one article, Logan argued that Point Four remained an "enigma" because the US developmental mission was not sufficiently linked to a strong anticolonial commitment, which would require the United States to refute, for example, Dutch sovereignty over Indonesia, or Italy's reassertion of control over its African colonies. Without such a commitment, it was reasonable to wonder whether Point Four was simply designed to advance the "strategic interests of the Western powers," or even to "mak[e] the underdeveloped areas more profitable for private capital." Logan's vision for development politics was thus tied to his longstanding ideas regarding the impossibility of true political sovereignty without economic self-determination.[33]

Many Black activists on the left, meanwhile, turned the same idea into a forthright argument against the Point Four program's existence. The Council on African Affairs (CAA), an organization founded by Paul Robeson and Max Yergan, was a primary critic of the NAACP's position on Point Four. Though the CAA stood at the leading edge of African American anticolonial advocacy throughout the 1940s, anticommunist pressures near the end of the decade created rifts within the organization. Yergan left the CAA in 1948, turning away from Communism and wholeheartedly embracing American Cold War priorities. Logan, who had joined the board of CAA in 1944 to "show that as a Liberal [he] could not be frightened by red-baiting," also left the organization in support of Yergan. But he consistently refused to denounce Robeson, Du Bois, or other Black Americans who maintained Communist affiliations or pronounced their wholesale rejection of US foreign policy. In this regard, Logan exemplified historian Doug Rossinow's claim that "Popular Front liberalism was never extirpated among African Americans."[34]

The CAA nonetheless skewered Logan's advocacy for Point Four in their publication *New Africa*. In the minds of the CAA's leaders, Logan had put his weight behind a policy that promised nothing but the further extension of colonial economic arrangements under the auspices of American, rather than

European, capital. Horace Cayton agreed. As the international affairs columnist for the *Pittsburgh Courier*, Cayton observed in 1952 that "President Truman's Point Four and even the United Nations technical assistance program look more and more like a new form of imperialism rather than help for the backward areas of the world." Cayton focused on investments in territories that remained under colonial control, like the British protectorate of Northern Rhodesia and the Belgian Congo. Drawing on reporting conducted by the British historian of Africa Basil Davidson, Cayton claimed that "technical assistance" contributed to the uranium trade, where US investments through a British holding company wound up in the hands of the Belgian state-run company Union Minière de Haut Katanga. By placing American investments and technical assistance in the hands of colonial governments, and by failing to provide opportunities for input from colonial subjects themselves, the United States ensured that its developmental missions would reinforce rather than challenge European powers' political control across Africa. As Cayton wrote, echoing Logan's fears from before the passage of Point Four legislation, the continued control of development assistance by colonial powers meant that "it will be very easy for the Belgians or the French or the English to convince this country that it is better for them to rule and that to encourage movements toward self-government on the part of the Africans would be a mistake." Those who hoped US-led development aid might point toward a welfare world and smooth the way to independence, Cayton argued, underestimated the ease with which American capital could make peace with arrangements of formal colonial rule.[35]

W. E. B. Du Bois, who had been a crucial ally of Logan's in wartime debates about the shape of the UN, also argued against Point Four. Increasingly aligned with the foreign policy of the Soviet Union—unlike other critics of US development policy, such as Cayton—Du Bois described Point Four as "an effort to furnish capital and technique to backward countries if the owners of capital are assured traditional power and high profit from low wages and cheap land." Their differing policy positions masked a deeper common ground, however. While Logan and the NAACP hoped US development aid could serve as a means to protect against neocolonial incursions once independence arrived, many Black internationalists on the left saw the aid itself as representing just such an incursion. Though Logan and Du Bois had divergent views of Point Four, a shared understanding of colonialism as a form of racialized economic exploitation, which political independence alone would not solve, still undergirded their advocacy.[36]

As development politics coalesced into a vital terrain of struggle over the shape of the global order, a new question arose among many African

American internationalists who defined colonialism as a problem of racialized economic exploitation. Would access to Western capital enhance or
hinder the ability of the decolonizing world to achieve political-economic
self-determination? This question not only preoccupied Logan, the NAACP,
and their domestic critics on the left. In the same period, a transnational set
of Black thinkers, who were involved in debates about British colonial development policy, the Gold Coast independence movement, and, subsequently,
the independent government of Ghana, confronted the question of Western
capital as well. Their visions of development politics focused less on the establishment of international governance of political-economic planning and
more on the building of economic capacity within national states.

Development Politics from Other Shores

Debates about US foreign aid policy and the Point Four program occurred at a time when the major imperial powers of Western Europe had also turned to development as a new justification for their empires. During and after the Second World War, the British and French states reframed their imperial projects as developmental missions. Both governments created colonial development plans between 1940 and 1946 that promised to elevate the economic status of their colonies in Africa. Reformulating an older idea of an imperial civilizing mission in new, economic terms, the British and French governments devised their development plans in part to stem the tide of labor unrest that had spread across their African colonies during the Depression, the war, and the war's immediate aftermath.[1]

The turn to development served two main purposes for the governments of Britain and France. On the one hand, the growing importance of self-determination as an ideal in international politics compelled these imperial powers to find justifications for continued imperial rule in terms that appeared to benefit colonial subjects themselves. On the other hand, the devastation of the war had left both Britain and France in desperate need of resources—which, many officials argued, could be found through the more productive exploitation of colonies, especially in Africa. An obvious tension existed between these two aims. Was colonial development primarily designed to benefit the colonies, or the metropole? The protean nature of the development concept often allowed policymakers to evade answering that question, but the question nonetheless pervaded debates about colonial development programs in the late 1940s and beyond.[2]

In the United Kingdom, these debates provided another stage for African Americans' engagements with development politics. London played host to a transnational circle of Black anticolonial activists from Africa, the Caribbean, and the United States. Centered around the Trinidadian-born activist and intellectual George Padmore, this circle argued about how anticolonial activists should respond to the Colonial Welfare and Development Acts (CWDAs), the first of which was passed by Parliament in 1940. Throughout the late 1940s and 1950s, this group of thinkers debated the proper way to pursue economic development in the colonial world, while also organizing movements for colonial reform and independence.[3]

The relationship between national independence and postcolonial economic development was a central focus of these debates, just as it was in the United States. But the relationship looked different from the vantage point of the British empire. Padmore's circle evinced less faith in the prospect of international governance than did Rayford Logan and the NAACP, even as they shared similar fears about the potential for neocolonial exploitation after the achievement of national independence.

For this group, anticolonial nationalism, rather than international institution building or advocacy within imperial metropoles, appeared as the more promising route to achieving the aims of postcolonial development. One colony and one anticolonial nationalist movement in particular came to the forefront of their thinking and activism. Padmore, the St. Lucian economist W. Arthur Lewis, and the African American social anthropologist St. Clair Drake all became increasingly involved in the movement for independence in the Gold Coast beginning in the late 1940s. Kwame Nkrumah, a leader of this movement and the first president of the independent nation-state of Ghana, lived in London from 1945 to 1947, where he collaborated with Padmore in organizing the Fifth Pan-African Congress in Manchester. The close involvement of this circle with the Gold Coast independence movement, and, later, with Nkrumah's government in Ghana, shaped their evolving views on the relationship between national political autonomy and postcolonial economic development. Driven by fears of a neocolonial future and disappointment at the colonial development plans of European powers, Black internationalists from London to Accra came to vest their developmental hopes in projects of national state-building in the postcolonial world.

St. Clair Drake, the Padmore Circle, and Late Colonial Development in Britain

A key member of Padmore's circle was the African American social anthropologist St. Clair Drake, who arrived in Britain in 1946. Drake was a scholar and activist whose career bridged several countries and generations. His international connections, and his views of the historical relationships and political obligations linking African-descended people across the globe, would go on to influence both the intellectual frameworks and the concrete strategies of important civil rights and Black Power organizations. Drake's writings, Pan-African organizing, and service to two states—as an informal adviser to Kwame Nkrumah's Ghana and, later, as a leader of a training program for Peace Corps volunteers in the United States—illuminate a different side of the multifaceted linkages between African American internationalism and development politics between the Second World War and the early 1960s.

Born in 1911, John Gibbs St. Clair Drake was the son of a father from Barbados and a mother from Virginia's Shenandoah Valley. His family—the product of the forced migration of the slave trade and the post-Emancipation migration of Africans from the Caribbean—were among the six million African Americans who moved north during the Great Migration, eventually settling in Pittsburgh. Both the religious radicalism of Southern Baptist preaching and the global Black consciousness of the 1920s were among Drake's earliest influences, especially through his father, who organized with Marcus Garvey's Universal Negro Improvement Association. After his parents' divorce in 1924, Drake returned to the South, eventually enrolling at the historically Black Hampton University, where he participated in student strikes and gained his first exposure to the social sciences. At Hampton, he conducted research on tenant farming with anthropologist Allison Davis, an important figure in the emerging caste-and-class school of race relations scholarship. Continuing his political activities throughout the 1930s as an organizer with the American Friends Service Committee's "Peace Caravans," which traveled around the South advancing the Quaker position on nonviolence, Drake moved to Chicago in 1937 to study for his doctorate in anthropology. At the University of Chicago, Drake studied with Lloyd Warner, another leading member of the caste-and-class school, and Robert Redfield, an anthropologist who both influenced and departed from the paradigm of modernization theory that was soon to overtake the American social sciences.[4]

Both the caste-and-class school of Davis and Warner and the idiosyncratic version of modernization theory advanced by Redfield influenced how Drake viewed questions of racial inequality, economic development, and social transformation. According to the classic statement of the caste-and-class school's perspective, a brief article Warner wrote in 1936 in *The American Journal of Sociology*, the US South was defined by a unique accommodation between two competing forms of stratification. A system of "caste" stratification that prohibited intermarriage between Black and white southerners and made impossible any mobility from the group marked as inferior into the group marked as superior coexisted alongside a system of class stratification within each group. The use of the term "caste" to describe this system of stark racial subordination illustrated Warner's rejection of any biological foundation for racial differences, but it also reflected a misleading and thin understanding of the Indian social system to which it made reference. Although Warner argued that the social and economic progress of African Americans since Emancipation meant that stratification between the caste marked as white and that marked as Black was no longer complete, the continuing existence of this supposed caste hierarchy distorted class relations. This social system "skewed" the "social position of the upper-class Negro," whose class position would lead them to expect social advantages which the caste system continued to deny them.[5]

The caste-and-class school was the dominant sociological paradigm for understanding American race relations in the mid-1940s. Gunnar Myrdal, in his monumental study *An American Dilemma*, relied on the framing of southern racial hierarchy in terms of caste, while claiming that the existence of an egalitarian "American Creed" ensured that the caste system would ultimately be superseded. The sharpest criticisms of the caste-and-class school came from a group of Black sociologists who trained at the University of Chicago around the same time as Drake, most notably E. Franklin Frazier and Oliver Cromwell Cox. Frazier argued that the analogy with caste was "essentially static"—that it underestimated both how popular forces could contest the racial hierarchy and how defenders of the status quo had to actively work to protect it. While the language of caste sought to denaturalize racial hierarchy, it falsely portrayed a system of coercion and oppression as a stable tradition. Cox was even more critical. Cox saw racism as a product of capitalism and imperialist conquest, and he considered the caste-and-class school's arguments, which understood racial hierarchy as semipermanent features of human affairs, obfuscations of the material interests propping up the Jim Crow system.[6]

The ideas of Redfield, Warner, and critics of the caste-and-class school such as Cox all influenced Drake's writings during the 1940s. While studying for his doctorate, Drake cowrote with Horace Cayton *Black Metropolis*, a social anthropology of African American life in the Bronzeville neighborhood of Chicago. Although the book began as a three-person project including Drake, Cayton, and Warner, Drake drafted the majority of the book's chapters, with Cayton providing criticism and editing. After a dispute, Cayton ultimately insisted that Warner had not contributed enough to the book to merit credit as an author. Written with literary ambition as well as a comprehensive outlook on the life of the Bronzeville community, *Black Metropolis* was described at the time of its publication as "a 'Middletown' of Negro life in America." Drake and Cayton's study resembled Robert and Helen Lynd's not only in its attempt to bring the methods of cultural anthropology to bear on an American urban community but in its abiding concern with class formation and inequality.[7]

The crucial determinants of social life in Bronzeville, Drake and Cayton found, were the "job ceiling" and the "color line." The dynamics of labor exploitation, class formation, and worker mobilization characteristic of class societies operated within a circumscribed sphere for Black residents of Bronzeville, as neither capital nor labor could effectively transgress the strict lines of separation in employment and housing in search of higher profits or higher wages. Drake and Cayton thus took an insight of the caste-and-class school—the existence of distinct class structures for white and Black Americans—and combined it with an insight of the school's critics, by illustrating how these forms of stratification depended on material factors that were consciously maintained and frequently contested.[8]

The pace and drama of global anticolonial movements in the years after 1945 upended the lives of both Drake and Cayton. As Drake would later observe, he and Cayton "had planned to do a *Black Metropolis Revisited* in 1955, ten years after the original publication, as the Lynds had done with *Middletown*," but "by that time I was in Africa documenting the West African anticolonial revolution and Cayton was an observer of these events at the UN in New York." Cayton became the foreign affairs correspondent for the *Pittsburgh Courier*, where he would write some of the most influential analyses of world affairs in the Black press—including his critical commentary on Point Four. Drake, on the other hand, became involved in anticolonial movements firsthand while still a student at the University of Chicago. After the publication of *Black Metropolis*, he moved overseas, where he continued to combine academic research with political activism. In his dissertation, a social anthropology of a community of African, Caribbean, and Arab sailors in the Tiger Bay area of Cardiff, Drake drew heavily from the structural-functionalism of sociologist Talcott Parsons—widely regarded as the primary intellectual influence on modernization theory in the United States—in his understanding of racial ideologies and systems of racial hierarchy.[9]

By the early 1950s, Drake's analysis of the global racial order contained elements that aligned with Cold War liberalism alongside sharp criticisms of the continuing influence of the imperial system. Although he repeated the conventional wisdom that the US was "impelled, whether it desired the rôle or not, to assume leadership in international affairs," he was anything but a mouthpiece of State Department opinions. Beyond his writings, Drake forged

connections with anticolonial activists in London and engaged in feuds with
the State Department about their refusal of visas to Kenyan students studying in the United States, which made him wonder if he was "persona non
grata" with either the State Department or the British Colonial Office. Drake
further retained a belief in the structuring role of imperialism in world affairs
and a commitment to understanding racism as the byproduct of European
global expansion at odds with the growing view of racism in elite circles as
a problem of individual, psychological prejudice. Citing Oliver Cromwell
Cox approvingly, Drake argued that "race relations began as one aspect of
the overseas expansion of Europe which involved the African slave trade and
colonial imperialism" and that "ideologies of racism arose to sanction 'white
supremacy.'" Though he understood the global scope of processes of racial
formation, Drake saw the prospects of what he called "Pan-Movements" as
limited. Such movements, he argued, were easily "weakened by the counter-
forces of tribalism and nationalism, and cultural differences," making them
operational "only in localized race relations situations," like the joint African
and Indian actions against the apartheid government in South Africa. Nationalist mobilization presented a more viable path to overcoming the racialized hierarchies of the world order, in his view.[10]

Drake's writings also signaled the growing disillusionment of many African Americans with the United Nations as a vehicle for challenging racial
discrimination at home or for accelerating decolonization abroad. Though
he cited both the NAACP's *An Appeal to the World* and the Civil Rights Congress's *We Charge Genocide* as examples of the UN's ability to serve as a "forum where matters involving racial discrimination can be aired," he had little
hope that the institution would ever provide a true counterweight to the national and subnational exercises of sovereignty that maintained Jim Crow in
the United States.[11]

Instead, Drake claimed that the body could play symbolic and developmental roles. The UN could still promote the interests of the decolonizing
world, and of African Americans, by normalizing the equal status of people
of color on the world stage as more African and Asian states gained admis-
sion. This vision of "indirect and informal" influence, which would occur
through "conditioning" European and American populations to accept Africans, Asians, and Latin Americans as equally "mature world citizens," was
paired with a view of the UN as a developmental actor, "contributing . . . toward that rise in living standards which is necessary for breaking 'the vicious
circle.'" Drake's perspective on the relationship between political sovereignty
and economic development here marked a shift from the dominant understanding of the relationship between development and self-determination

among African American internationalists that had endured through the Second World War. Rather than seeing development as a precondition of sovereignty, Drake envisioned development and national independence as two coeval parts of the changing global racial order.[12]

While in Britain conducting research for his dissertation, Drake became part of the transnational circle of anticolonial thinkers and activists centered around the Trinidadian thinker and activist George Padmore. A Marxist thinker, who resigned from the Third International in 1933, Padmore became involved in Pan-Africanist politics in the 1930s. He was an early member of the International African Friends of Abyssinia (IAFE), and he helped found, along with C. L. R. James and Amy Ashwood Garvey, the IAFE's successor organization, the International African Service Bureau (IASB). Around the same time as the publication of Drake and Cayton's *Black Metropolis*, Padmore organized the Fifth Pan-African Congress in Manchester with his friend Kwame Nkrumah, whom he had met at the historically Black Lincoln University in Pennsylvania in the 1930s.

The Manchester congress pulled the center of gravity of Pan-African activity away from the United States and toward Europe and Africa. The conference's resolutions, beyond their rejection of all forms of trusteeship, signaled a broader shift toward an embrace of the national state as the vehicle of anticolonial aspirations. In the 1930s and early 1940s, anticolonial movements in metropolitan London and in British West Africa often sought to reform imperial space on terms of greater equality by demanding labor protections, an end to racial discrimination, and full citizenship rights in the colonies. During the late 1940s and 1950s, more and more anticolonial organizations, including Nkrumah's United Gold Coast Convention Party (UGCC), foregrounded national self-government in their political stances. The growing identification of anticolonialists' aspirations with the national space—even if, as the Manchester delegates declared, national independence was merely an intermediate station on the way to "inevitable world unity and federation"—influenced the approach of Padmore, Nkrumah, and their circle to the world of development politics.[13]

This approach first took shape in response to the British government's plans for colonial development during and after the war. The first Colonial Development and Welfare Act (CDWA), passed in 1940, provided a new justification for the British empire as well as new tools for governing it. The Act represented perhaps the clearest indication of an ascendant imperial imaginary that promoted Indigenous economic welfare and rising living standards as primary justifications for empire. It helped enshrine a greater reliance on technical experts from Britain and a new class of educated African elites, as

opposed to the traditional "chiefs" of the divided rule system, for the administration of colonial governance. The new justification for empire, in turn,
reflected a shift in colonial administrators' thinking about Africa itself. The
emergent discourse of development in the British colonial state charted a
path away from a vision of Africa as a timeless space defined by stable peasant lifestyles and coherent "tribal" divisions, and toward a view of Africans as
stuck between a "backward" past and a "modern" future.[14]

At first, Padmore's circle of Black anticolonial activists in London found
several reasons for optimism about the British government's developmental agenda. The first was a matter of personnel. The St. Lucian economist
W. Arthur Lewis, who maintained ties with the IASB in the 1930s and would
go on to serve as Nkrumah's economic adviser in Ghana, began working in
the Colonial Office in 1938. Although Padmore would later clash with Lewis,
initially he saw cause for hope in Lewis's rise through the ranks of the economics profession. When Lewis was appointed a lecturer at the London School of
Economics, the journal of the IASB published a front-page report, hopefully
imagining that the news might prompt a reconsideration of racist attitudes: "If
there still remain persons so ignorant as to believe that the peoples of African
descent in the West Indies 'cannot stand by themselves under the strenuous
conditions of the modern world,' their belief will suffer the shock which it
deserves" from learning of Lewis's new position. Moreover, Lewis's writings
and advocacy with the League of Coloured Peoples—a more politically moderate group, compared to the IASB, made up largely of Caribbean intellectuals
and activists in London—argued vigorously for sweeping colonial reform. By
1943, Lewis was named secretary of the Colonial Economic Advisory Committee (CEAC), which brought together conservative and social-democratic
economists along with representatives of business and labor to discuss plans
for colonial development. Lewis articulated themes in his reports for CEAC
that would be central to his economic thought in the postwar years. In these
reports, he first emphasized the argument that, in most colonies, agricultural
growth should take precedence over industrialization. Further previewing his
position in later debates about Gold Coast development, Lewis claimed in a
1943 report that the Colonial Office would need to recruit large amounts of
foreign—probably American—capital to achieve its development goals.[15]

Another appointment that raised expectations in anticolonial circles was
the selection of Arthur Creech-Jones for the position of secretary of state for
the colonies in the Labour government that swept to power in 1945. Creech-
Jones was a prominent voice for the developmentalist mission of empire
within the Labour Party. He was also one of very few British elites who had
some familiarity with the world of transnational Black politics, as he had been

an early patron of the IASB in the 1930s. During the war, in a parliamentary debate about colonial development, he introduced the term "decolonization" to British politics. Arguing that "the resources of the Colonies are their own," Creech-Jones framed decolonization as a process to be led by the metropole: "We have acknowledged the paramountcy of [the Colonies'] interests, yet on us falls the responsibility of rapidly creating the conditions under which the people can stand on their own feet, of associating them with other areas for economic and political needs, and of moving on to their own de-colonisation both in status and in stature." As historian Stuart Ward has noted, this definition of decolonization as a process directed by the colonial government became the dominant interpretation of the term until the 1960s. While Creech-Jones assigned little political agency to the subjects of British imperial rule, his familiarity with anticolonial circles in London and his foregrounding of the economic interests of the colonies themselves made him appear at least as a potential ally in the Labour Party for the advancement of anticolonial goals.[16]

The appointments of Lewis and Creech-Jones were coupled with an increased financial commitment in the second Colonial Development and Welfare Act, which was passed in 1945. While the first CDWA appropriated only five million pounds annually, the second act more than doubled this amount, providing for a ten-year total of 120 million pounds in development funding. This expansion reflected, in part, the government's anticipation of greater financial flexibility as it looked toward peacetime. But it also spoke to a challenge the government faced: that of justifying the empire to its subjects in the face of unrest by workers and returning soldiers across British colonies in the Caribbean and Africa. As the mission of British colonial development took shape, it became clear that the question of political reform was to be repeatedly deferred. Development, as a mission of the British government, was to be ensconced within an effort to rehabilitate rather than to end formal colonialism.[17]

This outcome only intensified the position held by Padmore and his circle that political autonomy was a precondition for, rather than a consequence of, economic growth and social transformation. Padmore and his partner, Dorothy Pizer, stressed this argument in their book *How Russia Transformed Her Colonial Empire*, which they completed amid the development debates of 1945. Though the nominal focus of the book was Russian development, its broader implications were clear. Padmore and Pizer opened the text with an analysis of the economy of Tsarist Russia, which, as they described it, "followed the by no means unique principle of keeping the colonial areas backward, using them only to provide raw materials for the industries of the European section of the Empire." After the Russian Revolution, the Soviet Union came to represent a multinational state—contrary to its depiction as an empire in American and British elite opinion—and a successful example of development. As much as Russia itself, Padmore and Pizer's object of analysis in the book was the contemporary British empire, which, they argued, should be transformed into a socialist federation along the lines of the Soviet Union.[18]

Padmore and Pizer also offered direct comments on contemporary development debates in Britain. They praised Creech-Jones, who "has so often championed the Colonial peoples in Parliament and exposed their grievances, while under no particular obligation to do so." But the authors criticized the way "the colonial theoreticians of the Labour Party fall back upon the Development and Welfare Act to correct the economic and social ills of the colonies." Development within an imperial structure amounted to nothing more than "more intensive exploitation of the natural resources and labour power of the Colonial territories." Through historical and contemporary analysis, Padmore and Pizer emphasized that political self-determination was the only way to reverse the economic "backwardness" that all empires enforced on their hinterlands. Other members of their circle, such as St. Clair Drake, were less committed to this sequence, seeing development and independence as coequal aims. But Drake, too, ultimately came to see British colonial development policy as motivated by the British drive to "short-circuit the desire for independence."[19]

From the vantage point of Black internationalists in London, colonial development had revealed itself to be a ruse. Padmore's circle increasingly focused their activities on Nkrumah's movement for self-government in the Gold Coast in the years that followed. Although the Pan-African ideal still animated the thinking of Padmore, Pizer, Drake, and Nkrumah, all four began to emphasize the necessity of building national states from which to embark on regional and continental projects.

Many in Padmore's circle in London wound up in Nkrumah's Ghana. Lewis, although never as committed a Pan-Africanist as the others, became one of Nkrumah's economic advisers in the early 1950s. Drake, after spending a year in Liberia, won a grant from the Ford Foundation to conduct research in Ghana in 1954. In his time there, he served as an occasional adviser to Nkrumah and as head of the sociology department at the University of Ghana. Padmore, meanwhile, maintained his close relationship with Nkrumah until Padmore's death in 1959. All three thinkers had distinct visions of how Ghanaian development should proceed. But they agreed that such development must take place within the framework of an independent, national state.

Debating Development in Decolonizing Ghana

Social unrest in the colonies reinforced the belief that colonial economic underdevelopment constituted a reason not for continued tutelage but for political autonomy. This effect appeared clearly after the 1948 Accra riots, which
began when African veterans who fought for the British empire in the Second
World War marched on the seat of the colonial government to demand their
unpaid pensions. After police fired on the former soldiers, killing three of
them, rioting broke out across the city. This unrest quickly became linked
to a longstanding grievance about the inflated prices that colonial subjects
in the Gold Coast paid for imported goods from Europe. It was not only anticolonial activists who identified the failure of the colonial state to improve
social and economic conditions—a failure that was increasingly articulated in
developmentalist terms—as a major reason for the unrest. The colonial government's own Commission of Enquiry into Disturbances in the Gold Coast
cited "the feeling that the Government had not formulated any plans for the
future of industry and agriculture, and that, indeed, it was lukewarm about
any development apart from production for export" as one of the causes of
the riots.[20]

The 1948 riots represented a turning point in the movement for Ghana's
independence. In the aftermath, the government arrested Nkrumah and five
other leading members of the UGCC. Following the release of the Commission's report, the British government agreed to reform the Gold Coast's
constitution to create a legislative assembly with an African majority, to be
elected by residents of the colony. As the elections approached, Nkrumah,
still imprisoned, broke away from the UGCC, whose social base consisted
largely of the professional class, and founded the Convention People's Party
(CPP). The CPP's mass support was based in urban market women, young
people attracted to the party's emphasis on education, and farmers opposed
to the colonial government's agricultural policies, especially its forced eradication of cocoa in some regions of the country.

Capitalizing on discontent with the UGCC's gradualist approach in the
aftermath of the 1948 riots, the CPP demanded immediate self-government
in the Gold Coast. In the first legislative elections, held in 1951, the CPP won
thirty-four of the thirty-eight elected seats. The CPP followed this resound-
ing victory by winning majorities—albeit smaller ones—in the 1954 and 1956
elections. Nkrumah's increasingly urgent demands for immediate independence and the clear and repeated endorsement of his party by Gold Coast
voters, combined with a shift in British official thinking toward acceptance

of an inevitable power transfer, led ultimately to the independence of Ghana on March 6, 1957.[21]

As Nkrumah and the CPP pushed for independence, a consensus formed among Black internationalists that postcolonial economic development should take place within the framework of the national state. Nkrumah and his supporters—including Drake and other African Americans—began to understand development aid as a means to bolster the position of Ghana in the international sphere after eventual independence, even as Nkrumah envisioned national independence merely as a first step toward a broader project of African unity. Within this national frame, debates about the relative priority of industrial or agricultural development, the trade-offs between social welfare and modernization, and the desirability of foreign investment capital proliferated.[22]

At the center of these debates was a proposal to build a large-scale dam across the Volta River to generate hydroelectric power. Like many development projects across the decolonizing world, this proposal drew inspiration both from the Tennessee Valley Authority (TVA) of the American New Deal and from Soviet electrification projects of previous decades. The plan's origins, however, dated back to the First World War. British economists and colonial officials had been interested in building a dam across the Volta River to generate electrical power for the production of aluminum from the bauxite that was mined in the colony. After the Second World War, the Labour government conducted an extensive survey of the electricity-generating potential of such a dam. As Nkrumah rose to power, he imagined the dam across the Volta River—what came to be called the Akosombo Dam—as the centerpiece of his vision for a modern and independent Ghana.[23]

As much as the "high-modernist" Volta project may seem like an uncritical adoption of a European developmental model, many anticolonial actors at the time saw it instead as a sharp break from colonial modes of governance. More often than not, anticolonial activists criticized the developmentalist turn in British colonial policy in the 1940s as being too small, not too big, in its ambitions. Colonial development policies such as the Colonial Development and Welfare Acts were viewed not only as last-ditch attempts to stave off movements for independence but as efforts to keep Africans confined to an agricultural mode of life. Considering the specific contours of dissatisfaction with British colonial development, Nkrumah's plans for industrial development through the Volta River dam promised not to replicate British late-colonial rule but to overcome its limitations.[24]

The debates about Volta among Nkrumah, his advisers, and African Americans invested in the Ghanaian independence movement revealed yet again the centrality of concerns about continuing economic domination after political independence to Black internationalists' engagement with development politics. These concerns operated on several levels. The issue of foreign capital investment was raised, alongside the more fundamental question of whether high-modernist, industrial schemes like Volta represented the best way to raise the living standards of ordinary Ghanaians. These questions in turn reflected the growing interest of this transnational circle of Black intellectuals in various versions of developmentalist thought, from W. Arthur Lewis's brand of development economics to St. Clair Drake's more sociological vision of the modernization process.

The issue of foreign capital divided W. Arthur Lewis and George Padmore as they advised Nkrumah on Ghana's developmental path in the years before independence. Padmore feared the political impact of the large amounts of foreign investment capital that the Volta project would likely require. Padmore argued that such a project would enable the British to retain concrete control over the Gold Coast economy as the territory moved toward independence. Both foreign capital and foreign technical experts were cause for concern, Padmore told Nkrumah as early as 1951, as "what the British are trying to do is to establish an economic stranglehold in your country, so that you will remain bound hand and foot to them even when you get dominion status." Although Lewis was skeptical of large-scale, capital-intensive industrial projects like the Volta River dam for other reasons, he argued that Padmore's fears about foreign capital were misguided. The dearth of investment capital and technical expertise in the Gold Coast outweighed Padmore's political considerations. "In my opinion," he wrote to Padmore, "what is important is not how much a firm takes out of a country but how much it puts in and how much it leaves there." Padmore's perspective made the mistake of focusing too much on the "size of the profits carried out" rather than "the size of the wealth created and left to the people of the country." Echoing his recommendations to the Colonial Office during the war, Lewis maintained that foreign capital would be necessary to finance any development project, whether on the scale of Volta or not.[25]

Lewis was hired by Nkrumah as an economic adviser, under the auspices of the UN, after the 1951 elections that swept Nkrumah's party, the CPP, to power. In this role, Lewis reiterated his belief in the necessity of foreign capital for the economic development of the Gold Coast. In his *Report on Industrialization and the Gold Coast*, he asserted this position clearly, even as he outlined a developmental vision somewhat at odds with Nkrumah's.

Previewing some of the arguments he would make famous in his 1954 paper, "Economic Development with Unlimited Supplies of Labour," which would help to found the subfield of development economics, Lewis argued in this report that the only way to stimulate industrial growth in the Gold Coast was through a modernization of agricultural techniques in food production. Whereas improved productivity in the primary export crop of cocoa would only serve to depress prices, Lewis argued, increased productivity in food production would enable farmers to escape conditions of subsistence and begin to consume industrialized goods. Rising productivity in agriculture would make possible a transfer of the labor force from agriculture to industry without sacrificing overall food production. Against those who posed agricultural development as an alternative to industrialization, Lewis proclaimed that "the truth is that industrialization . . . can make little progress unless agriculture is progressing vigorously at the same time, to provide both the market for industry, and industry's labor supply." The effort to increase agricultural productivity should be coupled with an effort "to improve the public services" which "will reduce the cost of manufacturing . . . and will thus automatically attract new industries, without the government having to offer special favours."[26]

Lewis's recommendations cast a critical eye on the Volta River dam proposal. But he nonetheless argued that countries like Ghana should welcome foreign capital for its development projects. He recognized that "foreign capital is unpopular in all countries which are or have been in colonial status." But Lewis, operating under a classical model of economic rationality, insisted that domestic and foreign sources of private capital would respond to the same incentives for investment. Using nearly identical language as he had used in his letter to Padmore a year earlier, Lewis maintained in his report that "from the point of view of economic development what matters with [foreign] profits is not how large they are, but how much goes out of the country." Moreover, if the alternative to accepting foreign investment was devoting more of the tax revenues of the Gold Coast government to industrial development than to public services, Lewis argued that the Gold Coast might as well "postpone industrialization rather than divert money to it from these more urgent purposes." Nkrumah's measured response to the report illustrated a willingness to adapt economic advice to his own political purposes. Despite Lewis's opposition to the Volta project, his arguments buttressed the idea that the Gold Coast should seek out and willingly accept foreign aid and investment for whatever development strategy it decided to pursue.[27]

Both the specific debates about the Volta River dam project and the broader interest in modernization and development in this Black internationalist milieu influenced the writings of Richard Wright during and after his visit to the Gold Coast in 1953.[28] St. Clair Drake was the first connection for Wright in this broader circle. He had gotten to know Drake in Chicago in the late 1930s and early 1940s, and he wrote the introduction to Drake and Cayton's *Black Metropolis*. Wright placed their sociological examination of Black life in Chicago, Wright's home city for a decade and the setting of his most celebrated work of fiction, *Native Son*, in the context of the global anti-colonial upsurge during and after the Second World War. Drake and Cayton's ethnographic account of Bronzeville, according to Wright, illuminated that "the problem of the world's dispossessed exists with great urgency, and the problem of the Negro in America is a phase of this general problem, con-taining and telescoping the longings in the lives of a billion colored subject colonial people into a symbol."[29]

George Padmore and Dorothy Pizer also played crucial roles in enabling Wright's trip to the Gold Coast in the spring of 1953. Interceding with Kwame Nkrumah, Padmore and Pizer helped secure Wright's visa, along with a letter of invitation from the prime minister. Wright's controversial account of his travels, published in 1954 under the title *Black Power: A Record of Reactions in a Land of Pathos*, has long faced criticism for the hostility it evinced toward African traditions and for its critical view of Ghanaian culture.[30] This work was part of a broader turn in Wright's career toward questions of decoloni-zation, postcolonial development, and Third World solidarity. In both *The Color Curtain*, his 1956 account of the Asian-African Conference at Bandung, and in *Black Power*, Wright envisioned movements for decolonization as vec-tors for the historical forces of secularization and industrialization that would bequeath a world order no longer predicated on racial domination.[31]

Wright's argument in *Black Power* that Nkrumah and the CPP should pur-sue an aggressive program of industrialization and modernization stemmed from Wright's fear of the continuation of colonial relations after formal inde-pendence. This motivation placed him firmly on Padmore's side of the debate about funding development projects with foreign capital. (The two thinkers nonetheless diverged on whether Ghana's decolonization had the potential to shift the balance of world power; Padmore objected to the title of Wright's ac-count, suggesting he change it to *Black Freedom*, because, as he wrote, "what power will they ever have in this atomic age.") In the final section of *Black Power*, an open letter addressed to Nkrumah, Wright claimed that borrowing money from the West might "industrialize your people in a cash-and-carry system" but would ultimately lead only "from tribal to industrial slavery, for tied to Western money is Western control, Western ideas." He warned: "Be-ware of a Volta Project built by foreign money. Build your own Volta, and build it out of the sheer lives and bodies of your people! With but limited outside aid, your people can rebuild your society with their bare hands." The idea of building an industrial, economically independent society through the "lives and bodies" of its people conjured, to some readers, images of authoritarianism and even, perhaps, forced labor. But in Wright's mind such a project required the wholesale transformation of the daily lives of the Gold Coast's inhabitants.[32]

Wright's infamous decree that "AFRICAN LIFE MUST BE MILITARIZED" reflected just this belief. Echoing the pragmatist philosopher William James's invocation of a "moral equivalent of war," Wright translated James's call for a revitalization of a service ethic among early twentieth-century American youth into the context of midcentury decolonization and development. Wright wanted this process to be directed "not for war, but for peace; not for destruction, but for service; not for aggression, but for production; not for despotism, but to free minds from mumbo-jumbo." Such a wrenching transformation, Wright believed, was both philosophically and politically necessary. It would force the residents of the Gold Coast, in the existential terms of much of Wright's writing at the time, to "face what men, all men everywhere, must face." Wright argued that European colonial powers, by forcing African economies into a state of dependency "because they feared disrupting their own profits," had prevented Africans from experiencing the modern condition of secularized, existential uncertainty. Politically, establishing the "military form of life" of a regimented, planned, industrial society could "free you, to a large extent, from begging for money from the West, and the degrading conditions attached to such money." Wright saw the modernization of the psyche—through the painful abandonment of traditional culture—as the necessary adjunct of the overcoming of political and economic dependency that preoccupied Lewis, Padmore, Pizer, and Drake.[33]

This circle of advisers and observers had varied reactions as Nkrumah and the CPP pushed forward with the Volta River dam project in the years after Ghana's independence in 1957. Lewis, although opposed to the vision of development through rapid industrialization that the Volta dam signified, continued to advise Nkrumah on the project through independence. After a sharp drop in the world price of aluminum in the mid-1950s caused British and Canadian financiers to abandon the project, and as Nkrumah sought a new deal to fund it with a mix of public financing and private funding from the US company Kaiser Industries, Lewis resigned, arguing that the dam's benefits to Ghana's development would not be worth the public expenditure Nkrumah now seemed committed to providing. Padmore, although he continually warned of the dangers of subjecting Ghana to the influence of Western capital, remained allied with Nkrumah, pouring his energy into projects like the 1958 All-African Peoples' Conference (AAPC) that aimed to realize

Pan-African unity. Drake, meanwhile, sensed a growing conflict in the minds of some Ghanaians between the ideal of a continental federation and the urgency of national development. After a lecture Padmore delivered in the fall of 1958 at the University of Ghana, where Drake taught, Drake observed that students' responses "revealed clearly that they have no interest in the Conference and feel that Ghana's time and money should be spent on internal development." If Wright and Padmore had envisioned development as part of a broader program of gaining independence from the West, Drake suggested, the more prosaic motivations of Ghana's citizens for higher-wage employment, wider access to electricity, and greater social mobility deserved equal attention in assessments of the progress of the Volta River dam.[34]

St. Clair Drake returned to the United States in 1961, after three years as head of the Department of Sociology at the University of Ghana. At home, he continued to operate as a conduit between Nkrumah and both his African American supporters and elements in the US government. Drake urged policymakers to understand the cultural significance of newly independent Ghana to African Americans. When it was revealed that Nkrumah would make a stop in Chicago on his first visit to the United States as head of state in 1958, he encouraged the State Department to reach out to the "Negro community of some 800,000 people in Chicago, many of whom feel a bit toward African states as the Irish do toward Eire and the Jews toward Israel."[35]

Drake further sought to build support for US development funding for the Volta River dam among Black Americans. In a letter to sociologist E. Franklin Frazier, he not only emphasized Ghanaians' "warmth toward Negro Americans" but sought to downplay the project's direct connection to Nkrumah—whose crackdown on opposition forces made him a more controversial figure in the United States than he had been before independence—by arguing that such a project could have longstanding effects for Africans "even after the present generation of leaders has passed." He insisted that Nkrumah "means it when he says he doesn't want Communist imperialism in Africa any more than Western imperialism, and that when he talks of 'African socialism' it is really a mixed-economy, welfare state which he has in mind." His outreach further aimed to build a coalition of "a very broad segment of inter-racial liberal opinion" in support of American aid for Volta, but "with no Communist or near-Communist signatories." Although Drake had been considered a fellow traveler of the Communist Party in the 1940s, his genuflection before the realities of Cold War geopolitics delimited the extent and content of his appeal.[36]

Drake's continued engagement with Ghanaian development politics after his departure from the country was not limited to his efforts to build African

American support for the Volta project. He also became involved with the Peace Corps, the signature developmental initiative of the administration of John F. Kennedy, who launched the "decade of development" at the UN with a highly publicized speech in September 1961. Drake trained American volunteers who were headed to Ghana in the first few years of the program. Working alongside David Apter, an expert on Ghanaian politics and leading modernization theorist, Drake developed curricula and taught in the eight-week summer program.[37]

Drake's decision to work with the Peace Corps training program again exemplified the linkages between Black internationalism and development politics in the early Cold War. Most volunteers he taught were assigned to be secondary and vocational schoolteachers. They received teacher training and some rudimentary instruction in the Twi language from Twi-speaking Ghanaians, and they took classes in American studies, international studies, and the contemporary politics of Ghana. George Carter, country director for the Peace Corps in Ghana, thought that these courses held much greater relevance than the supposedly practical training in educational methods: "We are persuaded that any time spent on practice teaching, classroom psychology and other such relics is time less well spent than on subjects such as the history of Ashanti and the CPP, the role of a one party system in the new African republics and the limits of American foreign policy in Africa. These are the kinds of problems which the volunteers will have to wrestle with." In his own teaching on these subjects, Drake argued that the political independence of Ghana was only a small part of the ongoing social transformation of the country. In his notes for the orientation of new volunteers, he wrote that one of the "basic facts" about the Ghanaian education system that "it would be well to always keep in mind" was "that a social revolution is underway in Ghana—a vast, thoroughgoing revolution—and the whole educational system is being profoundly affected by that revolution. The political shift from colonial status to sovereignty was only one aspect of this process of change." Drake's message to volunteers revealed both the radical hopes he invested in decolonization and his acceptance of some of the assumptions about modernization that animated the Peace Corps' mission.[38]

From Truman's Point Four program to Nkrumah's Volta River project, Black activists who engaged in development politics in the early years of the Cold War confronted a neocolonial future. They saw a looming threat of a world in which the economic domination of the colonial order outlived the end of formal empire, even as they disagreed about the potential of various development strategies to prevent such an outcome. Development politics provided the setting where the critique of colonialism as a form of racialized economic exploitation, which had pervaded African American internationalism in the early 1940s, endured in the Cold War era, despite its strictures. Postwar Black internationalism, in both its liberal and radical variants, thus constituted an ideological formation intertwined with, rather than external to, the modernization theory then emerging as a dominant paradigm in social-scientific and policy discourse. Even so, key Black thinkers and activists disagreed fervently with the social scientists and policymakers who were the strongest advocates of modernization theory about the *scope* and *meaning* of colonialism—and its relation to the history and social structure of the United States.

5

The Myth of the First New Nation

On Sunday, June 28, 1959, in the Grand Ballroom of the Waldorf-Astoria Hotel in New York, Senator John F. Kennedy rose to address the banquet of the annual meeting of the American Society for African Culture (AMSAC). This organization, founded three years earlier, had quickly become a leading promoter of cultural exchanges between African American writers and artists and their counterparts in Africa and across the diaspora. Kennedy, who had recently been appointed chairman of the Subcommittee on African Affairs in the Senate Foreign Relations Committee, spent much of his speech highlighting the potential of US development aid to contribute to economic growth on the African continent. At several moments in his speech, however, Kennedy cast his prosaic policy concerns in grand, world-historical terms. The decolonization of Africa, he suggested, was the culmination of a process inaugurated by the American Revolution of the eighteenth century. Quoting Thomas Paine's view of liberty radiating outward from the thirteen colonies—"From a small spark kindled in America, a flame has arisen not to be extinguished"—Kennedy insisted, "That very flame is today lighting what was once called 'the Dark Continent.'"[1]

At the same conference a day earlier, two African American writers engaged in a heated debate over how to understand a similar question to the one Kennedy raised: that of the relationship between the history of the United States and the present-day decolonization of Africa. J. Saunders Redding and Harold Cruse, both participants on a panel entitled "Negro Literature—African," came to sharply different conclusions. Whereas Cruse saw in African independence movements a sign that African Americans should shift their goals from integration to cultural "rebirth," Redding countered that African Americans, unlike the "new nations" on the continent, "are not a *people* in Cruse's sense of the word" and that seeing their situation as analogous to that of the decolonizing world would only "cut American Negroes off" from their American heritage. Redding and Cruse debated the status of African American literary culture and the direction of African American politics in terms not only of a shared culture across the African diaspora—a culture AMSAC was actively invested in building—but of a shared history of colonial oppression.[2]

Kennedy's speech and the debate between Cruse and Redding open a window onto a crucial feature of the political culture of the postwar United States, one that is obscured when their ideas are cordoned off from each other in our historical imagination. Kennedy's invocation of the American Revolution in a speech primarily dedicated to American foreign aid policy in Africa reflected a widely held view among American elites of the United States as the "first new nation"—the first national community to emerge from colonial rule to gain independent statehood. This idea, articulated by social scientists as well as policymakers and politicians, was an important element of modernization theory and the period in American foreign policy, particularly under the Kennedy and Johnson administrations, it helped to define. The debate between Cruse and Redding, meanwhile, marked a flashpoint in a decades-long conversation—one that would take on new importance in the 1960s—about how African Americans should understand the relationship between their own intellectual and political movements and those of the decolonizing world.[3]

Seen together, these two moments at the AMSAC Conference in June 1959 underscore the increasing relevance of debates about the nature and meaning of colonialism to American politics and intellectual life in the late 1950s and early 1960s. In the 1940s, comparisons between American racial hierarchy and European colonial rule suffused debates about the international order and the newly founded UN. Beginning in the late 1950s, the relationship between American history and governance and European colonialism became central to domestic political discourse. Tracing these discussions across the realms of the social sciences, the US foreign policy apparatus, and Black political thought helps illustrate the important place of decolonization in the ideological development of both American liberalism and the Black freedom movement in the early 1960s.

The debate over the image of the United States as the first new nation coincided with and was reinforced by John F. Kennedy's rise through American politics to the presidency. Dwight Eisenhower's secretary of state John Foster Dulles had claimed that the United States held "natural sympathy" for the decolonizing world because of its own experience as "the first colony

in modern times to have won independence," and others in both the Truman and Eisenhower administrations occasionally made similar references.
But the image of the United States as a political model for the decolonizing world resonated particularly strongly in the cultural and political milieu
of the Kennedy administration. Sociologist Seymour Martin Lipset, author
of the influential book *The First New Nation: The United States in Historical
and Comparative Perspective* (1963), later described his work as the product of
"those bygone almost bucolic days of the New Frontier." Lipset's association
between the discourse of the first new nation and that of the new frontier
suggests a close relationship between the "imperialist nostalgia," in anthropologist Renato Rosaldo's words, of Kennedy's slogan and the portrayal of
the United States as a natural ally of the decolonizing world. The discourse
of the first new nation served important purposes in Cold War liberalism, as
policymakers sought to portray the United States as preternaturally aligned
with anticolonialism—regardless of actual US policy—while seeking to steer
anticolonial movements away from an alignment with the Soviet Union.[4]

Kennedy himself, in his years in the Senate, distinguished himself in national politics as an advocate for anticolonial causes. He often condemned
the US posture of overarching support for British and French policies in their
colonies by invoking the idea of a postcolonial United States. In a speech critical of the Eisenhower administration's approach to the decolonizing world
in 1956, he argued that the "home of the Declaration of Independence" had
"appeared in the eyes of millions of key uncommitted people to have abandoned our proud traditions of self-determination and independence." This
criticism reached its zenith in a speech on Algeria he gave from the Senate
floor in 1957. This speech not only denied the official French line that the
Algerian conflict represented a matter internal to France but also decried the
Eisenhower administration's "retreat" from the "principles of independence
and anti-colonialism." Kennedy's focus on what historian Anders Stephanson
calls the "utopian deficit" between the United States and the Soviet Union
in the 1950s derived from his belief that a sense of the postcolonial heritage
of the United States had failed to install itself adequately in Asian and African imaginations. As Kennedy put it in another speech—with questionable
veracity—"every African nationalist 20 or 25 or 30 years ago quoted Thomas
Jefferson," whereas now they "quote Marx."[5]

Those who used the language of first new nationhood did more than simply seek to win friends in the Cold War, however. The language expressed a
distinctive historical imagination of the American Revolution and of early
American history.[6] Attempts to market the United States as a model for the
decolonizing world relied on an account of the American Revolution as

straightforwardly anticolonial, an account which denied the country's history of genocide against American Indians and marginalized Indigenous peoples' relationships to the early American state.[7] Further, in line with a dominant strand of historical scholarship, these efforts envisioned the American Revolution as a political revolution without a corresponding social or economic revolution.[8]

The scholars and policymakers who promoted the first new nation discourse not only portrayed the American Revolution as a model for *anti*colonial revolts, as other scholars have suggested, but also sought to shape *post*colonial politics. American elites in both governmental and nongovernmental positions promoted the federal system of the United States as a promising model for decolonizing states. Further, as political theorist Adom Getachew has shown, politicians and scholars from a variety of locations across what Paul Gilroy has termed the "Black Atlantic" also embraced the first new nation language in their own federalist projects, although they saw in federation a solution to a different set of problems than American elites did.[9]

The designation of the midcentury United States as the first *new* nation was the mirror image of a contemporaneous effort to cast decolonizing states in Asia and Africa as other than new. International lawyers from the Global South, such as Algerian jurist Mohammed Bedjaoui, rejected the designation of Algeria and other postcolonial nations as new states. Instead, Bedjaoui and his interlocutors presented the process of decolonization as the restoration of political communities that had existed before colonial rule. This argument, as historian Natasha Wheatley shows, was a means to challenge the inequality of an international order built on the principle of "sovereignty in sequence": a juridical hierarchy that placed established, presumably permanent states above new, potentially changeable ones. American elites' claims that the United States—by some measures the oldest constitutional order in continuous existence in the world—was in fact a special kind of new nation demonstrated that the sequence of sovereignty also mattered to US political and diplomatic objectives. Old states benefited from the presumption of permanence in international law; new states represented the frontier of political struggle for international allegiance. The language of the first new nation helped American politicians and intellectuals assert that the United States was both old and new at once.[10]

Those who pronounced the United States the first new nation further intervened in an ongoing global conversation about the definition of colonialism. Colonialism had emerged by the late 1950s as one of the most contested terms in international politics. Prominent social scientists and Kennedy administration policymakers invested in the idea of the United States as an example of decolonization put forth a narrow definition of colonialism as a system of political rule by a foreign power. In so doing, they defined colonialism more narrowly than did the new states themselves. Led by a cohort of newly independent nations in Africa and Asia, the UN General Assembly in 1960 passed a resolution denouncing "colonialism in all its manifestations" and asserting the right of nations to "freely dispose of their natural wealth without prejudice to any obligations arising out of international economic co-operation." The question of just what "colonialism in all its manifestations" meant was of substantial importance in the Cold War. US policymakers insisted on a stark distinction between formal political rule and continuing relations of economic dependence after decolonization, while simultaneously portraying Soviet domination in Eastern Europe and Central Asia as a form of colonialism worthy of condemnation from the Third World.[11]

These global debates about the definition of colonialism took on a new importance among African Americans in the early 1960s and contributed to an important turn in Black political and intellectual life. Harold Cruse was the most influential among a number of Black intellectuals in the United States who began to develop a new concept of "internal colonialism" to describe American racial hierarchy in this period. Although this concept took on greater political importance in the latter half of the 1960s and early 1970s, as later chapters will detail, one of its proximate intellectual sources was located in the early 1960s. In contrast to the policymakers and thinkers who promoted the image of the United States as the first new nation, those who imagined African Americans as an internal colony embraced a broad definition of colonialism that included cultural domination, spatial segregation, and racialized economic inequality, rejecting a definition that focused solely on political sovereignty.

Federalism, Pluralism, and the First New Nation

Ideas about constitutional design, national sovereignty, and civic values pervaded the portrayals of the United States as the first new nation in social science and political discussion. Leading modernization theorists were divided on the relative priority of economic growth, political institutions, and cultural value systems in the transition to what they saw as modern society. American elites both inside and outside government saw the relationship between formal institutions and cultural values as the key to the establishment of stable polities in postcolonial societies. This relationship was particularly important to Seymour Martin Lipset, whose book *The First New Nation* represented the most sustained and prominent attempt to elaborate the relevance of the political structure of the early United States—and not just its revolutionary heritage—to the decolonizing world.

Lipset grew up in New York and graduated from City College in 1943. After he was rejected by the Selective Service for nearsightedness, Lipset entered the graduate program in sociology at Columbia University, where he studied with Robert Merton and Paul Lazarsfeld. Lipset was a Trotskyite in his youth, but, according to his own recounting, his exposure to German sociologist Robert Michels's *Political Parties* (1911) influenced his gradual abandonment of Marxist theory and politics. Michels argued that there was an "iron law of oligarchy": that the internal structure of all parties and organizations, regardless of their ideological orientation, would be oligarchical. Lipset's early scholarship was driven by the questions that Michels's work raised, and by the perennial question of why socialism had not succeeded in the United States. His first two books focused on the internal democracy of trade unions and the comparative development of socialism in the United States and Canada. By the late 1950s, he had built a reputation as an expert in the sociology of political parties and civil society organizations.[12]

After moving to the University of California at Berkeley in 1956, Lipset began to consider the question of political modernization, chairing a group of social scientists devoted to investigating the Third World. His new interest in the decolonizing world grew out of his longstanding interest in the comparative political analysis of socialism. As he put it, his "concern for the failure of social democracy or the conditions for the success of socialism was in a sense transmuted into analyses of the transition to democracy in comparative perspective." Lipset's 1960 book *Political Man: The Social Basis of Politics* offered a first attempt to understand the conditions for political development in the decolonizing world. In the closing chapter of *Political Man*, Lipset suggested that, if the ideological conflicts that had defined modern politics in the United States and Europe had transformed into narrower contests over the management of mixed-economy welfare states, this shift did not render ideology meaningless. The nations of the North Atlantic were not facing the "end of ideology," as Lipset's friend and sometime collaborator Daniel Bell suggested, but rather its migration from the arena of domestic politics to the "larger political struggle in the world as a whole with its marginal constituencies, the underdeveloped states." While acknowledging that the nations of the North Atlantic should align with "radicals, probably socialists" in the decolonizing world in order to keep the "new nations" in the West's Cold War camp, Lipset did not think the role of Western thinkers should be limited to picking sides. Rather, he argued, analyses like his own, which sought "to clarify the operation of Western democracy in the mid-twentieth century," might "contribute to the political battle in Asia and Africa." Rejecting a narrowly technocratic view of social science, Lipset saw the wholesale analysis of social and political development as a heroic task in the struggle for democracy in the global Cold War.[13]

In the early 1960s, Lipset grew more engaged with intellectual questions relating to the decolonizing world. As a member of the program committee for the 1962 World Congress of Sociology, Lipset contributed to the decision to make "development" the focus of the conference, in keeping with efforts by the United Nations and John F. Kennedy to brand the 1960s the "decade of development." In the world of modernization and development theory, Lipset was a joiner, not a pioneer. Yet he believed that his expertise in the history of political parties and trade unions in the United States could be reframed in the terms of development and modernization that were then prevailing in his fields of sociology and political science. As he reflected at the 1962 conference, "perhaps the first new nation can contribute more than money to the latter-day ones; perhaps its development can show how revolutionary, equalitarian and populist values become incorporated into a stable nonauthoritarian polity." Insisting on the relevance of sweeping, historical comparison as complementary to narrow, technical analysis, Lipset further claimed that reflecting on the experiences of the "first new nation" ought to generate an appreciation of the scale of the challenges facing the decolonizing world. He took aim at those policymakers and intellectuals who "view[ed] with impatience the internal turmoil of new nations," insisting that "a backward glance into our own past should destroy the notion that we proceeded easily toward the establishment of democratic political institutions." Lipset argued that postcolonial states faced problems similar to those facing the early United States, from economic weakness and the absence of a unifying central authority to the divisions of a pluralistic society. The United States had overcome all of these problems, in Lipset's analysis, only through a slow process of institutional development over the course of the early republic.[14]

While Lipset claimed that the political institutions of the United States could serve as a model for the decolonizing world, he also suggested reasons why the new nations of the twentieth century might have difficulty achieving the same level of stability as the United States had achieved. These reasons, according to Lipset, were rooted less in an unequal international political economy than in cultural values. Like many modernization theorists, Lipset was influenced by Talcott Parsons's emphasis on "value-orientations" as causal forces in social change. Expanding his account from the 1962 World Congress of Sociology in his book *The First New Nation*, he argued that the "key values" of the United States, which "stem from our revolutionary origins," are the values of "equality and achievement." The cultural emphasis in Lipset's approach ultimately left little that appeared directly transferable from the experience of the early United States to the decolonizing world—where such values, in Lipset's mind, were not as well established.[15]

Yet Lipset was not entirely pessimistic. If he perceived the "value-orientations" of postcolonial societies as incompatible with the full complement of American institutions, he envisioned federalism as a potentially transferable institutional form. He shared this belief with elements of the state policymaking apparatus, notably the State Department's Benjamin Gerig. Gerig had served in the Information Section of the League of Nations in the 1930s and became director of the Division of Dependent Area Affairs at the US State Department, where he worked alongside Ralph Bunche, during the Second World War. He held this position until his retirement in 1961, helping to shape US policy toward the decolonizing world as more and more so-called dependent areas gained their independence. Observing this transformation, Gerig argued not only that the revolutionary birth of the United States made the country a "natural" ally to postcolonial nations, but that its early history, up to and including its civil war, offered a lesson for "new states" about the dangers of secession and fragmentation. A "federal system which balances a large degree of autonomy with effective centralized government," Gerig claimed, could offer regions that might otherwise seek their own states a degree of self-determination short of national independence.[16]

Whereas Gerig saw federalism as a way to provide a form of autonomy without nationhood to groups that challenged a new state's authority, Lipset imagined other advantages. Federalism, to him, offered a means of managing racial and ethnic pluralism by creating a cross-cutting source of division. Democracy was only sustainable, in Lipset's mind, if social differences of class, race, religion, and language were not the primary sources of citizens' allegiances and political mobilizations. "Democracy needs cleavage within linguistic or religious groups, not between them. But where such divisions do not exist, federalism seems to serve democracy well." Federalism served to produce difference along a new axis, to ensure that existing social divisions did not determine political alignments in a new polity. Political development theorist William Nisbet Chambers, another social scientist who promoted the image of the United States as the "first new nation," argued that the two-party system played a similar role, as the two large, national parties served "to contain the forces of pluralism" and to "set a pattern for a responsible opposition."[17]

Some anticolonial leaders in Africa and the Caribbean also embraced the idea that the federal system of the United States could serve as a useful model for the decolonizing world. But they took from the American experience different lessons than the ones American academics and policymakers hoped they would. Both Kwame Nkrumah, president of Ghana, and Eric Williams, prime minister of Trinidad and Tobago, looked to the federal system of the early United States as an example in their own attempts to build postcolonial federations among newly independent states in West Africa and the Caribbean. For Nkrumah and Williams, as political theorist Adom Getachew has shown, the federal system of the United States was not only an intellectual interest but an inspiration for concrete projects of federation in the decolonizing world.[18]

In 1956, after years of anticolonial struggle, Caribbean political leaders agreed with the British colonial office to establish provisions for a West Indian Federation that would rule independently over ten British colonies beginning in January 1958. This short-lived federation disbanded in 1961, in large part due to disputes between Williams, who sought a more centralized federal state, and Jamaican prime minister Norman Manley, who insisted on greater national autonomy within the federal structure. Williams's arguments for the federation, both before its creation and during its existence, often relied on his understanding of the federalism of the early United States. The decision of the colonies to unite in 1776, in Williams's reading, enabled them to overcome their peripheral economic status in relation to their former colonial power. This lesson from the American colonies in the eighteenth century remained relevant to anticolonial movements of the mid-twentieth century: "The colonies were condemned to an agricultural specialization, as they still are today in so many parts of the world, except where the necessities of modern production require the refining of oil and the mining of gold." Federation, in this account, provided a way for former colonies to build greater power in the realm of international political economy.[19]

Across the Atlantic, Nkrumah and Ahmed Sékou Touré, the president of Guinea, formed the Union of African States in 1958, after Guinea became the only French colony to vote against joining the reorganized French Community in a referendum organized by Charles de Gaulle. Mali, another former French colony, joined the federation in 1960. The Ghana-Guinea-Mali union had limited power and no formal administrative body, but it represented a practical step toward Nkrumah's overarching political goal: greater political unification on the African continent for the sake of staving off continued economic domination of newly independent states.[20]

Although this federation disbanded in 1963, just two years after the end of the West Indian Federation, Nkrumah continued to assert the necessity of such a political union. In his book *Africa Must Unite*, published in the same year, he drew an analogy between the economic conditions of contemporary Africa and the British colonies in North America in the eighteenth century. In both places and times, he claimed, "local industry was deliberately discouraged" by Great Britain, which sought to maintain its position as the industrial workhouse to which its colonial possessions supplied raw materials. Ghanaian writer Tetteh Amakwata, in the state-run journal *Voice of Africa*, explored the connection provocatively. In the 1770s, the "internal peace" of the American colonies was "threatened by external imperialism." Drawing on the title of Nkrumah's book, Amakwata argued that through the experience of defying British attempts to assert political and economic control, "the American States saw that they could not survive by living separately and managing their own affairs independently. America Must Unite." The federal system that brought together the American colonies into a single political and economic unit was attractive as a model for a state seeking to overcome the problem of holding formal, political sovereignty while remaining economically dependent on one's former colonial rulers.[21]

Some postcolonial leaders thus shared with US policymakers and intellectuals the belief that American federalism was a useful and potentially transferable model for the constitutional design of newly independent states. Nkrumah's and Williams's embrace of this element of the first new nation discourse, however, reflected an understanding of the definition of colonialism and of the central problems facing the decolonizing world that diverged sharply from the priorities of their American counterparts. Both figures discounted the salience of internal pluralism, whether within their own states or in the regions they sought to unify politically through federations. Rather, both Nkrumah and Williams turned to federation for external reasons: to strengthen the economic and political positions of their states in an international society that was defined by hierarchy even after formal decolonization. If postcolonial elites agreed with US thinkers and policymakers that the federal system established by the "first new nation" was something to emulate, they saw different possibilities in the political form. Federation was an answer not to the problem of pluralism, but to the problem of neocolonialism—a form of imperial domination that implicated the "first new nation" itself.[22]

"In All Its Manifestations"

Debates about the applicability of American political institutions to newly independent states were intertwined with contestations over the meaning of colonialism at the height of decolonization. The scope of what should and should not be labeled "colonial" was a matter not only of academic interest but of intense political concern in the late 1950s and early 1960s. Conflicts over the meaning of colonialism were paralleled by the rising popularity and shifting meanings of the term "decolonization." As historians Todd Shepard and Stuart Ward have shown, many European elites began to portray decolonization as an irresistible, world-historical force in order to deflect blame for the loss of their colonial empires. Ward further illustrates that many anticolonial actors in the colonies were long suspicious of the term "decolonization," believing it suggested a process directed from the metropole. At the same time, anticolonial thinkers and statesmen constructed their own definitions of colonialism, even as they worked to dismantle it.[23]

At the Bandung Conference in 1955, representatives of twenty-nine Asian and African states declared themselves against "colonialism in all its manifestations." This same locution was repeated in the UN General Assembly's Declaration on the Granting of Independence to Colonial Countries and Peoples in December 1960.[24] The phrase captured several ambiguities of the moment. "All its manifestations" could include both Soviet domination in Eastern Europe and Central Asia and continuing forms of political and economic control by the United States and its Cold War allies across Africa, Asia, and Latin America.[25]

Even before 1960, when seventeen countries in Africa gained independence in a single year, American diplomats had identified the *lexicon* of empire as an arena in which US foreign policy goals were at stake. State Department official Francis T. Williamson argued that decolonization presented a "semantic" problem for the United States, and he expressed a desire for new language that might "avoid . . . the emotionalism and partisanship surrounding the word 'anti-colonial.'" While some figures joined Williamson in his outright objection to the terms "colonial" and "anti-colonial," the more common move among liberal intellectuals and state policymakers was to embrace a narrow definition of colonialism as a strictly political system that had the unfortunate, but largely unintended, effects of producing racial and cultural hierarchies. The image of the United States as the first new nation proved useful to this ideological project.[26]

The writings of Rupert Emerson, the foremost expert on decolonization among US political scientists, were representative of American elites' understanding of colonialism as defined fundamentally by alien political rule and only incidentally by international hierarchy or racial domination. Emerson studied with British Fabian socialist Harold Laski at the London School of Economics in the interwar period and served in both the Foreign Economic Administration and the Department of State in the 1940s. Prior to the late 1950s, his area of scholarly focus was Southeast Asia. In his academic work,

Emerson evinced a sympathy for the movements for independence in Asia and Africa alongside an admiration for the European nationalists of the nineteenth century, for whom "the virtue of nationalism lay at least as much in the belief that it would be a bridge to the brotherhood of man as in the calculation of the benefits it would bring to the particular nation concerned." Influenced by Laski's conception of pluralism, he hoped that anticolonial nationalism would ultimately be tempered into a liberal internationalism and a plural world government.[27]

To make such a transition possible, Emerson thought it particularly important to decouple the problem of colonialism as foreign rule from the problem of racial hierarchy. Emerson recognized that contests over the meaning of colonialism were becoming increasingly salient as empire was delegitimized and as newly independent nations gained a greater voice on the world stage. He sought to defend a narrow definition: "It is idle to think that the well-established category of colonies . . . can be merged with the other comparable evils of mankind." Instead, he defined colonialism as "the establishment and maintenance for an extended time of rule over an alien people which is separate from and subordinate to the ruling power." In Emerson's view, postcolonial rulers and citizens were more likely to be seduced by the dangerous elements of nationalism when they identified their former rulers with ideologies of racial superiority and practices of racial discrimination, and they were more likely to overreach in their criticisms of capitalism and "the West" when they identified both with a project of asserting and protecting a global system of white supremacy.[28]

For this reason, Emerson was sharply critical of the white minority regimes in the settler colonies of Kenya, Algeria, Northern and Southern Rhodesia, and South Africa. The existence of these governments, he argued, lent credence to the dangerous linkages made by certain anticolonial nationalists. Although he emphasized that "an African nationalism which seeks to get its own back through an expropriation and expulsion of Europeans on the Indonesian model would lead to painful consequences for all concerned," Emerson eagerly anticipated the end of the political domination of white minorities in those states. Even in his support for majority rule in settler colonies, however, Emerson saw the problem of white settlers in a distinctive way. White settlers posed a challenge, Emerson argued, primarily because their presence revealed "the lack of that national homogeneity which any simple version of self-determination presupposes"—not because their privileges represented an extreme manifestation of the racial logic underlying the entire colonial project.[29]

Many African American journalists and intellectuals agreed with Emerson that European settler colonies in Africa were particularly volatile examples of colonialism's potential for racial violence. But they typically interpreted the relationship between the settler colonies and other forms of colonial rule differently. Several events in 1960—the mass exodus of Belgian settlers during the Congo Crisis, the Sharpeville Massacre in South Africa, and Charles de Gaulle's rejection of a ceasefire in the Algerian War of Independence—rendered this relationship especially relevant. St. Clair Drake identified the settler colonies as crucial test cases for the United States in the Cold War struggle for Third World loyalties: "If South Africa and the other settler areas are sought after to join into military bastions for the West, all the African people will be turning away from the West in revulsion." Drake's onetime coauthor Horace Cayton, then serving as foreign affairs correspondent for the *Pittsburgh Courier*, turned the attention of his weekly column to Algeria for months on end in 1960, highlighting the potential danger *pied noir* "extremists" posed to the possibility of a peace settlement centered around Algerian independence.[30] Drake and Cayton, unlike Emerson, believed that European settler colonies in Africa served as acute demonstrations of the racial violence at the foundation of the colonial project writ large. Moreover, these settler colonies exemplified continuities between the colonial system now deemed anachronistic in world governance and the racial order of the United States itself—contrary to the language of the first new nation, which presented an image of the country as both prototypically modern and structurally and ideologically aligned with the decolonizing world.

Although Emerson's *From Empire to Nation* was written for academic audiences, some readers saw in it an approach to the decolonizing world that policymakers should follow. Modernization theorist David Apter, an expert on the politics of Ghana who worked with Drake in the Peace Corps training program, proclaimed that Emerson's book "ought to be a guidebook for a new frontiersman." While Emerson's channels of policy influence were never quite so direct as Apter hoped, his analytical treatment of colonialism and racism as only incidentally linked ultimately came to support the public diplomacy of the Kennedy administration. The common understanding in the decolonizing world of colonialism and racism as inherently tied together posed a problem for US policymakers, who insisted that Soviet control over Eastern Europe was the more severe and pressing instance of colonialism than European control over Africa, Asia, and the Middle East.[31]

John F. Kennedy himself acknowledged links between domestic racial inequality and European imperialism in Africa in his discussions of civil rights. He regularly brought up his interest and experience in African affairs and his sympathy for anticolonial movements in his attempts to win the support of African American voters during his 1960 presidential campaign. When dealing with foreign actors, though, Kennedy and his advisers disavowed any connection between the history of European colonial rule and the US racial order. Even in his famous speech expressing support for Algerian independence on the Senate floor in 1957, which helped Kennedy build a reputation as a friend to the decolonizing world, he reserved his strongest expressions of concern for the idea that "Western imperialism" was viewed as a more significant problem than "Soviet imperialism" in the eyes of much of the world.[32]

As president, Kennedy pursued a policy of engagement with newly independent nations that were nonaligned in the Cold War. This approach marked a shift away from the posture of deference to European powers in their colonial conflicts that had predominated in the Eisenhower administration.[33] Other elements of Kennedy's policy of engagement, however, were deeply implicated in the ongoing global debates surrounding the definition of colonialism. Kennedy's expansion of foreign aid packages to the Third World moved well beyond what was first authorized under Truman's Point Four program and included significant commitments for police assistance designed to quell rebellious activity—raising new accusations of American neocolonialism.[34] Kennedy's foreign policy also relied to a significant degree on presidential diplomacy. Kennedy met personally with many heads of state from the postcolonial world during his tenure and in some cases successfully built amicable relationships with them.[35] Further, the presence of increasing numbers of African diplomats in Washington, DC, and their encounters with the city's regime of housing segregation, made decolonization a "social force" on the "landscape" of the American capital, as historian Andrew Friedman explains.[36] In these more intimate spheres of presidential and diplomatic sociality, in particular, the notion that deep commonalities connected the colonial order Kennedy seemed at pains to reject and the racial order of the United States posed a problem for the Kennedy administration's Cold War strategy.

G. Mennen Williams, Kennedy's assistant secretary of state for African Affairs, noted this problem after making an unprecedented three trips to the African continent in the first year of the administration. Williams had been chosen for his position in part because of his support for civil rights and his popularity among Black voters in his home state of Michigan. Once inside the administration, he aligned with Undersecretary of State Chester Bowles in seeking to make Africa a more central concern of US foreign policy. Williams simultaneously worked to make the administration take Jim Crow more seriously as an impediment to their foreign policy agenda and sought to convince African Americans that they must separate the issues of colonialism and racism in order to see the threat of Soviet imperialism clearly. "Colonialism, for many Africans, doesn't mean domination of one people by another, but the

domination of Black men by white men," he claimed in a speech at the Episcopal Society for Cultural and Racial Unity in Chicago: "Such definitions dis-
tort and obscure our whole fight for freedom and our struggle against communism." Williams's appeal, later published in *Negro Digest*, urged African
Americans to view colonialism in a narrowly political light in an effort to
secure their loyalty to American foreign policy in the Cold War. As this call
came in the middle of a speech calling for "racial peace" at home, however,
his entreaty betrayed a deeper anxiety about the separability of domestic and
foreign spheres of racial governance. Indeed, Williams delivered his speech at
a moment when African Americans were rethinking the nature and meaning
of colonialism themselves.[37]

African Americans and the Scope of Colonialism

Between the late 1950s and the middle of the 1960s, more and more Black
Americans began envisioning the relationship between decolonization and
the Black freedom struggle in a new way. In the late 1950s, the relationship
was primarily seen as one of exemplarity and inspiration. Martin Luther
King Jr. spoke in these terms in a sermon delivered after his return from the
independence ceremonies in Ghana in 1957. The anticolonial movement
there, in his estimation, served as an example from which Black Americans
might draw inspiration, strategic lessons, and philosophical reinforcement in
their parallel, but conceptually distinct, struggle for freedom. By the middle of
the 1960s, however, an increasing number of Black intellectuals—including,
if only on occasion, King—began to describe American racism *as* a kind of
colonialism.[38]

This new terminology had several crucial effects. First, it provided a new
way for Black thinkers and activists to call into question the self-image of
the United States as a liberal democracy, by associating the country not with
the vanguard of newly independent nation-states but with the recently dis-
credited form of rule those states had thrown off. Second, it portrayed the
struggles of African Americans in the United States and those of colonized
peoples in Africa and Asia as part of the same global movement, offering civil
rights and Black Power groups who tried to build connections across borders
a language of transnational solidarity not reliant on the racial essentialism
of older notions of a "dark world."[39] Third, it presented a novel social theory
of the origins and operation of racial hierarchy in the United States. As the
remainder of this chapter shows, the wider embrace of an understanding of
Black Americans' position in American society as a form of colonial status
operated in part as a response to the competing way of thinking represented

in the first new nation discourse. These debates in the Kennedy era conditioned the more contentious politics of colonial comparison that accompanied the rise of the Black Power movement in the latter half of the decade.

The emergence of civil rights as a problem for Cold War foreign policy and the recognition that decolonization would play a transformative role in reshaping American racial politics were not simultaneous processes. Harold Isaacs, who by the early 1960s was working at the Massachusetts Institute of Technology Center for International Studies, a leading center for modernization theory, observed this asynchrony. In his influential book *The New World of Negro Americans*, Isaacs commented that, when he began his research in 1957, "it had become common . . . to hear about the effect of American race problems on American standing in the world, but much less common to give heed to the reverse effect, that is, the way in which changes in the world were forcing changes in the American society."[40] By the time of the publication of Isaacs's book in 1963, the "reverse effect" had become equally important.

The Pan-Africanist scholar and activist John Henrik Clarke located the moment of transition precisely, at least for his own experience. The protests by African Americans at the United Nations in February 1961, after the CIA-backed assassination of Congolese president Patrice Lumumba, marked the moment when "the plight of the Africans still fighting to throw off the yoke of colonialism and the plight of the Afro-Americans, still waiting for a rich, strong and boastful nation to redeem the promise of freedom and citizenship, became one and the same." The precepts of modernization theory filtered into Clarke's understanding of the relationship between African Americans and Africans as well. Both groups, in his mind, faced the dual challenge of insisting upon the value and equal stature of Afro-diasporic cultures after centuries of Euro-American cultural hegemony while simultaneously adjusting these cultures to the industrialized world. Africans were "looking back and reevaluating the worth of old African ways of life, while concurrently looking forward to the building of modern and industrialized African states," a dualism that was "basically the same" for African Americans. The "new Afro-American nationalists" in organizations such as the Nation of Islam and the New Alajo Party in Harlem "feel that the Afro-American constitutes what is tantamount to an exploited colony within a sovereign nation." Clarke's argument and phraseology reflected a growing sense among some African American intellectuals that decolonization offered not only an inspiring example but a new framework for understanding American society.[41]

Although the phrases "domestic colonialism" and "internal colonialism" had been used in earlier discussions of the relation between domestic and global inequalities, they became keywords of Black political thought only in the 1960s. Debates about the postwar peace settlement formed the setting for philosopher Alain Locke's argument, in 1944, that the United States' attempts to assert global leadership would be complicated by the fact that "we have internal colonies, as well as ghettos legal and illegal, and . . . the empires of the world have only the external, colonial analogue of what we have at home." In the late 1950s and early 1960s, the phrases began to spread more widely, popping up in discussions of racial inequality globally. Leo Marquard, a white South African liberal and president of Johannesburg's influential Institute of Race Relations, in 1957 described apartheid as a system of "internal colonialism" due to its political subjugation of the country's Black majority. In the same year, the conservative African American journalist George Schuyler described African Americans as "an internal colony yearning for freedom and integration (but not autonomy) and wielding considerable political power in the USA." The Senegalese poet and politician Léopold Sédar Senghor used the term when describing the danger of replacing formal colonial rule with tyrannical self-government. "What good is our independence," he asked, "if it is only to imitate European totalitarianism, to replace external colonialism by domestic colonialism?" Across these usages, the phrase "internal colonialism" facilitated the articulation of ideas about spatial segregation, unequal citizenship, authoritarian rule after independence, and minority group power. Colonialism encompassed more than alien political control in each instance, even if the language of internal colonialism operated more as a fluid signifier than a fixed concept.[42]

Internal or domestic colonialism emerged as a keyword in discussions of American racial hierarchy in the early 1960s largely through the writings of Harold Cruse. Cruse was born in 1916 in Petersburg, Virginia, and moved in his teenage years to New York, first to Queens and then to Harlem. Drafted into the army at age twenty-five in 1941, he served in North Africa and Italy during the Second World War. According to Cruse's autobiographical reflections, a personal experience serving in North Africa initially illuminated the global dimensions of racial formation. After he landed in Oran, Algeria, two Algerian women stopped Cruse and a friend on the street and asked if they were Arabs. Cruse told them that they were not Arabs, but rather Americans. The women "insisted that we were Arab *but didn't know it because our fathers had been stolen from Africa many years ago*." This incident, in Cruse's recollection, opened his eyes to his "ingrained provincialism about America." Whether exaggerated or not, this anecdote provoked Cruse to reconsider the national identity of African Americans in light of the global history of colonialism and the slave trade.[43]

After the war, Cruse, a budding writer, became involved with the Communist Party in New York. In addition to writing plays, stories, and essays, he earned his living writing for the *Daily Worker* for several years in the late 1940s and early 1950s. The novelist and critic Julian Mayfield, a younger member of the New York left at that time, would later describe Cruse as an "up-and-coming Marxist theoretician" in this period. For reasons both political and personal, which remain not entirely well explained, Cruse broke from the Communist Party in 1952.[44]

As for so many other writers in this period, Cruse's split from the party had a defining influence on his politics. Cruse spent much of the 1950s living in Greenwich Village, moving between periods of unemployment and jobs in retail and service work while writing scripts for plays and musicals, nearly all of which went unproduced. Although the difficulties he faced as a Black playwright would go on to influence his later advocacy of greater Black control over the means of cultural production, for much of the 1950s political concerns appeared marginal in his writing. Still, Cruse's departure from the Communist Party developed into a thoroughgoing animosity toward Black Americans who made common cause with it. By the middle of the 1950s, he was calling on Black intellectuals to abandon their "sacred cows," particularly "those loud and wrong voices from the leftwing who have gotten themselves so tied up with the white folks' version of Marxism and the Negro Question that they can't think straight on Negro affairs anymore."[45]

After the frustrations of his commercially unsuccessful playwrighting efforts in the 1950s, Cruse shifted his focus to writing essays of political and social criticism. His elaboration of domestic colonialism as a framework for understanding the American racial order developed out of this turn to criticism. It also emerged from a period of intensifying international engagement between 1957 and 1960. Cruse became affiliated with the American Society for African Culture (AMSAC), which was established in 1958 as the US arm of the Society for African Culture in Paris. After his departure from the Communist Party, Cruse "transferred [his] cultural loyalties in th[e] direction" of AMSAC, and he warned the AMSAC staff to avoid collaborations with Communists, who, Cruse claimed, were "too aggressive to be allowed to wield influence behind the scenes with no opposition."[46] Cruse wrote an essay entitled "An Afro-American's Cultural Views" for *Présence Africaine*, the official journal of the Society for African Culture in Paris. Here, he articulated an early version of an argument that would pervade his writing throughout the 1960s: that African Americans needed to develop a cultural front to place alongside their political struggle, and that the integrationist outlooks of civil rights leaders were preventing such a development.[47]

Cruse's argument relied on an explicit comparison between African Americans and nations struggling against formal colonialism, a reference that both spoke to the audience of *Présence Africaine* and indicated Cruse's own developing thinking on colonial affairs. Cruse insisted that, although "when one thinks of the liberation of oppressed peoples one assumes a rebirth and a flowering of that people's native 'culture,'" in the American case, "there has been no cultural upsurge commensurate with our stepped up struggle for political and social equality." Cruse's explanation for this supposed failing reflected the influence of E. Franklin Frazier, the Howard University sociologist whose critical examination of the Black middle class in his book *Black Bourgeoisie* had been published earlier in 1957. Cruse made a parallel argument to Frazier's critique of Black leaders for abandoning what Frazier saw as an internally coherent Black vernacular culture. Cruse emphasized Harlem and the cities of the North as the geographical centers of "Afro-American traditions in a group sense"—rather than the rural South, which had been Frazier's focus. The reaction of certain Black leaders to anticolonial struggles indicated, to Cruse, their failure to understand the problems Black Americans faced. The response of Martin Luther King Jr., to the Egyptian revolution and the Suez Crisis exemplified the problem, as King associated the "new order of freedom and justice" that emerged from the end of British domination with a "promised land of cultural integration." To Cruse, the emphasis on "cultural integration" misrepresented the nature of anticolonial revolt and indicated that "it is we Afro-Americans who are out of step with the rest of the colonial world."[48]

Cruse's view that Black American cultural politics should take its cues from anticolonial struggle generated friction within AMSAC. The year after the publication of "An Afro-American's Cultural Views," Cruse shared the stage with J. Saunders Redding at the Second Annual AMSAC Conference in New York, where John F. Kennedy was the keynote speaker. Redding attacked Cruse's essay, proclaiming that Black Americans, unlike the "new nations" on the continent, "are not a *people* in Cruse's sense of the word." Seeing their situation as analogous to that of the decolonizing world would only "cut American Negroes off" from their American heritage. Redding's full response, published in the *New Leader*, insisted that Cruse's attempt "not only to link but to equate the American Negro's struggle for full citizenship with the African Negro's struggle for political independence as the ultimate goal of race nationalism" was a sign of his "total blindness to the truth." This conflict with Redding pushed Cruse to break with AMSAC entirely. But it only inspired him further to pursue his attempt to envision Black American culture in a colonial frame.[49]

In July 1960, two months after Redding's *New Leader* essay was published, Cruse traveled to Cuba with a delegation of Black writers under the auspices of the Fair Play for Cuba Committee (FPCC). Richard Gibson, cofounder of the FPCC—who would later inform on Black and Third World liberation movements for the Central Intelligence Agency—organized this group, which included Robert F. Williams, LeRoi Jones (later Amiri Baraka), John Henrik Clarke, and Julian Mayfield. Two months later, Cruse helped organize a grand reception for Fidel Castro at the Theresa Hotel in Harlem. Although he was sympathetic to Castro, Cruse's Cuban engagements did not motivate him to undertake more overt political activity. Instead, his travels prompted him to think differently about the relations among Third World nationalism, revolutionary ideologies born in the West, and the place of African Americans within the US social system.[50]

In several essays written after his departure from the AMSAC fold and his trip to Cuba, Cruse elaborated on his vision of the relationship between African Americans and the decolonizing world. The image of the United States as the first new nation featured prominently in Cruse's work as a foil for his developing understanding of African Americans as subjects of a regime of domestic colonialism. In the midst of decolonization, the revolutionary traditions of the West lost their force, as "the Americanism of 1776 becomes an expression of a frightening reactionary military might in 1960," while "the symbol of French liberty of 1798 [sic] becomes the barrier to national independence in the hills of Algeria." Far from serving as an inspiration to the decolonizing world, the American Revolution and the early history of the United States were, to the world of the early 1960s, symbols of the exhaustion of the revolutionary traditions of the West as a whole.[51]

Beyond his rejection of the anticolonial self-image of the United States, Cruse developed an understanding of American racial hierarchy as parallel to the colonial system. While he claimed that the United States was "never a 'colonial' power . . . in the strictest sense of the word"—ignoring both the nation's history as a settler empire and its territorial holdings in the Caribbean and the Pacific—Cruse suggested that "the nature of economic, cultural and political exploitation common to the Negro experience in the U.S. differs from pure colonialism only in that the Negro maintains a formal kind of halfway citizenship within the nation's geographical boundaries." Cruse went further in his 1962 essay, "Revolutionary Nationalism and the Afro-American," which he published in the fledgling New Left journal *Studies on the Left*. There, Cruse contended that decolonization demanded a complete realignment in the way that African Americans should conceive of their status within the United States. He rejected the frameworks of analysis promoted by both the Marxist left and the civil rights leadership. "The Negro," Cruse wrote, was not simply an exploited worker or a second-class citizen of American democracy but rather "the subject of domestic colonialism." The connected histories of the slave trade and European colonial expansion meant that "from the beginning, the American Negro has existed as a colonial being." Even after Emancipation, in Cruse's narrative, African Americans only attained the status of "semi-dependent[s]," not recognized as "an integral part of the American nation."[52]

Scholars have largely considered Cruse's arguments in "Revolutionary Nationalism and the Afro-American" in relation to his evolving thinking about race, Marxism, and cultural nationalism.[53] Less often remarked upon is the essay's conception of colonialism itself. Cruse's broad conception of colonialism intervened in a global discourse about the scope and nature of colonial rule that reached a peak of intensity at the moment of his writing.[54] Although he characterized his own views as antithetical to the analyses offered by the Marxist left, Cruse's formulation was clearly influenced by the endorsement of "self-determination in the Black belt" by the Communist Party of his youth. Detached from any particular territory and looking beyond questions of political sovereignty and alien rule, Cruse's conception of domestic colonialism depicted colonial status as one of legal subordination and, more importantly for him, of cultural degradation and racialized forms of economic exploitation.

Cruse's language both reflected and contributed to the ongoing global debate about the semantics of colonialism during the period of decolonization. At the same time that Kennedy administration officials such as G. Mennen Williams were invested in narrowing the term's meaning in order to gain African American support for the United States' Cold War efforts, Cruse sought to widen it. Cruse's embrace of the language of colonialism, though inflected by his experiences in Cuba and his interpretations of nationalist movements in Africa, primarily derived from his domestic political leanings. His dissatisfaction with prevailing strategies in Black politics and his desire to reorient Black politics away from what he saw as a narrow goal of desegregation, more than a deep engagement with anticolonial struggles, inspired his initial articulation of the idea of domestic colonialism.[55]

Cruse's writings were not the only efforts by African Americans in the early 1960s to reframe the Black freedom struggle in the language of decolonization. Two others who traveled with Cruse to Cuba in 1960, Robert F. Williams and LeRoi Jones, also articulated influential visions of Black politics and Black art modeled on anticolonial struggles. And as John Henrik Clarke noted, several other Black nationalist groups began to develop programs premised on the idea of internal colonialism in the early 1960s. Even so, the direct influence of Cruse's "Revolutionary Nationalism and the Afro-American" should not be understated. The San Francisco-based Afro-American Association, a study group that included future Black Panther Party founders Huey P. Newton and Bobby Seale, read and debated Cruse's work. Max Stanford (later Muhammad Ahmad) of the Revolutionary Action Movement (RAM) cited it as a significant influence on his politics. Most strikingly, Malcolm X was so taken with the article that he began to carry *Studies on the Left* in the bookstore of his Harlem mosque. Both Cruse's particular writings and the broader intellectual milieu of which they were a part turned the idea of internal colonialism into a touchstone of Black politics in the years to come. If the semantics of colonialism were largely the concern of diplomatic officials like Francis T. Williamson and G. Mennen Williams at the start of the 1960s, Black politics brought them to the center of national debate by the middle of the decade.[56]

The decolonizing world had already emerged as the decisive object of strategic concern for many US foreign policymakers by the middle of the 1950s. But decolonization and its consequences became a more *visible* concern in US foreign policy in the late 1950s and early 1960s, from John F. Kennedy's 1957 speech on Algeria to the growing American involvement in Vietnam and Laos during Kennedy's administration. Foreign policy, moreover, was not the only sphere in which questions raised by the accelerating pace of global decolonization interceded on American public life in this era. Through the 1940s and early 1950s, the politics of colonial comparison had largely factored into debates about international politics, from postwar planning to foreign aid policy. In the late 1950s and early 1960s, as the keywords of the first new nation and the internal colony spread to new corners of political debate, the politics of colonial comparison seeped into domestic political culture. As the 1960s progressed, this process would only accelerate, as competing understandings of decolonization and its relevance to US domestic politics ran through the contentious politics of the War on Poverty and the Black Power movement.[57]

The War on Poverty and the Search for
Indigenous Leadership

In the same year that Seymour Martin Lipset urged the "first new nation" to "contribute more than money to the latter-day ones," another American writer suggested that the more meaningful contributions might run in the other direction. Also writing in 1963, the socialist journalist Michael Harrington observed that within the United States there existed an "underdeveloped nation." This "underdeveloped nation" did not "suffer the extreme privation of the peasants of Asia or the tribesmen of Africa," but "the mechanism of the misery is similar." The poor in the United States, whose plight Harrington sought to bring to greater public consciousness, "are beyond history, beyond progress, sunk in a paralyzing, maiming routine." The "new nations" had an advantage over the United States in their ability to address this poverty, however. Because "poverty is so general and so extreme . . . every resource, every policy, is measured by its effect on the lowest and most impoverished," whereas in the United States, "because so many are enjoying a decent standard of life, there are indifference and blindness to the plight of the poor." Harrington's faith that the eradication of poverty in the decolonizing states "becomes a national purpose that penetrates to every village and motivates a historic transformation" reflected a more positive outlook on the developmental aspirations of decolonizing states than the attitude held by many liberals in the Kennedy administration. But his vision of the United States as characterized by internal problems of underdevelopment extended well beyond the democratic socialist left. This view suffused the rising consciousness of the problem of poverty among liberal social scientists, foundation officials, and policymakers.[1]

The increasing importance of colonial comparisons in domestic political life can be seen clearly in debates over social policy that Harrington himself did much to influence. Alongside a conception of the United States as the first new nation—a model for the decolonizing world and the *telos* of the modernization process—a view of the United States as internally underdeveloped proved equally important to liberal statecraft in the 1960s. Despite their apparent contradiction, the two ideas both took hold among a set of liberal policymakers, social scientists, and philanthropists. Intent as they were on influencing decolonizing states to pursue American forms of political and social organization, these figures simultaneously set out to address the pockets of US underdevelopment that remained at home.[2]

Policymakers' understandings of internal underdevelopment evolved in part due to changes in US overseas development programs. Throughout the 1950s, there were numerous calls for a domestic Point Four program, from economists, labor leaders, government officials, American Indian activists, and others. These proposals typically reflected a regionalized understanding of US underdevelopment, derived from the New Deal and refracted through the language of international development politics. Contained in small pockets amid a general affluence, domestic underdevelopment, in this understanding, represented the outcome of technological shifts and out-migration of working-age adults that left certain areas of the country behind, particularly older industrial cores in the Northeast and rural areas in Appalachia and the Midwest. National efforts to address the problem of so-called depressed areas promoted capital investments, incentives for business formation and expansion, technical assistance for the development of local economic plans, and worker retraining.[3]

A different conception of underdevelopment permeated US overseas community development programs. Community development focused neither on capital investment nor on technical assistance for large-scale modernization projects. Rather, it focused on overcoming what its advocates saw as the cultural underdevelopment of the people of the Third World. The core tenets of community development were local participation and decision-making, which could be stimulated by volunteers and experts from the outside. Through the experience of local participation, community development theorists and administrators believed, the people of the Third World would form a new set of behaviors and attitudes more in tune with modern life. As the 1950s progressed, community development schemes became increasingly important to the US development mission abroad, from India to the Philippines. The signature development initiative of the 1960s, the Peace Corps, reflected the participatory ideals of community development much more than had the Point Four program that predated it.[4]

A cohort of experts who administered and witnessed community development projects abroad returned to the United States to work in housing policy, urban redevelopment, and antipoverty policy. The influence of these figures extended beyond any single field. Observations of and experiences in the Third World had an enormous impact on the worldview of social policymakers in the era of New Frontier and Great Society. As historian Amy Offner has written, "their comparisons between home and away generated as many practical experiments and stylized pieces of wisdom as there are political traditions in the United States." But if the domestic spread of policy ideas drawn from international development work has been well traced, the deep effects of such colonial comparisons on the fault lines of US politics have not been adequately examined.[5]

One such fault line emerged between the policymakers and foundation officials who developed the War on Poverty and Black activists and commentators who engaged with this policy. A centerpiece of the Johnson administration's War on Poverty was the Community Action Program (CAP). A domestic community development program of sorts, the Community Action Program encouraged widespread participation by poor people themselves. Yet the foundation officials and policymakers who designed this program, in part because of their understanding of the postcolonial world, emphasized that such participation had to be mediated through community leaders— often referred to as "indigenous leaders"—whose political stances and tactics were acceptable to those disbursing antipoverty funds.

"Indigenous leadership" was particularly important to Paul Ylvisaker, a Ford Foundation official who led the Gray Areas program, which served as the model for the Johnson administration's Community Action Program. Ylvisaker's conception of indigenous leadership derived from his understanding of the politics of the postcolonial world, which he formed during a brief stint in 1961 on a Ford Foundation project in India. The search for indigenous leadership, in both the Ford Foundation and the Johnson administration, sought to transform community action into a form of brokerage politics. The identification of acceptable leaders was seen as the best means of ensuring the integration of underdeveloped communities into modern American society on terms that would maintain political stability.

Discussions of the role of indigenous leadership in antipoverty efforts extended beyond the realms of the federal government and large philanthropies, bringing activists and social critics into a shared community of discourse with state and foundation officials. In Black politics, the discourse surrounding indigenous leadership in antipoverty policy became the initial site of an anticolonial critique of urban political economy, as the next chapter will show. As colonial comparisons spread through American political debate in the early 1960s, antipoverty policymaking emerged as the site of their greatest salience. Americans' understandings of colonialism and decolonization both shaped the contours of Great Society liberalism and formed the basis for its immanent critique.

Territories and Cultures of Poverty

The recursive and intertwined nature of "domestic" and "foreign" policymaking was on full display in American debates about domestic underdevelopment. The joining together of capital investment for infrastructural improvement with technical assistance in the New Deal had provided a model for the Point Four program in the Truman administration, even as the latter policy operated on a much smaller budgetary scale. And, in the years after US foreign aid began, activists and policymakers began to look to Point Four as a model for addressing domestic poverty.

In 1951, D'Arcy McNickle, a founding member of the National Congress of American Indians (NCAI), described a proposal to address Indian impoverishment through the return of some tribal lands and the provision of technical and financial assistance to tribal governments as "a domestic Point 4 Program."[6] When Congress adopted a policy of termination and moved to end federal recognition of Indian tribes—as well as the federal aid that accompanied such recognition—both the NCAI and the Association on American Indian Affairs (AAIA) called for continued tribal autonomy and federal assistance as elements of a "domestic Point Four." Advocates of American Indian sovereignty framed their demands as a natural extension of the popular aid program that appeared to reflect the United States' best ideals in foreign policy.[7]

Indigenous activists were not alone in defining their political agenda in these terms. The president of the United Steelworkers, Philip Murray, described his union's support for a guaranteed annual income as a call for a "domestic Point Four program for backward, or under-developed areas of American economic stability." Reflecting the embrace of US foreign policy goals by much of the leadership of organized labor in the early years of the Cold War, Murray appealed to the "solid and justifiable sense of satisfaction from the pioneering efforts of our government to help our less fortunate neighbors overseas." Both of these calls for a domestic Point Four ascribed a distinctly territorial dimension to American poverty. Whether poverty was located in Indian reservations or in "under-developed areas of American economic stability," and whether the solutions proposed involved a national wage floor or targeted federal aid, American underdevelopment was imagined as a regional problem.[8]

A similar vision of regional underdevelopment pervaded economic thinking within the federal government. The Bureau of Employment Security (BES) in the Department of Labor began to keep track of "major labor areas with substantial labor surplus" in 1955, as part of an effort to understand regional patterns of structural unemployment. These figures defined "substantial labor surplus" as an unemployment rate of 6 percent or higher. In 1960, the BES started to label a subset of these areas as characterized by "substantial and persistent" unemployment. A region qualified as having "substantial and persistent" unemployment if its unemployment rate was at least 50 percent higher than the national average for three of the previous four calendar years, 75 percent higher for two of the previous three years, or 100 percent higher for one of the previous two years. While the absolute number of these areas varied with the fortunes of the national economy—reaching peaks of 89 out of 149 major industrial areas in the middle of the 1958 recession and 101 out of 150 areas during the 1961 recession—the purpose of collecting this data was to identify regions still mired in high rates of unemployment even when the US economy as a whole was growing. The regional outlook of the Labor Department was in keeping with an emerging emphasis among academic economists on structural unemployment. As Gunnar Myrdal wrote in *Challenge to Affluence*, the coexistence of high unemployment with "overfull employment in important sectors of the labor market" generated a need for targeted, regionalized interventions over and above the pursuit of national GDP growth.[9]

The growing consensus on the regional nature of US underdevelopment in the 1950s included Arthur F. Burns, chairman of Eisenhower's Council on Economic Advisers (CEA), who proposed a program of targeted domestic technical assistance explicitly modeled on Point Four. Whereas Point Four's architects had defined underdevelopment as the condition of two-thirds of the world, Burns imagined American poverty as contained in small areas amid a general condition of affluence. As part of Eisenhower's legislative agenda beginning in 1955, the proposal for a "domestic Point Four" identified "small pockets of depression" based on the new metrics of the BES, and Eisenhower endorsed it as a means of "extending the good times" to every section of the country.[10]

Despite the support for a "domestic Point Four" within Eisenhower's administration, Eisenhower vetoed two area redevelopment bills that reached his desk in his second term, citing fiscal limitations and the bills' overly broad mandate. John F. Kennedy, meanwhile, envisioned area redevelopment as a central part of his campaign's broader emphasis on poverty and underdevelopment both at home and abroad. After he was elected, a similar bill passed Congress for a third time, and Kennedy signed the first Area Redevelopment Act into law.[11]

The four-year program authorized $300 million in treasury loans for busi-
nesses to undertake factory construction, land redevelopment, and capital
upgrades. It contained an additional $75 million in federal grants for public
facilities in designated "redevelopment areas," which had to meet the thresh-
old for "substantial and persistent unemployment" set by the BES. As with
Point Four abroad, however, this sum was far from sufficient to address the
needs of the areas designated as eligible for assistance. The bill's effects were
similarly limited by broader economic conditions. The bill passed just as the
1961 recession hit, when most businesses were seeking to cut, not expand,
their workforces. As unemployment rose nationwide, businesses that were
hiring could find what additional labor they might need in places less remote
than the "depressed areas" where the federal government was attempting to
stimulate job growth. Area redevelopment thus not only took inspiration
from Point Four but in many ways replicated the foreign aid program's mis-
match between ambition and effect.[12]

In addition to the regional emphasis of antipoverty policymaking, an influential vision of American underdevelopment as a cultural phenomenon
also arose in this period. This view came out of direct engagement with
social-scientific research on the Third World, which blossomed in the 1950s
and early 1960s thanks in part to government and philanthropic funding.[13]
Anthropologist Oscar Lewis formulated his influential and notoriously slip-
pery idea of a "culture of poverty," in two studies, *The Children of Sánchez*
(1961), and *La Vida: A Puerto Rican Family in the Culture of Poverty—San
Juan and New York* (1966), which he wrote after spending time observing the
pioneering national community development program in India.[14] Although
Lewis argued that material factors created the conditions of poverty, he emphasized that poor people suffered from a shared set of cultural and psychological ailments that perpetuated it. These ailments included, in Lewis's
mind, fatalism, a sense of helplessness, present-orientation, and alienation
from society.

An inconsistency ran through Lewis's writings about how widely these
traits were shared across the poor people of the world. At times, he argued
that the term could not be applied to the "two-thirds of the world's population who live in the underdeveloped countries," because there poverty was
the norm rather than the exception, and as such its psychological and cultural
impact was diminished. Instead, the culture of poverty was "a subculture of
the Western social order" that emerged as "an adaptation and a reaction of
the poor to their marginal position in a class-stratified, highly individuated,
capitalistic society." In this rendering, the "culture of poverty" was a mental-
ity forged in the specific crucible of Western capitalist modernity. At other

times, however, Lewis posited the "culture of poverty" as a universal concept. Insisting that the culture of poverty transcended racial, national, regional, religious, and rural-urban differences, Lewis argued that poor people in the West and the Third World shared a similar set of character traits and psychological responses to the conditions of material deprivation.[15]

Prominent writers and policymakers who adapted Lewis's "culture of poverty" thesis over the course of the 1960s either ignored this ambiguity or resolved it in favor of its universalist interpretation. Michael Harrington, a self-proclaimed socialist, former editor of the *Catholic Worker*, and contributor to the *Village Voice*, helped to popularize the concept of the "culture of poverty" in his 1962 book *The Other America: Poverty in the United States*. Harrington argued that the cultural traits of the "underdeveloped nation" within American borders were remarkably similar to those of the underdeveloped nations across the world: "Like the Asian peasant, the impoverished American tends to see life as a fate, an endless cycle from which there is no deliverance." With poverty defined as a totalizing culture, the remedies for it must go beyond the provision of social services, employment, or income guarantees. Rather, "any attempt to abolish poverty in the United States must seek to destroy the pessimism and fatalism that flourish in the other America." Harrington agreed with proponents of area redevelopment that American underdevelopment was located in territorial "pockets," from urban and rural slums to declining industrial regions. Yet the tools of area redevelopment—capital investment, worker retraining, and so forth—were far from sufficient to achieve what he had in mind: a "comprehensive" campaign against poverty with the goal of "establishing new communities, of substituting a human environment for the inhuman one that now exists." Only a cultural program aimed at the transformation of behavior could solve the problem of American underdevelopment.[16]

Harrington's *The Other America* was a major intellectual influence on politicians and policymakers in the early 1960s. An extended review of the book by Dwight MacDonald in the *New Yorker* made its arguments known to John F. Kennedy. Along with John Kenneth Galbraith's *The Affluent Society* (1958) and a series of articles about rural Kentucky in the *Herald Tribune*, *The Other America* was a key component of the public discourse surrounding Lyndon Johnson's declaration of an "unconditional war on poverty" in January 1964.[17] As policymakers turned their attention to domestic poverty with greater urgency, they often embraced Harrington's image of the American poor as a culturally underdeveloped community, just like their counterparts in the decolonizing world. Even more than the comparison between underdeveloped regions of the US and underdeveloped countries, which reinforced the idea that a "domestic Point Four" might be necessary, the universalizing language of the culture of poverty lent credence to the notion that the same tools the US used to fight underdevelopment abroad might be used at home.[18]

The tools of community development seemed particularly transferable, inspiring an approach to domestic social policy called community action. The animating principle behind community action was that local communities, although they might share a similar "culture of poverty," were the best arbiters of their own needs. The way to fight poverty was to involve the people of these communities in identifying their most urgent priorities and addressing them, whether that be a day care center or street repairs. Encouraging and channeling their participation, as much as providing financing and expertise to the projects they devised, was the task of government and philanthropic actors. Poor people would not only gain material benefits from these projects. Through their participation in activities that helped their communities, poor people would come to see that they were neither helpless nor fated to the lives they led. Community action, it was imagined, would catalyze a rejection of the "culture of poverty."

Both the intellectual underpinnings of community action and its remarkable rise in popularity owed a great deal to American international development policies, as historian Daniel Immerwahr has demonstrated. American experts, technocrats, and policymakers, some of whom got their start in agricultural development in the New Deal, shaped the establishment of a national community development program in independent India and contributed to community development programs from the Philippines to Vietnam. An influential cohort of those with experience in overseas community development became the architects of domestic community action, in both the philanthropic organizations that germinated the idea and the Johnson White House that made it central to national policy. Their ideas about postcolonial politics—and especially about the forms of leadership necessary to overcome the condition of postcolonial underdevelopment—would reverberate in the conflicts that the War on Poverty generated.[19]

Community Action and the Search for "Indigenous Leadership"

The development of community action programs generated an intense focus on what many policymakers and thinkers called "indigenous leadership." Scholars often fixate on the role of the volunteer in community action and community development, emphasizing the continuities between the Peace Corps and the War on Poverty's Office of Economic Opportunity (OEO)—not least because both agencies were headed by the same man, Sargent

Shriver. And it is true that Shriver's vision of middle-class, well-educated, usually white Peace Corps volunteers serving as catalysts for broader transformations in the expectations and social norms in the communities they served was repatriated through War on Poverty programs, especially Volunteers in Service to America (VISTA).[20]

In the minds of most foundation officials and policymakers, though, the catalytic potential of volunteers paled in comparison to the importance of finding and empowering the right kind of indigenous leadership within the target communities themselves. The structure of community action enabled a wide range of groups, including many with radical political affiliations, to pursue foundation and governmental support for their agendas. Increasingly aggressive surveillance and policing strategies served as a primary means for the state to manage this subversive potential. For civilian officials, however, the empowerment of alternative indigenous leaders offered a way to channel the participatory energies community action sought to unleash in ways that would foreclose the possibility of insurgent politics. More than the fresh-faced volunteer, the respected "indigenous leader" occupied center stage in the drama of community action.[21]

Conflicts over indigenous leadership in the War on Poverty furnish a crucial example of the importance of colonial comparisons in 1960s liberal statecraft. Black Studies scholar Cedric Robinson describes political leadership as the "actualization of a myth, a legend or . . . a social ideology," which becomes realized in a particular set of "crisis-experiences." The linked crisis-experiences of the end of European empire as an organizing principle of global politics and the rediscovery of poverty in the increasingly affluent United States provoked a reconceptualization of the ideology of leadership at the highest levels of American society. With the embrace of community action, policymakers emphasized leadership not at the national or state level, but at the level of the local community. They took pains to stress that an appropriate leader must be "indigenous" to their community—by which they meant an authentic representative of that community's history, traditions, and desires. Almost always, an indigenous leader meant a leader of the same racial identity as his or her (usually his) community.[22]

Such a broad usage of the category of indigeneity, of course, masked the settler foundations of the United States, and the continued existence of American Indians, by casting indigeneity as a quality to which all Americans potentially had access. Antipoverty policymakers' designation of American Indians as merely one in a long line of impoverished communities further marginalized American Indians' demands for sovereignty and for US adherence to treaty obligations. At the same time, the designation of poor communities as generative of a separate category of indigenous leaders extended the linkage between poverty and foreignness. It cast the policy analyst, foundation official, and OEO bureaucrat in the role of the colonial administrator, dispensing largesse and conducting governance through the mechanisms of indirect rule.[23]

Indigenous leaders, in policymakers' minds, needed both to have credibility with a particular community and to serve as willing conduits of the visions of national policymakers, foundation leaders, and others who supplied them with funding and legitimacy. As a result, a common feature of the figures identified as suitable indigenous leaders was a history of militant social action that had since been tempered into an orientation toward modest social reform. This pattern—forged through policymakers' engagements with postcolonial politics—helped to transform the War on Poverty, with its stated emphasis on grassroots participation, into a form of elite brokerage politics.

The Ford Foundation was particularly important in this process. It devised its main antipoverty initiative, the Gray Areas program, around a focus on identifying and cultivating the right kinds of indigenous leadership. The driving force behind the Gray Areas program was Paul Ylvisaker, a political scientist hired by the Ford Foundation in 1955. Ylvisaker was born in Minnesota to a Norwegian American family and graduated from Mankato State Teachers College in 1942. A beneficiary of the expansion of elite higher education in the immediate postwar years, Ylvisaker attended Harvard for a master's degree in public administration and earned a doctorate in government in 1948. He taught constitutional law and public administration at Swarthmore College and served briefly in the reform administration of Mayor Joseph S. Clark in Philadelphia before joining Ford. Ylvisaker was quick to engage with the emerging paradigm of pluralism in American political science, as he assigned Robert Dahl's and Charles Lindblom's *Politics, Economics, and Welfare* in his Swarthmore class on the British welfare state in the fall of 1953, the same year the book was published. In Philadelphia, where Clark portrayed his regime as a modern, technocratic upgrade in a city long governed by a patronage machine, Ylvisaker encapsulated the administration's spirit of expertise and optimism. Ylvisaker approached urban renewal, industrial decline, suburbanization, and rural-to-urban migration with a view of the metropolis as an interdependent system. He helped turn Philadelphia into a nationally recognized model of modern approaches to urban administration in the 1950s. After less than three years in city government, he was hired in 1955 by the Ford Foundation to run their newly established Public Affairs program. Over the course of the late 1950s, Ylvisaker transformed Public Affairs into the primary agency in the Ford Foundation dealing with domestic policy, especially on issues of urban development and poverty.[24]

When Ylvisaker first took this position, he often blamed white flight and urban segregation for the problems of American cities. His writings and speeches in the late 1950s condemned white residents' "search for homogeneity" for its effects on both desegregation efforts and urban economies. White flight particularly exacerbated the problems in the "growing range of deteriorated real estate between central business district and suburb." Ylvisaker designated these regions as "gray areas" to signify both their geographical locations between central business districts and suburbs and their "shabby" infrastructure. In previous generations, these regions had served the ends of "transition and aspiration and self-improvement—for the immigrant from abroad, for the rural uprooted, for a wide assortment of human beings who are at the bottom rung of their life's ambitions." Now, they were becoming blighted and stagnant, in large part because suburban homeowners were "blocking the suburban exit" for new migrants to the city. The declining fortunes of the "gray areas" could be ascribed to the "sin of segregation, not only of color but also of class, of taste, of way of life." In the late 1950s, Ylvisaker saw urban poverty as the responsibility of the most prosperous and advantaged members of the metropolitan system.[25]

Ylvisaker's opinions about urban policy and the causes of poverty changed during his time in charge of Public Affairs. While this shift has been observed by some historians, the influence of international development politics on his views has not been adequately explored. In 1960 and 1961, as he was developing the Gray Areas program in the United States, Ylvisaker got involved in the Ford Foundation's work in India. The foundation had forged early connections with the government of independent India, opening its first office outside the United States there in 1952. Ford's India office was led by Douglas Ensminger, an expert in rural sociology and former official in the US Department of Agriculture, who ran the foundation's pilot project in rural community development in the villages of Etawah in Uttar Pradesh. By the late 1950s, Ford's office in India had become a common stopping point for American urban planners, as the foundation increasingly involved itself in urban community development projects there. This cohort included Albert Mayer, who worked on the Etawah villages project and was a key architect of the "new town" movement in the United States, as well as Ed Logue, who worked for Ambassador Chester Bowles in India and who, by the late 1950s and 1960s, was overseeing ambitious urban renewal projects in New Haven and Boston.[26]

Ylvisaker, a good friend of Logue's, was another member of this cohort. In 1960, Ford began a pilot project in Calcutta, following closely on the heels of a pilot project in Delhi. The rapidly growing city of Calcutta, located in the state of West Bengal in India's Northeast, appeared to the foundation's leaders as an extreme case of the stress that rural-to-urban migration could place on all cities, including those in the United States. Ford Foundation officials hoped to "make possible full exploitation of the Calcutta 'laboratory' as a case example for students of urban problems of the relation of rapid urbanization to development (and vice-versa)." And so the foundation sent Ylvisaker, whose portfolio as director of Public Affairs was otherwise entirely domestic, to India for the project's opening.[27]

Ylvisaker's work on community development and urban renewal projects in India would change his thinking about urban policy in fundamental ways. It prompted a shift in his thinking from a structural understanding of metropolitan life to an emphasis on the cultures and attitudes of urban residents themselves. His time in India particularly shaped his emphasis on indigenous leadership as the key variable in what was coming to be known in the United States as the urban crisis.

In India, Ylvisaker traveled first to Delhi and then to Calcutta, working closely with Douglas Ensminger and with another city planner, Edward Echeverria. Although the planning tasks Ylvisaker and Echeverria envisioned were unremarkable, such as building a bridge and clearing land for future development, Ylvisaker was taken aback by the political environment in Calcutta. The Communist Party of India held twenty-four of twenty-seven seats on the municipal corporation council in Calcutta. From Ylvisaker's perspective, this group of local leaders stood as an obstacle to both the foundation's immediate aims in the city and the broader agenda of its Overseas Development program, which aimed at diminishing Communist influence in the Third World. Ylvisaker took the rare step of writing directly to Ford Foundation president Henry Heald to request approval for the foundation's continued involvement in Calcutta. The challenge facing Calcutta, he told Heald, was "exactly the same as any urban problem—99% a matter of politics, and we'd be living in a fool's paradise if we presumed otherwise." Far from the purview of disinterested experts, the foundation's development work in Calcutta required a political strategy.[28]

The bulwark against complete Communist control over Calcutta's development was Bidhan Chandra Roy, the chief minister of the state government of West Bengal. Roy was a British-educated medical doctor who had once been Mohandas Gandhi's personal physician. A prominent figure in Congress Party politics, he had served as mayor of Calcutta in the 1930s and as chief minister of West Bengal from 1948 onward. Roy made an immediate impression on Ylvisaker. The foundation official described him as "shrewd as hell," a "master politician," and someone "against whom Churchill at his

mightiest looks feeble." Ylvisaker's positive comparison of an Indian nationalist official—especially one in Bengal—to Winston Churchill was deeply
ironic and born of an ignorance of the history of imperialism characteristic of
many American elites. Churchill's colonial policies during the Second World
War, especially a "scorched earth" policy of destroying rice crops in Bengal in
order to deny the Japanese army access to food in the event of an invasion,
was a leading cause of a famine that killed somewhere between a million and
a half and three million people in the region.[29]

For Ylvisaker, Roy's involvement in the Indian independence movement
counted as a positive asset to the foundation. His credibility in laying claim
to his country's anticolonial traditions would only help him in his battle with
the Communist members of the municipal council. Ylvisaker recognized that
the foundation could help Roy "win" in his battle for control in the city. Ford
would serve, in Ylvisaker's vision, as Roy's "passport to the big money" and as
a "foil in his public relations" that would allow him, when challenged by local
opposition, to say, "my experts agree with me."[30]

Both Ylvisaker and Ensminger agreed that supporting Roy should be
the immediate focus of the foundation's involvement. This meant "raising
Echeverria's sights from professional city planning to politics and strategy."
Achieving the foundation's long-term objectives in Calcutta's economic development required the short-term political success of Roy. Even projects that
city planner Echeverria was "dubious" of, such as a proposal to fill fifty-five
thousand acres of land to the south of the city for the construction of housing
for new migrants, were worthy of support if they helped Roy. Roy's success
was the key to the foundation's success in Calcutta, above all else—even the
judgments of Ford's own experts. And he came to represent the model of indigenous leadership that Ylvisaker would soon try to replicate in cities across
the United States through the Gray Areas program.[31]

During and after his time in India, Ylvisaker began to formulate new
explanations for the problems of American cities. Rather than viewing the
destiny of the "gray area" as bound up with the central business district and
the suburb, as he had in the late 1950s, Ylvisaker now traced the problems of
the "gray area" to its residents and their community leaders. Softening his
portrayal of white flight, he argued that the color barrier was "being eroded
by the undercurrent of class and taste differentiation which flows beneath it,"
while noting that "Negroes no less than whites aspire to the system of self-
determined segregation which the suburb at heart represents." As he continued to develop the Ford Foundation's urban policy program, he later recalled,
the primary issue occupying his attention was the "people problems" of the
"vast migration to the central city," which he defined as neither a problem of

"bricks and mortar" nor of the "power structure." In particular, he believed, the "new black" migrants had "pulled out from the old black coalition," threatening to destabilize the brokerage politics of many cities in the North. Ylvisaker's new focus on rural-to-urban migrants—especially African American ones—as the source of urban problems reflected a similar perspective to the one that animated the Ford Foundation's approach in Calcutta. This view became, in short order, the leading rationale behind the Gray Areas program.[32]

Ylvisaker envisioned the Gray Areas program as a means for the holistic transformation of the communities he had identified as both cause and epicenter of the urban crisis, which typically lay between a city's central business district and its wealthier suburbs. Gray Areas combined projects of educational reform, vocational training, and housing development with efforts to facilitate access to city services. Rather than seeking to coordinate across existing municipal agencies, Ylvisaker devised the independent community action agency, which he described as a "new instrumentality" in the history of urban policy. Ylvisaker believed that these independent agencies had a unique capacity to enable the adjustment of new migrants to the modern city, both because of their separation from municipal bureaucracies and their ability to work on multiple issues at once. Four cities—Boston, Philadelphia, Oakland, and New Haven—along with the state of North Carolina were chosen as the initial sites for the demonstration of community action programs.[33]

The identification and development of indigenous leadership was emphasized in the Gray Areas program from the very beginning. In Oakland, foundation officials sought to work with the Bay Area Urban League to "develop a parallel program of leadership identification and training in the Negro community," which would be "aimed at inactive members of the middle class as well as those potential leaders to be found in the in-migrant group." In public commentary in the second half of the 1960s, and in much scholarship since, community action would be associated with bottom-up participation by the poor. At its origin in the Gray Areas program, however, community action had more to do with finding the right people to direct and channel such participation.[34]

In 1963, Ylvisaker gave a speech at an urban planning conference in Indianapolis that exemplified the prominent place of indigenous leadership in his vision of urban renewal. While he reiterated his longstanding belief that cities and suburbs could not be treated in isolation from each other, his sharp condemnation of suburban segregation was now blunted. Instead, he defined the American metropolis as a continuous "system" for the attraction and assimilation of largely working-class migrants—"once the Scotch, the Irish, the Jews, the Italians, now the Negroes, the Puerto Ricans, the mountain Whites,

the Mexicans, and the American Indians"—which turned "third-class newcomers into first-class citizens." This system worked relatively well, in Ylvisaker's estimation. Its main problem was inefficiency: the conversion of "third-
class newcomers" into "first-class citizens" took three generations on average.
Ylvisaker mused that urban planners might make it their collective purpose
"to do in one generation for the urban newcomer what until now has taken
three." He acknowledged that his approach, which reframed basic ideas of
Chicago-school sociology in the language of "systems analysis" that was rapidly entering the world of urban planning, might strike observers as "mecha-
nistic." Yet because "a social system can't be perfected by clever manipulators,"
he maintained, "the problem we regard as the toughest to lick—and we see no
easy answers—is that of generating indigenous leadership (we're still looking
for a down-to-earth definition of that elusive term) and the spirit of self-help."
Finding the right indigenous leaders was not only important to the success of
community action. It was the key that would unlock the entire urban crisis.[35]

But who were the right leaders? The sheer variety of urban communities,
with "political and social organization ranging from the closed country club
to the open door, with leadership ranging from the greatest statesmanship to
the basest demagoguery," ensured that "urban social change will express itself
in diverse, often militant form." If militancy often frightened foundation officials, Ylvisaker, drawing on his experience in Calcutta, argued that it could
serve a useful purpose. After all, he reasoned, "American independence, too,
came by fiery patriots as well as by cool-headed generals and far-sighted diplomats." Although both elements were necessary, there was no doubt in his
mind which needed to win out in the end: "One supplemented the other; one
without the other was ineffective; but at one stage, the first had to give way to
the second to avoid the negation of every hope by permanent civil war." The
anticolonial revolutionary turned anticommunist bulwark B. C. Roy exemplified this substitution. Imagining a continuum that spanned the American
Revolution, anticolonial and postcolonial politics in the twentieth century,
and the US urban crisis, Ylvisaker depicted the tempering of militancy as a
necessary ingredient in the indigenous leadership he prized.[36]

The conflicts that arose after the Gray Areas program was established
only reinforced the foundation's emphasis on empowering some indigenous
leaders and weakening others. In Philadelphia, the Ford Foundation became
embroiled in a struggle for power between the president of the city's NAACP
chapter, Cecil Moore, and the pastor of Zion Baptist Church, Reverend Leon
Sullivan. The two figures had worked together in the late 1950s, as Sullivan had
recruited Moore, a veteran of the Second World War and a civil rights lawyer,
to work for the local Citizens Committee Against Juvenile Delinquency. In

1963, Moore was elected president of the Philadelphia chapter of the NAACP, in part on the strength of his populist appeal and his willingness to engage in the confrontational tactics of boycotts and pickets that the NAACP often avoided.[37]

Shortly after his election, Moore organized protests of the new community action agency that the Ford Foundation had established, the Philadelphia Council for Community Advancement (PCCA). Moore criticized the agency for "conduct[ing] an expensive but meaningless survey" while it "has brought forth no practical proposals." Further, although the PCCA was "demanding and accepting tax exempt provision under the guise of benefiting the greater masses of Negro people in North Philadelphia," Moore claimed, "none of those benefits are conferred upon the group other than those of the high salaries which are being paid to the director." This was "tantamount to fraud," in Moore's opinion, and only exacerbated the "undesirable status quo among Negroes." Moore also understood that the foundation's fortunes were linked to the company that gave it its name. "Since your foundation is a large shareholder of Ford Motor Company," he warned in a telegram to foundation officials, he would "be compelled to take direct action against your dealers and outlets in this area" if they did not withdraw their support for the PCCA. Although Moore was unable to mobilize a sustained mass protest among Black Philadelphians against the PCCA, Ford Foundation officials treated Moore's threat of organizing a Ford boycott as a problem that had the potential to derail the entire Gray Areas program.[38]

Ylvisaker saw the solution in the elevation of an alternative leader who could challenge Moore and his confrontational politics. While Ylvisaker blamed Moore for the negative responses to the PCCA in the Black community, he hoped that "middle-ground Negro leadership—as represented by the Reverend Leon Sullivan, for example" would embrace the Ford Foundation's projects if they saw that "more than talk and tokenism are involved." Sullivan, who several years earlier had led "don't buy where you can't work" campaigns that encouraged Black Philadelphians to boycott local businesses that refused to hire Black workers, had turned away from direct action and toward educational solutions to the problem of employment discrimination by 1963. He opened the Operations Industrialization Center, Inc. (OIC), which sought to provide job training to unemployed and underemployed Black Philadelphians, in a building that was once a city jail in January 1964.[39]

Sullivan's history of militancy made some Ford Foundation officials wary. So, too, did his organization's attempts to circumvent existing vocational training schools in the city and his initial reluctance to work with the PCCA. But others at the foundation, including Ylvisaker, held a different view. They believed that Sullivan's efforts to work with sections of the Black community that foundation officials referred to as "the unemployed, the unemployables, the drop-outs, and others who have . . . inadequate motivation to achieve" made him Ford's best hope to counteract Moore's influence. Ylvisaker described Sullivan approvingly as "certainly the most constructive and one of the most powerful (and militant) of Philadelphia's Negro leaders." He recast Sullivan's initial discomfort at working with Ford as an admirable sign of his "pride and determination not to let this become just another job-training program *for* rather than *by* Negroes." To Ylvisaker, Sullivan's past militancy was an asset—just as B. C. Roy's had been in Calcutta—in the foundation's effort to ward off a challenge from more radical corners of Philadelphia politics.[40]

In what he later called a "Machiavellian act," Ylvisaker orchestrated a meeting between Sullivan and the Ford Foundation trustees in an attempt to win their support for funding the OIC. He arranged what seemed to be a chance encounter between Sullivan and Ford Foundation officials just as a trustees' meeting was ending. According to Ylvisaker's later recollection, Sullivan "from six feet six . . . looked down at Henry Ford [II] and [John J.] McCloy and all these guys" and "had the . . . trustees around him like the Sermon on the Mount in a few seconds." Henry Ford II was so taken with Sullivan that he asked, in a revealing statement of elite philanthropy's vision of Black Americans, "My God, how do we manufacture more of you?" to which Sullivan supposedly replied, "By giving me some money."[41]

After this meeting, Ylvisaker encountered little resistance in gaining the support of his Ford Foundation superiors for Sullivan's organization. The foundation authorized an initial grant of $201,200 for Sullivan's OIC. If Calcutta's B. C. Roy was the model of indigenous leadership that Ylvisaker hoped Sullivan would equal, Sullivan became the foundation's model for the rest of the United States. Yet the foundation quickly found that it was unable to "manufacture" more Sullivans, a failure that would only grow more concerning as the pace of urban uprisings increased after 1965. After the Watts uprising in August 1965, Ylvisaker suggested that the absence of "indigenous leadership" was a primary reason for the unrest. He noted the difficulty of "find[ing] a leader who can combine the indigenous qualities of Sullivan with the 'expert stuff' of [Mitchell] Sviridoff," an urban policy expert and director of the Gray Areas–sponsored community action agency in New Haven, lamenting, "We can't find anybody in Watts or all of Los Angeles to match these two men." Ford Foundation officials saw the right kind of indigenous leadership as a rare commodity—which made it all the more valuable as the uprisings of the 1960s only magnified the problems of urban poverty.[42]

By this time, the Gray Areas program, along with the President's Committee on Juvenile Delinquency (PCJD) in the Kennedy administration, had provided the models of community action embraced by Lyndon Johnson's Task Force on Poverty.[43] The elevation of community action as the centerpiece of the War on Poverty involved a rejection of other approaches to fighting poverty, especially those that relied on direct job creation by the federal government, which Secretary of Labor Willard Wirtz had pushed for throughout the policy planning process.[44] The Community Action Program received more funding than any other single element of the Economic Opportunity Act of 1964, garnering $300 million of the $800 million in total that went to the newly created Office of Economic Opportunity (OEO).[45] Community action agencies across the country were able to apply for this funding. In the first years of the program, the OEO financed hundreds of such agencies, sometimes under the auspices of existing local governments and sometimes independently of them.[46]

The policymakers in the Johnson administration who embraced the principles of community action also listened to Ylvisaker's ideas about indigenous leadership. Ylvisaker was personally involved in the task force from a very early stage, and he was considered for the job of second-in-command at the OEO. Task force members debated the form community action should take as much as they argued over its place in the overall War on Poverty. Sargent Shriver, among others, continued to believe that the identification of indigenous leadership would contain the potentially radical implications of the provision of the Economic Opportunity Act that called for the "maximum feasible participation of residents of the areas and members of the groups served." In Shriver's ideal vision, community action agencies would be "composed of distinguished people at the local level: private businessmen, private philanthropy people, poor people, and government people." Class divisions were meant to be minimized in the community action agency: "Ours was not the poor community versus the rich community, or the business community versus the labor community." Through the identification of indigenous leadership, the centrifugal energies of community action could be redirected toward a politics of consensus.[47]

Leon Sullivan and his Operations Industrialization Center exemplified the type of agency, and the type of leadership, that the Johnson administration wanted to support. After its success in winning the financing of the Ford Foundation, the OIC quickly became a favorite target of federal funding, receiving over two million dollars from the Department of Labor and the OEO by the middle of 1965 and growing even more rapidly after that. By 1967, the OEO was providing $2.7 million per year in funding for the Philadelphia OIC, and the first eight branches established outside of Philadelphia relied on funding from three other federal agencies. Sullivan credited the early support of Ylvisaker, in particular, for enabling his organization's initial survival and extraordinary growth.[48]

Sullivan was careful to present his organization's purpose in terms of class harmony. By 1966, after the Community Action Program came under fire for providing material support to radical groups, Sullivan was careful to draw a contrast between the OIC and the community action agencies that were accused of provoking popular challenges to urban power structures. In testimony before a Senate committee hearing on urban problems, Sullivan stressed the benefits of the OIC's job training programs to private industry and to state and city taxpayers, rather than to the poor themselves. "Industry," he proclaimed, was the OIC's "closest friend;" the OIC served as the "Vestibule of Industry." Moreover, the program, in Sullivan's accounting, "added six million dollars a year in new purchasing power to the Philadelphia economy" and saved "a million dollars a year in tax revenue that otherwise would have to go to the people on the relief rolls." Testifying at a time when calls for Congress to roll back the War on Poverty because of its associations with urban uprisings were growing louder, Sullivan presented his brand of indigenous leadership as the alternative to the unrest the Senators feared. "Either this leadership can be supported and new hope given to the depressed peoples in our urban areas everywhere," Sullivan argued, or "the potentially explosive forces within the community [will] set our people toward other paths of violence and mass disorder." If some community action agencies had indeed become vehicles for the poor to challenge the hierarchies of their cities, Sullivan's realized the vision of community action as a new form of elite brokerage politics.[49]

The community action program of the War on Poverty represented perhaps the clearest instance of the transfer of international development thinking into US domestic policymaking. More than that, it exemplified how the politics of colonial comparison in the early 1960s pervaded not only intellectual discussions about the character of the American nation but concrete social policies as well. Policymakers' and philanthropists' engagements with postcolonial politics bequeathed to them an image of indigenous leadership that they sought to replicate in poor communities across the United States. In pursuit of the right brand of indigenous leadership, these policymakers delimited the potential for grassroots participation that the community action program promised. But this brand of indigenous leadership did not go unchallenged. Its challengers derived a different language of antipoverty politics from their own understandings of colonialism and decolonization.

Welfare Colonialism and the Limits
of Community Action

The first sustained attempt by African American thinkers to understand US urban politics in terms of colonialism grew out of the swirling debate about community action and indigenous leadership during the War on Poverty. The rising significance of the concept of indigenous leadership in discussions of poverty reinforced a longstanding tendency in American political discourse to understand Black politics not as a struggle among classes, competing interests, or opposed ideological alignments, but as an arena of racial representation, in which a leader or set of leaders spoke for an undifferentiated African American populace. One prominent 1960 study of Black politics in the urban North, James Q. Wilson's *Negro Politics: The Search for Leadership*, exemplified this view. Wilson's book was one of the few texts by a white political scientist to take Black politics as its central subject since Harold Gosnell's *Negro Politicians* (1935). He assumed that the best way to understand Black politics was through a comparison of the leadership styles of two notable Black politicians, William Dawson of Chicago and Adam Clayton Powell Jr. of New York.[1]

The inclination to understand Black politics in terms of a bifurcation between leaders, on the one hand, and the community, on the other, crossed racial as well as political lines. Among Black thinkers, questions of leadership structured debates about the character and trajectory of the civil rights movement, at times with explicit reference to decolonization. This discussion reached new levels of intensity after the Montgomery Bus Boycott and the rise to national prominence of Martin Luther King Jr. One "participant-observer" of the boycott, Lawrence Dunbar (L. D.) Reddick, described King as a "bourgeois leader of the masses" in his 1959 biography, *Crusader without Violence*. Privately, he described the minister as a charismatic leader in much

the same mold as Kwame Nkrumah and other statesmen of the decolonizing world. The organizer and intellectual Ella Baker famously split with King
and the Southern Christian Leadership Conference (SCLC) in part because
of her frustration with what she saw as an overreliance on charismatic, male
leadership in the organization. Her disagreements with the SCLC's leaders
precipitated her attempt to develop an alternative brand of civil rights leadership in the Student Non-Violent Coordinating Committee (SNCC), where
she sought to bring young people and the rural poor into positions of self-
conscious leadership within the broader movement. Movement politics thus
shaped the contours of debate on the question of Black leadership.[2]

In the early 1960s, Black intellectuals and activists also debated the politics
of leadership in the context of the new politics of community action.[3] If Leon
Sullivan embraced the designation of "indigenous leader" bestowed upon
him by the Ford Foundation and the Johnson administration, other African
American thinkers and activists bristled at the way antipoverty agencies selected and empowered local intermediaries. Just as philanthropists and policymakers looked to the colonial world and the evolving process of decolonization to understand urban poverty within the United States, so too did many
Black Americans who were the targets of their interventions. But they did not
draw the same lessons. According to Black activists and thinkers, government
and philanthropic agencies engaged in the identification and promotion of
"indigenous leaders" too often took on the role of a colonial state, seeking to
govern the American metropolis through mechanisms of indirect rule.

The terms of this colonial comparison evolved over the course of the early
1960s. The practices of social welfare agencies first came under fire as forms
of "social welfare colonialism" after the New York City Youth Board decided
to fund a social service agency from outside Harlem to lead efforts against
juvenile delinquency there. This decision generated outrage among community activists and ministers in Harlem, who pressured the city to change its
plan. One leader of the local protest movement was the noted psychologist
Kenneth Clark. Clark, a liberal social scientist, was initially a strong believer
in the potential of community action. His and other activists' criticisms of
the "social welfare colonialism" of the city's Youth Board only reinforced the
emphasis on indigenous leadership in antipoverty policy.

Over the next few years, Clark became increasingly involved in the politics of community action through the organization he cofounded with his wife
Mamie Phipps Clark, Harlem Youth Opportunities Unlimited (HARYOU). As
his engagement with the War on Poverty deepened, his initial faith in community action faded. Clark extended the critique of social welfare colonialism into a more substantial analysis of how American urban political economy

replicated, on the scale of the city, the racialized exploitation that characterized colonial rule. Clark's ghetto-as-colony thesis was a more thoroughgoing challenge to metropolitan political economy in colonial terms than the idea of social welfare colonialism had been. The ghetto-as-colony thesis would become a central element in the political thought of the Black Power movement in the second half of the 1960s. But it first emerged in Clark's writing both as a product of the Black internationalist ideas about colonialism formulated over the previous decades and as a timely response to the emphasis on the development of indigenous leadership in antipoverty policy. The anticolonial analysis of urban political economy that would become a touchstone of Black radical thought in the late 1960s had an important precursor in Clark's immanent critique of Great Society liberalism.

The Critique of Social Welfare Colonialism

The description of liberal antipoverty policy as a form of social welfare colonialism originated in a dispute in Harlem involving the funding of antidelinquency programs. In the early 1960s, Manhattan's Lower East Side was home to the most prominent experimental program designed to combat juvenile delinquency in the country, called Mobilization for Youth (MFY). Mobilization For Youth was founded by Lloyd Ohlin and Richard Cloward in 1959 as an experiment to test the "opportunity theory" of delinquency the two criminologists were developing at the time. Ohlin and Cloward argued in their *Delinquency and Opportunity* (1960) that a society that encouraged high ambitions and provided few opportunities to satisfy them bred the conditions for youth crime and the development of gangs, and their theory gained significant attention in both law enforcement agencies and antipoverty policy-making circles.[4]

Inspired by the prominence of Mobilization for Youth, a group of local organizations in Harlem sought to attract city resources for an antidelinquency project in their own neighborhood. Among these organizations was the Northside Child Development Center, which had been founded by psychologists Kenneth and Mamie Clark in 1946. Northside originally provided only clinical services, including talk therapy and diagnostic testing, but over the course of the 1950s the Clarks expanded its offerings to include nutritional and educational programming. While Kenneth Clark taught at City College, Mamie Clark ran the day-to-day operations of Northside. The Clarks' clinical approach at Northside reflected their shared skepticism of orthodox Freudianism, with its emphasis on the internal roots of individual mental disorders through the ultimate and universal influence of the parent-child relationship, as well as their resistance to the increasing medicalization of psychiatry in the postwar United States. Instead, the Clarks emphasized the social sources of psychological health—highlighting, in particular, the influence of racism on the psychological development of young Black people in Harlem. This viewpoint influenced the Clarks' efforts to involve social workers in Northside's activities, and it undergirded the organization's turn to advocacy on health and education issues in the city.[5]

In May 1961, when the New York City Youth Board announced a plan to establish a "psychiatric unit" that would monitor "high delinquency areas" in Harlem that summer, neither Northside nor other agencies operating in the neighborhood were consulted. The Youth Board's far-fetched plan involved sending psychiatrists, social workers, and an anthropologist to attempt to identify gang members, approach them on the street, and either provide immediate psychiatric assistance or convince them to begin sustained treatment. Youth Board Commissioner Ralph Whelan, according to the *New York Times*, supported the proposal "because of the reluctance of the youngsters to go to established mental health centers and . . . because the conventional forms of help had not always been effective." Beyond the program design itself, which the *Amsterdam News* editorial board ridiculed as "snatching [juvenile delinquents] off the streets and forcing them on some white psychiatrist's couch," the city government faced criticism for its to decision to contract with the Jewish Board of Guardians, rather than an organization in Harlem, to carry out the project.[6]

A group of Harlem ministers and directors of neighborhood organizations, including Kenneth Clark, came together to protest the city's refusal to consult with local agencies. In a letter to Whelan, they cited the emerging consensus in community action circles that "one cannot reasonably hope for a community program of this type to be successful if it is imposed upon a community from 'above.'" The city's choice to pay an outside organization for services that overlapped with the mission of several local organizations "could indeed be interpreted as a deliberate attempt to weaken the existing agencies in the community." The city's handling of the process, as Clark and his colleagues put it, was "an example of the 'lady bountiful' approach to the problem of the people of the community" and "a form of social welfare colonialism." Reverend Eugene Callender, another signatory of the letter, repeated the charge of "social welfare colonialism" from the pulpit of the Church of the Master on 122nd St. and Morningside Avenue. This phrase updated a longstanding criticism of social work practices as out of touch and counterproductive for the era of decolonization, associating the city government not with the extractive and violent elements of colonial rule but with its ideology of a civilizing mission. The opposition by Harlem residents forced city officials to abandon their plan for a "psychiatric unit" to monitor delinquency in Harlem.[7]

Notably, in applying the label of colonialism, Clark and his colleagues did not question the Youth Board's plan at its roots. They sought instead to delegitimize the board's reliance on white experts from outside Harlem. Despite misgivings about the specific design of the Youth Board's program, Clark and his colleagues shared a belief in the existence of juvenile delinquency as a problem needing to be solved as well as a faith in the value of psychiatric interventions in the lives of young people classified as delinquent. In fact, they argued that a principal danger of the city's decision was that it "threaten[ed] to undo much of the public confidence in the psychiatric approach to troubled and disturbed children and youth."[8]

The controversy with the New York City Youth Board stimulated greater interest in developing antidelinquency programs within Harlem. Mamie and Kenneth Clark met with leaders of other voluntary agencies throughout the summer of 1961, drawing up a proposal for a new organization that would provide a greater range of services than Northside did. Out of these conversations came the idea for Harlem Youth Opportunities Unlimited (HARYOU). Aware of the support for Mobilization for Youth in the Kennedy administration, the Clarks sought the advice of James Jones, a Black sociologist who worked alongside Cloward at MFY, in the planning process. HARYOU won a planning grant of $230,000 from the President's Committee on Juvenile Delinquency and an additional grant of $100,000 from the city government. David Hackett, the executive director of the PCJD, was involved in the formation and early operations of HARYOU, and the organization was discussed in the Johnson administration's Task Force on Poverty. HARYOU's emergence out of the frustration of Harlem reformers with the Youth Board's approach exemplified the early common ground between activists who criticized the "social welfare colonialism" of philanthropic agencies run by outsiders to a particular community and policymakers who increasingly saw the development of "indigenous leadership" as the most important factor in antipoverty work.[9]

A few years after the Youth Board controversy, a bestselling book brought the charge of social welfare colonialism into the national consciousness. Written by the white journalist Charles Silberman, *Crisis in Black and White* (1964) captured a rising tide of discontentment with philanthropic practices. Silberman, who grew up in New York and taught economics at Columbia University and City College, joined the staff of *Fortune* magazine in 1953, where he covered urban policy and education during the 1950s and early

1960s. In *Crisis in Black and White*, Silberman framed his commentary in the terms of indigenous leadership on which foundation officials relied. Failures of social policy directed at African Americans, Silberman concluded, often resulted from the narrow band of Black leaders that policymakers consulted. "Businessmen and civic leaders must realize that when they talk only to the eight or ten most prosperous or most socially polished Negroes in town, they are not really talking to the Negroes at all," which meant that they could be "badly misled as to the temper and desires of the Negro community." In Silberman's mind, "nothing rankles Negroes quite so much as the 'power structure's' habit of choosing the Negro 'leaders' whom it wants to reward or with whom it wants to deal."[10]

Silberman singled out Paul Ylvisaker and the Ford Foundation's Gray Areas program for criticism along these lines, even though Ford had helped fund Silberman's research. Silberman cited the foundation's treatment of NAACP leader Cecil Moore in Philadelphia as a particularly egregious example. The foundation's actions there had not only run counter to the best practices of community action but had inflamed the very sentiments they hoped to counter. Even "middle-class Negroes who regarded Moore as a dangerous rabble-rouser," he argued, "felt constrained in this instance to support him out of resentment at this example of white welfare colonialism." Throughout the final chapter of *Crisis in Black and White*, entitled "The Revolt against 'Welfare Colonialism,'" Silberman used the language of colonialism to emphasize the "self-defeating" nature of liberal social reform efforts.[11]

Silberman contrasted the efforts to cultivate indigenous leadership by Ylvisaker with the work of Saul Alinsky and The Woodlawn Organization (TWO) among African Americans in Chicago. TWO was the latest organizing vehicle founded by Saul Alinsky, who began his career in the 1930s under the tutelage of CIO president John L. Lewis and in the 1940s founded the Industrial Areas Foundation (IAF), which he directed using his distinctive principles of community organization. Alinsky's approach to organizing focused on building power by uniting residents of a neighborhood around immediate demands, and using the collective power of these groups—made manifest through petitions, boycotts, or direct action—to extract concessions from local elites. Deeply suspicious of Communist and socialist ideologies, Alinsky argued that the practical-minded organizer who could bring people together around modest demands and help them understand their own power was the key to social change.[12]

The idea of indigenous leadership had been an element of Alinsky's theories of organizing since the 1940s. The form of indigenous leadership that Alinsky favored differed, in some ways, from what policymakers desired. For

Alinsky, the willingness to engage in disruptive action to win concessions from city elites was not a mark against a leader, but a requirement.[13]

Nonetheless, Alinsky's ideal vision of an indigenous leader shared important elements with Ylvisaker's. In particular, both men emphasized the ability to coordinate disparate groups within a community and a close, organic connection to the most disempowered populations in a city. Silberman's portrayal of a complete divergence between the Gray Areas program and the work of Woodlawn disguised important similarities in their philosophies and overlooked the close ties between the foundation and community action agencies that resembled Woodlawn across the country.[14] When Alinsky wrote to Ylvisaker after the publication of *Crisis in Black and White* suggesting that the foundation must have been unhappy to have funded a work that cast the Gray Areas program in such a negative light, he, too, overlooked the ways that Silberman's book endorsed the premises underlying the foundation's view of community action. It was precisely the perception that Ford had been successful at identifying and developing a class of leaders close to the grassroots that made Gray Areas such an attractive model for the policymakers who developed the OEO.[15]

Writers and activists who leveled the charge of social welfare colonialism thus had more in common with the policy and foundation officials seeking to identify indigenous leadership in their efforts to fight poverty than either group liked to admit. Both Silberman and those involved with the formation of HARYOU shared an underlying faith that a version of community action, implemented through the right leaders, represented the best means of addressing urban poverty and juvenile delinquency. Like the policymakers and foundation officials who devised community action, they believed that the unequal distribution of power in the American metropolis could be overcome through the elevation of a certain brand of leadership.

From Social Welfare Colonialism to the Ghetto-as-Colony

Crisis in Black and White spent ten weeks on the *New York Times* bestseller list, bringing the phrase "social welfare colonialism" into the mainstream of American commentary. Almost simultaneously, Kenneth Clark was developing a broader application of the language of colonialism to the urban crisis. In the 1964 HARYOU report *Youth in the Ghetto: A Study of the Consequence of Powerlessness and a Blueprint for Change* and the 1965 book *Dark Ghetto*, Clark developed an analysis of the ghetto-as-colony that would deeply influence the Black Power movement—which Clark himself would come to oppose. Clark's analysis of the ghetto-as-colony applied the label of colonialism not to the attitudes of individuals or the actions of city agencies but to the structure of urban political economy. His transition from a narrow critique of social welfare colonialism to a broader analysis of the ghetto-as-colony marked his growing ambivalence about the premises—and not just the practices—of liberal antipoverty policy.[16]

Clark's first discussion of the political economy of the Harlem ghetto in colonial terms came in the HARYOU report *Youth in the Ghetto*. Spanning 600 pages and authored primarily by Clark, *Youth in the Ghetto* aimed to provide a comprehensive social survey of Central Harlem, defined as the area between "110th Street on the south; Third Avenue on the east; the Harlem River on the northeast; and the parks bordering St. Nicholas, Morningside, and Manhattan Avenues on the west." HARYOU employed over two hundred young people as research associates, who compiled the document alongside adult consultants and research directors. The report combined a statistical portrait of stark differentials in economic, educational, and health indicators between Harlem and the rest of the city with a "blueprint for change" centered on a distinctive vision of community action.[17]

Although HARYOU attracted the eye of policymakers, its original orientation had more of an activist bent than the agencies, such as Leon Sullivan's Operations Industrialization Center, that were the darlings of the Ford Foundation and the Johnson administration. As historian Daniel Matlin argues, Clark's psychological thought, which emphasized the therapeutic benefits of social action by the disempowered members of a community, made *Youth in the Ghetto* more of a call for social and political struggle than a plan for the technocratic administration of social services by local elites. *Youth in the Ghetto* suggested that HARYOU's community action wing would work alongside groups such as SNCC, CORE, and the Community Council on Housing—a group led by legendary Harlem housing activist and Communist Jesse Gray, which had organized successful rent strikes in 1963—in order to "insur[e] the participation of Harlem's young people in programs of social action and social protest." Clark thus expected that grassroots civil rights protest would constitute one part of HARYOU's version of community action.[18]

An embryonic analysis of the ghetto-as-colony anchored *Youth in the Ghetto*. As the introduction to the report put it: "Ghettoes in contemporary America may be defined primarily in terms of racial and color-determined restrictions on freedom of choice and freedom of movement. Ghettoes are the consequence of the imposition of external power and the institutionalization of powerlessness. In this respect, they are in fact social, political, educational, and—above all—economic colonies. Those confined within ghetto walls are subject peoples. They are victims of the greed, cruelty, insensitivity, guilt, and fear of their masters." This colonial position diminished the capacity of grassroots organizations, including HARYOU itself, to alter the conditions of the neighborhood: "The precarious plight of social agencies in Harlem reflects not only the general predicament of the community, its pattern of powerlessness, but also the specific fact that Harlem is an economic, business, and industrial colony of New York City."[19]

Clark's analysis here posed HARYOU's vision of community action as analogous to a struggle for decolonization. At the same time, by insisting that Harlem's problems were inseparable from the political economy of the city writ large, Clark suggested that community-level politics were insufficient. Although Clark did not state his definition of colonialism outright, it clearly referred to something other than political sovereignty over a distant people and something different from what the label of "social welfare colonialism" implied. Rather, the economic exploitation of a racialized, territorially defined population, which had been at the center of internationally minded Black thinkers' understandings of colonialism for decades, exemplified the colonial relationship between the Harlem ghetto and the broader metropolis. In his protest of the Youth Board decision two years earlier, Clark and his allies employed a colonial analogy to emphasize paternalism. Here, he used one to illuminate a pattern of exploitation.

The HARYOU report was distributed among policymakers in New York and Washington. But it was also intended for uptake in Harlem itself. To that end, it was adapted into a comic book for young people in the neighborhood who were the target of HARYOU's programs. Hardly a vessel for entertainment, the comic book combined a narrative of HARYOU's formation with an abridged presentation of some of *Youth in the Ghetto*'s findings about racial inequality in the neighborhood. It also contained testimony from young people about HARYOU and a membership form for its readers to sign. While its narrative was often clunky and uninspired—one panel contains an image of Kenneth Clark telling his staff, "It is most important we involve *youth* in the project . . . too often adults are wrong about what is best for youth"—its depiction of the deprivation imposed on Harlem residents was more compelling. The comic presented the social scientific findings of the HARYOU report through humor as well as horror. A page about Harlem's old and deteriorating housing stock highlighted that 40 percent of the housing in Central Harlem was built between 1880 and 1901, while depicting a passerby telling their companion, "I hear a crazy fellow just invented something called an elevator!" and the companion responding, "What's that?" Another panel presented dire statistics on youth unemployment in Central Harlem over an image of the faces of young Black people, stretched out in the manner of Edvard Munch's painting *The Scream*, being sucked down a drain. The presentation of social scientific data in comic book form reflected HARYOU's attempt to democratize the expertise of its research staff for the benefit of its target audience—the young people of Harlem.[20]

The *Youth in the Ghetto* comic illustrated the centrality of the ghetto-as-colony thesis to HARYOU's analysis. In the foreground of one key panel, which was replicated on the comic's cover, was a young man with his open hands raised—in a position of surrender—and a fearful look in his eyes. Bearing down on him, as if from the tips of his own fingers, were the forces of oppression and exploitation, represented by a policeman wielding a nightstick as well as a loan shark. Also menacing the young man were images of narcotics and gambling, reflecting HARYOU's view of these vices as originating outside the ghetto and contributing to misery within it. Above this figure, the text read: "Our ghetto is the sum total of outside pressures denying our community self-guidance. Making it, in fact, a powerless political, social, educational, and above all—an economic colony!" Clark's ghetto-as-colony thesis, which undergirded the social-scientific analysis of the HARYOU report, here appeared in a vernacular form, intended for circulation among the young Black people of Harlem.[21]

Clark also hoped he could turn the insights of *Youth in the Ghetto* into a popular book that would reach a wide audience. Time for writing was freed up when HARYOU's activities did not go as he planned. Shortly after the establishment of the agency, Harlem's congressman, Reverend Adam Clayton Powell Jr., worked to bring the independent organization under his control. First, he orchestrated the creation of a second community action agency, called Associated Community Teams (ACT), which also won a grant from the President's Committee on Juvenile Delinquency. Then, Powell proposed a merger between the two organizations, which Clark vehemently opposed. In Clark's mind, the goal of HARYOU was to build up an independent base of power from which Harlem residents could agitate for change. A merger would only create an organization beholden to Powell's political interests. Policymakers in Washington, however, largely supported Powell, in part because his position in Congress gave him leverage over antipoverty legislation. The merger between HARYOU and ACT went through with the support of Robert F. Kennedy and the PCJD. Clark was left off the board of the newly formed HARYOU-ACT. He resigned in July 1964, only a few months after the release of *Youth in the Ghetto*.[22]

After leaving the organization he helped found, Clark turned toward revising *Youth in the Ghetto* for public consumption. The book he produced, *Dark Ghetto: Dilemmas of Social Power* (1965), combined social-scientific analysis

Panel from "Harlem Youth Report #5: Youth in the Ghetto and the Blueprint for Change," Kenneth Bancroft Clark Papers, Library of Congress.

based on HARYOU's research and activism with Clark's personal reflections as a resident of Harlem for over forty years. Released in the aftermath of the Harlem riots, *Dark Ghetto* was one of several books printed in 1965 by prominent New York publishers that sought to capitalize on growing nationwide interest in the subject of Black urban life, and the book reached wide audiences. Although much of the analysis in *Dark Ghetto*, and even large sections of the text, were drawn from *Youth in the Ghetto*, the two documents contained important differences and served different purposes for their author. Clark wanted *Youth in the Ghetto* to serve as the authoritative report on conditions in Harlem. *Dark Ghetto*, meanwhile, was "no report at all, but rather the anguished cry of its author," even if it was a "cry" still "controlled in part by the concepts and language of social science." Clark hoped to combine expert analysis and literary skill to dramatize the problems of the American ghetto for what he saw as a largely apathetic public audience.[23]

Dark Ghetto opened with the same evocative description of the ghetto-as-colony originally included in the introduction to *Youth in the Ghetto*. British philosopher Bertrand Russell highlighted this point in an extended blurb that was printed on the book's front cover in its first edition. "The Negro in America enjoys what can only be described as colonial status," Russell wrote, arguing, more stridently than the author himself, that Clark's analysis confirmed "the necessity of radical, even revolutionary action." Clark did not go so far as to endorse revolution—although the way he substantiated the colonial analogy with an account of social conditions in Harlem would inspire others to argue that his book pointed in that direction. His analysis of labor, capital investment, and housing in the third chapter of *Dark Ghetto* provided the strongest support for his description of American ghettos as "above all—economic colonies." Segregation and employment discrimination meant that residents of the ghetto either worked elsewhere or were forced to work in low-wage jobs. The ghetto's housing stock was dilapidated and deteriorating; its schools were substandard and underfunded; and, crucially, most of its businesses were owned by outsiders, who took their profits out of the neighborhood. Clark saw this last factor as the main reason that the ghetto could only be understood in relation to the surrounding metropolis. Absentee ownership left the ghetto with a lack of investment capital and a surplus of businesses geared toward low-quality consumer goods. Federal highway construction and racially discriminatory federal mortgage underwriting further ensured that "the suburbs drain the economy of the city—through subsidized transportation, housing development, and the like."[24]

Clark's analysis was among the first to link the language of colonialism with the territorially specific space of the Black ghetto. The Communist

Party's call for self-determination in the Black belt had seen the clearest connections to colonialism in the plantation society of the post-Emancipation US South. Harold Cruse and other writers in the early 1960s deployed a colonial analogy to emphasize the cultural domination and economic exploitation that characterized the American racial hierarchy on a national scale. In contrast, Clark's ghetto-as-colony thesis emphasized that urban political economy was the crucial arena of racial domination in American life.

Clark's analysis of the political economy of ghetto and metropolis in colonial terms reflected a greater ambivalence about community action than he had exhibited in previous writings. His conflict with Powell and his departure from HARYOU-ACT diminished his faith in the independent community organization as an effective social actor. Powell's ability to muster political support in Washington for his takeover of the agency suggested to Clark that the same forces that made the ghetto a "colony" presented overwhelming obstacles to successful mobilization from within its confines. In a subtle repudiation of his belief in community action that animated so much of the HARYOU report, Clark insisted that "the dark ghetto is not a viable community." The assumption that the development of indigenous leadership could transform ghetto conditions similarly struck Clark as false. "Negro leaders can no longer control the pace of change in America," he wrote, and "in fact they are no longer, if they ever were, literally *leaders*." This was a consequence, Clark argued, of the "successful movement of democracy in America and throughout the world," which turned the leadership class through which liberal antipoverty policy sought to work into "mere interpreters or executives." Examining the strategies on offer in the civil rights movement, from the "strategy of accommodation" to the "strategy of law and maneuver" to the "strategy of direct encounter," Clark concluded bleakly that these strategies held only limited promise. "If racism has so corroded the American society" that white Americans felt no identification with Black ghetto residents, "then no strategy or combination of strategies can transform the ghetto and save the society." Community action might play some role in the sought-after transformation, but the notion that it could be at the center of a "blueprint for change," as Clark had described it in *Youth in the Ghetto*, no longer seemed viable.[25]

A few years later, Clark would reject community action entirely. Clark and Jeannette Hopkins, an editor at Harper & Row who had worked on *Dark Ghetto*, jointly wrote a stinging critique of the way community action had been incorporated into the War on Poverty. Their book, *A Relevant War against Poverty* (1968), focused on the turn by Congress and the administration away from the "maximum feasible participation" mandate. Clark and

Hopkins leveled criticisms, informed by Clark's experience with HARYOU, at the way that community action agencies had been subsumed by existing local political machines.[26]

A year later, in a speech titled "Problems of the Ghetto," Clark disparaged not only the implementation of community action but its underlying ideals as well. Clark no longer saw community action as a promising means to build up indigenous leadership and local sources of power that could put pressure on urban political machines. Instead, the emphasis on community action in the War on Poverty represented an abdication of responsibility by those who truly held power over the ghetto. Clark argued that the "maximum feasible participation" mandate of the EOA "ask[ed] the victims of America's social and racial cruelty to assume the primary responsibility for overcoming the manifestations of this cruelty." In his analysis, "the victims of the ghetto are not in themselves able to overcome the burdens and problems of the ghetto." Clark's ambivalence about the possibilities of community action in the middle of the 1960s had transformed into outright rejection. He no longer believed that participatory politics within the boundaries of American liberalism could decolonize the internal colony.[27]

By the time Clark delivered his "Problems of the Ghetto" address, the ghetto-as-colony thesis had traveled far from the debates about antipoverty policy, community action, and indigenous leadership from which it had emerged. Influenced by an enduring line of Black internationalist thought about the nature and meaning of colonialism and its connections to American society, intellectuals and activists associated with the Black Power movement embraced elements of both Harold Cruse's recasting of American racial hierarchy as a form of domestic colonialism and Kenneth Clark's analysis of the ghetto-as-colony. A committed integrationist, Clark's distaste for Black nationalism made him a consistent opponent of the Black Power movement. But his claim that the relationship between the Black ghetto and the American metropolis was a fundamentally colonial one profoundly influenced many Black Power thinkers whose political positions he rejected. Through this argument, the politics of colonial comparison took center stage in the struggles of the Black Power era.

The Crisis of Vocabulary in the
Black Freedom Movement

In the period after the legislative victories of the Civil Rights Act of 1964 and the Voting Rights Act of 1965, the Black freedom movement faced a crisis of vocabulary. A wide range of Black activists and thinkers—some but not all of whom identified with the protean call for Black Power—argued that the Black freedom movement needed to develop a new conceptual register for a new phase of struggle.[1]

The idea that African Americans faced a regime of internal colonialism emerged as a central part of this new conceptual register. Thanks in part to the unexpected reach of Harold Cruse's writings and the social-scientific legitimacy bestowed by Kenneth Clark's vision of the ghetto-as-colony, the concept of internal colonialism proliferated across African American politics and intellectual life in the middle of the 1960s. The colonial analogy, in various formulations, played a prominent role in the debates about the strategic direction and ideological definition of the Black freedom movement. Leading activists in the Student Nonviolent Coordinating Committee (SNCC), such as James Forman and Stokely Carmichael, and the Southern Christian Leadership Conference (SCLC), such as Jack O'Dell, turned to the language of internal colonialism in their attempts to formulate a new ideological framework and strategic direction both for their own organizations and for the Black freedom struggle as a whole.

Often dismissed as an inappropriate analogy or an irrelevant rhetorical device, the invocation of the internal colony instead indexed important shifts in the Black freedom movement. First, a burgeoning, international discourse on the psychological consequences of colonialism deeply influenced the intellectual life of the Black Power movement. In particular, the emphasis in the writings of Martinique-born psychiatrist and anticolonial revolutionary

Frantz Fanon on the "inferiority complex" that colonial racism produced resonated with various segments of the Black Power movement. This vision of a shared "inferiority complex" affecting African Americans and colonial subjects around the world prompted some in the movement, such as Amiri Baraka, to identify the therapeutic potential of actions that would cultivate a sense of Black pride, from artistic production to violent rebellion.[2]

Second, the question of cultural degradation pointed to further similarities between the colonial project and the American racial order. Racist depictions of Black culture in the United States, in both popular culture and scholarly writing, comprised an important part of the broader vision of a global cultural hierarchy that had long justified European colonial rule. The rising fortunes of movements for decolonization in Asia and Africa after the Second World War provided additional ballast to longstanding challenges to these notions of European cultural superiority. A language of cultural decolonization thus pervaded African American thought and activism in the 1960s and 1970s. Writers, activists, educators, and artists invoked the language of decolonization to support a wide range of cultural nationalist activities and agendas, from greater levels of Black control over the industries of cultural production, to the adoption of African modes of personal appearance and dress, to curricular reform at all levels of education.[3]

Third, the colonial analogy deeply influenced understandings of violence in the Black Power movement. The recasting of the quotidian acts of state violence inflicted by police in African American communities as part of a global continuum of imperial warfare occupied a particularly central place in the political imaginary of the Black Panther Party. As historian Sean Malloy writes, the Panthers propagated an "anticolonial vernacular" for understanding the links between policing at home and warfare abroad through Black urban communities in the late 1960s and early 1970s.[4] Moreover, Black Power organizations that countenanced revolutionary violence, including segments of the Panthers, often justified this position by arguing that the movement for Black liberation in the United States must adopt the strategies of movements for liberation from colonial rule in Africa and Asia. Unsurprisingly, the use of the colonial analogy in justifications of violent resistance generated extensive critical commentary from state actors and a range of intellectuals at the time. Hannah Arendt, famously, condemned the embrace of the philosophy of Frantz Fanon by some African American activists because she believed it elevated and aestheticized violence. The connections between the language of internal colonialism and the question of violence in the Black Power movement often occupies the most prominent place in existing historical examinations of the concept, often to the exclusion of its other entailments and implications.[5]

In particular, it is underappreciated that thinkers and activists across the Black freedom movement who embraced the concept of the internal colony often did so to analyze the political economy of racial inequality in the United States. Developing theorizations of the persistence of economic dependency after political independence by both Frantz Fanon and Kwame Nkrumah found a ready audience among African American thinkers and activists, as these ideas resonated with the longstanding debate among African American internationalists over the political-economic organization of the postcolonial world. Black Power thinkers' analyses of metropolitan political economy in colonial terms further intersected with prominent currents in the social sciences, as ethnic pluralism and the place of African American communities in the political economy of the postwar metropolis became prominent subjects of social-scientific debate. The shifting meanings of internal colonialism in debates over metropolitan political economy revealed growing fissures among advocates of Black Power over the movement's relationship to mid-century racial liberalism and Fordist capitalism.[6]

The New Left, the Colonial Analogy, and the Revolutionary Subject

The proliferation of the colonial analogy among activists in the civil rights and Black Power movements in the middle of the 1960s owed its impetus to the shifting circumstances of that moment. But earlier evocations influenced the ways this language was adopted anew. The writings of Harold Cruse from the early 1960s particularly shaped the way that movement activists in the second half of the decade understood the concept of internal colonialism. Cruse's writings left a conceptual imprint, creating grooves in which later thinkers and activists would work.

As discussed in chapter 5, Harold Cruse's theorization of American racism as a form of domestic colonialism in his 1962 essay "Revolutionary Nationalism and the Afro-American" was a signal contribution to global debates about the scope of colonialism in the early 1960s. But the essay is more widely remembered as a key intervention in the reconsideration of the revolutionary subject by the New Left. As sociologist C. Wright Mills claimed in his "Letter to the New Left" of 1960, the belief that the industrial working classes of advanced capitalist societies represented the preeminent agent of social change represented a "labor metaphysic" that "is now quite unrealistic." In this account, the decline of industrial labor militancy since its height in the 1930s and 1940s, and the perceived integration of trade unions into the corporatist structure of the American state, demanded that social movements and social critics alike identify a new agent of wide-ranging social transformation. Mills, whom Cruse admired and whose work he cited regularly, articulated a widespread belief. The young people who flocked to Students for a Democratic Society (SDS) in the early 1960s—those to whom Mills addressed his letter—shared the conviction that a new social base, perhaps consisting of people like themselves, was necessary for the flowering of radical politics.[7]

Cruse's experiences in the Communist Party had already made him skeptical of the major organizations of the US left by the late 1950s. The success of the Cuban Revolution in 1958 and 1959 only intensified Cruse's belief in the inadequacy of the CPUSA's presumption that industrial workers in the Global North represented the vanguard of revolution. Many on the American left, Cruse wrote, "were unable to foresee" the revolt against the US-backed dictator Fulgencio Batista in Cuba, and "indeed opposed Castro until the last minute." And this failure "to work out a meaningful approach to revolutionary nationalism" in Cuba "has special significance for the American Negro"— precisely because African Americans were subject to a regime of "domestic colonialism."[8]

For Cruse, domestic colonialism entailed a condition of political and economic underdevelopment. "The Negro is the American problem of underdevelopment," he wrote, because "like the peoples of the underdeveloped countries, the Negro suffers in varying degree from hunger, illiteracy, disease . . . urban and semi-urban slums, cultural starvation, and the psychological reactions to being ruled over by others not of his kind." Cruse had little interest in the proposals of foundation officials and antipoverty policymakers who identified similar parallels, though. He instead saw in the conditions of domestic colonialism an opportunity to reinvigorate the organized left. The "realities of the 'underdeveloped' world" suggested that the "revolutionary initiative has passed to the colonial world, and in the United States is passing to the Negro." Like many figures in the developing New Left, Cruse identified a shift in the source of radical energy. Rather than in students or the youth, however, he located its new sources among colonized peoples at home and abroad.[9]

This shift demanded a new orientation toward Black nationalism, both from the white-dominated organizations of the US left and from Black intellectuals. The organized left, especially the Communist Party with which Cruse was once affiliated, had failed to engage effectively with Black nationalism since the age of Marcus Garvey's Universal Negro Improvement Association, which, in Cruse's account, was an example of "revolutionary nationalism being expressed in the very heart of Western capitalism." Garvey's adoption of elements of the economic philosophy of Booker T. Washington, which drew sharp criticism from thinkers on the left, simply "paralleled the bourgeois origins of the colonial revolutions then in their initial stages in Africa and Asia." Meanwhile, the Communist Party's simultaneous attempt to analogize the condition of African Americans to counterparts in the colonial world—the policy of self-determination in the Black Belt developed by Harry Haywood—struck Cruse as an ineffective imitation. This effort to promulgate a "national question without nationalism" failed to capture what made the UNIA the largest mass movement of African Americans in history.[10]

Cruse was loath in this essay to offer a full-throated defense of Black nationalism. But he argued that the left must accept its "validity," for it drew from the same well as did the anti-imperialist consciousness in Asia, Africa, and Latin America. Widespread Black nationalist opinion, whatever its faults or merits, was a social fact. If, as Cruse believed, "the Negro [was] the only potentially revolutionary force in the United States today," then the path forward for any revolutionary movement in the US went *through* Black nationalism—even if it aimed ultimately to transform its agenda.[11]

As Cruse relied on the concept of domestic colonialism to level an unequivocal criticism at the organizations of the US left, he advanced an ambiguous economic philosophy of his own. This ambiguity emerged in his discussion of the parallels between Black politics in the United States and anticolonial politics abroad. In contrast to his portrayal of the economic vision of Garveyism as a variety of anticolonial nationalism, he argued that "the would-be Negro bourgeoisie in the United States confronted unique difficulties quite unlike those experienced by the young bourgeoisie in colonial situations." Cruse observed that African Americans could not premise their economic advancement on a process of imperial withdrawal that would redirect rents, profits, and patronage into the hands of the colonized. Further, in an argument that drew explicitly on E. Franklin Frazier's *Black Bourgeoisie*, white control over the "Negro market" meant that the Black middle class "derive[d] its income from whatever 'integrated' occupational advantages it has achieved." This predicament not only drove a wedge between middle-class and working-class African Americans but turned those who "thriv[ed] off the crumbs of integration" into a "de-racialized" and "decultured" class, unable to fulfill the historic role of a national bourgeoisie in the colonial world.[12]

The inability of the Black middle class to play the role of a revolutionary colonial bourgeoisie had its counterpart in the unrealistic visions of economic autarky that Cruse saw in working-class Black nationalism. The "sense of a need for economic self-sufficiency" contributed to the growth of nationalist ideology among Black workers. Slogans such as "Buy Black" reflected an ambition for "economic control over the segregated Negro community." But this ambition failed to grapple with the structural impediments to economic advancement through consumerism and entrepreneurship within a segregated economy. Devising an exaggerated division between integrationism and nationalism as the ideological consequence of the divergent interests of the Black working and middle classes, Cruse refused to endorse either program. His analysis of "domestic colonialism" in "Revolutionary Nationalism and the Afro-American" thus bequeathed a new theory of the revolutionary subject without a clear program for the political economy of Black America.[13]

Cruse was not alone in turning to the language of colonialism and decolonization to identify a new revolutionary subject in the early 1960s. James Boggs and Grace Lee Boggs, two influential left activists based in Detroit, similarly embraced a colonial analogy out of a desire to capture the unique impact of capitalism on African Americans. James Boggs, a writer, activist, and autoworker at the Chrysler-Jefferson plant in Detroit, and Grace Lee Boggs, a Chinese American philosopher and activist, had organized with a range of small organizations on the non-Communist left in the 1940s and 1950s. Grace Lee Boggs was a cofounder, along with C. L. R. James and Raya Dunayevskaya, of the Johnson-Forest Tendency within the Trotskyite Socialist Workers' Party, which in 1950 broke from the party and renamed itself Correspondence. A few years later, this small organization fragmented as well.[14]

Conflicting interpretations of the importance of decolonization to global politics contributed to the split in the late 1950s between James and Grace Lee Boggs and other members of Correspondence, including C. L. R. James. In 1956, just after the Asian-African Conference at Bandung, and with the Hungarian uprising and Suez Crisis pointing to the instability of both the British empire and Soviet control in Eastern Europe, the Boggses contested C. L. R. James's push for the organization to identify Hungary as the most promising site of popular revolt. The belief in working-class self-activity as the heart of any revolutionary movement had been central to this group's political thought ever since the earliest days of the Johnson-Forest Tendency. To James, the Hungarian uprising offered a validation of his central critique of the Soviet Union, as well as a model which American workers might seize upon. James and Grace Lee Boggs countered by appealing to their own experiences in Detroit. The predominantly African American workers James Boggs toiled alongside, they argued, did not identify with the Hungarian Revolution to nearly the same degree as they did the anticolonial revolts. They further claimed that the nationalization of the Suez Canal demonstrated that

Third World nationalism had the potential to disrupt the economies of Europe and the United States in ways that the uprising in Hungary did not. While this debate caused tension within Correspondence, it pushed them to develop further their analysis of the relation between the political economy of decolonization and their daily lives among autoworkers in Detroit.[15]

Like Cruse, both James and Grace Lee Boggs doubted the prospects for social revolution in the industrial working classes of the developed world. In an article in 1963, after their break from C. L. R. James, Grace Lee Boggs insisted that the civil rights "revolution" was "a totally new and uniquely American revolution, a revolution without historical precedent anywhere in the world." Picking up this language, James Boggs, in his 1963 work *The American Revolution: Pages from a Negro Worker's Notebook*—which first appeared in a special double issue of the independent socialist magazine *Monthly Review* and was published as a paperback later that year—questioned the identification of Western industrial workers as a potentially revolutionary force. Indeed, he insisted that the fact that "the emerging nations of Asia and Africa, which have all these years been dominated by a little corner of the globe known as Western Civilization, are clashing with that civilization" called for a rethinking of the "basic philosophy" of radicals within the United States.[16]

It was not only decolonization abroad but automation at home that instigated the Boggses' reflections on revolutionary subjectivity. Beginning in the late 1940s, the Big Three automobile manufacturers in Detroit had introduced new automated processes in car production. The introduction of new technologies on assembly lines in engine production and stamping provided a means for employers to assert greater authority over production, weaken unions' control of the shop floor, and speed up the labor process, contributing to workers' exhaustion and a greater risk of injury. In conjunction with these technological changes, job losses in Detroit auto plants in the decade and a half after the Second World War had reconfigured the Boggses' social world—an early wave of the deindustrialization that would hit the city even harder in the decades to come. At the Ford River Rouge plant alone, employment fell from eighty-five thousand in 1945 to only thirty thousand in 1960. Detroit's Black communities felt the effects of automation and deindustrialization particularly acutely. Black unemployment outstripped white unemployment substantially, and those who remained in industrial employment were forced to work in the lowest-paying and most dangerous positions.[17]

For James and Grace Lee Boggs, these developments presented new challenges and opportunities for the industrial labor movement and for the broader US left. Grace Lee Boggs noted that the "remarkable historical coincidence of the Negro revolt and the technological revolution" could allow revolutionary struggles to aim beyond material questions of production and distribution to center instead around "the dignity of man." At the same time, the prospect of increasing automation and unemployment augured a widespread alienation of Black workers from the Fordist social compact of the midcentury United States. Such alienation, James Boggs wrote, held the potential to parallel the alienation colonial subjects felt from the regimes that ruled over them. The predominantly young, Black workers most vulnerable to automation might become "outsiders," whose relation to US society Boggs analogized to the relation of a colonized people to their imperial ruler: "Being workless, they are also stateless. They have grown up like a colonial people who no longer feel any allegiance to the old imperial power and are each day searching for new means to overthrow it."[18]

Like Harold Cruse, the Boggses saw the world-historical transformation of decolonization as an event to unseat the working classes of the industrialized West from their presumptive role as the revolutionary subjects of history. The thinkers' emphases were different, with Cruse offering an antidote to the historic obliviousness to Black nationalism on the US left and the Boggses presenting a clearer analysis of the political-economic circumstances of African American workers in 1960s industrial capitalism. But for all three figures, analogies with colonialism were the centerpiece of an emerging *social theory* of African American oppression in the early 1960s—just as many thinkers and activists began to search for new terminology.

Beyond Second-Class Citizenship

The turn to the colonial analogy as a conceptual framework for interpreting Black oppression by a small group of thinkers on the Black left preceded a crisis of vocabulary in the broad-based civil rights movement. The keywords of the long civil rights movement were not unchanging. As victories were won, and as new challenges emerged, activists, strategists, and commentators defined and redefined the objectives of the Black freedom movement and the obstacles it faced. Beginning in 1964 and 1965—at the end of what historian Peniel Joseph labels the "heroic period" of the movement, which culminated in the passage of the Civil Rights and Voting Rights Acts—efforts to reframe the twentieth-century Black freedom struggle and its significance intensified. These redefinitions emanated from what political theorist Brandon M. Terry describes as a "felt need for more adequate metaphors to characterize those *structural* and *cultural* dimensions of the racial order," dimensions that were not captured by the terms of "prejudice," "discrimination," or "second-class citizenship." This crisis of vocabulary motivated many writers and activists to turn to the language of colonialism and decolonization.[19]

The phrase "second-class citizenship" furnishes a useful example of the crisis of vocabulary in the Black freedom movement. Throughout the 1950s and early 1960s, it was common for participants and commentators alike to describe civil rights protests as part of a struggle against second-class citizenship. On this account, the regime of Jim Crow—characterized by its distinctive combination of disfranchisement; segregation in schools and public accommodations; discrimination in housing, education, and employment; exposure to state and state-sanctioned violence; and pressures to adhere to a rigid code of deference—constituted a moral and political wrong insofar as it kept Black Americans from full membership within the American polity. Even when linked to transformative demands, as it often was, the language of second-class citizenship enclosed the freedom struggle within the normative bounds of the US state.

Defining the civil rights movement as a struggle for first-class citizenship did not rule out an internationalist perspective. For example, at the founding conference of the SCLC in Atlanta in 1957, delegates affirmed that the "determined drive of Negro Americans to become first class citizens" was "inextricably bound together" with "Asia's successive revolts against European imperialism, Africa's present ferment for independence, [and] Hungary's death struggle against Communism."[20]

But the terminology more often accompanied efforts to define the movement in the terms of creedal nationalism. What political theorist Aziz Rana calls the "creedal narrative" of postwar racial liberalism, articulated most famously by Gunnar Myrdal, held that racial inequality marked the incompleteness of the American project, defined as a commitment to liberty and equality. For Roy Wilkins, executive secretary of the NAACP, appeals to the creedal narrative were at the heart of the NAACP's legal strategy that aimed to challenge segregation in education and public accommodations in the courts. Writing in 1957, the same year as the founding conference of the SCLC, Wilkins described the "colored people of the South" as "tired of second-class citizenship" and declared that the movement for civil rights, especially in its legal manifestations, aimed at a "fuller realization of the democratic ideal" in keeping with the Fourteenth Amendment's guarantee of "equal protection of the laws." In its description of the civil rights movement's aim as the fulfillment of existing American legal principle rather than the transformation of American public life, Wilkins's language of first- and second-class citizenship foreshortened the horizon of the Black freedom movement.[21]

The creedal associations of the language of second-class citizenship made this term a central target of Malcolm X's challenges to the strategic and ideological orientation of the civil rights movement, especially after his departure from the Nation of Islam in early 1964. In his April 1964 speech "The Ballot or the Bullet," Malcolm X singled out this concept specifically—and proposed a colonial framework as an alternative. "What do you call second-class citizenship?" he asked rhetorically in his address: "Why, that's colonization." Unlike the leaders of the SCLC seven years earlier, Malcolm X declared that any attempt to align the Black freedom movement with movements in Africa and Asia required an embrace of Black nationalism and an explicit recognition that "America is just as much a colonial power as England ever was." Here, Malcolm X rejected the idea that the most salient or destructive feature of American racial hierarchy was its refusal to grant Black Americans full membership within the existing polity.[22]

At the same time, Malcolm X carefully distinguished his critique of the language of second-class citizenship from a call to spurn the US political scene entirely. In fact, his embrace of the colonial analogy accompanied recommendations for electoral organizing and partisan innovation by Black Americans. Revising his conception of revolution from the vision of a land-based, violent revolt that pervaded some of his earlier speeches, most notably "A Message to the Grassroots," here Malcolm X argued that political engagement, both domestic and international, could serve as an instrument for Black liberation. Internationally, he called for the United Nations to take up the issue of the American civil rights struggle, while domestically he insisted that Black Americans could be the "key factor" in electoral contests across the United States were disfranchisement to end. Both of these claims were, in some ways, restatements of important arguments from the late 1940s, when the NAACP first engaged in a politics of petition at the UN and when NAACP leader Henry Lee Moon declared that Black voters held the "balance of power" in the election of Truman in 1948. But Malcolm X broke from these precursors in his insistence that existing political channels—first and foremost the Democratic Party—were insufficient vehicles for the achievement of Black liberation.[23]

The antidemocratic features of the US constitutional order undergirded Malcolm X's embrace of a colonial analogy, just as they had for W. E. B. Du Bois in his 1944 book *Color and Democracy*. Federalism and committee seniority rules in both houses of Congress, combined with Jim Crow disfranchisement laws at the state level, ensured that southern Democrats held disproportionate power in shaping federal legislation. "Of the sixteen senatorial committees that run the government, ten are in the hands of southern segregationists," and "of the twenty congressional committees that run the government, twelve of them are in the hands of southern segregationists," he noted, asking acerbically: "And they're going to tell you and me that the South lost the war?" If the Democrats were the party of the Dixiecrats, as Malcolm X believed, then Black voters were placed in an intolerable bind. Black political participation could supply the margin of victory for Democratic candidates, as it had for Harry Truman in 1948 and John F. Kennedy in 1960. Theoretically, then, Black voters held the fate of the Democratic Party in their hands. But the antidemocratic elements of the constitutional order meant that there was no way to translate that power into durable influence over civil rights policy.[24]

To Malcolm X, this contradiction demanded an innovative approach to political organizing. In sharp contrast to his earlier condemnations of the civil rights leadership, here he endorsed the voter registration organizing that civil rights groups had undertaken across the South. At the same time, he called for a Black political convention to determine the directions that Black politics should take, including the possible formation of a new "Black nationalist party." And he further insisted that the need for violent, militant action outside formal politics—the bullet—might become necessary at any moment.[25]

"The Ballot or the Bullet" did not contain a programmatic message. It was neither an invitation to violent revolution nor an appeal to use the existing channels of American politics. The speech instead represented Malcolm X's clearest call for a conceptual reorientation of the Black freedom movement. The strategic measures he called upon Black Americans to consider, from the formation of a Black nationalist party to renewed appeals to the UN, reflected Malcolm X's underlying belief in the inability of the political system of the United States to address Black political demands. The language of second-class citizenship, however, obfuscated the fundamental unresponsiveness of the constitutional order by suggesting that Black inequality was a question of incomplete membership. The language of colonialism, on the other hand, underscored the basic injustice of the constitutional order, while simultaneously promoting a sense of a shared condition with peoples across the Third World.

The conceptual crisis that Malcolm X identified in early 1964 was felt more widely across the Black freedom movement over the course of 1964 and 1965. The passage of the Civil Rights and Voting Rights Acts, combined with the spread of urban unrest and police violence in cities of the North and West—punctuated by the Watts uprising in August 1965—left both participants and observers wondering what new direction the movement would take. For Martin Luther King Jr., this was the moment when "one phase of development in the civil rights revolution came to an end" and "a new phase opened." In this moment of transition, more and more activists and writers adopted the concept of internal colonialism as a language of *movement politics*.[26]

Frantz Fanon and the Proliferation of the
Colonial Analogy

The publication of Frantz Fanon's writings in the United States spurred on the embrace of vocabularies of colonialism and decolonization in this moment of conceptual reorientation for the Black freedom movement. The first English translation of Fanon's *Les Damnés de la Terre* was published in France under the title *The Damned* by the French publisher Présence Africaine in 1963, two years after Fanon died of leukemia in a hospital in Maryland. Its more famous English-language title—*The Wretched of the Earth*—was adopted with the American publication by Grove Press in 1965. Between 1965 and 1968, Fanon's other three books—*A Dying Colonialism, Toward the African Revolution*, and *Black Skin, White Masks*—were published in the United States, all by Grove or Monthly Review Press. In short order, the writings of the Martinique-born psychiatrist, revolutionary, and theorist of decolonization became a touchstone in the search for new concepts in the American Black freedom movement.

For his part, Fanon wrote that his analyses of colonialism and decolonization, born out of his upbringing in Martinique and his experiences as a spokesperson and diplomat for the National Liberation Front (FLN) in the Algerian revolution, had little direct applicability to struggles against racism in the United States. In *The Wretched of the Earth*, he wrote, "the Negroes of Chicago only resemble the Nigerians or the Tanganyikans in so far as they were all defined in relation to the whites. But once the first comparisons had been made and subjective feelings were assuaged, the American Negroes realized that the objective problems were fundamentally heterogeneous." Taking as his reference point the campaigns for integration and legal equality in the South, he argued that the US movement for Black freedom had "very little in common with the heroic fight of the Angolan people against the detestable Portuguese colonialism."[27]

Many of Fanon's first American readers thought differently. Fanon's stirring depictions of the phenomenology of racism and the psychology of the oppressed, his work in support of the Algerian revolution, and, not least, his analysis of how the colonial system functioned all had a profound influence on African American thought and politics in the second half of the 1960s. His description of violence as a "cleansing force" that the colonized should embrace—both to overthrow their colonial rulers and to overcome the "inferiority complex" that warped their own psychologies—garnered a substantial share of attention in the US reception of Fanon, especially after the increased pace of uprisings in US cities after 1967.[28]

In part, this emphasis on violence derived from the English-language translation of *The Wretched of the Earth* by Constance Farrington. An Irish writer, librarian, and translator living in the *banlieues* of Paris, Farrington became aware of Fanon's writing through her involvement with a small, clandestine group that supported the efforts of the FLN. Although deeply sympathetic to Fanon's political project, Farrington often elided the author's philosophical groundings, especially his indebtedness to the writings of Négritude poet and philosopher Aimé Césaire and to the existential Marxism of Jean-Paul Sartre. In the process, she minimized Fanon's analysis of a dialectical relation between colonizer and colonized. She further misconstrued Fanon's nuanced understanding of the multiplicity of the forms of colonial violence, and the implications of this analysis for his description of anticolonial violence as a necessary component of the process of decolonization. As a result, Farrington's translation often left the reader with a simplified portrait of Fanon's thought as defined by a straightforward embrace of violence against an oppressive power as a cleansing, unifying force.[29]

Just as it would be misleading to suggest that a celebration of violence was at the center of Fanon's work, so too would it be misleading to see this theme as the most important feature of his US reception. The reception of Fanon among Black Americans is most often remembered through the quotation of Dan Watts, editor of *Liberator* magazine, that "every brother on a rooftop can quote Fanon." Delivered to a reporter in the aftermath of the Newark and Detroit uprisings of 1967, and frequently misattributed to Black Panther Party leader Eldridge Cleaver, the line signified the growing popularity of Fanon after the acceleration of urban uprisings and the rise of the Black Power movement. But even before 1967, Fanon's ideas about psychology, culture, and political economy contributed to the ongoing reconceptualization of the Black freedom movement among some of his first American readers.[30]

Grove Press played a key role in mediating the spread of Fanon's work in the United States. Run by the eccentric publisher Barney Rosset, Grove built its reputation on publishing avant-garde, modernist literature. Rosset took pride in Grove's publications of the latest European existentialist theatre and philosophy, as well as works frequently banned in the United States for their sexual content, such as novels by D. H. Lawrence and Henry Miller. Publishing *The Wretched of the Earth*—which came with the infamous preface of Sartre—inaugurated Rosset's list of Black radical texts. The press would later release editions of *The Autobiography of Malcolm X* and works by both Julius Lester and Amiri Baraka. When Grove first published Fanon's work in 1965, at an early stage in its turn to more overtly political releases, the press thus incorporated Fanon into an evolving canon of aesthetic radicalism, linking it to the existential rebellion of Albert Camus and Samuel Beckett more than to the anticolonial revolution of the FLN in Algeria. Only after the emergence of the Black Power movement on the national stage, and the spread of uprisings across American cities, did the press change its marketing strategy for the book, altering the subtitle from "A Negro Psychoanalyst's Study of the Problems of Racism and Colonialism in the World Today" in 1965 to "The Handbook for the Black Revolution That Is Changing the Shape of the World" in 1968.[31]

The publication of *The Wretched of the Earth* in English had an immediate impact in African American intellectual life, especially in the pages of *Negro Digest*. Under the editorship of Hoyt Fuller, *Negro Digest*—which was renamed *Black World* in 1970—became, as historian Jonathan Fenderson explains, the foremost journal of the Black Arts movement and a setting for Fuller's "efforts to amplify an emergent Black nationalist politics as a counter to civil rights liberalism." The journal published excerpts of *The Wretched of the Earth*, including Jean-Paul Sartre's infamous preface, in 1965, and tracked with interest the commercial success of the Grove Press edition, noting that it had "sold more than 17,000 copies in its first year of publication." By the fall of 1966, Fanon was a key reference point in a symposium the journal sponsored on "Negro Rights and the American Future," which included civil rights and Black Power activists such as Stokely Carmichael and Julian Bond as well as literary figures such as poets Lawrence Neal and Roland Snellings. "When our generation speaks," Snellings wrote, in a characteristic statement of the symposium's perspective, "it is the Tongue, the Voice of the 'Wretched of the Earth' within this land." The publication of *Wretched* in the United States in the very same year as the passage of the Voting Rights Act and the Watts rebellion contributed to a growing sense that a new phase of the Black freedom movement had opened, one that would be led by a new generation into new strategic and ideological directions.[32]

Small-circulation magazines of the predominantly white New Left and the emergent counterculture were also among the first publications to print excerpts of Fanon's writings. The San Francisco–based *Ramparts*, which originated as a liberal Catholic publication but would become an important magazine of the New Left in the Bay Area, was one such magazine, publishing two excerpts of *The Wretched of the Earth* in early 1966. The editor of *Ramparts*, Ralph Gleason, framed Fanon's writings as casting a spotlight on issues of race and empire that the white left too often ignored. Gleason further argued that Fanon's depictions of colonial violence and the Manichaean nature of colonial society had relevance in the United States precisely because Americans did not think of their country as a colonial power. But Gleason advertised Fanon's work to his predominantly white readership as above all a social psychology of Black revolt, capable of explaining the attitudes of figures such as Malcolm X and Amiri Baraka. In doing so, he missed the importance of Fanon's active presence in a revolutionary movement in shaping his thought. He further underestimated the degree to which Fanon's writing served as both an analysis of the colonial system against which he rebelled and as a vision and inspiration for social action.[33]

A more sustained and faithful engagement with Fanon's work came in the magazine *Streets*. A shoestring operation printed on the Lower East Side of Manhattan, *Streets* printed its own translation of Fanon's essay "Racism and Culture" nearly two years before this text was published in English as part of *Toward the African Revolution*. Edited by Maro Riofrancos, Paul Jaspers, and Stefan Uhse, *Streets* emerged out of a Marxist discussion group at City College, where Riofrancos had organized a sympathy strike during the mass boycott of New York City public schools by Black students and parents in 1964. Despite running for only two issues (and an additional issue under the name *Chalk Circle*), *Streets* was notable for its engagement with the literature and cultural criticism of the global left, as it published translations of Mexican, Cuban, and German writers, as well as work by both Sartre and Milan Kundera. Publishing Fanon's "Racism and Culture" was a natural extension of this engagement.[34]

In this essay, first delivered as a speech at the 1956 Congress of Black Writers and Artists in Paris, Fanon denied the individual and psychological explanations of racism that had gained currency across the Western world in the previous decade. Racism, Fanon insisted, existed as part of the "social constellation" and the "cultural whole." Its forms changed along with modes of economic exploitation and political domination: "The perfecting of the means of production inevitably brings about the camouflage of the techniques by which man is exploited, hence of the forms of racism." Fanon's address further included a sustained criticism of the cultural philosophy of Négritude that predominated the proceedings of the Congress. In contrast to the ideas of the luminaries of Négritude who had organized the gathering, including Aimé Césaire, Fanon declared that "rediscovering tradition" was a "defense mechanism," and that "falling back on archaic positions having no relation to technical development" was "paradoxical." In Fanon's mind, the rediscovery and celebration of "traditional" culture would not undermine colonialism. Instead, the destruction of the colonial system would generate a new cultural equilibrium: one in which the culture of "the Native" was not "hardened" but transformed, and in which it was finally possible to "recognize and accept the reciprocal relativism of different cultures." This dynamic view of cultural change, which envisioned an ultimate state of "universality" defined by the mutual recognition of cultures as possible only once the "colonial status is irreversibly excluded," resonated with the grand, if quixotic, ambition of providing a home for the global writing of the New Left that animated the fledgling *Streets*.[35]

During the brief run of *Streets*, its editor Maro Riofrancos also commissioned a review of *The Wretched of the Earth* from James Boggs. Though the magazine shut down before the review could be published, Boggs's unpublished review reveals how Fanon's writing helped provide answers to questions Black activists and writers were asking about the strategic direction and ideological development of the Black freedom movement in the middle of the 1960s. Fanon's view of decolonization as a revolutionary struggle inspired Boggs to criticize the integrationist thrust of the "leaders of the civil rights movement," who were, in Boggs's mind, "still begging for entrance into the system." Boggs identified *The Wretched of the Earth* as not merely a sociology explaining the causes of revolution, but as the "first scientific philosophy" of the revolt of the "colonized, semi-colonized, and enslaved peoples all over the world." To Boggs, one of the most appealing aspects of Fanon's writing was that it offered a version of *totality* that could be applied to the African American struggle.[36]

The question of violence was secondary in Fanon's thought, to Boggs. Instead, in Boggs's mind, Black Americans should learn from Fanon that the fight against racism and colonialism required a complete rejection of the ideologies and social arrangements of the dominant society—including, most notably, its economic orientation toward the pursuit of profit. Fanon's theorization of economic underdevelopment was thus a central feature of Boggs's unpublished review of *The Wretched of the Earth*. Boggs, unlike most reviewers in the United States, evinced a familiarity with the English-language edition first published in France, entitled *The Damned*. The title change, Boggs argued, reflected an unfortunate domestication of Fanon's political-economic ideas by his American publisher, Grove Press. Unlike the word "damned," which connoted an active process of being cast out and condemned by a superior power, the word "wretched" merely suggested a passive condition of abjection. This substitution allowed readers to "evade facing the historical fact that the underdevelopment of [Third World] countries is the result of the over-barbarism in the developed countries." Putting his own gloss on Fanon's famous assertion that "Europe is literally the creation of the Third World," Boggs emphasized that Fanon's work helped African American activists understand the causal relationship between economic development in the West and underdevelopment in Asia, Africa, and Latin America.[37]

This claim echoed a long tradition of African American internationalist thinking that defined the problem of the colonial project in terms of racialized economic exploitation. It also resonated with an emergent set of arguments by a group of academic social scientists, including most notably the German American sociologist Andre Gunder Frank and the Egyptian-French economist Samir Amin, who argued that the underdevelopment of the Third World derived from its integration in a global capitalist system, not from its supposed isolation. Fanon's insistence that, because of the legacy of underdevelopment, "colonialism and imperialism have not paid their score when they withdraw their flags and their police forces from our territories" would come to play a larger role in Black Americans' invocations of his work later in the decade. But Fanon's analysis of the political economy of colonialism resonated as early as 1965 for activists such as Boggs, who saw in Fanon's writing a useful set of concepts for understanding the uneven dynamics of capitalism—whether between nations or between white and Black communities in the United States.[38]

As Boggs turned to Fanon from the vantage point of the urban North, key figures in the southern freedom movement also came under Fanon's influence beginning in 1965. James Forman, executive secretary of SNCC from 1961 to 1966, was foremost among them. Reading Fanon so influenced Forman's perspective that the Martinican thinker would become a lifelong fascination. Over the course of the late 1960s and 1970s, Forman began work on a biography of Fanon, for which he traveled to Martinique and Algeria. He further sought to establish a Frantz Fanon Institute in the United States, which he hoped would serve as both a beacon for the promotion of Fanon's work and a think tank for Black radicalism within the United States. Forman's sense of a close connection with Fanon shaped his push for SNCC to adopt the language of internal colonialism in its public statements as it grappled with how to define the struggle for Black freedom after the passage of the Civil and Voting Rights Acts. Although SNCC had lost much of the vigor of its southern organizing efforts by 1966, it remained a key organization in national discussions of the direction of the Black freedom movement. SNCC's turn, under Forman's influence, toward envisioning its activism as part of a struggle for internal decolonization provided a key indication of the increased purchase of the colonial analogy in organizing and activist circles after 1965.[39]

Forman's connections to Pan-African intellectual currents and his early interest in international affairs had shaped SNCC's orientation toward global problems since the organization's founding in 1960. As a student at Roosevelt University in Chicago in the 1950s, Forman studied with St. Clair Drake, who inspired him to pursue graduate education in African Studies at Boston University. Forman complained that the Boston University program exhibited overt support for US Cold War policies, in keeping with the broader orientation of area studies programs nationwide. But his experience of studying African politics during the Little Rock school desegregation battle had a lasting influence on his political orientation. As Forman recounted in his autobiography, in the fall of 1957 and the spring of 1958, "Every time I read about some pass law or some restriction on the rights of Blacks in South Africa, the more I thought about home—the South." Forman took from his brief foray into Cold War African studies a sense of the parallels between the governing structures of South African apartheid, European colonial rule in Africa, and the Jim Crow system in the US South.[40]

In the early years of SNCC's existence, Forman led the group's organizing efforts abroad. He coordinated attempts to organize a protest by visiting African students of American racial discrimination at the United Nations in 1963. With John Lewis, he organized a trip to Guinea in 1964, where SNCC members were official guests of President Sékou Touré. Lewis and Donald Harris extended this trip to Liberia, Ghana, newly independent Zambia (formerly Northern Rhodesia), and finally to Egypt, returning with a proposal to set up an "African Bureau" within SNCC.[41]

The adoption of the language of decolonization as a central piece of SNCC's conceptual repertoire, however, began only after the organization's wrenching transformation over the course of 1966. SNCC's public denunciation of the Vietnam War in January 1966, after the murder of SNCC activist and veteran Sammy Younge, was quickly followed by the contentious election of Stokely Carmichael as chair later that spring and the group's new self-definition as a Black Power organization. These shifts followed a sharp reduction in the size of SNCC's volunteer corps after the passage of the Voting Rights Act. Amid a reckoning with its new status, SNCC's leaders renewed the group's efforts to make direct connections to movements on the African continent. At SNCC's May 1967 meeting, Forman was named director of international affairs, after which he traveled to Lusaka, Zambia, to represent SNCC at the UN-sponsored International Seminar on Apartheid, Racial Discrimination, and Colonialism in Southern Africa. Forman and Howard Moore Jr. delivered SNCC's "position paper" for the occasion, entitled "The

Indivisible Struggle Against Racism, Colonialism, and Apartheid," which they had prepared with the help of Forman's old mentor, St. Clair Drake.[42]

This trip, and Forman's new organizational role, bespoke SNCC's desire to emphasize its international connections. It also reflected the organization's changing understanding of its own work against racial oppression in the United States. After reiterating SNCC's stances against apartheid and the Vietnam War and highlighting its attempts to engage the Asian-African bloc at the United Nations, Forman and Moore punctuated their speech with an assertion of SNCC's organizational adoption of the colonial analogy: "We also come to assert that we consider ourselves and other Black people in the United States a colonized people; a colony within the United States in many ways similar to colonies outside the boundaries of the United States and other European nations." Forman and Moore did not explore how this similarity operated, but their assertion of a shared history of colonization reflected SNCC's shifting self-image after its endorsement of Black Power. Forman and Moore closed their "position paper" with a series of recommendations, most of which urged the "full and immediate implementation" of UN General Assembly resolutions related to South Africa, Israel/Palestine, and Vietnam. The position paper imagined SNCC as a component in a global coalition, but it left unanswered how this new identity might reinforce and revive SNCC's weakening organizing presence within the United States.[43]

Another veteran of the southern freedom movement who saw in the language of colonialism a promising new conceptual framework after the legislative battles of 1964 and 1965 was Jack O'Dell. A veteran of the labor movement and the Popular Front left, O'Dell began his involvement with the civil rights movement through the National Maritime Union (NMU) and the Communist Party in the 1930s and 1940s. O'Dell left the CPUSA in the late 1950s, as he grew more involved with voter registration organizing efforts for the Southern Christian Leadership Conference (SCLC), although he never repudiated his involvement with the party. A close associate of Martin Luther King Jr., O'Dell resigned from SCLC in 1962 after the FBI, which had surveilled O'Dell for decades, leaked information about his Communist past to the press in an effort to weaken SCLC.[44]

The attempt by the national security state to discredit O'Dell—which formed part of a systematic policy intended to weaken the influence of the organized left on the civil rights movement—pushed O'Dell out of a leading organizing role in the SCLC. But it did not push him out of the movement. After his resignation, O'Dell became associate managing editor of the journal *Freedomways*, where he would devote his energy toward what he later termed "the intellectual life of the movement." O'Dell's writings in *Freedom-ways*, where he authored unsigned editorials in addition to dozens of articles under his own name, comprised commentaries on day-to-day politics and movement strategy as well as theoretical and historical analyses of the broad contours of African American politics and history.[45]

O'Dell first analyzed American racism as analogous to colonialism in a 1964 essay entitled "Foundations of Racism in American Life." The essay consisted of a consideration of the outsized influence of the forms of white supremacy dominant in the South on national politics, from the American Revolution through the Goldwater campaign of 1964. It centered on an analysis of how the racial state known as Jim Crow was shaped in the late nineteenth century: a process that included the overthrow of Reconstruction, the intellectual ascent of the "Teutonic Origins theory" of American political development, and imperial conquests in the Pacific and Caribbean. To O'Dell, this new political-economic formation operated on a continuum with both European colonialism and fascism. His characterization of Jim Crow as "of a colonialist-fascist type" reflected the continuing influence of the Popular Front Black left on movement activists of the 1960s.[46]

Central to O'Dell's narrative of US history was the argument that the segregationist order benefited, rather than hindered, American economic development. The Jim Crow system "served a functional role in the economic development of this nation that was similar, in all respects, to the role of colonialism in the development of Western Europe." The combination of racial disfranchisement, segregation, and racial violence, along with their legitimating discourses in popular culture and intellectual life, contributed to the rapid growth of the American capitalist economy between the 1870s and 1920s by guaranteeing the continued existence of a territorially confined and politically subjugated agricultural labor force. For O'Dell, this structural feature of the Jim Crow order helped explain the conjunctural appeal of Barry Goldwater, who in his 1964 campaign combined a revanchist embrace of segregation with a staunchly probusiness, free market economic platform derived from business conservatives' decades-long assault on the New Deal.[47]

In this adoption of a colonial comparison with the Jim Crow South, O'Dell did not articulate its implications for Black politics. Shortly thereafter, though, he would turn to the language of colonialism in a reevaluation of the premises of the Black freedom movement, in a two-part essay in *Freedom-ways* published in late 1966 and early 1967. O'Dell rejected, on the one hand, the notion that colonialism could only be termed a mere analogy for forms of racial oppression in the United States, just as he rejected, on the other, that African Americans and colonial subjects could be united through the "bonds of color." Instead, he argued that the social structure of the United States represented a *variety* of colonialism, and that its historical development was one iteration of a global process of European expansion for which racism was the "chief ideology." In the first essay, he identified the use of racial slavery as a means for capital accumulation as a central mechanism of colonial rule, and he argued that the defeat of Reconstruction should be seen in its "world context" of European imperial impositions. Noting the concurrence between the withdrawal of federal troops from the US South in 1877 and the "scramble for Africa" of the 1870s and 1880s, O'Dell identified how the post-Reconstruction South and colonial Africa shared four structural conditions: a "monopoly on land ownership by the few"; regimes of forced labor; racialized restrictions on the franchise, such as the Poll Tax; and the establishment of systems of residential segregation. These historical developments suggested not simply a parallel between African and African American experiences, but a shared structure of domination.[48]

In his second essay for *Freedomways*, O'Dell elaborated an understanding of colonialism that rested not on control over territory or on alien political sovereignty but on the "institutional mechanisms of colonial domination." Anticipating criticisms of the internal colonialism analysis that assumed its economic implications pointed toward Black separatism, O'Dell acknowledged that "there is obviously no separate colonial economy under which Negro Americans live." Yet the relegation of most Black workers to the "agricultural and industrial labor force of the highly developed United States economy" and the persistence of employment discrimination even after the passage of the Civil Rights Act produced a "kind of 'under-development' similar in essence (though perhaps somewhat less severe in degree) to that suffered by other peoples in Asia, Africa, or Latin America." Further, in an overt attempt to link the southern freedom struggle in which SCLC had played such a prominent role with accelerating activism in the North, O'Dell emphasized that the mechanisms of colonial rule affected African Americans both northern and southern, both urban and rural. These mechanisms, he proclaimed, "serve to unite Harlem and Alabama; the colonized in the squalid ghettos and on the plantations across the country." Strategically, if Forman linked the language of internal colonialism to his efforts to build support for African Americans abroad, O'Dell argued that the adoption of this language enabled a greater recognition of the overarching unity of struggles for Black equality across the country and in diverse arenas of public life.[49]

Notwithstanding their different emphases and aims, James and Grace Lee Boggs, James Forman, and Jack O'Dell embraced the terminology of internal colonialism in response to the crisis of vocabulary in the Black freedom movement in the middle of the 1960s. The concept gained wider acceptance as an answer to a question that civil rights and Black Power activists had to face in those years: How should the durability of American racial hierarchy be explained following the legislative achievements of the Civil and Voting Rights Acts? Between 1965 and 1967, an important set of leading civil rights and Black Power activists came to believe that the vocabulary of internal colonialism provided such an explanation, and that the Black freedom movement should orient itself around a vision of internal decolonization. The flexibility of the concept's implications contributed to its growing popularity, to be sure. But those who adhered to an internal colonial analysis in this period shared a critique of the uneven, racialized development of American capitalism that reflected decades of Black internationalist thinking about the nature of colonialism on a global scale. In the years after 1967, a wider range of thinkers, activists, and even politicians would employ the idea that African Americans were subject to a regime of internal colonialism in new ways—some of which extended this critique, and some of which abandoned it altogether.

Pluralism and Colonialism in the Black Power Era

The attempt to resolve the crisis of vocabulary of the Black freedom movement involved figures and organizations who embraced the designation of Black Power and those who did not. But it was predominantly in the Black Power movement where thinkers and activists adopted and transformed the idea of the internal colony in the second half of the 1960s. Black Power thinkers and activists saw in this concept a compelling new way to understand and address the problems of racialized economic inequality within American cities.

The associations Black thinkers drew between colonial rule and urban politics in their engagements with antipoverty policy during the War on Poverty contributed to the proliferation of the colonial analogy in the middle of the 1960s. The mass popularity and critical acclaim of Kenneth Clark's *Dark Ghetto*, as discussed in chapter 7, placed an imprimatur of social-scientific respectability on the analogy between ghetto and colony. Clark had pointed to an interconnected set of factors that ensured predominantly Black urban neighborhoods remained impoverished while turning them into sources of profit for wider metropolitan areas—from the housing segregation produced by government and private lending and insurance agencies to the refusal of businesses to reinvest profits locally. While figures such as James Forman and Jack O'Dell queried whether the concept of internal colonialism could guide the strategy of the Black freedom movement on the national and global scales, other influential activists, especially Stokely Carmichael, turned to the analysis of the ghetto-as-colony to recast the political economy of the American metropolis in colonial terms.[1]

The publication in 1967 of Stokely Carmichael's and Charles V. Hamilton's book, *Black Power: The Politics of Liberation in America*, was a landmark event for the politics of colonial comparison in the Black freedom movement. This work sought to outline a social theory of American racial inequality and define a political program for the protean Black Power movement, in which Carmichael was a leading figure. Carmichael and Hamilton invoked the language of internal colonialism to criticize the paradigms of pluralist political science, while simultaneously arguing that the pluralist paradigm and the colonial analogy were compatible. This linkage proved a turning point in the career of the concept of the internal colony. A deep antinomy existed between the image of urban politics as a balancing act of the interests of ethnic groups holding relatively (or at least potentially) equal amounts of power and the understanding of systematic exploitation implied by previous uses of the colonial analogy. This tension pervaded *Black Power*, as Carmichael and Hamilton both suggested that African Americans might simply enter the pluralistic contest for power and indicated that broader changes to metropolitan political economy were required. The linkage of the colonial analogy with theories of ethnic group pluralism set the stage for the appropriation of the language by a wide range of figures, on all sides of the political spectrum, by the end of the decade—stretching the concept to what some of its early promoters considered a breaking point.

Pluralism, Urban Politics, and the Antinomies of *Black Power*

The vision of Black urban politics as analogous with colonialism developed in a relation of proximity and tension with the theory of political pluralism then dominant in American political science and influential in public discourse. In the early years of the Cold War, leading scholars across the social sciences had turned away from an understanding of democracy as a process of popular participation—including frequent mass mobilization through the labor movement and other civil society organizations—in a policymaking process imagined as an ongoing experiment. Prominent voices across the social sciences grew suspicious of popular politics, embracing an understanding of totalitarianism that linked fascism and Communism and portrayed both as outgrowths of mass politics unchecked by elite supervision.[2]

Within political science, the "Yale school" of political pluralism recast American democracy as a carefully balanced, ultimately effective system of elite negotiation. Aiming to counter the analysis of C. Wright Mills, who argued that an intersecting "power elite" of military leaders, politicians, businessmen, and even labor leaders set the political priorities of the United States, pluralists insisted that power was scattered widely across social groups. The leading member of the "Yale school," Robert Dahl, defined this system as "polyarchal democracy" in his book *A Preface to Democratic Theory* (1956), building on the definition of "polyarchy" he had coined with Charles Lindblom several years earlier. In Dahl and Lindblom's formulation, "polyarchy" was a way of solving "the antique and ever recurring problem of how citizens can keep their rulers from becoming tyrants," by forcing "leaders" to "win their control by competing for the support of non-leaders." Dahl presented "polyarchal democracy" as both empirically more accurate than descriptions of American government as a system of majority rule and normatively superior to visions of democracy that stressed popular participation and mass mobilization.[3]

It was not only this overarching vision of a decentralized power structure of competing interest groups that shaped the trajectory of the language of internal colonialism. More specifically, the application of this theory of politics to the world of racially and ethnically heterogeneous municipalities appealed to Black thinkers seeking to translate the colonial analogy into programs of action. Dahl's celebrated study of New Haven's political institutions, *Who Governs?: Democracy and Power in an American City* (1961), provided a crucial source for the attempt to apply the theory of pluralism to urban politics. In *Who Governs?*, Dahl elaborated his model of political conflict. Dahl asserted that the ethnic composition of the city's social groups shaped the alliances among the organizations and individuals that constituted the urban elite. Crucially, Dahl denied that ethnic politics operated as a "substitute" for class politics or as a class politics in disguise. Instead, he argued that "an awareness of ethnic identification," over and above class consciousness, "is created by the whole social system." Even after immigrants underwent what Dahl called the "third stage" of political assimilation, ethnic identifications would drive political loyalties, even though the issues around which ethnic blocs might mobilize, from urban redevelopment to support for the Cold War, might be different. Throughout his work, Dahl denied the existence of a structural division in American politics along racial or class lines. He insisted that the combination of a "widespread belief in the democratic creed" and a supposedly low correlation between wealth and direct influence on the political process transformed Americans of all classes into interest groups operating in the roughly level playing field of a pluralist democracy.[4]

The place of Black politics in this struggle for power among ethnic groups in the American city was seen as a particularly important problem by some American social scientists in the 1960s. Nathan Glazer and Daniel Patrick Moynihan addressed this question in their *Beyond the Melting Pot: The Negroes, Puerto Ricans, Jews, Italians, and Irish of New York City* (1963). Glazer and Moynihan, like Dahl, insisted on the persistence of ethnic identification across multiple generations, arguing against an assimilationist reading of immigrants' experience in America. Although they observed that "language and culture are very largely lost in the first and second generations," which made "the dream of 'cultural pluralism' . . . as unlikely as the hope of a 'melting pot,'" they insisted that the power of ethnicity did not disappear. Over the course of two generations, ethnicity was transformed from a source of shared cultural practices and dense social networks to a source of a thinner, but still potent, sense of group belonging. The continuing power of one's "group" meant that New York's municipal politics became a stage for conflict and alliance among these ethnic groups, each of which acted as a political bloc: "ethnic groups in New York are also *interest groups*."[5]

Glazer and Moynihan declared African Americans' position in this field of ethnic interest groups distinct and precarious. Drawing on arguments from Gunnar Myrdal and E. Franklin Frazier, Glazer and Moynihan argued that African Americans lacked both a cultural identity distinct from the national culture of the United States and the "same kind of clannishness" of other ethnic groups. This argument, in addition to reflecting the authors' ignorance of Black Americans' forms of sociality and cultural production, was one way for Glazer and Moynihan to overlook the distinctive harms of slavery, Jim Crow, and anti-Black racism. Portraying African Americans as merely one among many "ethnic groups" in the postwar American city, Glazer and Moynihan deflected responsibility for racial inequality from white racism, segregation, and discrimination to the purported internal flaws of Black culture. Such deflections would, of course, become foundational to the political thought of the emergent neoconservative movement, in which Glazer and Moynihan would play major roles. Distinctive in their formulation at this stage, however, was their emphasis on the development of a Black leadership class as a potential solution. The lack of cultural cohesion among African Americans, Glazer and Moynihan argued, diminished their opportunities to develop a robust market for goods produced and sold within their community. The challenge for Black politics, in Glazer and Moynihan's mind, was to direct the "income and resources of leadership of the group . . . inwards." The path to Black advancement, then, ran through the empowerment of an elite leadership class.[6]

Stokely Carmichael and Charles V. Hamilton brought the language of internal colonialism into extended conversation with these strands of pluralist political science in their 1967 book *Black Power: The Politics of Liberation*. Hamilton was most responsible for establishing this association. Beginning in the 1950s, Hamilton had worked with the Tuskegee Civic Association in Macon County, Alabama, which brought him into contact with SNCC volunteers in the very earliest days of the organization's existence. Simultaneously,

he gained exposure to the latest writings in modernization theory and pluralist political science while studying at the University of Chicago, from which
he received his PhD in 1964. Starting in the fall of 1966, at the urging of Random House publishers, Hamilton and Carmichael began collaborating on a
book that aimed to illuminate the political and intellectual underpinnings of
the rising Black Power movement.[7]

The composition of *Black Power* coincided with Stokely Carmichael's rise
to a new status on the national and international political stages. Carmichael's
election as chair of SNCC and his defiant proclamation of the necessity of
"Black Power" during the "March against Fear" in June 1966 had, according
to his biographer Peniel Joseph, "elevated him alongside Martin Luther King
as one of the most influential and reviled figures in American politics." With
SNCC's organizational capacity in the US South waning, Carmichael em-
barked on a series of overseas journeys, traveling to the US territory of Puerto
Rico, European capitals, and the revolutionary hubs of Cuba, Vietnam, Algeria, Guinea, Egypt, and Tanzania between the fall of 1966 and the fall of 1967.
Under constant surveillance by the FBI and foreign intelligence services,
Carmichael attempted to establish concrete connections with postcolonial
regimes while affirming the view of US Black politics as defined by a colonial
relationship to white society. Between trips, Carmichael joined Hamilton to
write chapters of their book, which was released in November 1967.[8]

An antinomy between the implications of the colonial analogy and the
principles of pluralist political science pervaded Carmichael and Hamilton's
analysis in *Black Power*. The two authors constructed their analysis around
Kenneth Clark's evocative portrayal of ghettos as "social, political, educational, and—above all—economic colonies": a line that served as the book's
epigraph. The language of internal colonialism undergirded perhaps the
most influential conceptual innovation of *Black Power*—the distinction between individual and institutional racism, the latter of which Carmichael and
Hamilton equated with colonialism. "Institutional racism," they proclaimed,
which was "less overt, far more subtle, [but] no less destructive of human
life" than the individual variety, had "another name: colonialism." Following
Clark, they argued that predatory lending, price-gouging in retail establishment, and high rents maintained by outside landowners rendered the Black
ghetto a source of profit for the rest of American society. In American ghettos, capital and labor, rather than the natural resources that constituted the
economic prize in classical models of colonialism, were extracted from a spatially segregated, racialized population.[9]

The relationship of extraction between ghetto and metropole that formed
the basis for Carmichael's and Hamilton's colonial analogy contradicted two

central tenets of pluralist political science. First, it gave the lie to the idea that the "American Creed," as Gunnar Myrdal defined it, characterized political attitudes across a meaningful swathe of American society. Second, it countered pluralists' argument that belief in the "American Creed" reduced the level of antagonism in political conflicts. To Carmichael and Hamilton, "there is no 'American dilemma' because Black people in this country form a colony, and it is not in the interest of the colonial power to liberate them." Here, Carmichael and Hamilton counterposed a view of internal colonialism as a system of exploitation to pluralism's creedal and consensual picture.[10]

Carmichael and Hamilton further relied on the colonial analogy to argue that the pluralist theory of American politics failed to capture the relatively unified position of white Americans regarding Black economic advancement. The ruling elite did not fragment, as Dahl and others had argued, into a set of ethnic blocs and interest groups in competition with each other. Rather, the "white power structure" held an overarching, shared interest in the maintenance of Black economic subordination, forming a class as monolithic "as the European colonial offices have been to African and Asian colonies." The language of internal colonialism thus purported to offer a fundamentally different understanding of the struggle for power than the language of pluralism. The American metropolis was not a place where competition over resources among relatively equal groups enabled a tenable balance of power. Rather, it was a place where a territorially confined class of Black workers and the unemployed sought to escape the predations of a monolithic elite.[11]

Although Carmichael and Hamilton criticized the sanguine portrayal of American urban politics provided by pluralist social science, *Black Power* also reinforced several of pluralism's central tenets. Carmichael's and Hamilton's assertion that "the American pot has not melted" echoed the understanding of incomplete assimilation that Glazer, Moynihan, and Dahl embraced. Any political program organized under the sign of Black Power "must recognize" the "ethnic basis of American politics." This ethnic foundation required Black Americans to embrace thick forms of racial identification and solidarity. Only through racial unity, on this account, could Black people advance their interests. In one particularly controversial passage, Carmichael and Hamilton wrote, "the concept of Black Power rests on a fundamental premise: *Before a group can enter the open society, it must first close ranks. By this we mean that group solidarity is necessary before a group can operate effectively from a bargaining position of strength in a pluralistic society."* Recalling Du Bois's infamous declaration that African Americans should "close ranks" in support of Woodrow Wilson during the First World War, Carmichael and Hamilton appeared to countenance a papering over of potential divisions of class, gender, religion, and ideology in order to improve the "bargaining position" of the Black community writ large. Carmichael and Hamilton here portrayed the "internal colony" as an ethnic enclave in waiting, suggesting that a program of decolonization for Black America would mean the greater incorporation of African Americans into the existing landscape of municipal power politics.[12]

Black Power appeared alternately to demand a radical revisioning of the American political economy and to promote a conventional model of interest-group competition. This central tension revolved around the meaning of the colonial analogy. Carmichael and Hamilton's text, moreover, would mark a turning point in the career of the concept of internal colonialism. The antinomy between an understanding of the internal colony as a site of extractive capitalism and a view of the internal colony as one ethnic group among many would define debates about Black urban politics over the next several years.

The changing ideas of Harold Cruse further contributed to this tension. Cruse's writings in the early 1960s had spurred other Black thinkers to embrace the language of internal colonialism as an alternative to dominant formulations of African American inequality, such as "second-class citizenship," that aligned with the creedal narrative of American history on which pluralist political science depended. In the 1962 essay "Revolutionary Nationalism and the Afro-American," Cruse had made this point explicitly: "The Negro is not really an integral part of the American nation beyond the convenient formal recognition that he lives within the borders of the United States." By 1967, however, Cruse advocated a form of pluralistic politics that took the US nation-state as the inevitable container of Black politics and saw ethnic-group advancement as its ultimate destination.[13]

Cruse's *The Crisis of the Negro Intellectual: A Historical Analysis of the Failure of Black Leadership*, published in the same year as Carmichael and Hamilton's *Black Power*, quickly emerged as a touchstone for many Black nationalists for its critique of what Cruse termed the "integrationism" of most civil rights leaders and Black intellectuals. The work also became infamous, for three main reasons: first, for Cruse's acerbic critiques of nearly every prominent Black literary writer associated with the organized Left, from Lorraine Hansberry to Julian Mayfield; second, for his disparaging statements about Caribbean migrants to the United States; and third, for his anti-Semitic argument that the predominance of American Jews in the Communist Party of the United States had turned the party's politics into a vehicle for Jewish cultural nationalism.

The numerous controversies surrounding *The Crisis of the Negro Intellectual*, both at the time of its publication and since, have obscured its ambiguous relationship to the internationalist language of Cruse's earlier writings. A few years after he outlined a theory of American racism as a form of "domestic colonialism," Cruse criticized his own successors who sought to apply the language of decolonization to the African American freedom struggle. Cruse's understandings of economic and cultural exploitation, his portrayal of the relationship between Black intellectuals and their counterparts in the decolonizing world, and his calls to reframe the Black freedom struggle as a contest within a pluralistic order of American ethnic groups all reflected his changing ideas about the meanings of colonialism and decolonization.[14]

Although Cruse focused most of his attention in *The Crisis of the Negro Intellectual* on literary and political culture, his analysis of urban economics reflected ideas about exploitation shared by other exponents of the internal colony thesis. Harlem, in Cruse's mind, not only stood on the verge of becoming "deracinated culturally" as a result of integration, but also remained "an impoverished and superexploited economic dependency," whose residents served as no more than "captive consumers and cheap labor reserves, maintained for the extraction of profits." This economic condition placed Harlem in a global context of colonial labor exploitation that had spurred the previous decades' anticolonial revolts: "The ghettoes of color, which exist all over the United States and the non-Western world, have today become the endemic wellsprings of revolutionary ideologies that will change the social relationships of races for decades to come." While Cruse used this comparison to denounce those who thought integration could make the "Harlems of the world" disappear, he also refuted those who sought to apply the "revolutionary ideologies" of anticolonial struggle in the United States.[15]

Cruse's changing understanding of the relationship between African American and anticolonial struggles provided one reason for this denial. In his writings of the early 1960s, Cruse saw the African American struggle as lagging behind its counterparts in the colonial world, and he urged his fellow intellectuals to understand the politics of decolonization to better develop a theory and strategy of social action for African Americans. By 1967, he argued that this attempt to connect with the decolonizing world had failed.

Cruse advanced this argument by distancing himself from the younger writers and activists whom he had accompanied to Cuba in 1960. The "generation" of new nationalists that became "deeply impressed by the emergence of the African states, the Cuban Revolution, Malcolm X, and Robert Williams" had not, in Cruse's mind, heeded his call for a homegrown strategy of struggle but had instead been seduced by two romanticized visions of the foreign. (Black cultural nationalists at the time who celebrated Cruse's critique of "integrationism" rarely acknowledged this side of his work.) Cruse declared that both the thrust of Robert Williams's embrace of armed self-defense and the "naïve idealization of everything African" by what he termed "Harlem nationalists" reflected failures to parse the differences between "domestic colonialism" and colonialism proper. Despite the fact that "the social forces that have created both the Afro-American and the modern African are so similar," their two "revolutions" were "so related, and yet so uniquely different" that neither could fully understand the other. "The problem of Afro-American nationalism," Cruse proclaimed, was not a variety of the revolutionary nationalisms that had emerged across the colonial world; instead, it was "as American as are its historical roots." Cruse now believed the colonial analogy, which he had done so much to popularize, did not show the way out of the ideological confusion of the post-1965 era. Instead, the language of decolonization simply added to it.[16]

Cruse's newfound view that racial domination in the United States and colonialism abroad were irreconcilably distinct related to his growing conception of US politics as a pluralistic struggle for power among a variety of ethnic groups. By 1967, Cruse viewed American racial inequality as a "group power problem, an interethnic group power play," rather than an outgrowth of a global history of exploitation and uneven development.[17]

Even as he abandoned the language of domestic colonialism of his essays of the early 1960s, Cruse expanded on his political-economic vision, which centered on Black Americans' taking control over the industries of cultural production. In the early 1960s, Cruse had articulated this vision in an idiom of revolution and class struggle, arguing that, because "the weakest sector of American capitalist 'free enterprise'" was the "ownership and administration of the cultural communications," the only way for the "Negro rebellion to become revolutionary" was to "project the Concept of Cultural Revolution in America." But, by 1967, Cruse's agenda for Black cultural politics appeared to fit neatly with the precepts of ethnic pluralism. "The path to the ethnic democratization of American society is through its culture, that is to say its cultural apparatus," Cruse argued in *Crisis*, "which comprises the eyes, the ears, and the 'mind' of capitalism and its twentieth-century voice to the world." Greater autonomy over cultural production would give African Americans the resources and respect they needed to achieve a level of power on par with other ethnic groups within the United States. Winning power over the culture industry would prove especially beneficial because it would help to expunge the damaging and derogatory images and stereotypes of Black people that pervaded every aspect of American mass culture. In Cruse's argument, though, this cultural front was no longer envisioned as a wedge to overturn the political-economic order. Instead, he argued, "to democratize the cultural

apparatus" would "revolutioniz[e] American society itself into the living realization of its professed ideals." Abandoning his view that African Americans
should measure their struggle against the anticolonial revolutionaries of the
Third World, Cruse now looked forward to the achievement of the American
Creed.[18]

Over the course of 1967, the writings of Harold Cruse and Stokely Carmichael and Charles V. Hamilton brought the language of internal colonialism
into conversation with major currents of pluralist political thought. Cruse,
arguably the thinker most responsible for adoption of the colonial analogy in African American thought and activism, abandoned the language of
colonialism for a vision of Black political struggle as an effort to rebalance
power relations across America's ethnic groups, albeit one focused on achieving material control over cultural production. Carmichael and Hamilton,
meanwhile, left the antinomy unresolved: their vision of the internal colony
appeared simultaneously as a territory of exploitation set apart from the ordinary rules of pluralist competition, and as an ethnic enclave like any other.
This tension coursed through the career of the concept of the internal colony
at the end of the 1960s and into the 1970s, as it gained new prominence in the
national political vocabulary.

The Colonial Analogy in National Politics

During the summers of 1967 and 1968, as urban uprisings reached a new
level of intensity, national political debate began to orbit around the political economy of racism in the American metropolis. The wave of urban disturbances that spanned 1963 to 1971 constituted, in the words of sociologist
Peter B. Levy, a "Great Uprising." Far from merely expressive outbursts of
discontent, urban revolts reflected the simultaneous influences of the civil
rights and Black Power movements and of declining industrial employment
in cities that had been major destinations during the Great Migration, most
often sparked by unchecked police violence against Black people.[19]

President Lyndon Johnson convened the National Commission on Civil
Disorders, also known as the Kerner Commission, in 1967, after disturbances
in over two hundred US cities, including the major metropolises of Newark
and Detroit. Assessing the causes of these disorders, the commission painted
a picture of the political economy of the American metropolis not dissimilar to the one described by Kenneth Clark in *Dark Ghetto*. "White society,"
the Kerner Commission report argued, "is deeply implicated in the ghetto.
White institutions created it, white institutions maintain it, and white society
condones it." With the urban crisis occupying such a prominent place in the

national imagination, the language of internal colonialism briefly and unexpectedly moved to the center of US political discourse.[20]

The spread of the colonial analogy and its linkage with pluralist political thought made this language available across a wider political spectrum. The tensions between the two visions of the internal colony—as a pluralist enclave or a territory of exploitation—only grew in importance. Conservative reaction to the growing embrace of the concept of the internal colony was divided between fear of its implications and attempts to appropriate the concept for the promotion of entrepreneurial solutions to the urban crisis. At the highest levels of national politics, some Republican supporters of a politics of Black capitalism adopted internal colonialism as part of their political vocabulary. Some liberal Democratic politicians, meanwhile, began to embrace the image of Black ghettos as subject to forms of colonial exploitation, incorporating a language initially developed to excoriate the limitations of the Great Society in their continued advocacy for developmentalist solutions to urban poverty. The adoption of the colonial analogy by national politicians, from Walter Mondale to Richard Nixon, illustrated the "semantic drift" of the concept since its origins among writers and activists on the Black left in the early 1960s.[21]

With the rise of Black Power and the spread of urban uprisings, the shifting language of the Black freedom movement did not go unnoticed on the right. Some conservative thinkers reacted to the proliferation of metaphors of colonialism with dismay. Defense intellectuals Albert and Roberta Wohlstetter authored the most substantial conservative commentary on the adoption of the colonial analogy. Staff members of the RAND Corporation from the early 1950s until the mid-1960s, the Wohlstetters worked at the intellectual epicenter of Cold War national security policy. Roberta's historical study of the intelligence failures that left the US military unprepared for Japan's attack on Pearl Harbor, entitled *Pearl Harbor: Warning and Decision*, exhibited a dramatic concern about US readiness for a possible Soviet nuclear attack. Albert, trained as a mathematician, emphasized in his writings on nuclear strategy the looming threat of Soviet nuclear aggression and consistently urged US policymakers to adopt a more offensive nuclear posture.[22]

The Wohlstetters' turn, in the summer of 1968, to an examination of anticolonial language in the Black Power movement reflected a widespread view in the national security establishment of both urban rebellions and more sustained forms of Black Power activism as components of a transnational continuum of insurgency that threatened the security of the United States.[23] The Wohlstetters worried that the influences of Malcolm X, Che Guevara, and Frantz Fanon on the spokespeople of the Black Power movement would lead to an embrace of revolutionary violence—often rendered as "guerrilla war"— and that urban uprisings augured the beginning of a trend in this direction. Labeling the uprisings "expressive," they saw in Black activists' identification with the revolutions in Cuba and Algeria an existential, "nihilist" posture rather than a meaningful political stance.[24]

A concern about insurgent violence comprised only one part of the Wohlstetters' critique of the colonial analogy. The economic implications of the language of internal colonialism equally troubled them. Taking note of the lure of postcolonial developmentalism for many Black thinkers, they argued that, despite the "rich source of varied metaphor" that the history of colonialism provided, the language of internal colonialism only "evoke[d] a cloud of ideologies of economic development." Ignoring proposals for fair housing, welfare rights, full employment, and anti–employment discrimination legislation that littered the platforms of Black Power groups, the Wohlstetters reduced the economic message of Black Power to simplified demands for what they called economic "autarkies," consisting of Black ownership of businesses and Black political power in predominantly Black communities.[25]

Yet the Wohlstetters did not deny wholesale the potential relevance of international economics to the political economy of race in America. Rather, they argued, following libertarian economist Gary Becker's influential 1957 study *The Economics of Discrimination*, that "the theory of international trade," rather than "the rhetoric of imperialism," could apply to domestic circumstances of racialized economic inequality. The solution to discrimination in the labor market, in Becker's model, lay simply in reducing the barriers to free market competition, as unfettered markets would cause firms with a higher "taste for discrimination" to fail. Arguing that the economic relations between white and Black Americans were roughly analogous to the relations between a nation that is a source of capital and one that is a source of labor, Becker suggested that the low-wage work to which many African Americans were confined actually served as the source of their comparative advantage. Adopting Becker's analysis, the Wohlstetters countered theories of internal colonialism that envisioned an extractive relationship between the dominant institutions of American society and the Black ghetto.[26]

Outright rejection, however, was not the only reaction of American conservatives to the spread of the colonial analogy. Appropriation was another. In the same month that the Wohlstetters wrote their RAND Corporation analysis, Richard Nixon invoked the idea of the internal colony in his speech accepting the Republican Party's nomination for president in the 1968 election. Like many of Nixon's campaign speeches, his acceptance address reflected the influence of both Raymond Price, his chief speechwriter and a moderate Republican who had supported Lyndon Johnson in 1964, and the conservative firebrand Pat Buchanan. Nixon's speech, which centered on the themes of crime control and policing that dominated much of his campaign, also advanced his argument that antipoverty programs inaugurated under the Johnson administration fostered dependency among African Americans. Nixon argued that Black people would benefit from a retreat from the War on Poverty and the empowerment of an entrepreneurial business class in Black communities.[27]

Nixon grounded this argument in an appeal to the image of the United States as the first new nation, recasting the nation's revolutionary beginnings as the origin point of a continuous tradition of entrepreneurial economic development. "The war on poverty didn't begin five years ago in this country," but rather "when this country began." Contemporary African Americans, especially those in impoverished urban areas, should "turn to the American Revolution for the answer." "They don't want to be a colony in a nation," Nixon announced. "They want the pride, and the self-respect, and the dignity that can only come if they have an equal chance to own their own homes, to own their own businesses, to be managers and executives as well as workers, to have a piece of the action in the exciting ventures of private enterprise." Decolonization as entrepreneurship: Nixon's acceptance speech starkly illustrated the semantic drift of the language of internal colonialism since the early 1960s.[28]

Nixon's entrepreneurial vision was part of a long history of conservative promotions of ideologies of Black self-help that disclaimed the responsibility of the broader polity to combat structural inequality.[29] It also signaled a newfound support for "Black capitalism" as an explicit aim of the American right. The support in Nixon's campaign for the business-led community development efforts of the Congress of Racial Equality (CORE) illustrate the budding, if temporary, alliances between certain elements in Black politics, including Black nationalist politics, and the resurgent Republican Party.[30] Floyd McKissick, who authored CORE's shift to an identification as a Black Power organization in 1966, and his successor as CORE chairman, Roy Innis, forged these alliances through their advocacy for the Community Self-Determination Act of 1968. This act proposed the formation of locally administered, for-profit Community Development Corporations (CDCs) and community development banks, the profits of which would be used to bolster social services within areas of concentrated poverty.[31] Innis and McKissick presented the plan to both the Robert F. Kennedy and Nixon campaigns in 1968. After

Kennedy's assassination, the CORE leaders were drawn closer into Nixon's orbit. Facing opposition from liberals and the left, Innis and McKissick, too, defended both their substantive vision and their strategic decision to partner with Nixon and the Republican Party by referring to the concept of internal colonialism. Their proposal, Innis argued, represented the first step toward a "new social contract" that would elevate Black communities above the status of "sub-colonial appendages," allowing them to enter into the interest-group competition of metropolitan politics.[32] The linkage of the colonial analogy with the politics of ethnic group advancement had paved the way for its conservative appropriation.

Some Democratic politicians, too, turned to the concept of internal colonialism, integrating elements of its critique of racialized exploitation into their existing understanding of Black ghettos as zones of underdevelopment. In a hearing on "Financial Institutions and the Urban Crisis" in September 1968, Minnesota Senator Walter Mondale cited a "growing awareness . . . that the problems of the inner city are similar to the problems of underdeveloped countries." But, as historian Keeanga-Yamahtta Taylor has shown, Mondale went further than the liberal consensus in stating that "urban ghettos may also share another characteristic with some undeveloped countries—and that is the problem of colonial exploitation." In addition to "fast-buck operators" and "unscrupulous lenders," residents of poor Black communities were subject to other, "more subtle forms of colonialism, such as absentee merchants who collect high prices on sales in the ghetto, but invest the profits outside the ghetto." Financial institutions were implicated, too, as "many savings institutions located in or near ghetto areas might be tapping the savings of the ghetto and reinvesting them in mortgages in white suburbia." The overall outcome of residential segregation, and the captive rental and consumer markets it created, was a "substantial capital outflow." Mondale's description of the exploitation of the ghetto resembled the most stirring passages of the writings of Black radicals who employed the colonial metaphor in service of a critique of extractive capitalism. He offered more conventional prescriptions, however. Citing Michael Harrington, Mondale reiterated the widespread view among liberal policymakers that, like underdeveloped countries, Black ghettos needed a combination of technical assistance, the cultivation of local leadership, and capital investment, which the federal government could encourage through modest incentives to lending institutions.[33]

Allusions to internal colonialism by both conservative and liberal figures at the highest levels of US politics represented a significant departure in the career of the concept. On the one hand, these arrogations reflected transparent attempts to domesticate the language of the Black Power movement—to deny that it might represent a fundamental challenge to creedal narratives of American national identity or colorblind understandings of democracy. On the other hand, these references called attention to the proximate, if often conflictual, relationship between Black internationalist politics and more conventional registers in the American political vocabulary that existed throughout the midcentury decades.

The Challenge of Decolonization in America

The promotion of Black capitalism by the Nixon administration prompted a shift in the way many Black activists and intellectuals formulated their agendas for economic self-determination. The fragmentation of the Black freedom movement in the final years of the 1960s, combined with the semantic drift of the language of the internal colony, invited several reconsiderations of this vocabulary.

For some, such as the writer and activist Robert L. Allen, the rise to power of Black political leaders in cities such as Newark, Cleveland, and Detroit amid the failure of the civil rights and Black Power movements to achieve broad-based economic redistribution offered evidence of the continuing relevance of the decolonizing world to issues of American political economy. Some on the Black left, especially those involved in the 1969 National Black Economic Development Conference, tried to rescue the colonial analogy from its pluralist associations and to design concrete programs for Black economic development as a means to achieve internal decolonization.

At the same time, efforts to forge coalitions with American Indian, Puerto Rican, and Chicano activists also relied on the analysis of the United States as a multifaceted colonial power, although these efforts at times revealed the limitations of the concept of internal colonialism for making sense of settler and territorial forms of colonization. Moreover, from the late 1960s through the 1970s, activism and intellectual production by Indigenous peoples, Chicanos, and Puerto Ricans—some of which engaged directly with African American discourses of internal colonization—increasingly presented an image of the United States as a colonial power exercising illegitimate and exploitative authority over racialized peoples residing within its borders.[1]

Yet the proliferation of the language of internal colonialism across the political spectrum also raised new problems for Black radicals who had been among the first to promulgate this analysis. For some observers, shifting configurations of global power diminished the relevance of colonialism and even neocolonialism as the paradigmatic forms of international domination. For others, the association of the idea of the internal colony with a pluralistic politics of ethnic group advancement, and its appropriation by conservative forces, provided reason enough for the idea of internal colonialism to be abandoned altogether.

The most sustained attempt to return the colonial analogy to its associations with the global dynamics of racialized economic exploitation emerged from a young journalist and sociologist named Robert L. Allen. A student activist involved in civil rights protests while at Morehouse College in the early 1960s, Allen moved to New York in 1963, where he became an early participant in the antiwar movement while studying for a master's degree in sociology at Columbia University. Writing for the leftist newspaper the *National Guardian*, Allen reported on the antiwar and Black Power movements. He traveled to North Vietnam in October 1967 to write about the progress of the war with a small group of peace activists and journalists. Allen's reporting on the Newark Black Power Conference in the summer of 1967 provided the impetus for his 1969 book *Black Awakening in Capitalist America*, an extended, critical appraisal of what he saw as conservative tendencies in the Black Power movement. Allen turned to the language of "domestic neocolonialism" to emphasize the failure of a new generation of Black political leadership in American cities to adequately address racialized economic inequality and, further, to highlight the common dynamics affecting the global political economy after formal decolonization and the political economy of the American metropolis.[2]

Allen's concept of domestic neocolonialism marked a recognition of the changes that the civil rights movement and the election of a new group of Black politicians to political office had wrought. The passage of the Civil Rights Act of 1964 and the creation of new jobs in antipoverty agencies had sparked a dramatic rise in public sector employment for African Americans in the second half of the 1960s. In Baltimore, for example, as historian Jane Berger demonstrates, African Americans occupied half of the city's municipal jobs by 1970, which represented a significant increase since the middle of the 1960s. This increase was the result of the work of activists who "leveraged the power of the Black electorate" in many municipalities—a power that also brought about the election of Black mayors in major cities, from Cleveland and Detroit to Newark and Washington, DC, between 1967 and 1975.[3]

Allen acknowledged these political-economic transformations as significant breakthroughs for Black political power and economic advancement. But he also interpreted them as components of a broader effort by American elites to guarantee Black Americans' allegiances to the US state and its institutions. The colonial position of Black America, Allen argued, had historically meant that "the colonized blacks were prevented from developing a strong bourgeois middle class." The civil rights and Black Power movements and the urban rebellions of the 1960s posed an unprecedented challenge to the nation's traditional forms of racialized economic inequality, exemplified by the Jim Crow system. One aspect of the response by white political and corporate elites, in Allen's analysis, was a politics of law and order—a repressive crackdown on poor and working-class Black people through policing and incarceration. But another side of their response was a politics of incorporation. The elite's "deeper interest," Allen wrote, "is in reorganizing the ghetto 'infrastructure,' in creating a ghetto buffer class clearly committed to the dominant American institutions and values." Black political leadership and Black employment in municipal bureaucracies were thus recast by Allen as the means through which the American elite now sought to manage the rebellious potential of poor and working-class Black people: "It is the educated and trained blacks who are slated to become the new managers of the ghetto, the administrators of the black colony." This novel strategy marked one of the ways in which "Black America is now being transformed from a colonial nation into a neocolonial nation."[4]

Allen's analysis of American political economy in terms of neocolonialism also reflected a belated adaptation of a language that had taken hold in the decolonizing world several years earlier, most prominently with the publication of Kwame Nkrumah's *Neo-Colonialism: The Last Stage of Imperialism* in 1965. Nkrumah's analysis of the continuing control of important sectors of postcolonial economies by American- and European-owned businesses after formal independence gave a new name and a new urgency to the longstanding emphasis in Black internationalist writing on the dangers that faced states that won their political independence without achieving economic sovereignty.[5]

Stokely Carmichael and Charles Hamilton had already incorporated an understanding of the insufficiency of the transfer of political power to Black leaders in their theorization of internal colonialism in *Black Power*. In this analysis, they drew on the scholarship of Martin Kilson, a Black political scientist and member of AMSAC who had studied with Rupert Emerson at Harvard, on so-called indirect rule in the British colonies of Africa.[6] The changing social base of the Black leadership class rendered *neocolonialism* a more adequate reference point than colonial indirect rule, in Allen's mind. The cultivation of nationalist consciousness in colonial territories, and the struggle for political independence itself, produced a new elite fluent in the languages of militancy and revolt and dependent on political support from national-ist elements of the populace. Using Ghana as an example, where Kwame Nkrumah and the CPP had appeared to supplant the system of chieftaincy through which Britain had long exercised its authority, Allen argued that, in the first years after political independence, the new, "Nkrumahan political elite" continued to serve the interests of foreign, especially British, capital. The coup that brought down Nkrumah in 1966—which exposed the "face of neocolonialism"—only occurred after his turn toward a socialist develop-mental model for Ghana, which threatened these prerogatives and drove a wedge between Nkrumah and other members of his party.[7]

Ghana's experience illustrated that even the empowerment of a political elite comprised of "militant nationalists" offered no guarantee of an end to co-lonial processes of economic exploitation. This lesson, Allen argued, applied equally well to the cities of the United States. In cities ranging from Newark to Cleveland, a new leadership class had emerged that "denounced the old Black elite of Tomming preachers, teachers, and businessmen-politicians" and "an-nounced that it supported Black power." In Allen's analysis, the sincerity of this new elite's support for Black nationalism did not change the fact that its structural position in metropolitan politics was to mediate the relationship between corporate power and the "rebellious colony." In addition to Nkru-mah's analysis of the economic structures of neocolonialism, Allen turned to the writings of Frantz Fanon to provide a fuller picture of how nationalist political leaders and intellectuals turned their militancy into a currency that could advance their own aims. Fanon's argument that postcolonial leaders of-ten relied on cultural nationalist appeals to maintain popularity while under-mining democratic processes provided a striking parallel, in Allen's eyes, to the strategies of the first generation of Black political leaders holding elected office in the United States since Reconstruction.[8]

Allen continued to believe that the colonial analogy offered resources for a radical analysis of the dynamics of race and capitalism in American cit-ies. Yet he acknowledged that the force of this language had been blunted by semantic drift. Noting the similarities between Carmichael and Hamilton's *Black Power* and pluralist analyses in American political science, Allen ar-gued that Carmichael and Hamilton's manifesto put forward "another form of traditional ethnic group politics" that was in keeping with the "reformist ten-dency in Black nationalism." Allen further criticized Harold Cruse's cultural program, even while relying on and adapting Cruse's language throughout. Acknowledging that the idiosyncratic Cruse "stands outside the pale of ac-cepted categories," Allen argued that his emphasis on the "cultural apparatus" and his desire for a "cultural revolution" would only "exacerbate" class divisions among African Americans. Cruse's program of increasing Black control over the cultural apparatus would only serve to empower a new Black intelligentsia, a goal that aligned well with "corporate America's agenda for the Black colony." Similarly, Allen contended that the mere appearance of "cultural democratization" through the greater visibility of Black leaders would end up undermining Cruse's broader aims. If, as Cruse had written, "the American social system quite easily absorbs all foreign, and even native, radical doctrines and neutralizes them," then surely, Allen argued, Cruse's own program for greater Black control of the cultural apparatus was susceptible to this neutralization as well.[9]

The uncompromising critiques Allen leveled at other Black intellectuals and political leaders did not indicate complete pessimism about the prospects of a domestic decolonization. Recalling the analyses advanced by James and Grace Lee Boggs, Allen argued that automation and growing redundancies in the US industrial workforce that it created would soon force the labor movement into a crisis. This crisis, he argued, had already caused Black industrial workers and former industrial workers to seek new alliances and organizations to advance their political goals. He struck an optimistic tone about both the Black student movement and the Black Panther Party as signs of the potential for new forms of Black activism to build coalitions that would work against the "neocolonial" leadership of American cities at the end of the 1960s. Yet the promising signs he saw in each case were provisional. The agent of a more thoroughgoing reconstruction of metropolitan politics remained obscure. Allen's "neocolonial" critique of prevailing forms of Black political authority thus ultimately pointed backward, toward the question of the revolutionary subject that underlay earlier adoptions of the colonial analogy.[10]

Developmentalism and the Black Manifesto

The most sustained effort to link the language of internal colonialism to a practical program at the end of the 1960s emerged out of the National Black Economic Development Conference (NBEDC). Held in Detroit from April 25 to April 27, 1969, the conference aimed to develop alternatives to Nixon's program of "Black capitalism." The conference was sponsored by the Interreligious Foundation for Community Organization (IFCO), an ecumenical organization founded in 1967 to provide funding and technical assistance to community groups, both religious and secular, in the United States and abroad. The conference, which brought together between six hundred and eight hundred attendees, provided an economic counterpart to the Newark

Black Power Conference of 1967. Planned speakers included civil rights movement veterans such as Fannie Lou Hamer and Julian Bond, who had recently been elected to the Georgia House of Representatives, along with local Black Power leaders in Detroit, such as James Boggs and Milton Henry, one of the founders of the Republic of New Afrika. Best remembered as the site where James Forman launched the "Black Manifesto," the conference in fact entertained a range of visions and proposals. This gathering was a crucial moment in the Black Power movement's debates over political economy. It marked the apex of a way of thinking about racialized economic inequality and Black economic advancement in the United States in the idiom of post-colonial developmentalism.[11]

On the first day of the conference, Robert Span Browne and James Boggs outlined two distinct visions of Black economic development, both of which derived from their analyses of the similarities and differences between the conditions of Black America and the conditions of postcolonial states. Browne, who was trained as a development economist, had worked for the International Cooperation Agency (later the United States Agency for International Development, or USAID) in Cambodia and South Vietnam in the late 1950s and early 1960s. After his time in Southeast Asia, he became a key figure in linking the civil rights and antiwar movements, and his was among the most influential voices in lobbying Martin Luther King Jr. to speak out against the war. By 1969, Browne was teaching economics at Fairleigh Dickinson University, and his political focus had shifted to the Black Power movement. His professional training and experiences in the decolonizing world influenced his thinking on how Black Americans should conceive of their own programs of what the conference called "national" economic development.[12]

Invited to deliver the keynote address at the conference in Detroit, Browne struck a downbeat note. Though he castigated the conservative call for Black self-help that undergirded Nixon's Black capitalism initiatives— "There is no question of 'pulling ourselves up by our bootstraps' . . . We have no bootstraps"—Browne nonetheless cast a skeptical eye on some of the most popular economic ideas in Black radical circles. Much of his speech focused on the obstacles to formulating "five-year plans" for economic development for Black America that resembled those of the Soviet Union and many postcolonial states. The primary obstacle was the lack of sovereignty: economic development plans depended on "the existence of a nation which . . . exercises *sovereignty* over both *itself as a community* and over its members." Because "Black America clearly fails . . . these tests," plans for Black economic development must work "within the existing limitations of our *NOT* enjoying national sovereignty."[13]

In the face of these limitations, Browne proposed more modest action. Working within existing Great Society programs, Black Americans could advance "local development projects, small business programs, job training, consumer education, vocational guidance, [and] school improvement" that might alleviate Black poverty without threatening the political establishment, which remained staunchly opposed to Black advancement. Browne further criticized the popular notion of developing a "parallel economy" in cities with newly elected Black political leadership, such as Cleveland and Gary. Such a program faced severe challenges because a city "is a relatively limited economic unit" and "usually not a viable financial unit these days." This vision of Black separatism, derived from the pluralist reading of the internal colonial analysis, foundered because the only political space in which African Americans could exercise sovereignty was limited to the urban centers suffering the most severe effects of deindustrialization. Instead, Browne pointed toward the eventual aim of a "legal takeover" of an American state through the forging of Black political unity on questions of fiscal and social policy. This political strategy might then serve as a precursor to the formation of a true economic development plan for Black America.[14]

James Boggs outlined a competing approach to Black economic development in the next speech. For Boggs, the question of Black economic development required precisely the approach that Browne rejected—that is, "comprehensive planning for at least a five year period." Titling his address "The Myth and Irrationality of Black Capitalism," Boggs began his analysis from the standpoint of the radical reading of the internal colony thesis that he had held since the early 1960s: "Black America is underdeveloped today because of capitalist semi-colonialism, just as Africa, Asia and Latin America are underdeveloped today because of capitalist colonialism." The intertwined nature of capitalism, colonialism, and racism made the idea of Black capitalism a "dream and a delusion," a vision of the continuing exploitation of Black labor by a new class of exploiters now "of the same color." Yet here Boggs insisted that the differences between overseas colonialism and domestic colonialism were significant for understanding the political economy of underdevelopment. Colonialism in the Third World, he argued, served to arrest the process of national development, forcing nations to remain "pre-industrial or agricultural" to "supply raw materials or agricultural produce to the Western imperialists." But Black communities in the United States faced a different problem. Capital flight and automation had "turned these communities into wastelands, abandoned by industry as it has undergone technological revolutions." Domestic colonialism had not enforced a "pre-industrial" condition but a "post-industrial" one.[15]

This distinction shaped Boggs's positive vision of Black economic development. His speech linked together three traditions of political-economic thought: traditional socialist proposals for social housing and public ownership of productive enterprises; Black nationalist proposals for the establishment of a land base for Black political struggle in both the rural South and the urban North; and techno-futurist ideas about the transformations that automation would cause in the US labor force. The third of these elements derived directly from the distinction Boggs had drawn between the "pre-industrial" world colonialism had created and the "post-industrial" world of domestic colonialism. In language that resonated with the emergent ideas of social critics such as Daniel Bell, who envisioned a "new class" emerging to lead the "post-industrial society," Boggs emphasized the importance of higher education of African Americans for the "jobs of the future." Unlike Bell, however, Boggs stressed that such jobs—primarily professional, technical, and managerial positions—would appeal to young Black people born in the "space age," because they were "particularly aware not only of the racism which has always confined Blacks to dead-end jobs but of the revolutionary changes which are a routine part of modern industry." Young Black workers and students, who faced the direst consequences of deindustrialization and automation, thus constituted the focal point of Boggs's multifaceted agenda, which derived from his specific view of what internal colonialism entailed.[16]

The next day, the tenor and purpose of the conference changed dramatically. James Forman, who had recently left his position as director of international affairs for SNCC, led a faction of attendees that commandeered the proceedings, disrupting its scheduled program. This faction also included a representative of IFCO, Rev. Lucius Walker, and two leaders of the League of Revolutionary Black Workers in Detroit, Mike Hamlin and John Watson. Forman, who was initially scheduled to give an address on "Co-operatives as a Vehicle for Meeting the Economic and Social Needs of Black People," instead delivered what he called the "Black Manifesto."

The Black Manifesto turned the conference in a new direction—toward the question of reparations for African Americans. "For centuries," Forman declared, Black people "have been forced to live as colonized people within the United States, victimized by the most vicious, racist system in the world." As recompense for the suffering that African Americans experienced in "help[ing] to build the most industrial country in the world," the manifesto demanded $500 million in reparations payments from "the white Christian churches and Jewish synagogues which are part and parcel of the system of capitalism." Forman's decision to direct the manifesto's reparations demand at churches, specifically, derived from his understanding of the historical relation between organized Christianity, European colonization of Africa and the Americas, and the establishment of the slave trade. "We were kept in bondage and political servitude," Forman wrote, "by the military machinery and the Christian church working hand in hand." By making Christian churches a primary target of the reparations demand, Forman also denied the moral authority of the Black church within the civil rights movement. Though the manifesto declared, "we do not intend to abuse our Black brothers and sisters in Black churches," the document suggested plainly that the prominent role of Black ministers and churchgoers in the civil rights movement had delimited its potential. Framing his demand for reparations in relation not only to the history of slavery but to ongoing forms of racial violence and racialized economic inequality, Forman denied that the civil rights movement—especially its ministerial leadership—had successfully achieved its aims of Black freedom or equality within the boundaries of the American polity.[17]

While the announcement of the Black Manifesto radically shifted the direction of the NBEDC Conference, its reparations demand shared the idiom of postcolonial economic developmentalism that pervaded the conference. The demand for reparations, Forman argued, required a reframing of the Black freedom struggle not in terms of creedal nationalism or Christian redemption but in terms of the internal colony thesis. Forman justified the manifesto's reparations demand by citing the essential and uncompensated role of Black labor in American national economic development. More than that, Forman's vision for how the funds secured through reparations should be spent reflected his understanding of African American underdevelopment as a variant of the underdevelopment inflicted upon the entire colonial and postcolonial world. Forman's proposals for how the $500 million he demanded should be allocated—including the establishment of a "Southern land bank" to assist Black tenant farmers in purchasing land, the opening of publishing houses and "futuristic audio-visual networks," the creation of a national Black university, the development of a skills and training center, and the support of existing organizations such as the NWRO—were very much in keeping with the developmentalist orientation of the conference as a whole.[18]

After delivering his speech, Forman commandeered the rest of the conference. He arranged a vote among the delegates to adopt the Black Manifesto as the official program of the organization. The vote was 187 to 63 in favor of Forman's proposal, with less than half of the six hundred or more delegates registering a vote on either side. Forman took this vote as approval of both his message and his tactics, although his takeover of the proceedings was not universally welcomed.[19]

The next weekend, on May 4, 1969, the Black Manifesto captured the attention of a nationwide audience when Forman interrupted Sunday services at Riverside Church in New York. After striding to the lectern, Forman read out the demands of the Black Manifesto to the congregation. This public and visible reparations demand, delivered at one of the most prominent churches in the largest city in the country, made national news. The *New York Review of Books* published the Black Manifesto later that summer, along with multiple response pieces. The manifesto's indictment of predominantly white churches such as Riverside instigated a reckoning in religious communities across the country, especially in liberal Protestant denominations. The question of reparations dominated conversation in Protestant denominations in the Detroit metropolitan area in particular, where Hamlin, Watson, and other allies of Forman used similar tactics to disrupt church services throughout the spring and summer.[20]

In the aftermath of these dramatic pronouncements of the manifesto's reparations demand, Forman and his group adopted the name of the conference where the manifesto had been initially proclaimed for the organization that would pursue its aims. They soon dropped the word "National," becoming the Black Economic Development Conference (BEDC). Black Power activist Mae Mallory, Beulah Sanders of the National Welfare Rights Organization (NWRO), and Robert Browne, whose own speech at the Detroit Conference had been overshadowed by Forman's actions, were among those who took leadership roles in the new organization. As the group garnered attention, it also came under surveillance from law enforcement. FBI officers contacted IFCO leaders, and over a dozen individuals involved in the initial NBEDC Conference were served federal grand jury subpoenas.[21]

Though Forman had outlined a range of projects in the manifesto, BEDC struggled to make material progress. By August 1969, the organization had an income of only $18,212, which forced the organization to focus its attention on fundraising among denominations and individual churches that responded sympathetically to the manifesto. BEDC ended up raising close to $500,000 from a range of church sources, with $200,000 coming from an additional grant from IFCO. Chapters of BEDC were officially established in Chicago, Philadelphia, Cleveland, and Detroit, but they struggled to sustain themselves. By late 1970, Mae Mallory reported that "she has no office, her equipment was stolen from her, and she is having great difficulty getting reparations from her Cleveland operation." The most successful of the BEDC chapters was in Philadelphia, where, under the leadership of former Mississippi Freedom Democratic Party activist Muhammad Kenyatta, BEDC both engaged in successful negotiations with leaders of the Episcopal Church for capital donations and took part in a growing coalition of Black Power organizations in the city. Working alongside the Philadelphia Welfare Rights Organization (PWRO), one of the most vibrant chapters of the NWRO, Kenyatta and the Philadelphia chapter of BEDC worked to forge a united coalition of white New Left and Black Power activists in the city that linked demands for higher welfare benefits with a call to end the Vietnam War.[22]

Despite the challenges of sustaining active chapters, BEDC made several lasting contributions to Black thought and cultural production. It provided some of the financing for Black Star Press and Black Star Productions in Detroit, which served as the publishing house and production company for the League of Revolutionary Black Workers. In addition to printing collections of James Forman's writings and other materials by LRBW activists, these establishments released the memorable documentary *Finally Got the News . . .* (1970), which documented the league's organizing of wildcat strikes among Black autoworkers in the face of harsh opposition by both automobile manufacturers and the predominantly white leadership of the UAW. BEDC further contributed to the establishment of the Black Economic Research Center, an organization founded by Robert Browne to collect data on the economics of Black communities, which founded and published the *Review of Black Political Economy*.[23]

The most significant consequence of BEDC and the Black Manifesto, though, came in its raising of the issue of reparations. Dismissal and outright opposition to the manifesto's language and demands were the prevailing responses in elite circles. Journalist and commentator Murray Kempton, writing in the *New York Review of Books*, described the manifesto's analysis as fanciful and unreal, while claiming its primary accomplishment was to serve as a milestone in the "history of publicity." Yet, by pushing the issue of reparations to the forefront of conversation in Methodist, Presbyterian, Episcopal, and United Church of Christ denominations, it is undeniable that the manifesto forced hundreds of thousands of white Americans to consider the relation between present-day racial inequality and the history of slavery and Jim Crow, possibly for the very first time. The very choice to target BEDC's reparations demands against "white Christian churches and Jewish synagogues" remained puzzling to some other Black Power groups, however. The Republic of New Afrika (RNA), for instance, which also made reparations central to its vision of Black nationalist self-determination, refused to endorse the manifesto on the grounds that it did not aim its demands at the federal government. Ironically, the voluntaristic nature of church funding made it possible for BEDC to raise capital that a governmental body would never have considered handing over, even if the organization predictably fell wildly short of its stated demand for $500 million.[24]

The choice to target nongovernmental organizations in the manifesto's reparations demand also reflected the belief, held by Forman and BEDC members, that the creedal vision of the US state as an agent of Black progress was illegitimate.[25] Although the national attention the manifesto garnered after Forman's disruption at Riverside Church obscured its origins in the Detroit Conference, this element of the document clearly reflected the debates from which it emerged. The Black radicals and Black nationalists who gathered in Detroit in April 1969 offered a range of programmatic responses shaped by a shared rejection of Nixon's promotion of Black capitalism. Whatever their differences, however, Browne, Boggs, and Forman shared an idea of internal colonization as a form of racialized economic exploitation that called into question the possibility of Black economic development within the framework of the post–Great Society United States. The lingua franca of debates over Black economic development at the end of the 1960s relied on the concept of the internal colony.

The Challenges of Coalition

Many Black activists who embraced the language of internal colonialism at the end of the 1960s sought to make common cause with other colonized peoples within the United States. With the rise of the Young Lords Party (YLP) and the American Indian Movement (AIM) in 1968 and 1969, respectively, the question of how to relate the forms of colonialism faced by Black Americans, Puerto Ricans, and American Indians grew in importance in radical circles. Both the YLP and the AIM drew explicitly on the language, symbolism, and tactics of the Black Panther Party, from the YLP's adoption of a Thirteen-Point Program to the establishment of an "AIM Patrol" that monitored and responded to police activity in heavily Native neighborhoods of Minneapolis.[26] The Panthers, for their part, forged common cause with both organizations: the Chicago Young Lords were prominently involved in Fred Hampton's "Rainbow Coalition" in 1969, while the *Black Panther* newspaper publicized the occupation of Alcatraz by AIM activists in the same year.[27] Yet, despite these bonds, efforts to think through the differing positionality of those affected by territorial colonization, settler colonialism, and internal colonialism were sporadic and often unspecific, as Panther activists frequently subsumed the specific questions raised by American Indian and Puerto Rican claims to land, sovereignty, treaty recognition, and independence under broad proclamations of "solidarity with all oppressed peoples."[28]

Standing Rock Sioux writer Vine Deloria Jr. authored a significant, if controversial, analysis of the possibilities and challenges of a synthesis between
Black theories of internal colonialism and Indigenous critiques of settler colonialism in this period. The former executive director of the National Congress of American Indians (NCAI), Deloria had presided over an unprecedented period of growth for the organization, during which it moved from
representing 19 tribes to representing over 150. He led the NCAI's push for
tribal self-government in the era of the federal government's disastrous policy
of termination. Deloria emerged as a major intellectual of the "Red Power"
movement with the publication of *Custer Died for Your Sins: An Indian Manifesto* in 1969. Published just months before the takeover of Alcatraz and the
occupation of the Bureau of Indian Affairs offices in Washington, DC, by the
American Indian Movement, *Custer Died for Your Sins* represented Deloria's
attempt to make sense of "the unrealities that face *us* as Indian people" at the
end of the 1960s.[29]

The differing regimes of racialization, exploitation, and expropriation
faced by Black Americans and American Indians was a major topic of Deloria's manifesto. A fundamental historical difference existed between the
forms of colonization based on land expropriation and enslavement: or, as
Deloria put it, "We gave up land instead of life and labor." This basic distinction, in Deloria's mind, undergirded the different forms of prejudice Black
Americans and American Indians continued to face, as well as the different
ways each group related to the American polity. The tendency of "white liberals" to lump together American Indians with all other minority groups—the
largest of which was African Americans—meant that "the Indian is defined"
by many white Americans "as a subcategory of Black." This attitude could
lead policymakers as well as Black activists to overlook the significance of
land and sovereignty in American Indian politics. For Deloria, a failure to
recognize that demands for antipoverty measures and civil rights meant little
to peoples who sought the restoration of lands and the upholding of treaty
obligations produced conditions of estrangement and misunderstanding that
threatened coalitional politics.[30]

The shifting currents in the Black freedom movement presented both
challenges and opportunities for coalition building across peoples subjected
to regimes of settler and internal colonization. The drive for integration and
legal equality in the civil rights movement, Deloria claimed, overlooked the
true problem of anti-Black racism, which was "one of culture and social and
economic mobility." More troubling to Deloria was the way some civil rights
leaders turned the demand for "equality" into a call for "sameness." From the
perspective of American Indians, he argued, the aim of integration seemed

too close to the settler project of assimilation: an effort that, for centuries, had sought to dissolve tribal identities. Deloria cited these objections in part to justify the perception that American Indians had done too little to support the mainstream civil rights movement, from the March on Washington to the Poor People's Campaign. The turn toward Black Power, on the other hand, was "a godsend to other groups" that "clarified the intellectual concepts which had kept Indians and Mexicans confused." With its emphasis on "peoplehood," the Black Power movement "allowed the concept of self-determination suddenly to become valid." Stokely Carmichael's announcement of "Black Power" as the new aim of the Black freedom movement in 1966 spurred on a period of intensifying lobbying, both in the NCAI and in individual tribes, against the termination policy. For Deloria, the Black Power turn to self-determination as an ideal renewed American Indians' hopes that a politics of tribal self-determination might also gain traction.[31]

Deloria's analysis of Black politics both overlooked key components of the regimes of dispossession that African Americans faced and neglected the range of goals and ideologies in the Black freedom movement. His emphasis on a complete separation between the modes of expropriation and exploitation faced by American Indians and Black peoples—"We gave up land instead of life and labor"—failed to reckon with the fact that enslaved Africans in the Americas had also been forcibly removed from their ancestral homelands. Even more problematic for Deloria's attempt to ground a coalitional politics of American Indian and Black struggles was his dismissiveness toward major strands in Black activism. His disparaging remark that "for many people, particularly those Indian people who had supported self-determination a decade earlier, Stokely Carmichael was the first black [person] who said anything significant," bordered on contemptuousness. Deloria's perspective not only neglected the long history of Black advocacy for various forms of self-determination, including emigration outside the American polity, but it also failed to reckon with prominent critiques of the imperial character of the US state by figures he characterized as fixated only on "integration" and "civil rights," including Martin Luther King Jr. As Afro-Indigenous studies scholar Kyle Mays writes, "the assumption that African Americans' conception of belonging was exclusively about integration into US empire flattens Black history." Deloria's expressions of support for the emergence of Black Power were thus tempered by his trivialization of the wider stream of Black politics from which it emerged.[32]

Though Deloria's arguments could minimize the rich analysis of American colonialism in Black political thought, his account shared with many concurrent writings in the Black Power movement a critical engagement with prevailing discourses of developmentalism and pluralism. Development politics provided a potent language of American Indian self-assertion. The NCAI's antitermination campaign in the 1950s, Deloria noted, was framed as a Point Four program against US policies aimed at the extermination of Indigenous nations as cohesive political actors. And, in his own time at the head of NCAI, the community development programs of the War on Poverty had deeply influenced Deloria's vision for American Indian self-determination, as Deloria worked within OEO's Indian Division to make demands for tribal self-government. In his mind, "the Indian people are in a good position to demonstrate to the nation what can be done in community development in rural areas," especially considering the "overcrowding of urban areas." Beyond its intersections with the politics of international and community development, *Custer Died for Your Sins* also often presented a pluralistic image of American politics as made up of a series of competing ethnic-cum-interest groups. Deloria often referred to undifferentiated "groups" of American Indians, Chicanos, and Black Americans as having shared interests and aspirations and moving in concert in the US political arena: "Each group has its own road to travel . . . but the obstacles faced by each group are different and call for different solutions and techniques." But Deloria, like Carmichael and Hamilton in *Black Power*, also chafed against the limitations of the pluralist framework. The history of Indigenous sovereignty over the land, the fact of tribal membership, and the existence of treaty obligations all set American Indians apart, in Deloria's mind—not only from the white ethnics who formed the initial basis of pluralist theorizing, but from Black Americans as well.[33]

Perhaps the most significant effort to forge a coalitional politics based on an acknowledgment of the intersecting but distinct conditions of internal, external, and settler colonization occurred a year after the publication of *Custer Died for Your Sins*. The Revolutionary People's Constitutional Convention (RPCC), organized by the Black Panther Party and held in Philadelphia in 1970, included representatives of AIM, the YLP, the Chicano activist group the Brown Berets, Asian American activist group I Wor Keun, and other radical, Third Worldist, and feminist organizations. Representatives of these groups came together with the ostensible goal of drafting a replacement for the 1787 Constitution that still set the framework for US politics. Here, as political theorist Aziz Rana writes, participants grappled with the problems of coalitional politics under "the same overarching structures of colonial power" but as representatives of groups which were "located in collective life in profoundly distinct ways." The project generated grand proposals for institutional reform: from calls for a plebiscite among Puerto Ricans and

American Indians to determine their future political status; to a guarantee of proportional representation of women, Black Americans, and other "Third World people" in the institutions of US government; to an extensive roster of feminist demands, including the socialization of housework and a constitutional guarantee of maternity leave. But the energy on display in the RPCC was not sustained beyond this initial gathering, as plans for a second convention later that year were called off.[34]

Efforts to sustain a coalition of the colonized would continue after 1970, but often in the form of episodic expressions of solidarity, as when Panthers organized demonstrations in support of the AIM-led occupation of Wounded Knee in 1973. But, increasingly, the translation of solidarity into a durable coalition became harder to achieve. Accelerating state repression was one prominent culprit: the FBI worked tirelessly to discredit and divide radicals of color, and activists associated with groups all across this formation were incarcerated, forced into exile, and even, in some cases, murdered by the state. Linked to this outright repression were growing internal fissures— which agents of the state did much to exacerbate—such as the 1971 split in the Black Panther Party. These divisions diminished the possibility of constructing a cohesive political movement that could challenge the rightward turn in the nation's politics. Nonetheless, the spread of the language of internal colonialism within the Black freedom movement had generated momentum for forming common bonds across new activist formations among American Indians, Puerto Ricans, and Chicanos—even as it often failed to speak directly to the varieties of American colonization that these groups confronted.[35]

"There Are No More Colonies or Neo-Colonies"

The profusion of the colonial analogy in 1969 and 1970, in debates about Black economic development and in efforts to formulate a politics of solidarity across "Third World peoples" in the United States, marked the high point of the influence of the concept of internal colonialism in circles of movement politics. Beginning in 1970, vocal and influential segments of the Black left, most notably the Oakland-based leadership of the Black Panther Party, turned away from the understanding of African Americans as colonial subjects that had undergirded much of their internationalist activism. While the writings of BPP cofounders Bobby Seale and Huey Newton referred to the "Black colony" as early as 1966, a more programmatic understanding of internal colonialism in Panther ideology only emerged in 1968, as the organization grew nationally and engaged in more overt efforts at establishing international connections. In the spring and summer of 1968, the BPP collaborated with the Student Nonviolent Coordinating Committee, building on the work of Forman and others to establish SNCC's international connections in the previous year. Despite growing animosity between Forman and Carmichael, both figures joined a delegation from the Panthers for a series of rallies in New York and Newark to promote the Panthers' new demand: a call for a UN-sponsored plebiscite on the political status of Black Americans.[36]

The demand for a plebiscite grew out of the call by Malcolm X in the last year of his life to bring the US Black freedom struggle before the forum of the United Nations. Similar petitions existed in the platforms of other Black Power organizations, notably the Republic of New Afrika, which sought to establish an independent state in the "Black Belt" of the South. Underscoring the centrality of this demand to Black Panther Party leaders, especially Minister of Information Eldridge Cleaver, the party expanded the final point of its Ten Point Program to include a call for the plebiscite.[37]

The revised program listed as the party's "major political demand" a "United Nations sponsored plebiscite to be held throughout the Black colony in which only Black colonial subjects will be allowed to participate, for the purpose of determining the will of Black people as to their national destiny." For Cleaver, the internal colony thesis and the Panthers' appeal for a UN plebiscite signified a sharp rebuke to the common understanding of Black inequality as a form of "second-class citizenship." Rather than an extension of the rights of citizens, Cleaver argued, the Panthers' program, and indeed the broader Black Power movement, constituted a "projection of sovereignty," a symbolic manifestation of Black people's rejection of the authority of the American state and a positioning of African Americans within a global majority of the Third World.[38]

The call for a plebiscite further reframed the colonial analogy around the question of Black people's political status, rather than the economic questions that seemed to bedevil other attempts to forge a political program around the concept. By linking the analogy to the question of Black people's "political destiny" within or outside the United States, the demand for a plebiscite sidestepped the question of what resources Black ghettos possessed that made them comparable sources of profit for white society as colonies had been for imperial powers. The "decentralized colony" of "Afro-America," as Cleaver described it, must assert itself as a nation-in-waiting via the international forum of the United Nations, before a concrete alteration of the colonial relationship between "Black colony" and "white mother country" could be achieved.[39]

Although Cleaver had argued for the plebiscite most forcefully, other Black Panther Party members supported its addition to the Ten Point Program in 1968. In the coming years, both the failure of this demand to win traction in the international community and the widening fissures in the organization's leadership generated a turn away from the language of internal colonialism altogether.[40] With very few exceptions, postcolonial states in Asia and Africa refrained from endorsing the Panthers' call for a UN plebiscite, both because it risked alienating the much more powerful United States, and because these nations feared that the success of any claim to national self-determination by a group that could be categorized as a "national minority" might prompt additional claims that threatened their own national integrity.[41] The well-known division between Cleaver and his allies, who relocated to Algiers in 1969, and the circle around Newton and his allies in Oakland, stemmed from a variety of sources, from state repression to growing personal animosity to conflicting visions of the purpose of the party. Cleaver and the International Section continued to advocate revolutionary violence and guerrilla warfare, while the leadership in Oakland, and most chapters throughout the United States, engaged more deeply in the local community service programs—"survival programs," as Newton now labeled them—that had been established over the course of 1969 and 1970.[42]

Before the backdrop of this growing division, Huey Newton articulated a new analysis of the relationship of the Black Panther Party, and of the African American freedom struggle more broadly, to the global dynamics of capitalism and empire. In a speech at Boston College in November 1970, and in a joint speech with psychologist Erik Erikson in February 1971, Newton introduced his concept of "intercommunalism." For Newton, the language of internal colonialism, even in the neocolonial variant endorsed by Robert L. Allen, failed to register what made the world order of the late twentieth century distinctive from the imperial and colonial orders that preceded it. The globe-spanning power of the United States, and its ability to achieve global hegemony with minimal control of foreign territories, rendered colonial models inapplicable. Strategically, the Panthers had adopted the analysis of internal colonialism as a force multiplier, he declared. Because "Black communities throughout the country" held "many similarities" with the "traditional kind of colony," he declared, "we thought that if we allied with those other colonies we would have a greater number, a greater chance, a greater force; and that is what we needed, of course, because only force kept us a colonized people." Shifts in the configuration of global power, however, had rendered these alliances untenable. Technological transformations, especially in mass media, communications, and transportation, had undermined the power of the nation-state and the appeal of the "revolutionary nationalism" that Harold Cruse had once advanced and that the Panthers had initially defined as their ideological lodestar.[43]

"There are no more colonies or neo-colonies," Newton proclaimed, in an explicit renunciation of the language of internal colonialism, "only a dispersed collection of communities." Even the analysis of neocolonialism, in which the continuing economic power of former imperial rulers and foreign corporations undermined the sovereignty of a purportedly independent polity, failed to capture the deterritorialized nature of imperial power. The replacement of colonialism and even neocolonialism by a spatially diffuse system of technologically advanced, US-backed transnational capitalism made it "impossible to 'decolonize,'" in Newton's mind. The "waning of territoriality," as historian Charles Maier characterizes this shift, demanded a rethinking of the language and the spatial imaginary of Black struggle. A more pervasive form of domination existed, Newton claimed, than the relations of dependency and exploitation between colony and metropole—or between internal colony and wealthy suburb.[44]

"The communications revolution, combined with the expansive domination of the American empire," Newton announced, "has created the 'global village.'" This global unity, Newton suggested, provided the basis for an archipelago of struggle among a "dispersed collection of communities," united only by a desire to "determine their own destinies" against the "small circle that administers and profits from the empire of the United States." This vision contradicted the emphasis on the territorial specificity of the Black ghetto that had held an important place in analyses of internal colonialism from Kenneth Clark's *Dark Ghetto* onwards. For all their differences, visions of the internal colony as an enclave-in-waiting in a pluralistic city and visions of it as a site for the extraction of rents, profits, and cheap labor shared this understanding of territorial specificity. To Newton, however, this territorial specificity no longer held true. Without explicitly addressing the entailments of the language of internal colonialism in the previous few years, Newton framed the Panthers' abandonment of the colonial analogy as a revision to their analysis of the political-economic order at both local and global scales.[45]

After the Panthers discarded the idea of the internal colony, many other African Americans on the left followed suit. Some key thinkers moved away from the vision of an internal colony specifically because its many uses over the previous few years had deprived it of any clear political content. James Boggs, for his part, determined by 1973 that the ideological promiscuity of the colonial analogy in the late 1960s and early 1970s—especially its uses in support of a conventional politics of interest-group advancement—had rendered it useless for American radicals. "Concepts that grew out of and are relevant to the African struggle against colonialism and neo-colonialism," which Boggs himself had played a key role in introducing, now only "confuse[d] the struggle for a U.S. revolution," he confided in a letter. Those who continued to employ such language to frame movements for democracy and economic equality among Black Americans only engaged in a form of "self-indulgence." Structural commonalities between the decolonizing world and the deindustrializing United States had appeared to Boggs to provide an opening for radical politics in the early 1960s. Even in 1969, at the NBEDC Conference, Boggs continued to reflect on the relevance of the colonial analogy to the systematic analysis of American capitalism. But, by 1973, he viewed the language as no more than a radical veneer.[46]

The weakening political purchase of the internal colony thesis on the Black left did not slow its profusion in academic venues. Ongoing debates over the analytical clarity and usefulness of internal colonialism played out in several new publications and institutions created through the movement for Black studies.[47] *The Black Scholar*, founded in 1969 following the firing of sociologist Nathan Hare from San Francisco State University's pioneering Black Studies department for supporting a student strike in the university, and the *Review of Black Political Economy*, founded in 1970 by Robert S. Browne with the help of funding from BEDC, hosted many of these discussions.[48] In the same period, several heterodox white social scientists, most notably sociologist Robert Blauner and economist William Tabb, promoted the concept of internal colonialism within their disciplines.[49] As these scholars sought to bring the concept to bear on narrower disciplinary debates throughout the 1970s, other strands of thought that had once been organized under its sign, from James and Grace Lee Boggs's vision of a new revolutionary subject to Robert L. Allen's challenge to Black nationalist political elites, fell away. The migration of the concept of the internal colony into academia signaled the end of its purchase in movement politics.

In 1975, St. Clair Drake surveyed the role the internal colony thesis had played in Black life and thought in the preceding years. Drake's writings and political activities over the previous three decades had, in fact, laid some of the groundwork for the appeal of this comparison. In *Black Metropolis*, composed at the end of the Second World War, Drake and Horace Cayton had observed that the average resident of Chicago's Bronzeville ghetto "found the problems of the Chinese, the Indians, and the Burmese strangely analogous to his own," while insisting that "a blow struck for freedom in Bronzeville finds its echo in Chungking and Moscow, in Paris and Senegal." From his involvement in George Padmore's circles of activism in London and his experiences teaching in Ghana, to his training of Peace Corps volunteers and his mentorship of civil rights organizers such as James Forman, Drake's influence coursed through major currents in Black internationalist thought and activism.[50]

Drake's own role was not his concern as he looked back on the career of the language of internal colonialism, however. Rather, he sought to interrogate whether the language operated as a "mere analogy" or a "scientific concept." Drake lauded that the widespread embrace of the idea of the internal colony in the middle of the 1960s had "been useful in raising the consciousness of the young Black American" and in "generating sentiments of Third World solidarity." Further, its ability to capture shared features of the "process" of racial subordination and the psychological effects of resistance rendered it more than a "mere" analogy and reinforced that the language of internal colonialism had a "heuristic value" for African Americans.[51]

Its legacy as a guide to political-economic change appeared more ambiguous. For one, Drake argued that the colonial analogy had an insoluble problem of scale. Did it apply "only to the discretely bounded ghettos—to Harlem, Bronzeville, and the others large and small, North, South, and West? Or is this whole far-flung Black population in the United States 'the colony'?" Variations between urban and rural areas and among regions, Drake argued, had not been adequately addressed by proponents of the colonial analogy, who moved too quickly from analyses of the political economy of Black ghettos to characterizations of a national population. Drake acknowledged some parallels between "the concept of 'Black Capitalism'" and "the Colonial Development Welfare schemes during the final stages of Britain's decolonization process," implying that the internal colony thesis might have continuing purchase for the critique, rather than the advancement, of business-led programs of community development. Overall, however, the diminishing economic prospects of Black workers amid rising unemployment and deindustrialization in the mid-1970s indicated a broader set of problems than the language of internal colonialism could address. "As inflation persists and Black unemployment [ratios] not only stay high as compared to whites but also begin to increase," Drake argued, the galvanizing and consciousness-raising features of the language of internal colonialism diminished in importance. A decade after the internal colony thesis gained widespread adoption in the Black freedom movement, Drake argued that "the concept of 'internal colony' as ideology . . . may have outlived its usefulness to Black Americans."[52]

The Lost Promise of Decolonization

The difficulty Black activists faced in turning the language of internal colonialism from a potent metaphor into a concrete program of action resulted, in part, from internal conflicts within the Black freedom movement itself, which were consistently exacerbated by the forces of state repression. But the downfall of this language of politics also resulted from the devaluation of postcolonial sovereignty that increasingly took hold in US elite opinion by the middle of the 1970s. Rising authoritarianism and ethnic conflict in post-colonial states fractured African American anticolonial alliances, with the Nigerian-Biafran War at the end of the 1960s playing a particularly crucial role. Within the circle of US policymakers, already suspicious of expansive visions of decolonization, the trajectories of postcolonial states called into question the normative foundations of Third World self-determination itself. To some, war, repression, and famine in the postcolonial world appeared to wide swathes of the American elite to prove that decolonization had failed—or had arrived too quickly. To others, the growing voice of the Third World on the international stage suggested that the ambitions behind decolonization needed to be curtailed.[53]

On May 1, 1974, the United Nations General Assembly adopted Resolution 3201, the "Declaration on the Establishment of a New International Economic Order" (NIEO). Proposed by the "Group of 77" (G-77)—a coalition of developing states across Asia, Africa, and Latin America—the NIEO aimed to ensure Third World states' sovereign ownership over natural resources, to affirm their authority to regulate multinational corporations, to provide for a global mechanism for commodity price stabilization, and to address the uneven terms of trade that afflicted developing economies. Broadly, the NIEO sought to enact the redistributive mechanisms of the welfare state at a global scale. The resolution framed these efforts as an extension of the process of decolonization into the economic realm: it proclaimed both that "the greatest and most significant achievement during the last decades has been the independence from colonial and alien domination of a large number of peoples and nations" and that "the present international economic order is in direct conflict" with that achievement.[54]

The declaration of the NIEO came just a year after the oil embargo enacted by the Arab countries of OPEC, which caused the price of oil to rise fourfold in the United States. The response among policymakers in the Ford administration, especially Secretary of State Henry Kissinger, involved both rejection and conciliation. In a speech before the General Assembly in the days before the adoption of the NIEO resolution, given in response to an address by Algerian leader Houari Boumédiène that outlined the program's aims, Kissinger forthrightly denounced the proposal's framework. "The notion of the northern rich and the southern poor has been shattered," he proclaimed. The world economy, rather than being defined by exploiters and exploited, was a "sensitive set of relationships," a "common enterprise." Despite this posture, Kissinger pursued an accommodation with the NIEO's demands on several policy fronts, promising that the United States would work with individual developing countries on commodity price stabilization and pledging a significant increase in American food aid to the developing world. Kissinger's strategy aimed to divide the Third World between oil-exporting and oil-importing nations, thereby diminishing the political forces behind the NIEO and stabilizing the existing order.[55]

For many elite thinkers—especially the emergent group of neoconservatives—Kissinger's pragmatic strategy underestimated the threat the NIEO posed. This position crystallized, as historian Michael Franczak has shown, in the magazine *Commentary*. Seeing the NIEO not as a concrete program of international economic policy but as a civilizational challenge to Western liberalism, writers Daniel Patrick Moynihan, Irving Kristol, and Robert W. Tucker portrayed it as an exemplar of how the anticolonial independence movements of the middle of the century had gone wrong.[56]

Moynihan declared this verdict with particular fervor. In March 1975, after returning from a two-year stint as US ambassador to India, Moynihan penned an article in *Commentary* denouncing the demands for global wealth redistribution emanating from the postcolonial world. Moynihan argued that US policymakers must begin by recognizing that the NIEO represented a flowering of a "distinctive ideology at work in the Third World." Refusing to credit the thinkers and statesmen of the decolonizing world with an original political outlook, Moynihan ascribed their ideology to the influence of British Fabian socialism—conveyed through Harold Laski, who had indeed forged connections with key anti- and postcolonial leaders—mixed with a fixation on the "ethnic discrimination corresponding to class distinctions in industrial society." The existence of this ideology required that the United States adopt a posture of "opposition" to the "new majority" of postcolonial states in the United Nations. This opposition must include not only a rejection of the NIEO's policy demands, he argued, but an overt denunciation of the argument that colonialism was primarily responsible for the underdevelopment and poverty so pervasive in the Third World. Economic conditions in postcolonial states are "of their own making and no one else's, and no claim on anyone else arises in consequence." The NIEO was, in this rendering, an unjustified call for help directed at those who had no responsibility over the conditions in the decolonizing world.[57]

The NIEO also represented, to Moynihan and other neoconservatives, a global analog to the excesses of the New Left and Black Power movements at home. Just as "American liberalism experienced [a] depreciation in the 1960s" in the face of domestic radical movements, Moynihan argued, "international liberalism" was undergoing the same devaluation in the face of the "radical demands" of the NIEO. Robert Tucker, striking a similar chord in another article for *Commentary*, declared that the supposedly permissive response by the United States to the NIEO "extends earlier confusions and mistakes about domestic equality into the debate about global equality." Accusations that liberal guilt over slavery, colonialism, and segregation had blinded Americans to the need to defend the Western liberal capitalist order against radical challengers, both domestic and international, pervaded this commentary. The "obsession with the West's past sins," as Tucker put it, constituted a "failure of will." On this account, the affective response of American liberals both to decolonization and to movements against racial and economic inequality at home had been one of extreme permissiveness—not of co-optation and rejection. And this response, in the eyes of conservatives, had allowed movements for decolonization and civil rights to transform into radical challenges to the existing order.[58]

Although the neoconservative response to the NIEO was not universal, it became widely influential both among policymakers and in the broader climate of opinion. Despite Moynihan's criticisms of the Ford administration's policy—or perhaps because of them—Ford appointed him ambassador to the United Nations in the months after the publication of his article in *Commentary*. The longstanding efforts by American foreign policy elites to delimit and contain the meaning of decolonization, which had been pronounced in the debates over the definition of colonialism in the early 1960s, transformed in the 1970s into a growing mistrust of postcolonial sovereignty writ large. The NIEO seemed to bear out the concern that the definition of colonialism had been expanded too far—a concern which was only amplified by the association of the language of colonialism with Black Power at home.[59]

Ever the astute observer, St. Clair Drake identified the common thread in Moynihan's views about the decolonizing world and his opinion of the Black freedom movement. In an article in *The Nation*, published just after Moynihan's appointment to the UN ambassadorship, Drake observed a parallel between Moynihan's ideas about the NIEO and his earlier pronouncements on African American poverty. Moynihan's 1965 report on *The Negro Family: The Case for National Action*, written when he worked in the Johnson administration's Department of Labor, had grown infamous for its racist demonization of Black families, and especially Black mothers. Although advocating job creation programs for Black men that exceeded the War on Poverty's commitments, the report insisted that the internal structure of Black families was defined by a "tangle of pathology" that held the greatest share of responsibility for perpetuating Black poverty. At the end of the 1960s, Moynihan argued—in a memo to Richard Nixon that gained almost equal notoriety to his 1965 report—that issues of racial discrimination might benefit from a period of "benign neglect" in national politics. These perspectives on Black inequality, Drake argued, "have now been transferred to the world scene." Moynihan's "refusal to accept concepts of 'exploitation' and 'reparations'" in the global arena represented no more than the "international extension of his oft-reiterated refusal to consider 'white racism' in the United States as the basic cause of Black poverty." Nor was this linkage limited to Moynihan alone. Deep commonalities remained in the ways US policymakers treated Black Americans and the postcolonial world, in Drake's view—especially when it came to demands for economic redistribution.[60]

Drake wrote his rebuke to Moynihan around the same time that he argued that the idea of the internal colony had "outlived its usefulness to Black Americans." The specific analogy had faltered as a guideline for Black political thought because of the ambiguities in its economic implications and the scale of its applicability. But Drake held onto central insights of the Black internationalist politics from which the language of internal colonialism had emerged. Black Americans, he insisted, should continue to link their struggles against racial and class inequality in the United States with hopes for a more egalitarian global order. Whatever the language used, Black internationalism, for Drake, must pursue a broad reconstruction of both domestic and world economies to repair the racialized economic exploitation at the heart of the colonial project.[61]

Epilogue

The politics of colonial comparison influenced vital struggles over the meaning of American democracy from the Second World War through the era of Black Power. The waning political salience of the idea of internal colonialism does not erase its significance as both an agent and an emblem of political conflict in the midcentury decades. From the 1940s through the middle of the 1970s, global decolonization generated new political vocabularies in the United States—for liberal, radical, and conservative elements in the Black freedom movement, for social policymakers and social scientists, and for politicians at the highest levels of American politics.

Three main factors explain why the impact of global decolonization on American political discourse faded. One was the continuing fragmentation of the Black Power movement. Already apparent by the early 1970s, the movement's divisions only grew as the decade wore on. Many cultural nationalist organizations, from the US Organization to the widespread independent Pan-African nationalist school movement, increasingly turned inward, abjuring political engagement aimed at systemic transformation in favor of the pursuit of Afrocentric educational and cultural forms. As the membership of the Black Panther Party declined due to state repression and internal division, its national leadership turned its focus to electoral politics in Oakland, devoting resources and organizing energy to supporting the unsuccessful candidacies of Bobby Seale for mayor and Elaine Brown for city council. Black-led feminist groups, such as the Third World Women's Alliance (TWWA), continued to fly the banner of Third World solidarity in the late 1970s, incorporating imperialism alongside sexism and racism as the three pillars of the "Triple Jeopardy" against which they struggled. All of these efforts demonstrate the continued potency of the symbols, organizing strategies, and ideologies of

Black Power beyond the years of its peak influence in the late 1960s and early 1970s. Yet the ambitious idea of formulating a national program for political-economic change under the rubric of internal decolonization—the vision that had animated the National Black Economic Development Conference of 1969—had largely receded from view a decade later.[1]

A second major factor was the diminishing significance of decolonization to US foreign policymakers. Although President Jimmy Carter appointed former SCLC leader Andrew Young as ambassador to the United Nations, where he repudiated Moynihan's positioning of the United States "in opposition" to the organized efforts of the G-77, this brief period of rapprochement was an exception to the broader trend. The rise of human rights rhetoric both in activist circles and among American foreign policymakers during the late 1970s marked the continuing decline of postcolonial sovereignty as a fundamental normative principle in global politics. With the election of Ronald Reagan and the ascent of the New Right in US domestic politics, moreover, came a thorough disparagement of the place of the decolonizing world in international affairs. The new administration's approach, exemplified by UN ambassador Jeane Kirkpatrick, combined Moynihan's sense of US aggrievement by G-77 demands with an even deeper belief that US interests were coterminous with the world's. At the same time, the Third World debt crisis put an end to calls for a New International Economic Order. Sparked by Mexico's default on $80 billion of its sovereign debt, the crisis—which had its worst effects in Latin America but hit dozens of countries across the Middle East, Africa, and Asia as well—represented the signal global consequence of the "Volcker Shock," or the US Federal Reserve's decision to increase interest rates dramatically after 1979. In the absence of an organized push to restructure the global economy, and with dozens of Third World nations appealing to the International Monetary Fund (IMF) and Western creditors for debt relief, US policymakers could safely see the postcolonial world as a less significant priority. As the New Right ascended in domestic politics, and as the Third World debt crisis altered the perception of the postcolonial world in international politics, views of African Americans as part of a global majority of oppressed peoples were increasingly met with suspicion.[2]

Third, the worsening effects of deindustrialization changed the terms of debate for Black thinkers and activists who examined metropolitan political economy. A pastoralist tradition in Black nationalist thought, which linked demands for Black self-determination to the agrarian land of the US South and often described urban life as beset by pathology—sometimes in language not wholly dissimilar from the conservative obsession with urban disorder—gained adherents in the early 1970s. While the challenges to achieving widespread Black landownership, let alone sovereignty, in rural settings caused many Black nationalists to revise this pastoralist vision, the appeal of an escape from the postindustrial urban environment persisted. For those who continued to focus on urban political economies, the rise of the concept of the "underclass" to characterize the class position of Black people living in areas of concentrated poverty displaced earlier frameworks beginning in the early 1980s. Although some proponents of the "underclass" idea, including William Julius Wilson, endorsed social-democratic reforms, the concept shared with the earlier idea of a culture of poverty a focus on supposed behavioral differences of poor city dwellers, and, in doing so, often buttressed arguments for limiting welfare and other forms of aid to the poor. The language of internal colonialism, for all its imprecision, had authorized a broader political vision than the vocabulary of the "underclass" that came to supplant it. For James and Grace Lee Boggs, for instance, the comparison between postindustrial disinvestment and postcolonial underdevelopment inspired their efforts to reconstruct global and metropolitan political economies on a more equal basis.[3]

To be sure, the vision of US racial hierarchy as enmeshed with a system of global inequality that emerged from the history of colonialism has continued to hold a place in African American political thought since the middle of the 1970s. Organizations such as TransAfrica, led by Randall Robinson, brought a version of this argument to its interventions in antiapartheid activism and the politics of international development in Africa and the Caribbean, often in conjunction with important voices in the Congressional Black Caucus, such as Mickey Leland and Shirley Chisholm. These ideas broke through to the highest levels of national politics in the presidential campaigns of Rev. Jesse Jackson in 1984 and 1988, which brought unprecedented attention to a Black internationalist politics that linked American racial oppression with both the system of apartheid in South Africa and the Israeli occupation of Palestine. But, in the decades since the denouement of decolonization and the fragmentation of the Black Power movement, this global vision has often been looked upon as a rejected strain in Black politics.[4]

The backlash against Black Power within American liberalism took special aim at its internationalism. A plethora of examples of this phenomenon can be found in the public statements of former president Barack Obama. Undoubtedly, Obama's decision to frame his personal narrative and political success in terms of American exceptionalism and the triumph of multiculturalism derived from his exceptional political instincts as a politician in a majority-white country, combined with a well-founded fear of racist criticisms of the first Black president, especially one with an African father.

Contrary to conservative conspiracy theories that labeled Obama a rabid anti-colonialist, the former president argued consistently that an orientation toward decolonization and its legacies is a dead end for global Black politics in the twenty-first century.[5]

A prime instance of this attitude shone through in a town hall Obama hosted in 2014. The attendees were the first class of the Mandela Washington Fellowship for Young African Leaders, which brings African students and young people to the United States for academic training and professional development. A young Kenyan man in the group asked the president the most pointed question of the event. The young man laid the responsibility for continued problems of underdevelopment, disease, and starvation in Africa on the "very huge debts" owed by "our governments" to the IMF, the World Bank, and the wealthy nations of the world. "As a global leader in the family of nations," he asked, "when will the U.S. lead . . . in forgiving Africa these debts so that our governments can be in a position to deliver and provide . . . social, health care, and . . . infrastructural development services to our people?"[6]

Obama's response exemplified a common tendency to dismiss the legacy of colonialism on the contemporary world. Acknowledging that questions of dependency and the terms of trade among developing and developed countries were hot topics "when I was a college student," Obama dismissed arguments about the impact of colonialism on African underdevelopment as an academic fad. Now, he said, "we have to stop looking elsewhere for solutions." While acknowledging that a small number of loans and past practices might need to be reexamined on narrow grounds, his response insisted that failures of internal governance were the major cause of African poverty. The connection between the historical and the prescriptive portions of Obama's answer was clear. If the history of colonialism was ruled irrelevant, African debt service payments to the West should keep flowing.[7]

In fact, the condition of indebtedness represents perhaps the clearest instance of the continuities in the forms of racialized economic exploitation that face the American city and the postcolonial world today. As historian Destin Jenkins has written, US cities face a regime of "bondholder supremacy" that maintains an "infrastructural investment in whiteness" and condemns Black neighborhoods and majority-Black cities to continuing crises of austerity and disinvestment.[8] Similar conditions of creditor power enforce the primacy of debt service over social welfare spending, both in territories that continue to chafe under colonial rule, such as Puerto Rico, and postcolonial states, such as Ghana and Zambia, among others.[9] Debt has become a primary mechanism through which predominantly white financiers can override democratic decision-making in, and extract resources from, predominantly Black and

Brown cities and nation-states.[10] Colonial comparisons may not resonate in the same way they once did in the time of the world-historical transformation of decolonization. But regimes of racialized economic exploitation still operate across multiple scales—ensnaring localities and nations alike in a web of indebtedness, undemocratic rule, and violence. Any effort to confront such conditions requires a political vocabulary that makes these connections clear. A politics that envisions the domestic in light of the international remains essential.

Acknowledgments

No work is the product of one person alone. Whatever is valuable in this book owes much to the collaboration, critique, support, and solidarity of many other people. Any errors are, of course, my own.

First, at Harvard, I thank Jim Kloppenberg, who is a model of intellectual generosity. This book bears the imprint of innumerable conversations with him. His rigorous approach to the study of ideas and his openness to those he may not share are rare qualities. Evelyn Brooks Higginbotham has provided essential mentorship and commentary. Her encyclopedic knowledge of African American history and her ability to see the connections between small details and the largest historical questions shaped both the framing of this book and the way I approached its sources. Samuel Moyn helped me think through the international politics of decolonization and always pushed me to articulate the critical stakes of this project in the present. Nikhil Pal Singh's incisive comments helped me explore more deeply the relation between language and social action. Brandon Terry gave generously of his deep reservoir of knowledge of Black political thought and insisted that I never let narrative supersede careful conceptual analysis. His sharp mind and unwavering belief in this project have been invaluable, and this book owes a great deal to his intellectual engagement, practical support, and good humor.

Other scholars have given generously of their time, insight, and support. Elizabeth Hinton pointed me toward important sources and pushed me to think deeply about the relationship between Black activism and state power. Erez Manela offered numerous suggestions and urged me to consider the implications of my research for international history. Durba Mitra lent her support and gave helpful comments in several key moments. In the early phases of the project, Nancy Cott gave indispensable advice, and Walter Johnson provided a valuable model of how to pursue rigorous historical scholarship while speaking to the politics of the moment.

Several chapters of what became this book were originally tested and argued over in Harvard's Twentieth-Century US History Workshop. I am especially grateful to Lisa McGirr for encouraging me to situate my work in relation to major questions in US political history. The participants contributed significantly to what this book became: Jacob Anbinder, Ella Antell, Tim Barker, Rudi Batzell, Aaron Bekemeyer, Colin Bossen, John Gee, Balraj Gill, Tina Groeger, Elizabeth Katz, Abigail Modaff, Jacob Moses, Kristin Oberiano, Yukako Otori, Charles Petersen, Andrew Pope, Rachel Steely, Erica Sterling, and Gili Vidan. Erik Baker, Brandon Bloch, Jonathon Booth, Charles Clavey, Bradley Craig, Hardeep Dhillon, Ruodi Duan, Erin Hutchinson, Gili Kliger, Joseph La Hausse de Lalouvière, Charlotte Lloyd, Zachary Nowak, Samantha Payne, Sonia Tycko, Lydia Walker, Jackie Wang, and Azmar Williams further contributed to an intellectual community that left an indelible mark on this project.

I am grateful to a number of others who read and commented on chapters, conference papers, and workshop presentations, including Anne-Marie Angelo, Abou Bamba, Mari Crabtree, Manu Goswami, Daniel Immerwahr, Annette Joseph-Gabriel, Sarah Miller-Davenport, Maribel Morey, Tejasvi Nagaraja, Eric Porter, David Myer Temin, and Penny Von Eschen.

Special thanks go to Tom Arnold-Forster, Merve Fejzula, and Aziz Rana, who read the entire manuscript and gave me vital feedback. Adom Getachew and an anonymous reader provided sharp and discerning peer reviews of the manuscript for the press, and I am extremely grateful for their acuity and generosity.

I have further benefited from insightful discussions about the material in this book with Wendell Adjetey, Carol Anderson, Casey Nelson Blake, Stephanie DeGooyer, Christopher Dietrich, James Thuo Gathii, Jessica Levy, Daniel Matlin, Melani McAlister, Joanne Meyerowitz, Amy Offner, Sarah Reckhow, Russell Rickford, Barbara Savage, Stuart Schrader, Tommie Shelby, Brad Simpson, Christy Thornton, Katherine Turk, Robert Vitalis, Stephen Wertheim, and Chad Williams. Maro Riofrancos allowed me to interview him and gave generously of his time and recollections.

Several institutions provided financial support. The Radcliffe Institute for Advanced Study, the Edmond and Lily Safra Center for Ethics, the Weatherhead Center for International Affairs, and the Charles Warren Center for Studies in American History provided funding for research and writing at Harvard. Grants from the American Council of Learned Societies, the Lyndon B. Johnson Presidential Library, the Rockefeller Archive Center, and the Center for the Humanities at Loyola University Maryland also helped to support research travel. I am grateful for the assistance of many librarians and archivists, particularly at the Schomburg Center for Research in Black Culture at the New York Public Library, the Moorland-Spingarn Research Center at Howard University, the Walter P. Reuther Library at Wayne State University, the Harvard University Archives, the Bancroft Library at the University of California at Berkeley, the John F. Kennedy Presidential Library, the Rockefeller Archive Center, and the Library of Congress.

A fellowship at the Fox Center for Humanistic Inquiry at Emory University provided additional financial support and connected me with wonderful colleagues who helped expand my horizons and clarify my ideas. Keith Anthony and Colette Barlow were extremely welcoming and helped make my time there enjoyable and productive. Peter Kitlas, Kylie Smith, Nathan Suhr-Sytsma, Bethany Wade, and George Yancy gave perceptive comments at key moments. I am especially grateful to Trace Peterson for her insight, camaraderie, and support then and since.

A fellowship at the Charles Warren Center for Studies in American History at Harvard introduced me to an incredibly talented group of scholars. I am grateful to Martha Biondi, Charisse Burden-Stelly, Magana Kabugi, Traci Parker, J. T. Roane, Robyn Spencer Antoine, Jackie Wang, and Jasmin Young for their critical commentary and support. Special thanks to Jarvis Givens and Brandon Terry for the opportunity to participate in the "New Directions in Black Power Studies" seminar.

At Loyola University Maryland, I have been fortunate to share a department with welcoming and supportive colleagues. In particular, Nadine Fenchak, Matthew Mulcahy, Oghenetoja Okoh, Andrew Ross, Willeke Sandler, and the members of the Junior Faculty Symposium have supported my research and helped me navigate the demands of teaching while completing this book.

Parts of chapters 1 and 2 previously appeared in "The Phelps-Stokes Fund and the Institutional Imagination of Black Internationalism, 1941–1945," *Diplomatic History* 46, no. 4 (September 2022): 675–700. A portion of chapter 5 appeared in "First New Nation or Internal Colony? Modernization Theorists, Black Intellectuals, and the Politics of Colonial Comparison in the Kennedy Years," in *Globalizing the U.S. Presidency: Postcolonial Views of John F. Kennedy*, ed. Cyrus Schayegh (London, 2020), 19–33. Thanks to Oxford University Press and Bloomsbury Academic, an imprint of Bloomsbury Publishing Plc., for permission to reprint this material.

I have been fortunate to be able to test out some of the ideas in this book in different and less scholarly forms in several outlets. Many thanks to the editors I've worked with—Kaavya Asoka, Matt Lord, Ben Platt, Tim Shenk, and Usha Sahay—for helping to sharpen my thinking and my prose.

At the University of Chicago Press, Tim Mennel has been an ideal editor. His enthusiasm and support, along with his insight and skill, have been crucial to seeing this project through. I also thank Olivia Aguilar, Andrea Blatz, Carol McGillivray, and Adriana Smith for their help in making this book a reality.

I wrote much of what became this book amid an intense period of struggle in the academic labor movement, and my experiences as an organizer influenced my understanding of how history is made. I am deeply grateful to my companions involved in organizing the Harvard Graduate Students Union-UAW Local 5118 for their friendship, inspiration, and solidarity. There are too many to name—which is all the more gratifying—but I especially want to thank Ella Antell, Erik Baker, Rudi Batzell, Aaron Bekemeyer, Hyacinth Blanchard, Justin Bloesch, Cherrie Bucknor, Belle Cheves, Joe Cronin, Ellora Derenoncourt, Maggie Doherty, Andy Donnelly, Josh Gilbert, Jenna Grady, Tina Groeger, Ken Lang, Marena Lin, Brandon Mancilla, Jack Nicoludis, Felix Owusu, Sarah Schlotter, Niha Singh, Camille Traslavina, Abbie Weil, Lisa Xu, and Ege Yumuşak.

Two friends deserve special recognition for their role in helping this book come to fruition. Bradley Craig has been a kindred spirit, a source of warmth, care, sage advice, and good humor, and a major influence on my thinking. Merve Fejzula has been an intellectual companion of the highest order, and I thank her for sharing research materials, for collaborating on conference panels, for commenting incisively on various versions of this book, and, most importantly, for her enlivening and supportive friendship.

My greatest thanks go to my family. Jim and Kerry Joseph opened their home to me and welcomed me into their family, and I am grateful for all the encouragement they've given to my work over the years. My brother, Nate Klug, has been my biggest supporter ever since he taught me how to climb out of the crib. A wonderful companion in the life of the mind, he has been a source of guidance, inspiration, and joy throughout the writing of this book. My parents, Kate Stearns and Richard Klug, to whom this book is dedicated, are my first and greatest teachers. Their commitments to working hard, building a meaningful life, and taking care with language, ideas, and most of all people have inspired me, and they have given me boundless support and love. Maddy Joseph, to whom this book is also dedicated, is a true partner in thought and life. She has read, heard, and commented on countless versions of the ideas in this book. I owe a great deal to her brilliance and perceptiveness, but even more to her joyous and sustaining presence in my life.

Notes

Introduction

1. Stephen M. Ward, *In Love and Struggle: The Revolutionary Lives of James and Grace Lee Boggs* (Chapel Hill: University of North Carolina Press, 2016), 327.

2. James Boggs, "The Myth and Irrationality of Black Capitalism," *Review of Black Political Economy* 1, no. 1 (Spring–Summer 1970): 28, 30; Keith Dye, "The Debate on Reparations before the Debate on Reparations at the National Black Economic Development Conference in Detroit, 1969," *Michigan Historical Review* 46, no. 2 (Fall 2020): 175–76.

3. Albert Wohlstetter, "The Delicate Balance of Terror," *Foreign Affairs* 37, no. 1 (1958): 211.

4. Albert Wohlstetter and Roberta Wohlstetter, "Metaphors and Models: Inequalities and Disorder at Home and Abroad," RAND Corporation, D-17664-RC/ISA, August 27, 1968.

5. Wohlstetter and Wohlstetter, "Metaphors and Models."

6. Quoted in James Miller, *"Democracy Is in the Streets": From Port Huron to the Siege of Chicago* (Cambridge, MA: Harvard University Press, 1994), 232.

7. John Kenneth Galbraith, *The Affluent Society* (Boston: Houghton Mifflin, 1960); Daniel Bell, *The End of Ideology: On the Exhaustion of Political Ideologies in the Fifties* (Glencoe, IL: Free Press, 1960); Howard Brick, *Daniel Bell and the Decline of Intellectual Radicalism: Social Theory and Political Reconciliation in the 1940s* (Madison: University of Wisconsin Press, 1988); Howard Brick, *Age of Contradiction: American Thought and Culture in the 1960s* (New York: Twayne, 1998). On the "politics of nominalization," see Brent Hayes Edwards, "The Uses of Diaspora," *Social Text* 19, no. 1 (Spring 2001): 46.

8. See especially Peniel E. Joseph, *Waiting 'til the Midnight Hour: A Narrative History of Black Power in America* (New York: Henry Holt, 2006); Ashley Farmer, *Remaking Black Power: How Black Women Transformed an Era* (Chapel Hill: University of North Carolina Press, 2017); Sean Malloy, *Out of Oakland: Black Panther Party Internationalism during the Cold War* (Ithaca, NY: Cornell University Press, 2017); Christopher Tinson, *Radical Intellect: Liberator Magazine and Black Activism in the 1960s* (Chapel Hill: University of North Carolina Press, 2017). My work on the politics of colonial comparison in the United States owes a significant debt to the work of Ann Laura Stoler on the "politics of comparison" in colonial regimes and postcolonial studies. See especially Ann Laura Stoler, "Tense and Tender Ties: The Politics of Comparison in North American History and (Post) Colonial Studies," *Journal of American History* 88, no. 3 (December 2001): 829–65; and Ann Laura Stoler, *Carnal Knowledge and Imperial Power* (Berkeley:

University of California Press, 2010). Other important works on the politics of comparison include Michael G. Hanchard, *The Spectre of Race: How Discrimination Haunts Western Democracy* (Princeton, NJ: Princeton University Press, 2018); Manu Goswami, "Imaginary Futures and Colonial Internationalisms," *American Historical Review* 117, no. 5 (December 2012): 1461–85; Benedict Anderson, *The Spectre of Comparisons: Nationalism, Southeast Asia, and the World* (New York: Verso, 1998).

9. Martin Delany, *The Condition, Elevation, Emigration, and Destiny of the Colored People of the United States, Politically Considered* (1852; Baltimore: Black Classic Press, 1993), 12; Tommie Shelby, "Two Conceptions of Black Nationalism: Martin Delany on the Meaning of Black Political Solidarity," *Political Theory* 31, no. 5 (October 2003): 664–92. On the importance of intra-European empires, and their dissolution, for the intellectual history of empire and decolonization globally, see Natasha Wheatley, *The Life and Death of States: Central Europe and the Transformation of Modern Sovereignty* (Princeton, NJ: Princeton University Press, 2023).

10. Adom Getachew, "A 'Common Spectacle' of the Race: Garveyism's Visual Politics of Founding," *American Political Science Review* 115, no. 4 (November 2021): 1197–1209; Cyril Briggs quoted in Minkah Makalani, *In the Cause of Freedom: Radical Black Internationalism from Harlem to London, 1917–1939* (Chapel Hill: University of North Carolina Press, 2011), 38; *The 1928 and 1930 Comintern Resolutions on the Black National Question in the United States* (Washington, DC: Revolutionary Review, 1975), http://www.marx2mao.com/Other/CR75.html; W. E. B. Du Bois, "A Negro Nation within a Nation," *Current History* (June 1935).

11. Todd Shepard argues that, in the French case, policymakers and intellectuals portrayed decolonization as part of the "tide of history" in order to absolve the French state of responsibility both for colonial violence and for the condition of former French citizens in Algeria. See Todd Shepard, *The Invention of Decolonization: The Algerian War and the Remaking of France* (Ithaca, NY: Cornell University Press, 2008). For the British case, see John Darwin, *Britain and Decolonisation: The Retreat from Empire in the Post-War World* (London: Macmillan, 1988). On the diverse cultural, political, and intellectual effects of the Great Migration, see especially Davarian L. Baldwin, *Chicago's New Negroes: Modernity, the Great Migration, and Black Urban Life* (Chapel Hill: University of North Carolina Press, 2007); Keneshia N. Grant, *The Great Migration and the Democratic Party: Black Voters and the Realignment of American Politics in the 20th Century* (Philadelphia: Temple University Press, 2020); and Winston James, *Holding Aloft the Banner of Ethiopia: Caribbean Radicalism in Early Twentieth-Century America* (New York: Verso, 1998).

12. Daniel B. Schwartz, *Ghetto: The History of a Word* (Cambridge, MA: Harvard University Press, 2019); Mitchell Duneier, *Ghetto: The Invention of a Place, the History of an Idea* (New York: Farrar, Straus, and Giroux, 2016); Eric J. Sundquist, *Strangers in the Land: Blacks, Jews, Post-Holocaust America* (Cambridge, MA: Harvard University Press, 2005).

13. Aziz Rana, *The Constitutional Bind: How Americans Came to Idolize a Document That Fails Them* (Chicago: University of Chicago Press, 2024), 398.

14. Malcolm X, "Message to the Grassroots," in *Malcolm X Speaks*, ed. George Breitman (New York: Grove Press, 1965), 8; Dan Berger, *Captive Nation: Black Prison Organizing in the Civil Rights Era* (Chapel Hill: University of North Carolina Press, 2014), especially 49–90; Garrett Felber, *Those Who Know Don't Say: The Nation of Islam, the Black Freedom Movement, and the Carceral State* (Chapel Hill: University of North Carolina Press, 2020).

15. Berger, *Captive Nation;* Schwartz, *Ghetto;* Duneier, *Ghetto.*

16. While other scholars have at times drawn a distinction between the idea of a "colonial analogy" and the idea of an "internal colony thesis," this book uses the terms flexibly to avoid

constant repetition, except in such cases where this distinction mattered for the historical actors involved.

17. See, among others, Ras Makonnen, *Pan-Africanism from Within*, ed. Kenneth King (New York: Oxford University Press, 1973); Hakim Adi, *Pan-Africanism: A History* (London: Bloomsbury, 2018); Keisha N. Blain, *Set the World on Fire: Black Nationalist Women and the Global Struggle for Freedom* (Philadelphia: University of Pennsylvania Press, 2018); and Robin D. G. Kelley, *Freedom Dreams: The Black Radical Imagination* (Boston: Beacon, 2002). On the discourse of civilization, see Michael Adas, "Contested Hegemony: The Great War and the Afro-Asian Assault on the Civilizing Mission Ideology," *Journal of World History* 15, no. 1 (March 2004): 31–63. An incisive account of the importance of the Manchester Congress for African American internationalism is found in John James Munro, *The Anticolonial Front: The African American Freedom Struggle and Global Decolonisation, 1945–1960* (Cambridge: Cambridge University Press, 2017), 37–74.

18. Kevin K. Gaines, *American Africans in Ghana: Black Expatriates and the Civil Rights Era* (Chapel Hill: University of North Carolina Press, 2006), 5.

19. James Boggs and Grace Lee Boggs, "The City Is the Black Man's Land," *Monthly Review* 17, no. 11 (April 1966), reprinted in James Boggs, *Racism and the Class Struggle: Further Pages from a Black Worker's Notebook* (New York: Monthly Review, 1970), 39–50; Musab Younis, *On the Scale of the World: The Formation of Black Anticolonial Thought* (Oakland: University of California Press, 2022), 7.

20. Tiffany Lethabo King, *The Black Shoals: Offshore Formations of Black and Native Studies* (Durham, NC: Duke University Press, 2019).

21. David Myer Temin, *Remapping Sovereignty: Decolonization and Self-Determination in North American Indigenous Political Thought* (Chicago: University of Chicago Press, 2023), 27–62; Vine Deloria Jr., *Custer Died for Your Sins: An Indian Manifesto* (1969; Norman: University of Oklahoma Press, 1988).

22. This formulation owes an obvious debt to Matthew Connelly's declaration that international historians should "take off the Cold War lens." See Matthew Connelly, "Taking Off the Cold War Lens: Visions of North-South Conflict during the Algerian War for Independence," *American Historical Review* 105, no. 3 (June 2000): 739–69.

23. The monumental literature on the New Deal order, in particular, pays little to no attention to decolonization. See especially Steve Fraser and Gary Gerstle, eds., *The Rise and Fall of the New Deal Order, 1930–1980* (Princeton, NJ: Princeton University Press, 1989); James T. Patterson, *Grand Expectations: The United States, 1945–1974* (New York: Oxford University Press, 1997); Ira Katznelson, *Fear Itself: The New Deal and the Origins of Our Time* (New York: Liveright, 2013); Jefferson Cowie, *The Great Exception: The New Deal and the Limits of American Politics* (Princeton, NJ: Princeton University Press, 2017); and Gary Gerstle, Nelson Lichtenstein, and Alice O'Connor, eds., *Beyond the New Deal Order: U.S. Politics from the Great Depression to the Great Recession* (Philadelphia: University of Pennsylvania Press, 2019). On the language of "free enterprise," see Elizabeth A. Fones-Wolf, *Selling Free Enterprise: The Business Assault on Labor and Liberalism, 1945–60* (Urbana: University of Illinois Press, 1994); Wendy L. Wall, *Inventing the "American Way": The Politics of Consensus from the New Deal to the Civil Rights Movement* (New York: Oxford University Press, 2008); and Lawrence B. Glickman, *Free Enterprise: An American History* (New Haven, CT: Yale University Press, 2019). On defense spending, see Tim Barker, "Cold War Capitalism: The Political Economy of American Military Spending, 1947–1990" (PhD diss., Harvard University, 2022). On the chilling effects of Cold War anticommunism,

see especially Ellen Schrecker, *Many Are the Crimes: McCarthyism in America* (Princeton, NJ: Princeton University Press, 1998).

24. Odd Arne Westad, *The Global Cold War: Third World Interventions and the Making of Our Times* (Cambridge: Cambridge University Press, 2005); Odd Arne Westad, "Exploring the Histories of the Cold War: A Pluralist Approach," in *Uncertain Empire: American History and the Idea of the Cold War,* ed. Joel Isaac and Duncan Bell (New York: Oxford University Press, 2012); Odd Arne Westad, *The Cold War: A World History* (New York: Basic Books, 2017). One example of the literature on the "global Cold War" that acknowledges more clearly the autonomous dynamics of decolonization is Paul Thomas Chamberlin, *The Cold War's Killing Fields: Rethinking the Long Peace* (New York: Harper, 2018). Scholars of East Asian history and Asian American history and literature have produced some of the foremost attempts to rethink the Cold War paradigm. See, for example, Masuda Hajimu, *Cold War Crucible: The Korean Conflict and the Postwar World* (Cambridge, MA: Harvard University Press, 2015); and Jodi Kim, *Ends of Empire: Asian American Critique and the Cold War* (Minneapolis: University of Minnesota Press, 2010).

25. Raymond Williams, *Keywords: A Vocabulary of Culture and Society* (New York: Oxford University Press, 1976).

26. See especially Frederick Cooper, *Decolonization and African Society: The Labor Question in French and British Africa* (Cambridge: Cambridge University Press, 1996); Frederick Cooper, *Citizenship between Empire and Nation: Remaking France and French Africa, 1945–1960* (Princeton, NJ: Princeton University Press, 2014); Margaret Kohn and Keally McBride, *Political Theories of Decolonization: Postcolonialism and the Problem of Foundations* (New York: Oxford University Press, 2011); Gary Wilder, *Freedom Time: Negritude, Decolonization, and the Future of the World* (Durham, NC: Duke University Press, 2015); Adom Getachew, *Worldmaking after Empire: The Rise and Fall of Self-Determination* (Princeton, NJ: Princeton University Press, 2019); and Younis, *On the Scale.* For examples of the earlier view, see John Plamenatz, *On Alien Rule and Self-Government* (London: Longman's, 1960); and Hedley Bull and Adam Watson, eds., *The Expansion of International Society* (Oxford: Clarendon, 1984).

27. Glenda Sluga and Patricia Clavin, "Rethinking the History of Internationalism," in *Internationalisms: A Twentieth-Century History,* ed. Glenda Sluga and Patricia Clavin (Cambridge: Cambridge University Press, 2017), 5. On Black internationalism in the early Cold War, see Gerald Horne, *Black and Red: W. E. B. Du Bois and the Afro-American Response to the Cold War, 1944–1963* (Albany: State University of New York Press, 1986); Brenda Gayle Plummer, *Rising Wind: Black Americans and U.S. Foreign Affairs, 1935–1960* (Chapel Hill: University of North Carolina Press, 1996); Penny M. Von Eschen, *Race against Empire: Black Americans and Anticolonialism, 1937–1957* (Ithaca, NY: Cornell University Press, 1997); Cheryl Higashida, *Black Internationalist Feminism: Women Writers of the Black Left, 1945–1995* (Urbana: University of Illinois Press, 2011); Dayo F. Gore, *Radicalism at the Crossroads: African American Women Activists in the Cold War* (New York: New York University Press, 2011); Mary Helen Washington, *The Other Blacklist: The African American Literary and Cultural Left of the 1950s* (New York: Columbia University Press, 2014); Carol Anderson, *Bourgeois Radicals: The NAACP and the Struggle for Colonial Liberation, 1941–1960* (Cambridge: Cambridge University Press, 2015).

28. N. D. B. Connolly, "Notes on a Desegregated Method: Learning from Michael Katz and Others," *Journal of Urban History* 41, no. 4 (July 2015): 584–91; Juliet Hooker, *Theorizing Race in the Americas: Douglass, Sarmiento, Du Bois, and Vasconcelos* (New York: Oxford University

Press, 2017), 13. On the advantages of treating comparison as subject rather than method, see Micol Seigel, "Beyond Compare: Comparative Method after the Transnational Turn," *Radical History Review* 91 (Winter 2005): 62–90.

29. Frank B. Wilderson III, *Red, White & Black: Cinema and the Structure of U.S. Antagonisms* (Durham, NC: Duke University Press, 2010), 37; Frank B. Wilderson III, *Afropessimism* (New York: Norton, 2020). For an exceptionally lucid critique, including on this point, see Jesse McCarthy, "On Afropessimism," *Los Angeles Review of Books*, July 20, 2020, https://lareviewof books.org/article/on-afropessimism/.

30. Ann Laura Stoler, *Duress: Imperial Durabilities in Our Times* (Durham, NC: Duke University Press, 2016), 15. Emphasis added.

Chapter One

1. "Should I Sacrifice to Live 'Half-American'?" *Pittsburgh Courier*, January 31, 1942, 3. On the "Double V" campaign and efforts to frame anticolonial activity alongside it, see Plummer, *Rising Wind*; Kimberley L. Phillips, *War! What Is It Good For? Black Freedom Struggles and the U.S. Military from World War II to Iraq* (Chapel Hill: University of North Carolina Press, 2012); Vaughn Rasberry, *Race and the Totalitarian Century: Geopolitics in the Black Literary Imagination* (Cambridge, MA: Harvard University Press, 2016); James Meriwether, *Proudly We Can Be Africans: Black Americans and Africa, 1936–1961* (Chapel Hill: University of North Carolina Press, 2002); and Nico Slate, *Colored Cosmopolitanism: The Shared Struggle for Freedom in the United States and India* (Cambridge, MA: Harvard University Press, 2011).

2. On the "Hands Off Ethiopia" movement and its impact, see especially Joseph Fronczak, "Local People's Global Politics: A Transnational History of the Hands Off Ethiopia Movement of 1935," *Diplomatic History* 39, no. 2 (April 2015): 245–74; and Blain, *Set the World*. On left-liberal coalitions in Black internationalist activism during the war, see Von Eschen, *Race against Empire*; Horne, *Black and Red*; and Nikhil Pal Singh, *Black Is a Country: Race and the Unfinished Struggle for Democracy* (Cambridge, MA: Harvard University Press, 2004). An alternative view, which deemphasizes the left, is provided in Anderson, *Bourgeois Radicals*.

3. David Scott, *Conscripts of Modernity: The Tragedy of Colonial Enlightenment* (Durham, NC: Duke University Press, 2004), 4; David Scott, *Refashioning Futures: Criticism after Postcoloniality* (Princeton, NJ: Princeton University Press, 1999), 7.

4. Getachew, *Worldmaking after Empire*, 7; Christy Thornton, *Revolution in Development: Mexico and the Governance of the Global Economy* (Oakland: University of California Press, 2021), 13. On the history of the League of Nations mandates, see Susan Pedersen, *The Guardians: The League of Nations and the Crisis of Empire* (New York: Oxford University Press, 2015).

5. *The 1928 and 1930 Comintern Resolutions on the Black National Question in the United States* (Washington, DC: Revolutionary Review Press, 1975), http://www.marx2mao.com/Other /CR75.html.

6. Harry Haywood, *Black Bolshevik: Autobiography of an Afro-American Communist* (Chicago: Liberator, 1978), 230.

7. Ford quoted in Haywood, *Black Bolshevik*, 230. On the Black Belt thesis and Communist organizing among African Americans in the South, see Robin D. G. Kelley, *Hammer and Hoe: Alabama Communists during the Great Depression* (Chapel Hill: University of North Carolina Press, 1990); Oscar Berland, "The Emergence of the Communist Perspective on the 'Negro

Question' in America: 1919–1931: Part One," *Science & Society* 63, no. 4 (Winter 1999–2000): 411–32; Oscar Berland, "The Emergence of the Communist Perspective on the 'Negro Question' in America: 1919–1931: Part Two," *Science & Society* 64, no. 2 (Summer 2000): 194–217; Alec Fazackerley Hickmott, "'Brothers, Come North': The Rural South and the Political Imaginary of New Negro Radicalism, 1917–1923," *Intellectual History Review* 21, no. 4 (2011): 395–412.

8. Ralph Bunche, "Marxism and the 'Negro Question'" (1929), in *Ralph J. Bunche: Selected Speeches & Writings*, ed. Charles P. Henry (Ann Arbor: University of Michigan Press, 1995), 35–45, quoted at 36–37.

9. Bunche, "Marxism,'" 43–45.

10. John Crowe Ransom, "Land," *Harper's Monthly Magazine*, July 1932, 218. See also, Twelve Southerners, *I'll Take My Stand: The South and the Agrarian Tradition* (New York: Harper Brothers, 1930).

11. Rupert Vance, *Human Geography of the South*, 2nd ed. (1932; Chapel Hill: University of North Carolina Press, 1935), 467; Howard Odum, "Regionalism vs. Sectionalism in the South's Place in the National Economy," *Social Forces* 12, no. 3 (March 1934): 338–54. On Odum and Vance specifically, see Alice O'Connor, *Poverty Knowledge: Social Science, Social Policy, and the Poor in Twentieth-Century U.S. History* (Princeton, NJ: Princeton University Press, 2001), 67–73. On the political economy of southern regionalism, see Joseph J. Persky, *The Burden of Dependency: Colonial Themes in Southern Economic Thought* (Baltimore: Johns Hopkins University Press, 1992); and Natalie J. Ring, *The Problem South: Region, Empire, and the New Liberal State, 1880–1930* (Athens: University of Georgia Press, 2012). On the New Deal's influence on US international development policies, see David Ekbladh, *The Great American Mission: Modernization and the Construction of an American World Order* (Princeton, NJ: Princeton University Press, 2010).

12. Donna Jean Murch, *Living for the City: Migration, Education, and the Rise of the Black Panther Party in Oakland, California* (Chapel Hill: University of North Carolina Press, 2010), 15; Grant, *The Great Migration and the Democratic Party*, 154.

13. St. Clair Drake and Horace Cayton, *Black Metropolis: A Study of Negro Life in a Northern City* (1945; Chicago: University of Chicago Press, 2014), 762, 760. On the semantic history of the word "ghetto," see Schwartz, *Ghetto*; and Duneier, *Ghetto*.

14. Eric S. Yellin, "The (White) Search for (Black) Order: The Phelps-Stokes Fund's First Twenty Years, 1911–1931," *The Historian*, 65, no. 2 (Winter 2002): 319–52; Belinda H. Y. Chiu, *The One-Hundred-Year History of the Phelps-Stokes Fund as a Family Philanthropy, 1911–2011: The Oldest American Operating Foundation Serving the Educational Needs of the African Diaspora, Native Americans, and the Urban and Rural Poor* (Lewiston, NY: Edwin Mellen Press, 2012); Memorandum Regarding Preliminary Meeting of Committee on Africa and Peace Aims, folder 4, box 37, Phelps-Stokes Fund Papers, Schomburg Center for Research in Black Culture, New York Public Library (hereafter PSF).

15. Stephen Wertheim, *Tomorrow, The World: The Birth of U.S. Global Supremacy* (Cambridge, MA: Harvard University Press, 2020), 38. CAWPA also fits the mold of what Samuel Zipp calls the "jumble of mainstream organizations dedicated to organizing a new postwar world order" that were established early in the war. See Samuel Zipp, *The Idealist: Wendell Willkie's Wartime Quest to Build One World* (Cambridge, MA: Harvard University Press, 2020), 215.

16. Du Bois had clashed with Jones three decades earlier over his report on Black schools in the US South, which advised them to specialize in manual training. See Angela Zimmerman,

Alabama in Africa: Booker T. Washington, the German Empire, and the Globalization of the New South (Princeton, NJ: Princeton University Press, 2012), 202–3. On Du Bois's political thought in the 1940s, see Eric Porter, *The Problem of the Future World: W. E. B. Du Bois and the Race Concept at Midcentury* (Durham, NC: Duke University Press, 2010). On Logan's wartime experience, see Kenneth Robert Janken, *Rayford W. Logan and the Dilemma of the African-American Intellectual* (Amherst, MA: University of Massachusetts Press, 1993), 114–44.

17. Blain, *Set the World*, 116–27; Carter G. Woodson, review of *Progress in Negro Status and Race Relations, 1911-1946: The Thirty-Five Year Report of the Phelps Stokes Fund,* by Anson Phelps Stokes et al. (New York, 1948), Journal of Negro History, 34, no. 3 (1949): 369. On Du Bois and Jones, see Donald Johnson, "W.E.B. DuBois, Thomas Jesse Jones and the Struggle for Social Education, 1900–1930," *Journal of Negro History*, 85, no. 3 (2000): 71–95. On white philanthropists' views of Black Americans in this period, see Maribel Morey, *White Philanthropy: Carnegie Corporation's An American Dilemma and the Making of a White World Order* (Chapel Hill: University of North Carolina Press, 2021).

18. Memorandum Regarding Preliminary Meeting, folder 4, box 37, PSF; Anson Phelps Stokes to Claude A. Barnett, September 9, 1942, folder 1, box 37, PSF. On the prevalence of civilizationist views toward Africa among African American activists in this period, see Blain, *Set the World*, 133–65. On the place of these ideas in Black nationalist thought generally, see Wilson Jeremiah Moses, *The Golden Age of Black Nationalism, 1820-1925* (New York: Oxford University Press, 1988).

19. "The Atlantic Charter," in *The Avalon Project: Documents in Law, History, and Diplomacy*, https://avalon.law.yale.edu/wwii/atlantic.asp.

20. Von Eschen, *Race against Empire*, 25–28; Porter, *Problem of the Future World*, 74–77; "Hope Held Out for Revision of Atlantic Charter Aims to Include Darker Peoples," *Cleveland Call and Post*, November 28, 1942, 14.

21. Minutes of Meeting of the Executive Committee of the Committee on Africa and Peace Aims, February 7, 1942, p. 2, folder 4, box 37, PSF.

22. Minutes, Executive Committee, February 7, 1942, p. 2, PSF; Preliminary and Confidential Draft of Report for Members of the Executive Committee, p. 1, folder 5, box 37, PSF.

23. Minutes, Executive Committee, February 7, 1942, p. 4, PSF; Ernest Kalibala to Anson Phelps Stokes, March 9, 1942, p. 2, folder 4, box 37, PSF. Logan's emphasis on the link between personnel and policy also influenced his advocacy to integrate the Foreign Service after the Second World War. See Michael L. Krenn, *Black Diplomacy: African Americans and the State Department, 1945-1969* (Armonk, NY: M. E. Sharpe, 1999), 19–23.

24. W. E. B. Du Bois, "Memorandum for Committee on Africa and Peace Aims," November 1941, folder 4, box 37, PSF; W. E. B. Du Bois, "The African Roots of War," *Atlantic Monthly* 115 (May 1915): 707–14; J. A. Hobson, *Imperialism: A Study* (1902; Ann Arbor: University of Michigan Press, 1967); V. I. Lenin, *Imperialism, the Highest Stage of Capitalism: A Popular Outline* (1917; Chicago: Foreign Languages Press, 1996).

25. W. E. B. Du Bois to Anson Phelps Stokes, April 28, 1942, p. 4, folder 1, box 37, PSF.

26. Committee on Africa, the War, and Peace Aims, *The Atlantic Charter and Africa from an American Standpoint* (New York, NY, 1942), 16, 78. For the section on "indirect rule" in the initial draft, see Preliminary and Confidential Draft, pp. 15–17.

27. "The Covenant of the League of Nations," in *The Avalon Project: Documents in Law, History, and Diplomacy*, https://avalon.law.yale.edu/20th_century/leagcov.asp; Susan Pedersen,

"Samoa on the World Stage: Petitions and Peoples before the Mandates Commission of the League of Nations," *Journal of Imperial and Commonwealth History* 40, no. 2 (August 2012): 231–61; Arnulf Becker Lorca, "Petitioning the International: A 'Pre-History' of Self-Determination," *European Journal of International Law* 25, no. 2 (May 2014): 497–523.

28. Rayford Logan, "The Operation of the Mandate System in Africa," *Journal of Negro History*, 13, no. 4 (October 1928): 474; Ralph Bunche, "French Administration in Togoland and Dahomey" (PhD diss., Harvard University, 1934), especially 316–18 for Bunche's criticism of Jones.

29. Neta C. Crawford, "Decolonization through Trusteeship: The Legacy of Ralph Bunche," in *Trustee for the Human Community: Ralph J. Bunche, the United Nations, and the Decolonization of Africa*, ed. Robert A. Hill and Edmond J. Keller (Athens: Ohio University Press, 2010), 93–115; Pearl T. Robinson, "Ralph Bunche the Africanist: Revisiting Paradigms Lost," in *Trustee for the Human Community*, 84; Ralph Bunche, *A World View of Race* (Washington, DC: Associates in Negro Folk Education, 1936); Jeffrey C. Stewart, "A New Negro Foreign Policy: The Critical Vision of Alain Locke and Ralph Bunche," in *African Americans in U.S. Foreign Policy*, ed. Linda Heywood, et al. (Urbana: University of Illinois Press, 2015), 30–57, quoted at 32.

30. Preliminary and Confidential Draft, p. 45.

31. Minutes of the Meeting of Committee on Africa and Peace Aims, May 23, 1942, p. 5, folder 4, box 37, PSF.

32. Minutes, Committee on Africa and Peace Aims, p. 5.

33. Committee on Africa, the War, and Peace Aims, *Atlantic Charter and Africa*, 40, 57.

34. On these continuities, and the persistence of this ideology into the present, see Ralph Wilde, *International Territorial Administration: How Trusteeship and the Civilizing Mission Never Went Away* (New York: Oxford University Press, 2008).

35. For a critical analysis of the definition of empire as "alien rule," see Getachew, *Worldmaking after Empire*, 14–36.

36. On nonnational visions of a postimperial order, see Getachew, *Worldmaking after Empire*; Cooper, *Citizenship between Empire and Nation*; Wilder, *Freedom Time*; and Merve Fejzula, "The Cosmopolitan Historiography of Twentieth-Century Federalism," *The Historical Journal* 6, no. 2 (2021): 477–500.

37. Memo to Policy Committee from Henry Luce, November 3, 1943, folder 9, box 17, Time, Inc. File, Raymond Leslie Buell Papers, Library of Congress.

38. Committee on Africa, the War, and Peace Aims, *Atlantic Charter and Africa*, 22. On the intertwining of racial reform and US global power projection in *An American Dilemma*, see Singh, *Black Is a Country*; and Morey, *White Philanthropy*.

39. Committee on Africa, the War, and Peace Aims, *Atlantic Charter and Africa*, 19, 34.

40. Plummer, *Rising Wind*, 110.

Chapter Two

1. Brian Urquhart, *Ralph Bunche: An American Life* (New York: Norton, 1993), 102; Conyers Read to Thomas Jesse Jones, December 22, 1941, folder 1, box 37, PSF.

2. Ralph Bunche to Anson Phelps Stokes, July 15, 1942, folder 1, box 37, PSF; Urquhart, *Ralph Bunche*, 110.

3. W. A. Bennett to Anson Phelps Stokes, January 7, 1943, folder 1, box 37, PSF; "America and Africa," *Manchester Guardian*, September 18, 1942. On British colonial development during the

war, see Joseph Morgan Hodge, *Triumph of the Expert: Agrarian Doctrines of Development and the Legacies of British Colonialism* (Athens: Ohio University Press, 2007), 179–206.

4. "The Atlantic Charter and Africa," Broadcast by Dr. Anson Phelps Stokes, Town Hall on the Air, New York, NY, United Nations Day Program, January 25, 1943, folder 4, box 37, PSF.

5. "Put Africa in Peace, U.S. Urged," *Baltimore Afro-American*, June 27, 1942, 2; "Committee Suggests U.S. Protect African Interests," *Pittsburgh Courier*, June 27, 1942, 14; "All-American Committee on Africa Formed," *Chicago Defender*, June 13, 1942, 6; "African Problems Committee Releases Names of Members," *Norfolk Journal and Guide*, June 13, 1942, A18.

6. W. E. B. Du Bois, "The Future of Africa," *Phylon* 3, no. 4 (1942): 435–37.

7. Eric Williams, "Africa and the Post-War World," *Journal of Negro Education* 11, no. 4 (October 1942): 534–36.

8. "Says Africa Will Not Be Pawns for Alien Rulers: Author Urges Full Freedom on Continent," *Norfolk Journal and Guide*, August 22, 1942, 7.

9. Kwame Nkrumah, "Towards Colonial Freedom," in *Revolutionary Path* (London, 1973), 35–36. This essay, first published in 1962, was written between 1942 and 1945.

10. Merze Tate, "The War Aims of World War I and World War II and Their Relation to the Darker Peoples of the World," *Journal of Negro Education* 12, no. 3 (Summer 1943): 521–32. See also Barbara D. Savage, "Beyond Illusions: Imperialism, Race, and Technology in Merze Tate's International Thought," in *Women's International Thought: A New History*, ed. Patricia Owens and Katharina Rietzler (Cambridge: Cambridge University Press, 2021), 266–85.

11. Mark Mazower, *Governing the World: The History of an Idea, 1815 to the Present* (New York: Penguin Random House, 2012), 198–99.

12. Wm. Roger Louis, *Imperialism at Bay: The United States and the Decolonization of the British Empire, 1941–1945* (New York: Oxford University Press, 1978); Neil Smith, *American Empire: Roosevelt's Geographer and the Prelude to Globalization* (Oakland: University of California Press, 2003), 347–73.

13. Benjamin Gerig, *The Open Door and the Mandates System: A Study of Economic Equality before and since the Establishment of the Mandates System* (London: George Allen and Unwin, 1930); Louis, *Imperialism at Bay*, 114, 183.

14. Rayford Logan Diary, December 2, 1942, folder 7, box 3, Rayford W. Logan Papers, Library of Congress (hereafter RWL); Rayford Logan to Benjamin Gerig, "Memorandum on a Proposed New Mandate System," quoted in Janken, *Rayford W. Logan and the Dilemma of the African-American Intellectual*, 169; Louis, *Imperialism at Bay*, 183.

15. Louis, *Imperialism at Bay*, 231; Fred E. Pollock and Warren F. Kimball, "'In Search of Monsters to Destroy': Roosevelt and Colonialism," in Warren F. Kimball, *The Juggler: Franklin Roosevelt as Wartime Statesman* (Princeton, NJ: Princeton University Press, 1991), 127–57; Anderson, *Bourgeois Radicals*, 34–35; Elizabeth Borgwardt, *A New Deal for the World: America's Vision for Human Rights* (Cambridge, MA: Harvard University Press, 2005), 186–91.

16. Isaiah Bowman quoted in Louis, *Imperialism at Bay*, 239; On the exclusion of Indigenous self-determination claims from the international legal arena, see George Manuel and Michael Posluns, *The Fourth World: An Indian Reality* (1974; Minneapolis: University of Minnesota Press, 2019).

17. Leo Pasvolsky quoted in Louis, *Imperialism at Bay*, 241. A detailed account of Isaiah Bowman's place in postwar planning debates, including how his sympathy for the British exceeded that of many of his colleagues, is found in Smith, *American Empire*.

18. Ralph Bunche to Benjamin Gerig, January 7, 1945, pp. 1–2, folder 16, box 4, Benjamin Gerig Papers, Library of Congress. On Creech-Jones and the British Labour Party's orientation

toward the colonies, see Partha Sarathi Gupta, *Imperialism and the British Labour Movement, 1914–1964* (London: MacMillan, 1975).

19. Bunche, *A World View of Race*, 25, 49, 63; Ralph Bunche, "Africa and the Current World Conflict," *Negro History Bulletin* 4, no. 1 (October 1940): 13. For further analysis of Bunche's evolving views on the concept of race, see Jonathan Scott Holloway, *Confronting the Veil: Abram Harris Jr., E. Franklin Frazier, and Ralph Bunche, 1919–1941* (Chapel Hill: University of North Carolina Press, 2003), 162–74.

20. Ralph Bunche, "The International Implications of Far Eastern Colonial Problems," quoted in Urquhart, *Ralph Bunche*, 115.

21. "Proposals for Unity: Common Law Urged to Bind All Nations for Enduring Peace," *New York Times*, April 29, 1945, 65; Kim Cary Warren, "Mary McLeod Bethune's Feminism: Black Women as Citizens of the World," *Gender & History* 35, no. 1 (March 2023): 323–39; Plummer, *Rising Wind*, 126.

22. David Levering Lewis, *W. E. B. Du Bois: The Fight for Equality and the American Century, 1919–1963* (New York: Henry Holt and Company, 2000), 497–99; Gerald Horne, "Introduction," in W. E. B. Du Bois, *The World and Africa and Color and Democracy: Colonies and Peace*, ed. Henry Louis Gates Jr. (New York: Oxford University Press, 2007), 238.

23. W. E. B. Du Bois, *Color and Democracy: Colonies and Peace* (1945), in Du Bois, *World and Africa*, 253, 276, 300.

24. Du Bois, *Color and Democracy*, 249, 251.

25. Du Bois, *Color and Democracy*, 328.

26. Du Bois, *Color and Democracy*, 253. For more on Du Bois's capacious category of "colonialism" and "colonial peoples" in this period, see Adam Dahl, "Constructing Colonial Peoples: W. E. B. Du Bois, the United Nations, and the Politics of Space and Scale," *Modern Intellectual History* 20, no. 3 (September 2023): 858–82.

27. Du Bois, *Color and Democracy*, 254.

28. Du Bois, *Color and Democracy*, 270, 271.

29. Du Bois, *Color and Democracy*, 274, 253.

30. Du Bois, *Color and Democracy*, 294–96.

31. Alain Locke, "Race in the Present World Crisis," August 7, 1944, p. 3, folder 15, box 164–125, Alain LeRoy Locke Papers.

32. Lewis, *W. E. B. Du Bois, 1919–1963*, 500; Marika Sherwood, "'There Is No New Deal for the Blackman in San Francisco': African Attempts to Influence the Founding Conference of the United Nations, April–July, 1945," *International Journal of African Historical Studies*, 29, no. 1 (1996), 71–94.

33. George S. Schuyler, "Logan Gives Plan for Colonial Trusteeship," *Pittsburgh Courier*, April 14, 1945, 28.

34. Nkrumah quoted in Porter, *Problem of the Future World*, 90.

35. Rayford Logan Diary, April 11, 1945, folder 4, box 4, RWL; Porter, *Problem of the Future World*, 90.

36. Adi, *Pan-Africanism*, ch. 6; Munro, *The Anticolonial Front*, 37–74; "Declaration to the Colonial Workers, Farmers, and Intellectuals," in *History of the Pan-African Congress: Colonial and Coloured Unity, A Program of Action*, ed. George Padmore, 2nd ed. (London, 1963), 6; "Congress Resolutions. West Africa," in *History of the Pan-African Congress*, 55.

37. Crawford, "Decolonization through Trusteeship," 102; Urquhart, *Ralph Bunche*, 121; Ralph J. Bunche, "Trusteeship and Non-Self-Governing Territories in the Charter of the United Nations," *Department of State Bulletin*, December 30, 1945, 1037–1044.

38. "Testimony of W. E. B. Du Bois," ca. July 11, 1945, series 1A, General Correspondence, 1877−1965, W. E. B. Du Bois Papers, Special Collections and University Archives, University of Massachusetts Amherst, https://credo.library.umass.edu/view/full/mums312-b108-i336; Anderson, *Bourgeois Radicals*, 67.

39. Rayford Logan, "The System of International Trusteeship," *Journal of Negro Education*, 15, no. 3 (1946): 285−99; Rayford Logan, *The Negro and the Post-War World: A Primer* (Washington, DC: The Minorities Publishers, 1945), 88.

Chapter Three

1. Oliver Cromwell Cox, *Caste, Class, and Race: A Study in Social Dynamics* (1948; New York: Monthly Review, 1959), 580−81.

2. On the pre-1945 origins of "development," see Michael Adas, *Machines as the Measure of Men: Science, Technology, and Ideologies of Western Dominance* (Ithaca, NY: Cornell University Press, 1990); M. P. Cowen and R. W. Shenton, *Doctrines of Development* (London: Routledge, 1996); David C. Engerman, *Modernization from the Other Shore: American Intellectuals and the Romance of Russian Development* (Cambridge, MA: Harvard University Press, 2003); Thomas McCarthy, *Race, Empire, and the Idea of Human Development* (Cambridge: Cambridge University Press, 2009); Zimmerman, *Alabama in Africa*; Robert Vitalis, *White World Order, Black Power Politics: The Birth of American International Relations* (Ithaca, NY: Cornell University Press, 2015). On its postwar emergence, see Arturo Escobar, *Encountering Development: The Making and Unmaking of the Third World* (Princeton, NJ: Princeton University Press, 1995); Gilbert Rist, *The History of Development: From Western Origins to Global Faith*, trans. Patrick Camiller (New York: Zed Books, 1997); Amy L. S. Staples, *The Birth of Development: How the World Bank, Food and Agriculture Organization, and World Health Organization Changed the World, 1945−1965* (Kent, OH: Kent State University Press, 2006); Corinna Unger, *International Development: A Postwar History* (London: Bloomsbury, 2018); Sara Lorenzini, *Global Development: A Cold War History* (Princeton, NJ: Princeton University Press, 2019).

3. On African activists' appeals to the developmental missions of the British and French empires, see especially: Cooper, *Decolonization and African Society*; Frederick Cooper, "Development, Modernization, and the Social Sciences in the Era of Decolonization: The Examples of British and French Africa," in *The Ends of European Colonial Empires*, ed. Miguel Bandeira Jerónimo and António Costa Pinto (London: Palgrave Macmillan, 2015), 15−50; Mamadou Diouf, "Senegalese Development: From Mass Mobilization to Technocratic Elitism," trans. Molly Roth and Frederick Cooper, in *International Development and the Social Sciences: Essays on the History and Politics of Knowledge*, ed. Randall M. Packard and Frederick Cooper (Oakland: University of California Press, 1997), 291−319; and Priya Lal, *African Socialism in Postcolonial Tanzania: Between the Village and the World* (Cambridge: Cambridge University Press, 2015). On Bandung, see "Final Communiqué of the Asian-African Conference of Bandung," in *Asia-Africa Speak from Bandung*, ed. Ministry of Foreign Affairs, Republic of Indonesia (Djakarta: Ministry of Foreign Affairs, 1955), 161−69; and Frank Gerits, "Bandung as the Call for a Better Development Project: U.S., British, French, and Gold Coast Perceptions of the Afro-Asian Conference (1955)," *Cold War History* 16, no. 3 (2016): 255−72. On "development politics," see David Engerman, "Development Politics and the Cold War," *Diplomatic History* 41, no. 1 (2017): 1−19.

4. For one exception, focusing on the pre-1945 period, see Robert Vitalis, "The Lost World of Development Theory," *Perspectives on Politics* 14, no. 4 (December 2016): 1158−62.

5. Schrecker, *Many Are the Crimes*; Charisse Burden-Stelly, *Black Scare/Red Scare: Theorizing Capitalist Racism in the United States* (Chicago: University of Chicago Press, 2023); Gregory Briker and Justin Driver, "*Brown* and Red: Defending Jim Crow in Cold War America," *Stanford Law Review* 74 (March 2022): 447–514; Carole Boyce Davies, *Left of Karl Marx: The Political Life of Black Communist Claudia Jones* (Durham, NC: Duke University Press, 2007).

6. On the origins of Point Four, see especially Thomas G. Paterson, "Foreign Aid under Wraps: The Point Four Program," *Wisconsin Magazine of History* 56, no. 2 (Winter 1972–1973): 119–26; Sergei Y. Shenin, *The United States and the Third World: The Origins of Postwar Relations and the Point Four Program (1949–1953)* (Commack, NY: Nova Science Publishers, 1999); Ekbladh, *The Great American Mission*; Amanda Kay McVety, *Enlightened Aid: U.S. Development as Foreign Aid Policy in Ethiopia* (New York: Oxford University Press, 2012); and Stephen Macekura, "The Point Four Program and U.S. International Development," *Political Science Quarterly* 128, no. 1 (May 2013): 127–60.

7. Shenin, *United States*, 8; McVety, *Enlightened Aid*, 155. On the emergence of growth economics, see H. W. Arndt, *The Rise and Fall of Economic Growth: A Study in Contemporary Thought* (London: Longman Cheshire, 1978).

8. Harry S. Truman, "Inaugural Address," January 20, 1949, The American Presidency Project, accessed December 4, 2023, https://www.presidency.ucsb.edu/documents/inaugural-address-4.

9. Paterson, "Foreign Aid Under Wraps," 122; Shenin, *United States*, 64; Macekura, "Point Four Program," 143.

10. Mutual Security Act of 1951, Pub. L. 82–165, 65 Stat. 373 (1951), 373; Shenin, *United States*, 102. On the effects of loyalty investigations on left-leaning internationalists working in the federal government, see Landon R. Y. Storrs, *The Second Red Scare and the Unmaking of the New Deal Left* (Princeton, NJ: Princeton University Press, 2013), especially 206–21.

11. Macekura, "Point Four Program," 130.

12. Thomas Sugrue, *Sweet Land of Liberty: The Forgotten Struggle for Civil Rights in the North* (New York: Random House, 2008), 88–129; "The President's World Program," *Pittsburgh Courier*, January 29, 1949, 14; "Our Opinions: The Inaugural Address," *Chicago Defender*, February 5, 1949, 6.

13. The best account of the drafting and reception of *An Appeal to the World* is found in Carol Anderson, *Eyes off the Prize: The United Nations and the African American Struggle for Human Rights, 1944–1955* (Cambridge: Cambridge University Press, 2003), 58–112.

14. National Association for the Advancement of Colored People, *An Appeal to the World: A Statement on the Denial of Human Rights to Minorities in the Case of Citizens of Negro Descent in the United States of America and an Appeal to the United Nations for Redress*, ed. W. E. B. Du Bois (New York: National Association for the Advancement of Colored People, 1947), 49.

15. NAACP, *Appeal to the World*, 1, 14, 92. On the resonance of the *Appeal* with international legal principles regarding minority rights and the right to petition, see Emma Stone MacKinnon, "Declaration as Disavowal: The Politics of Race and Empire in the Universal Declaration of Human Rights," *Political Theory*, 47, no. 1 (February 2019): 57–81.

16. Anderson, *Eyes off the Prize*, 153.

17. Lewis, *W. E. B. Du Bois, 1919–1963*, 534.

18. Quoted in Patricia Sullivan, *Days of Hope: Race and Democracy in the New Deal Era* (Chapel Hill: University of North Carolina Press, 1996), 186.

19. Rayford Logan to Walter White, March 21, 1949, "Logan, Rayford, 1948–49" folder, General Office Files, Papers of the NAACP, Library of Congress. For an account of the NAACP's

advocacy related to Point Four that stresses the organization's anticolonialism, see Anderson, *Bourgeois Radicals*, 268–82.

20. "Point IV," *Fortune* (February 1950), 89–96, 177–82; Paterson, "Foreign Aid under Wraps," 123–24.

21. Charles Maier, "The Politics of Productivity: Foundations of American International Economic Policy after World War II," *International Organization* 31, no. 4 (1977): 607–33; Walter P. Reuther, *A Proposal for a Total Peace Offensive* (Detroit: International Union United Automobile, Aircraft, and Agricultural Implement Workers of America, CIO, 1950): 5–7; Congress of Industrial Organizations, Department of Education and Research, "Point 4: Helping People to Help Themselves," *Economic Outlook* 12, no. 11 (November 1951): 81–88. On US organized labor and the early Cold War, see especially Robert H. Zieger, *The CIO: 1935–1955* (Chapel Hill: University of North Carolina Press, 1995); George Lipsitz, *Rainbow at Midnight: Labor and Culture in the 1940s* (Urbana: University of Illinois Press, 1994); Victor I. Silverman, *Imagining Internationalism in American and British Labor, 1939–49* (Urbana: University of Illinois Press, 2000); and Robert W. Cherny, William Issel, and Kiernan Walsh Taylor, eds., *American Labor and the Cold War* (New Brunswick, NJ: Rutgers University Press, 2004).

22. Rayford W. Logan, "Bold New Program or Old Imperialism? Truman's 'Point Four' an Enigma," *Socialist Call*, May 13, 1949.

23. Logan, "Bold New Program or Old Imperialism?"

24. Nathan J. Citino, "Nasser, Hammarskjöld, and Middle East Development in Different Scales of Space and Time," in *The Development Century: A Global History*, ed. Stephen J. Macekura and Erez Manela (Cambridge: Cambridge University Press, 2018), 283–304; Quinn Slobodian, *Globalists: The End of Empire and the Birth of Neoliberalism* (Cambridge, MA: Harvard University Press, 2018).

25. James Warburg, "The 'Point Four' Program: Paper Presented before Post War World Council," October 29, 1949, "Point IV Program" folder, General Office Files, Papers of the NAACP; Raymond F. Gregory, *Norman Thomas: The Great Dissenter* (New York: Algora, 2008), 227–36; Zipp, *The Idealist*. Warburg was also a member of the United World Federalists (UWF), and the world federalist impulse was strong among the members of Thomas's organization. Stringfellow Barr, another member of the Post-War World Council's coordinating committee, served on the University of Chicago's Committee to Frame a World Constitution and directed an organization called the Foundation for World Government, which funded the publication of eight pamphlets in support of Point Four, including Harold Isaacs's *Two-Thirds of the World*. For more on the UWF and the Chicago Committee, see Or Rosenboim, *The Emergence of Globalism: Visions of World Order in Britain and the United States, 1939–1950* (Princeton, NJ: Princeton University Press, 2017), 168–208.

26. Rayford W. Logan to Roy Wilkins, October 31, 1949, "Logan, Rayford, 1948–49" folder, General Office Files, Papers of the NAACP; Harold Isaacs, *Two-Thirds of the World: Problems of a New Approach to the Peoples of Asia, Africa, and Latin America* (Washington, DC: Public Affairs Institute, 1950), 40, 45, 48; Harold Isaacs, *The Tragedy of the Chinese Revolution*, Revised Edition (Stanford, CA: Stanford University Press, 1951). For more on Isaacs, see Vitalis, *White World Order*.

27. Raymond Leslie Buell to Henry Luce, September 12, 1944, folder 3, box 23, Raymond Leslie Buell Papers.

28. Gunnar Myrdal, *Rich Lands and Poor: The Road to World Prosperity* (New York: Harper and Row, 1958). For a sustained analysis of Myrdal's version of this idea, see Samuel Moyn, *Not*

Enough: Human Rights in an Unequal World (Cambridge, MA: Harvard University Press, 2018), 89–118.

29. Isaacs, *Two-Thirds*, 58, 40.

30. Pearl S. Buck, "A Note on Point Four," *People* 4, no. 8 (1950), 3–6, in "Point IV Program" folder, General Office Files, Papers of the NAACP.

31. Arthur M. Schlesinger Jr., *The Vital Center: The Politics of Freedom* (1949; New Brunswick, NJ: Transaction, 1998), 233.

32. Warburg, "'Point Four' Program"; Isaacs, *Two-Thirds*, 62, 64.

33. Kenneth Robert Janken, *Walter White: Mr. NAACP* (Chapel Hill: University of North Carolina Press, 2003), 319; Rayford W. Logan, "Bold New Program."

34. Rayford Logan Diary, November 16, 1947, folder 4, box 4, RWL; Janken, *Rayford W. Logan and the Dilemma of the African-American Intellectual*, 192; Doug Rossinow, *Visions of Progress: The Left-Liberal Tradition in America* (Philadelphia: University of Pennsylvania Press, 2008), 214. On the formation of the CAA and the divisions within it, see Von Eschen, *Race against Empire*, especially 17–21, 115–16.

35. "Point Four Realities in Africa," *New Africa*, Volume 9 (July–August 1949), 9; Horace Cayton, "We Are Tied, With Cords of Gold, Into British Imperialism Because of Uranium," *Pittsburgh Courier*, September 20, 1952, 9; Basil Davidson, "Cashing in on Old Imperialisms," *The Nation*, September 13, 1952.

36. W. E. B. Du Bois, "Do We Want Peace with the Soviet Union?" March 26, 1953, Series 2: Speeches, W. E. B. Du Bois Papers, Special Collections and University Archives, University of Massachusetts Amherst, https://credo.library.umass.edu/view/full/mums312-b203-i027.

Chapter Four

1. Frederick Cooper, "Modernizing Bureaucrats, Backward Africans, and the Development Concept," in *International Development and the Social Sciences*, 64–92.

2. Cooper, "Modernizing Bureaucrats," 70. See also Cooper, *Decolonization and African Society*, especially 277–321; Hodge, *Triumph of the Expert*, 207–53; and Tiyambe Zeleza, "The Political Economy of British Colonial Development and Welfare in Africa," *Transafrican Journal of History* 14 (1985): 139–61.

3. Marc Matera, *Black London: The Imperial Metropolis and Decolonization in the Twentieth Century* (Oakland: University of California Press, 2015); Kennetta Hammond Perry, *London Is the Place for Me: Black Britons, Citizenship, and the Politics of Race* (New York: Oxford University Press, 2015).

4. Kevin Gaines, "Scholar-Activist St. Clair Drake and the Transatlantic World of Black Activism," in *The Other Special Relationship: Race, Rights, and Riots in Britain and the United States*, ed. Robin D. G. Kelley and Stephen Tuck (New York: Palgrave Macmillan, 2015), 77; Andrew Rosa, "The Routes and Roots of 'Imperium in Imperio': St. Clair Drake, the Formative Years," *American Studies* 52, no. 1 (2012): 49–75; Andrew Rosa, "'To Make a Better World Tomorrow': St. Clair Drake and the Quakers of Pendle Hill," *Race & Class* 54, no. 1 (2012): 67–90. On Davis, see David A. Varel, *The Lost Black Scholar: Resurrecting Allison Davis in American Social Thought* (Chicago: University of Chicago Press, 2018). On Redfield, see Nicole Sackley, "Cosmopolitanism and the Uses of Tradition: Robert Redfield and Alternative Visions of Modernization during the Cold War," *Modern Intellectual History* 9, no. 3 (2012): 565–95.

5. W. Lloyd Warner, "American Caste and Class," *American Journal of Sociology* 42, no. 4 (September 1936): 234–37; Daniel Immerwahr, "Caste or Colony? Indianizing Race in the United States," *Modern Intellectual History* 4, no. 2 (August 2007): 275–301; Slate, *Colored Cosmopolitanism*.

6. Gunnar Myrdal, *An American Dilemma: The Negro Problem and Modern Democracy*, Vol. I and Vol. II (1944; New Brunswick, NJ: Transaction, 1996); E. Franklin Frazier, "Sociological Theory and Race Relations," *American Sociological Review* 12, no. 3 (June 1947): 265–71; Cox, *Caste, Class, and Race*, 489–508.

7. Horace Cayton to W. Lloyd Warner, January 10, 1944, folder 29, box 5, St. Clair Drake Papers, Schomburg Center for Research in Black Culture, New York Public Library; *Boston Globe*, November 29, 1945, 20.

8. Drake and Cayton, *Black Metropolis*, 99–128, 214–263.

9. St. Clair Drake to Horace Mann Bond, January 6, 1980, folder 19, box 5, St. Clair Drake Papers; St. Clair Drake, "Value Systems, Social Structure, and Race Relations in the British Isles" (PhD diss., University of Chicago, 1954).

10. St. Clair Drake, "The International Implications of Race Relations," *Journal of Negro Education* 20, no. 3 (Summer 1951): 261–78; St. Clair Drake to E. Franklin Frazier, January 1, 1952, folder 2, box 131–9, E. Franklin Frazier Papers, Moorland-Spingarn Research Center, Howard University. On Drake's advocacy on behalf of Kenyan students in the United States, see Jerry Gershenhorn, "St. Clair Drake, Pan-Africanism, African Studies, and the Politics of Knowledge," *Journal of African American History* 98, no. 3 (Summer 2013): 422–33. On the predominance of theories of racism as individual prejudice, see Leah Gordon, *From Power to Prejudice: The Rise of Racial Individualism in Midcentury America* (Chicago: University of Chicago Press, 2015).

11. Drake, "International Implications," 277.

12. Drake, "International Implications," 277, 278.

13. "The Challenge to Colonial Powers," in *History of the Pan-African Congress*, 5. On the shift toward the nation-state in African anticolonial activism, see especially Cooper, *Citizenship between Empire and Nation*; and Jeffrey Ahlman, *Living with Nkrumahism: Nation, State, and Pan-Africanism in Ghana* (Athens: Ohio University Press, 2017).

14. Hodge, *Triumph of the Expert*, 179–80; Matera, *Black London*, 300; Cooper, "Development, Modernization, and the Social Sciences in the Era of Decolonization," 27.

15. "Editorial," *International African Opinion* (August 1938), 1; Robert L. Tignor, *W. Arthur Lewis and the Birth of Development Economics* (Princeton, NJ: Princeton University Press, 2006), 63–64.

16. *Hansard*, 5th ser. (Commons), Vol. 382, cols. 934–35, August 4, 1942; Stuart Ward, "The European Provenance of Decolonization," *Past and Present* 230 (February 2016): 227–60. On Creech-Jones's involvement with the IASB, see Matera, *Black London*, 84.

17. Cooper, *Decolonization and African Society*, 119–24.

18. George Padmore, in collaboration with Dorothy Pizer, *How Russia Transformed her Colonial Empire: A Challenge to the Imperialist Powers* (London: Dennis Dobson, 1946), 25. Although, as Carol Polsgrove notes, Padmore and Pizer had written much of this book by 1941, they did not find a publisher until 1946, and numerous additions were made in 1945, reflecting on the course of the war and the San Francisco Conference. See Carol Polsgrove, *Ending British Rule in Africa: Writers in a Common Cause* (Manchester: Manchester University Press, 2009),

62–65. See also Theo Williams, "George Padmore and the Soviet Model of the British Common-wealth," *Modern Intellectual History* 16, no. 2 (August 2019): 531–59.

19. Padmore, *How Russia Transformed*, 171, 173; St. Clair Drake, "Democracy on Trial in Africa," *The Annals of the American Academy of Political and Social Science* 354 (July 1964): 110–21.

20. Commission of Enquiry into Disturbances in the Gold Coast, "Report on the Riots of 1948," in *The Ghana Reader: History, Culture, Politics*, ed. Kwasi Konadu and Clifford C. Camp-bell (Durham, NC: Duke University Press, 2016), 261; Cooper, *Decolonization and African Society*, 248–60.

21. Ahlman, *Living with Nkrumahism*, 52–60.

22. Jemima Pierre, *The Predicament of Blackness: Postcolonial Ghana and the Politics of Race* (Chicago: University of Chicago Press, 2012); Getachew, *Worldmaking after Empire*.

23. Thomas J. Noer, "The New Frontier and African Neutralism: Kennedy, Nkrumah, and the Volta River Project," *Diplomatic History* 8, no. 1 (January 1984): 61–80; Tignor, *W. Arthur Lewis*, 194–95; Stephan F. Miescher, " 'Nkrumah's Baby': The Akosombo Dam and the Dream of Development in Ghana, 1952–1966," *Water History* 6, no. 4 (2014): 341–66.

24. Hodge, *Triumph of the Expert*, 265–68. The foundational critical analysis of "high-modernist" development projects is found in James C. Scott, *Seeing Like a State: How Certain Schemes to Improve the Human Condition Have Failed* (New Haven, CT: Yale University Press, 1998).

25. George Padmore to Kwame Nkrumah, November 22, 1951, folder 13, box 154–41, Kwame Nkrumah Papers, Moorland-Spingarn Research Center, Howard University; W. Arthur Lewis to George Padmore, April 16, 1952, box 9, W. Arthur Lewis Papers, Seeley G. Mudd Manuscript Library, Princeton University.

26. W. A. Lewis, *Report on Industrialization and the Gold Coast* (Accra: Government Print-ing Department, 1953), 2, 22. See also W. A. Lewis, "Economic Development with Unlimited Supplies of Labour," *Manchester School* 22, no. 2 (May 1954): 139–91.

27. Lewis, *Report on Industrialization*, 8, 9.

28. Although historian Kevin Gaines rightly acknowledges the "autobiographical dimension to Wright's affinity for the idea of modernization" that emerged from his understanding of "his own intellectual development in terms of a migration from tradition to modernity," Wright's full-throated advocacy of a program of modernization in the Gold Coast also emerged from this wider intellectual context. See Kevin Gaines, "Revisiting Richard Wright in Ghana: Black Radicalism and the Dialectics of Diaspora," *Social Text* 67, vol. 19, no. 2 (Summer 2001): 75–101, quoted at 82. The best account of the links between Wright's writings and modernization theory is found in Rasberry, *Race and the Totalitarian Century*, 305–54. For a broader account of mod-ernization as a master theme in Wright's writing, see Tommie Shelby, "Realizing the Promise of the West," in *African American Political Thought: A Collected History*, ed. Melvin L. Rogers and Jack Turner (Chicago: University of Chicago Press, 2021), 413–38.

29. Richard Wright, "Introduction," in Drake and Cayton, *Black Metropolis*, lxvii.

30. Contemporaneous critiques by Léopold Senghor and Camara Laye are discussed in Michel Fabre, *The World of Richard Wright* (Jackson: University of Mississippi Press, 1985), 209–11.

31. Richard Wright, *The Color Curtain: A Report on the Bandung Conference* (New York: World Press, 1956). For a treatment of Wright as a thinker deeply engaged with the condition

of modernity and its constitutive element of racial domination, see Cedric J. Robinson, *Black Marxism: The Making of the Black Radical Tradition* (London: Zed, 1983), 416–40.

32. Padmore quoted in Polsgrove, *Ending British Rule in Africa*, 136; Richard Wright, *Black Power* (1954), in *Black Power: Three Books from Exile: Black Power, The Color Curtain, and White Man, Listen!* (New York: Harper Collins, 2010), 414, 418.

33. Wright, *Black Power*, 415, 417; William James, "The Moral Equivalent of War" (1910), in *Essays in Religion and Morality*, ed. Frederick Burkhardt, et al. (Cambridge, MA: Harvard University Press, 1982), 162–74.

34. Miescher, "'Nkrumah's Baby,'" 355; Tignor, *W. Arthur Lewis*, 72–76. Drake quoted in Leslie James, *George Padmore and Decolonization from Below: Pan-Africanism, the Cold War, and the End of Empire* (Cambridge: Cambridge University Press, 2014), 181.

35. St. Clair Drake to Director, West African Section, Department of State, June 6, 1958, folder 41, box 70, St. Clair Drake Papers.

36. St. Clair Drake to E. Franklin Frazier, November 28, 1961, folder 2, box 131–9, E. Franklin Frazier Papers. As Drake later claimed in a 1979 letter reflecting on the writing of *Black Metropolis*, "It was generally assumed that I was a 'fellow traveler' and that Cayton was not, a fact that Richard Wright, by 1944, was warning Cayton to keep in mind and not to let what Dick considered Stalinism to influence the tone of the book." St. Clair Drake to Ron Bailey, June 8, 1979, folder 1, box 4, St. Clair Drake Papers.

37. On the importance of the Peace Corps and the development ideal to global politics in the 1960s, see Molly Geidel, *Peace Corps Fantasies: How Development Shaped the Global Sixties* (Minneapolis: University of Minnesota Press, 2015).

38. Rosemary George to St. Clair Drake, September 7, 1962, folder 1, box 79, St. Clair Drake Papers; George Carter to David Apter, March 14, 1961, folder 1, box 79, St. Clair Drake Papers; Notes, folder 23, box 66, St. Clair Drake Papers.

Chapter Five

1. John F. Kennedy, "The United States and Africa: A New Policy for a New Era," in *Summary Report: Second Annual Conference* (New York: American Society of African Culture, 1959), 8.

2. J. Saunders Redding, "Negro Writing in America," *The New Leader* (May 1960): 8; Lawrence P. Jackson, *The Indignant Generation: A Narrative History of African American Writers and Critics, 1934–1960* (Princeton, NJ: Princeton University Press, 2011), 467–69.

3. Despite increasing interest in African American intellectual history in recent years, other US historians have not, for the most part, incorporated the innovations of the growing field into their dominant narratives of American history. The best example of the recent upsurge in interest in Black intellectual history is the emergence of the African American Intellectual History Society and its blog, *Black Perspectives*. See also the following edited volumes: Adolph Reed Jr. and Kenneth W. Warren, eds., *Renewing Black Intellectual History: The Ideological and Material Foundations of African American Thought* (New York: Routledge, 2009); Mia Bay, Farah J. Griffin, Martha S. Jones, and Barbara D. Savage, eds., *Toward an Intellectual History of Black Women* (Chapel Hill: University of North Carolina Press, 2015); Keisha N. Blain, Christopher Cameron, and Ashley D. Farmer, eds., *New Perspectives on the Black Intellectual Tradition* (Evanston, IL: Northwestern University Press, 2018); and Leslie M. Alexander, Brandon R. Byrd, and

Russell Rickford, eds., *Ideas in Unexpected Places: Reimagining Black Intellectual History* (Evanston, IL: Northwestern University Press, 2022). A brief but compelling attempt to link policy discourse about the decolonizing world with the ideas of anticolonial thinkers in this period can be found in Vaughn Rasberry, "JFK and the Global Anticolonial Movement," in *The Cambridge Companion to John F. Kennedy*, ed. Andrew Hoberek (Cambridge: Cambridge University Press, 2015), 118–33.

4. John Foster Dulles, "International Unity," *Department of State Bulletin* 30, no. 782 (June 1954): 936; Seymour Martin Lipset, *The First New Nation: The United States in Historical and Comparative Perspective* (1963; New York: Norton, 1979), v; Renato Rosaldo, *Culture and Truth: The Remaking of Social Analysis* (Boston: Beacon, 1989), 68–69. Two useful overviews of Kennedy's foreign policy toward the decolonizing world are Robert B. Rakove, *Kennedy, Johnson, and the Nonaligned World* (Cambridge: Cambridge University Press, 2013); and Thomas G. Paterson, ed., *Kennedy's Quest for Victory: American Foreign Policy, 1961–1963* (New York: Oxford University Press, 1989).

5. "Remarks of Senator John F. Kennedy at the Los Angeles World Affairs Council Luncheon at the Biltmore Hotel on September 21, 1956," box 895, Speeches and the Press, Series 12, Senate Files, Pre-Presidential Papers, Papers of John F. Kennedy, John F. Kennedy Presidential Library and Museum, https://www.jfklibrary.org/archives/other-resources/john-f-kennedy-speeches/los-angeles-ca-world-affairs-council-19560921; "Remarks of Senator John F. Kennedy in the Senate, Washington, D.C., July 2, 1957," box 784, Legislation, Series 09, Senate Files, Pre-Presidential Papers, Papers of John F. Kennedy, https://www.jfklibrary.org/archives/other-resources/john-f-kennedy-speeches/united-states-senate-imperialism-19570702; "Remarks of Senator John F. Kennedy at State Capitol, Albany, New York, September 29, 1960," box 912, Speeches and the Press, Series 12, Senate Files, Pre-Presidential Papers, Papers of John J. Kennedy, https://www.jfklibrary.org/archives/other-resources/john-f-kennedy-speeches/albany-ny-19600929. On Kennedy and anticolonialism, see Anders Stephanson, "Senator John F. Kennedy: Anti-Imperialism and Utopian Deficit," *Journal of American Studies* 48, no. 1 (February 2014): 1–24; and Theresa Romahn, "Colonialism and the Campaign Trail: On Kennedy's Algerian Speech and His Bid for the 1960 Democratic Nomination," *Journal of Colonialism and Colonial History* 10, no. 2 (Fall 2009): 1–23.

6. This language provides an example of how historical narratives, both in the work of professional historians and in a general historical consciousness, contribute to imperial modes of self-understanding and structure policymakers' views of what is plausible, what is desirable, and what accords with national interest and national identity. For an examination of the impact of historical narratives on the imperial imagination in the context of the British Empire, see Duncan Bell, *Reordering the World: Essays on Liberalism and Empire* (Princeton, NJ: Princeton University Press, 2016), especially 119–47.

7. A useful examination of anti-imperialism in American history is found in Ian Tyrrell and Jay Sexton, eds., *Empire's Twin: U.S. Anti-Imperialism from the Founding Era to the Age of Terrorism* (Ithaca, NY: Cornell University Press, 2015). On the marginalization of Indigenous peoples from dominant narratives in American political thought, see David Myer Temin, "Custer's Sins: Vine Deloria Jr. and the Settler-Colonial Politics of Civic Inclusion," *Political Theory* 46, no. 3 (June 2018): 357–79.

8. See, for example, Louis Hartz, *The Liberal Tradition in America: An Interpretation of American Political Thought since the Revolution* (New York: Harcourt, Brace, 1955).

9. Getachew, *Worldmaking after Empire*, 107–41; Paul Gilroy, *The Black Atlantic: Modernity and Double-Consciousness* (Cambridge, MA: Harvard University Press, 1995). For a discussion

of how US policymakers appealed to the American Revolution in efforts to shape anticolonial revolutions, see Michael E. Latham, *The Right Kind of Revolution: Modernization, Development, and U.S. Foreign Policy from the Cold War to the Present* (Ithaca, NY: Cornell University Press, 2011). On adaptations of the American revolutionary heritage by twentieth century anticolonialists, see David Armitage, *The Declaration of Independence: A Global History* (Cambridge, MA: Harvard University Press, 2007).

10. Wheatley, *The Life and Death of States*, 255–82.

11. United Nations General Assembly Resolution 1514 (XV), "Declaration on the Granting of Independence to Colonial Countries and Peoples," December 14, 1960, http://www.un.org/en /decolonization/declaration.shtml, accessed March 5, 2018.

12. Robert Michels, *Political Parties: A Sociological Study of the Oligarchical Tendencies of Modern Democracy*, trans. Eden Paul and Cedar Paul (1915; repr., New York: The Free Press, 1968); Seymour Martin Lipset, *Agrarian Socialism: The Cooperative Commonwealth Federation in Saskatchewan, A Study in Political Sociology* (Oakland: University of California Press, 1950); Seymour Martin Lipset, *Union Democracy: The Internal Politics of the International Typographical Union* (New York: Free Press, 1956). For information on Lipset's early career and influences, see Seymour Martin Lipset, "Steady Work: An Academic Memoir," *Annual Review of Sociology* 22 (1996): 1–27.

13. Lipset, "Steady Work," 14; Seymour Martin Lipset, *Political Man: The Social Bases of Politics* (New York: Doubleday, 1960), 415–17. In short order, *Political Man* became the standard US text in political sociology, and eventually it was translated into twenty languages. For the paradigmatic statement of the "end of ideology" thesis, see Daniel Bell, *The End of Ideology: On the Exhaustion of Political Ideas in the Fifties* (Glencoe, IL: Free Press, 1960). On Bell, see Brick, *Daniel Bell and the Decline of Intellectual Radicalism*.

14. Lipset, "Steady Work," 15; Seymour Martin Lipset, "The United States—The First New Nation," *Transactions of the Fifth World Congress of Sociology, Washington, D.C., 2–8 September, 1962*, vol. 3 (Louvain: International Sociological Association, 1964), 308, 309.

15. Lipset, *First New Nation*, 2. On the extensive influence of Talcott Parsons on modernization theory, see Nils Gilman, *Mandarins of the Future: Modernization Theory in Cold War America* (Baltimore: Johns Hopkins University Press, 2003), especially 72–112. On the ways in which modernization theory reified views of Euro-American culture as coherent, unique, and superior, see J. M. Blaut, "The Theory of Cultural Racism," *Antipode* 24, no. 4 (October 1992): 289–99.

16. Very little scholarship exists on Gerig as an individual. Basic information about his career can be found in Gerlof D. Homan, "Orie Benjamin Gerig: Mennonite Rebel, Peace Activist, International Civil Servant, and American Diplomat, 1894–1976," *The Mennonite Quarterly Review* (1999): 751–82; Benjamin Gerig, "United States Attitude on the Colonial Question," folder 25, box 1, Benjamin Gerig Papers.

17. Lipset, *Political Man*, 92; William Nisbet Chambers, *Political Parties in a New Nation* (New York: Oxford University Press, 1963), 14.

18. The following discussion draws on Getachew, *Worldmaking after Empire*, 110–21.

19. Williams quoted in Getachew, *Worldmaking after Empire*, 111. On the history of the West Indian Federation, see Jason Parker, *Brother's Keeper: The United States, Race and Empire in the British Caribbean, 1937–1962* (New York: Oxford University Press, 2008), 140–60.

20. On the French Community referendum, see Cooper, *Citizenship between Empire and Nation*, 310–24. On the Ghana-Guinea-Mali union as an outgrowth of Nkrumah's vision, see Ahlman, *Living with Nkrumahism*.

21. Kwame Nkrumah, *Africa Must Unite* (London: Heinemann, 1963), 27; Tetteh Amakwata, "America Must Remember Her Past," *Voice of Africa*, November–December 1965, 8, 9.

22. Getachew, *Worldmaking after Empire*, 120–21; Kwame Nkrumah, *Neocolonialism: The Last Stage of Imperialism* (London: Thomas, Nelson, and Sons, 1965).

23. Shepard, *The Invention of Decolonization*, especially chapter 2; and Ward, "European Provenance of Decolonization." Ward also intriguingly suggests that Frantz Fanon's embrace of the term "decolonization" in *The Wretched of the Earth*—after he had, in earlier writings, identified it with a "European-inspired programme of incremental change designed to absorb the pressures of anti-colonialism at a minimal cost to metropolitan influence and prestige"—prompted a radical shift in the word's associations. Ward, "European Provenance of Decolonization," 254.

24. "Final Communique of the Asian-African Conference," in *The Asian-African Conference, Bandung, Indonesia, April 1955*, ed. George McTurnan Kahin (Ithaca, NY: Cornell University Press, 1956), 82; United Nations General Assembly Resolution 1514 (XV), "Declaration on the Granting of Independence to Colonial Countries and Peoples," December 14, 1960, http://www.un.org/en/decolonization/declaration.shtml, accessed March 5, 2018.

25. On the US diplomatic effort to convince the Third World to see Soviet expansion as a form of colonialism, see Jason Parker, "Cold War II: The Eisenhower Administration, the Bandung Conference, and the Reperiodization of the Postwar Era," *Diplomatic History* 30, no. 5 (November 2006): 867–92.

26. Francis T. Williamson, review of *The Idea of Colonialism*, ed. Robert Strausz-Hupé and Harry W. Hazard, *American Historical Review* 64, no. 2 (January 1959): 336.

27. Rupert Emerson, *From Empire to Nation: The Rise to Self-Assertion of Asian and African Peoples* (Boston: Beacon, 1960), 387. For more on Emerson's work, see Thomas Mallory Meaney, "The American Hour: US Thinkers and the Problem of Decolonization, 1948–1983" (PhD diss., Columbia University, 2017), 81–118; and Robert Vitalis, "What Time Was It?," *Comparative Studies of South Asia, Africa, and the Middle East* 40, no. 3 (December 2020): 621–27. For more on Laski's influence on transatlantic debates about international institutions, see Rosenboim, *The Emergence of Globalism*, ch. 8.

28. Emerson, *From Empire to Nation*, 310, 370, 382; Rupert Emerson, "Colonialism," box 1, Rupert Emerson Papers, Harvard University Archives.

29. Rupert Emerson, "The Character of American Interests in Africa," in *The United States and Africa*, ed. Walter Goldschmidt (New York: American Assembly, 1958); Emerson, *From Empire to Nation*, 341. Lorenzo Veracini emphasizes the ambiguity in how settler colonies were imagined in relation to other forms of colonial rule amid the anticolonial uprisings of the 1960s: "Settler colonialism was seen as fundamentally characterised by an inherent ambivalence, an ambivalence that required that settler colonial phenomena be considered simultaneously *part of* and *distinct from* colonialism at large." See Lorenzo Veracini, " 'Settler Colonialism': Career of a Concept," *Journal of Imperial and Commonwealth History* 41, no. 2 (April 2013): 313–33, quoted at 320.

30. St. Clair Drake, "Why Ghana's Nkrumah Supports Lumumba in Congo," *New Journal and Guide*, October 15, 1960, 19; Horace Cayton, "World At Large," *Pittsburgh Courier*, February 13, March 5, and March 26, 1960.

31. David E. Apter, Review of Rupert Emerson, *From Empire to Nation*, *The Journal of Politics* 23, no. 3 (August 1961): 590–91.

32. "Remarks of Senator John F. Kennedy in the Senate, Washington, D.C., July 2, 1957." On Kennedy's references to Africa on the campaign trail, see James H. Meriwether, " 'Worth a Lot of

Negro Votes': Black Voters, Africa, and the 1960 Presidential Campaign," *Journal of American History* 95, no. 3 (December 2008): 737–63; and Mary Dudziak, *Cold War Civil Rights: Race and the Image of American Democracy* (2000; repr., Princeton, NJ: Princeton University Press, 2011), 155–57.

33. Rakove, *Kennedy, Johnson*, 94–134.

34. On the differences between Kennedy's and Truman's foreign aid policies, see McVety, *Enlightened Aid*, 161–94; on police assistance, see Stuart Schrader, *Badges without Borders: How Global Counterinsurgency Transformed American Policing* (Oakland: University of California Press, 2019), 79–112.

35. Philip E. Muehlenbeck, *Betting on the Africans: John F. Kennedy's Courting of African Nationalist Leaders* (New York: Oxford University Press, 2012); Vanni Pettinà, "Whose Revolution? López Mateos, Kennedy's Mexican Visit, and the Alliance for Progress," in *Globalizing the U.S. Presidency: Postcolonial Views of John F. Kennedy* ed. Cyrus Schayegh (London: Bloomsbury, 2020), 168–82.

36. Andrew Friedman, "Decolonization's Diplomats: Antiracism and the Year of Africa in Washington, D.C.," *Journal of American History* 106, no. 3 (December 2019): 614–38.

37. Thomas J. Noer, *Soapy: A Biography of G. Mennen Williams* (Ann Arbor: University of Michigan Press, 2005), 247; G. Mennen Williams, "Why Racial Peace Is Imperative," *Negro Digest* 11, no. 12 (October 1962): 30. On the ongoing conceptual and practical slippage between "internal" and "external" racial frontiers, see especially Nikhil Pal Singh, *Race and America's Long War* (Oakland: University of California Press, 2017); and Vitalis, *White World Order*.

38. Martin Luther King Jr., "'The Birth of a New Nation,' Sermon Delivered at Dexter Avenue Baptist Church," April 7, 1957, in *The Papers of Martin Luther King, Jr., Volume IV: Symbol of the Movement, January 1957–December 1958*, ed. Clayborne Carson et al. (Berkeley: University of California Press, 2000), 155–67.

39. For two examples of how interwar African Americans often relied on a language of color in their proclamations of international solidarity, see W. E. B. Du Bois, "Worlds of Color," *Foreign Affairs* 3, no. 3 (April 1925): 423–44; and Ernest Otto Hauser, "The American Negro and the 'Dark World,'" *The Crisis* 44, no. 2 (February 1937): 38–40, 59.

40. Harold R. Isaacs, *The New World of Negro Americans* (New York: Viking, 1963), x.

41. John Henrik Clarke, "The New Afro-American Nationalism," *Freedomways* 1, no. 3 (Fall 1961): 285, 291, 293, 295. For more on the largely overlooked relationship between modernization theory and African American political thought, see chapters 3 and 4 of this book. See also Vitalis, "The Lost World of Development Theory."

42. Alain Locke, "Race in the Present World Crisis," August 7, 1944, p. 3, folder 15, box 164–125, Alain LeRoy Locke Papers; Leo Marquard, *South Africa's Colonial Policy: Presidential Address Delivered at the Annual Meeting of the Council of the South African Institute of Race Relations in the Hiddingh Hall, Cape Town, on January 16, 1957* (Johannesburg: South African Institute of Race Relations, 1957); George Schuyler, "Views and Reviews," *Pittsburgh Courier*, February 23, 1957; Léopold Sédar Senghor, *On African Socialism*, trans. Mercer Cook (1961; repr., New York: Frederick A. Praeger, 1964), 87.

43. Van Gosse, "More than Just a Politician: Notes on the Life and Times of Harold Cruse," in *Harold Cruse's The Crisis of the Negro Intellectual Reconsidered*, ed. Jerry G. Watts (New York: Routledge, 2004), 19; Harold Cruse, "Les Noirs et L'idée de la Révolte," in *Rebellion or Revolution?* (New York: William Morrow, 1967), 171. Emphasis in original.

44. Julian Mayfield, "Crisis or Crusade?" *Negro Digest* 17, no. 8 (June 1968): 14. Cruse himself later emphasized his frustration at the party's stance on Black nationalism as a reason for his

departure from the CPUSA, but Van Gosse, the scholar who has written most on the biographi-cal details of Cruse's life, suggests that this account may elide other factors. See Gosse, "More than Just," 20. No book-length biography of Cruse yet exists.

45. Gosse, "More than Just," 19, 21–22; Harold Cruse to *The Amsterdam News*, February 5, 1956, folder 6, box 2, Harold Cruse Papers, Tamiment Library and Robert F. Wagner Labor Ar-chives, New York University.

46. Harold Cruse to James T. Harris, Executive Secretary of AMSAC, folder 6, box 2, Harold Cruse Papers. Given AMSAC's covert funding from the CIA through the Congress for Cultural Freedom, such a warning was surely unnecessary, but it exhibited the degree to which Cruse believed that Black organizations should disassociate from the organized left. On this point, see Washington, *The Other Blacklist*, 249–52.

47. *Présence Africaine*, founded by the Senegalese writers and editors Alioune Diop and Christiane Yandé Diop, was the central organ of the literary-cultural movement known as Négritude and the major publication covering Black culture and politics in France. On *Présence*, see V. Y. Mudimbe, ed., *The Surreptitious Speech: Présence Africaine and the Politics of Other-ness, 1947–1987* (Chicago: University of Chicago Press, 1992); and Merve Fejzula, "Negritude and Black Cultural Citizenship across Senegal, Nigeria, and the United States, 1945–66" (PhD diss., University of Cambridge, 2019). On the specific influence of Négritude on Cruse, see Fejzula, "Negritude," 137–39, 154–57.

48. Harold Cruse, "An Afro-American's Cultural Views," *Présence Africaine* 17 (December 1957–January 1958): 31, 34, 40; E. Franklin Frazier, *Black Bourgeoisie* (Glencoe, IL: Free Press, 1957); Cruse, "Afro-American's Cultural Views," 35; Martin Luther King Jr., "Facing the Chal-lenge of a New Age," *Phylon Quarterly* 18, no. 1 (1957): 26.

49. Redding, "Negro Writing in America," 8; Jackson, *The Indignant Generation*, 467–69. Cruse provides his own account of his break from AMSAC in Cruse, *Rebellion or Revolution?*, 21.

50. This response differentiated Cruse from two of the younger members of the FPCC del-egation, Robert F. Williams and LeRoi Jones, both of whom sought to adapt the tactics and strat-egies of the Cuban Revolution to the US Black freedom struggle directly. On this divergence, see Cynthia A. Young, *Soul Power: Culture, Radicalism, and the Making of a U.S. Third World Left* (Durham, NC: Duke University Press, 2006), 18–53. Cruse was nine years older than Wil-liams and eighteen years older than Jones, who was only twenty-five at the time of this trip to Cuba. The importance of this generational difference is noted in Gosse, "More than Just," 20. For more on the FPCC trip to Cuba and the reception for Castro in Harlem, see Van Gosse, *Where the Boys Are: Cuba, Cold War America, and the Making of a New Left* (New York: Verso, 1993), 147–54; and Young, *Soul Power*, 8–9. Richard Gibson has recently been revealed to have worked as a CIA asset between 1965 and at least 1977, although thus far no public documents point to any involvement with the CIA as early as 1960. On this point, see Jefferson Morley, "CIA Reveals Name of Former Spy in JFK Files—And He's Still Alive," *Newsweek*, May 15, 2018, https://www.newsweek.com/richard-gibson-cia-spies-james-baldwin-amiri-baraka-richard-wright-cuba-926428.

51. Harold Cruse, "Cuba and the North American Negro," p. 43, folder 1, box 4, Harold Cruse Papers.

52. Harold Cruse, "Negro Nationalism's New Wave," in *Rebellion or Revolution?*, 69; Harold Cruse, "Revolutionary Nationalism and the Afro-American," in *Rebellion or Revolution?*, 74, 76, 77. On the underappreciated importance of the territorial empire of the United States, see Daniel

Immerwahr, *How to Hide an Empire: A History of the Greater United States* (New York: Farrar, Straus, and Giroux, 2019).

53. See, for example, Young, *Soul Power*, 18–53; Cedric Johnson, *Revolutionaries to Race Leaders: Black Power and the Making of American Politics* (Minneapolis: University of Minnesota Press, 2007), 3–41; Joseph, *Waiting 'Til the Midnight Hour*, 30–31; Nikhil Pal Singh, "Negro Exceptionalism: The Antinomies of Harold Cruse," in *Harold Cruse's The Crisis*, 73–91.

54. This argument runs counter to Frederick Cooper's claim that "colonialism . . . was an object of attack in the 1950s and 1960s, but not an object of careful examination," by illuminating the intellectual contributions and definitional contestations that occurred within the framework of such attacks. See Frederick Cooper, *Colonialism in Question: Theory, Knowledge, History* (Oakland: University of California Press, 2005), 33.

55. Cruse's acerbic critiques of his opponents often overshadowed his positive political vision, which receives more attention in chapter 9 of this book. Ultimately, he came to represent a politics that resembled what Michael Dawson labels "community nationalism," with a particular emphasis on the need for Black control over the institutions of culture and mass media. See Michael Dawson, *Black Visions: The Roots of Contemporary African-American Political Ideologies* (Chicago: University of Chicago Press, 2001).

56. On Williams, see Timothy B. Tyson, *Radio Free Dixie: Robert F. Williams and the Roots of Black Power* (Chapel Hill: University of North Carolina Press, 1999). On this aspect of the thought of Leroi Jones/Amiri Baraka, see especially Young, *Soul Power*. On the direct influence of Cruse's writings on the Black Panther Party and on RAM, see Murch, *Living for the City*, 71–96; Muhammad Ahmad, *We Will Return in the Whirlwind: Black Radical Organizations, 1960–1975* (Chicago: Charles H. Kerr Publishing, 2008). On Malcolm X and Cruse, see Cedric Johnson, "Between Revolution and the Racial Ghetto: Harold Cruse and Harry Haywood Debate Class Struggle and the 'Negro Question,' 1962–8," *Historical Materialism* 24, no. 1 (2016): 12–13; Gosse, "More than Just," 26–7.

57. On the centrality of the decolonizing world to US strategic thinking, see Robert J. McMahon, "How the Periphery Became the Center: The Cold War, the Third World, and the Transformation in US Strategic Thinking," in *Foreign Policy at the Periphery: The Shifting Margins of US International Relations since World War II*, ed. Bevan Sewell, et al. (Lexington: University Press of Kentucky, 2017).

Chapter Six

1. Lipset, "The United States—The First New Nation," *Transactions of the Fifth World Congress of Sociology*, 308; Michael Harrington, *The Other America: Poverty in the United States* (1962; repr., New York: Macmillan, 1964), 158–59.

2. For more on this point, see Alyosha Goldstein, *Poverty in Common: The Politics of Community Action during the American Century* (Durham, NC: Duke University Press, 2012).

3. Alice O'Connor, "Modernization and the Rural Poor: Some Lessons from History," in *Rural Poverty in America*, ed. Cynthia M. Duncan (New York: Auburn House, 1992), 215–33.

4. Sargent Shriver, "Two Years of the Peace Corps," *Foreign Affairs* 41, no. 4 (July 1963): 694–707. On the history of community development, see especially Daniel Immerwahr, *Thinking Small: The United States and the Lure of Community Development* (Cambridge, MA: Harvard University Press, 2015).

5. Amy Offner, *Sorting Out the Mixed Economy: The Rise and Fall of Welfare and Developmental States in the Americas* (Princeton, NJ: Princeton University Press, 2019), 12.

6. Goldstein, *Poverty in Common*, 83–84. Daniel M. Cobb, *Native Activism in Cold War America: The Struggle for Sovereignty* (Lawrence: University Press of Kansas, 2008), 8.

7. Cobb, *Native Activism*, chapter 1.

8. "Steelworkers Ask Minimum Annual Wage," *Washington Post*, February 2, 1952. On the turn away from labor internationalism in the late 1940s, see Lipsitz, *Rainbow at Midnight*; and Silverman, *Imagining Internationalism in American and British Labor*.

9. "Congress Enacts Area Redevelopment Bill," in *CQ Almanac 1961*, 17th ed. (Washington, DC: Congressional Quarterly, 1961), 247–56, http://library.cqpress.com/cqalmanac/cqal61 -1373049; Area Redevelopment Act of 1961, Pub. L. 87–27, 75 Stat. 47 (1961), 2; Gunnar Myrdal, *Challenge to Affluence* (New York: Pantheon Books, 1962), 23.

10. "Eisenhower Backs 'Point 4' Project for Parts of U.S.," *New York Times*, October 24, 1955; "Ike Approves Advisers' Wider Prosperity Plan," *Washington Post and Times Herald*, October 25, 1955.

11. Sar A. Levitan, *Federal Aid to Depressed Areas: An Evaluation of the Area Redevelopment Administration* (Baltimore: Johns Hopkins Press, 1964), 1–17. On the centrality of the development project to John F. Kennedy's political formation, see Sheyda F. A. Jahanbani, *The Poverty of the World: Rediscovering the Poor at Home and Abroad, 1941–1968* (New York: Oxford University Press, 2023).

12. Area Redevelopment Act of 1961, Pub. L. 87–27, 75 Stat. 47 (1961), 2; O'Connor, "Modernization and the Rural Poor," 229.

13. This research largely took place under the academic categories of area studies and modernization theory. On area studies, see especially Osamah F. Khalil, *America's Dream Palace: Middle East Expertise and the Rise of the National Security State* (Cambridge, MA: Harvard University Press, 2016); Zachary Lockman, *Field Notes: The Making of Middle East Studies in the United States* (Stanford, CA: Stanford University Press, 2016); and Fabio Lanza, *The End of Concern: Maoist China, Activism, and Asian Studies* (Durham, NC: Duke University Press, 2017). On modernization theory, in a crowded and growing field, see especially Michael E. Latham, *Modernization as Ideology: American Social Science and "Nation Building" in the Kennedy Era* (Chapel Hill: University of North Carolina Press, 2000); Gilman, *Mandarins of the Future*; David C. Engerman, Nils Gilman, Mark Haefele, and Michael E. Latham, *Staging Growth: Modernization, Development, and the Global Cold War* (Amherst: University of Massachusetts Press, 2006); Latham, *The Right Kind of Revolution*; Joel Isaac, *Working Knowledge: Making the Human Sciences from Parsons to Kuhn* (Cambridge, MA: Harvard University Press, 2012); Mark Solovey and Hamilton Cravens, eds., *Cold War Social Science: Knowledge Production, Liberal Democracy, and Human Nature* (New York: Palgrave MacMillan, 2012); Nicole Sackley, "Cosmopolitanism and the Uses of Tradition: Robert Redfield and Alternative Visions of Modernization during the Cold War," *Modern Intellectual History* 9 (2012): 565–95; Nicole Sackley, "Village Models: Etawah, India, and the Making and Remaking of Development in the Early Cold War," *Diplomatic History* 37 (2013): 749–78; and Immerwahr, *Thinking Small*. On the funding of social-scientific research, see especially Inderjeet Parmar, *Foundations of the American Century: The Ford, Carnegie, and Rockefeller Foundations in the Rise of American Power* (New York: Columbia University Press, 2012); Mark Solovey, *Shaky Foundations: The Politics-Patronage-Social Science Nexus in Cold War America* (New Brunswick, NJ: Rutgers University Press, 2013); and David H.

Price, *Cold War Anthropology: The CIA, the Pentagon, and the Growth of Dual Use Anthropology* (Durham, NC: Duke University Press, 2016).

14. Immerwahr, *Thinking Small*, 134; Oscar Lewis, *The Children of Sánchez: Autobiography of a Mexican Family* (1961; New York: Vintage, 2011); Oscar Lewis, *La Vida: A Puerto Rican Family in the Culture of Poverty—San Juan and New York* (New York: Random House, 1966).

15. Oscar Lewis, "The Culture of Poverty," *Scientific American* 215, no. 4 (October 1966): 21; Lewis, *Children of Sánchez*, xxxvi–xliii.

16. Harrington, *Other America*, 161, 166, 168. On this aspect of Harrington's career, see Maurice Isserman, *The Other American: The Life of Michael Harrington* (New York: PublicAffairs, 2000), 140–74.

17. Michael B. Katz, *The Undeserving Poor: From the War on Poverty to the War on Welfare* (New York: Pantheon Books, 1989), 82; Galbraith, *The Affluent Society*; Lyndon Johnson, "Annual Message to Congress on the State of the Union," January 8, 1964, The American Presidency Project, https://www.presidency.ucsb.edu/documents/annual-message-the-congress-the-state-the-union-25.

18. On the importance of the "culture of poverty" idea to antipoverty politics in the early 1960s, see especially Katz, *Undeserving Poor*; O'Connor, *Poverty Knowledge*; James T. Patterson, *America's Struggle against Poverty, 1900–1994* (Cambridge, MA: Harvard University Press, 1994); Jill Quadagno, *The Color of Welfare: How Racism Undermined the War on Poverty* (New York: Oxford University Press, 1994); and Robin Marie Averbeck, *Liberalism Is Not Enough: Race and Poverty in Postwar Political Thought* (Chapel Hill: University of North Carolina Press, 2018).

19. Immerwahr, *Thinking Small*; Stuart Schrader, "To Secure the Global Great Society: Participation in Pacification," *Humanity: An International Journal of Human Rights, Humanitarianism, and Development* 7, no. 2 (Summer 2016): 225–53.

20. See especially Elizabeth Cobbs Hoffman, *All You Need Is Love: The Peace Corps and the Spirit of the 1960s* (Cambridge, MA: Harvard University Press, 1998); Geidel, *Peace Corps Fantasies*; and Jahanbani, *The Poverty of the World*.

21. Schrader, *Badges without Borders*, 120, 237–42.

22. Cedric J. Robinson, *The Terms of Order: Political Science and the Myth of Leadership* (1980; Chapel Hill: University of North Carolina Press, 2016), 45.

23. On the centrality of demands for sovereignty to American Indian aspirations and the persistent marginalization of such demands by the United States, see especially Vine Deloria Jr. and Clifford M. Lytle, *The Nations Within: The Past and Future of American Indian Sovereignty* (1984; Austin: University of Texas Press, 1998); and Kevin Bruyneel, *The Third Space of Sovereignty: The Postcolonial Politics of U.S.-Indigenous Relations* (Minneapolis: University of Minnesota Press, 2007). On the relationship between American Indian communities and the Community Action Program, see Goldstein, *Poverty in Common*.

24. Syllabus for Political Science 18: The British Welfare State, Fall 1953, box 3, Paul N. Ylvisaker Papers, Harvard University Archives; Alice O'Connor, "Community Action, Urban Reform, and the Fight against Poverty," *Journal of Urban History* 22, no. 4 (July 1996): 586–625; Matthew J. Countryman, *Up South: Civil Rights and Black Power in Philadelphia* (Philadelphia: University of Pennsylvania Press, 2006), 13–14; Karen Ferguson, *Top Down: The Ford Foundation, Black Power, and the Reinvention of Racial Liberalism* (Philadelphia: University of Pennsylvania Press, 2013), 51–52.

25. Paul N. Ylvisaker, "Metropolitan Government—For What?" (1958), in *Conscience & Community: The Legacy of Paul Ylvisaker*, ed. Virginia M. Esposito (New York: Peter Lang, 1999), 86; Paul N. Ylvisaker, "The Deserted City" (1959), in *Conscience & Community*, 95, 96, 102.

26. Karen Ferguson marks the shifts in Ylvisaker's thought about urban problems but does not address his international development work. Ferguson even cites Ylvisaker's 1973 reference to urban gray areas as "the nation's 'Calcutta'" to illuminate how he "pathologized [rural-urban] migration," but does not acknowledge the influence of his direct experience in the Indian city. See Ferguson, *Top Down*, 58. On Ensminger, see Sackley, "Village Models." On the interchange between US urban planners and the Ford Foundation's office in India, see Sam Collings-Wells, "Developing Communities: The Ford Foundation and the Global Urban Crisis, 1958–66," *Journal of Global History* 16, no. 3 (2021): 336–54; Andrew Friedman, "The Global Postcolonial Moment and the American New Town: India, Reston, Dodoma," *Journal of Urban History* 38, no. 3 (2012): 553–76; and Lizabeth Cohen, *Saving America's Cities: Ed Logue and the Struggle to Renew Urban America in the Suburban Age* (New York: Farrar, Straus, and Giroux, 2019), 93.

27. Request for Foundation-Administered Action No. 0D-801G, February 17, 1961, box 5, Paul N. Ylvisaker Papers.

28. Request for Foundation-Administered Action; Paul Ylvisaker to Henry Heald, March 24, 1961, box 5, Paul N. Ylvisaker Papers.

29. Paul Ylvisaker to Robert Culbertson, March 19, 1961, box 5, Paul N. Ylvisaker Papers; Paul Ylvisaker to Henry Heald, March 24, 1961. On Roy, see Nitish Sengupta, *Dr. Bidhan Chandra Roy* (New Delhi: Ministry of Information and Broadcasting, 2002). On the Bengal famine, see Janam Mukherjee, *Hungry Bengal: War, Famine and the End of Empire* (London: Hurst Publishers, 2015).

30. Paul Ylvisaker to Henry Heald, March 24, 1961.

31. Paul Ylvisaker to Henry Heald, March 24, 1961; Paul Ylvisaker to Robert Culbertson, March 19, 1961. Ananya Roy, Stuart Schrader, and Emma Shaw Crane show how the territorial imagination of "gray areas" was linked to fears of insurgency in the decolonizing world and of violent uprisings in US cities, and how it originated in the context of Cold War foreign policy. See Ananya Roy, Stuart Schrader, and Emma Shaw Crane, "'The Anti-Poverty Hoax': Development, Pacification, and the Making of Community in the Global 1960s," *Cities* 44 (2015): 139–45.

32. Paul N. Ylvisaker, "Diversity and the Public Interest: Two Cases in Metropolitan Decision-Making," *Journal of the American Institute of Planners* 27 (1961), 108; Interview with Paul Ylvisaker by Charles T. Morrissey, 27 September 1973, p. 19, folder 227, box 40, Oral History Project (FA618), Ford Foundation Records, Rockefeller Archive Center.

33. O'Connor, "Community Action," 595–96; Paul Ylvisaker, "Community Action: A Response to Some Unfinished Business" (1963), in *Conscience & Community*, 24.

34. Henry Saltzman, Specifics of Oakland Program, December 5, 1961, Ford Foundation—Gray Areas—1963 (July–December) folder, box 5, Paul N. Ylvisaker Papers. The most prominent contemporaneous account of the War on Poverty that interpreted community action in this way is Daniel Patrick Moynihan, *Maximum Feasible Misunderstanding: Community Action and the War on Poverty* (New York: Free Press, 1969). Moynihan believed that the empowerment of the poor by community action programs was an irresponsible mistake. Many contemporary scholars share Moynihan's empirical assessment that community action was designed straightforwardly to provide avenues for greater direct political participation by the poor, even as they

oppose his political assessment and see instead radical democratic potential in the ideological origins and organizational forms of community action. In this vein, see Annelise Orleck, *Storming Caesars Palace: How Black Mothers Fought Their Own War on Poverty* (Boston: Beacon, 2005); Noel A. Cazenave, *Impossible Democracy: The Unlikely Success of the War on Poverty Community Action Programs* (Albany: State University of New York Press, 2007); and Annelise Orleck and Lisa Gayle Hazirjian, eds., *The War on Poverty: A New Grassroots History, 1964–1980* (Athens: University of Georgia Press, 2011).

35. Address by Paul N. Ylvisaker at the 1963 Citizen's Conference on Community Planning, Indianapolis, IN, January 11, 1963, pp. 3, 5, 6, folder 28, box 27, Office Files of Wilson McNeil Lowry, Ford Foundation Records. Excerpts from this speech are published as Ylvisaker, "Community Action." On "systems analysis" and its path from the military-industrial complex into antipoverty policy, see Jennifer S. Light, *From Warfare to Welfare: Defense Intellectuals and Urban Problems in Cold War America* (Baltimore: Johns Hopkins University Press, 2003).

36. Address by Paul N. Ylvisaker at the 1963 Citizen's Conference, p. 6.

37. Countryman, *Up South*, 85–86.

38. Cecil Moore telegram to Ford Foundation, January 6, 1964, box 5, Paul N. Ylvisaker Papers; Countryman, *Up South*, 129.

39. Paul Ylvisaker to Clifford Campbell, Christopher Riley, and Henry Saltzman, December 4, 1963, box 5, Paul N. Ylvisaker Papers; Leon H. Sullivan, *Build, Brother, Build* (Philadelphia: Macrae Smith, 1969). Sullivan's career is beginning to be treated by scholars as a prime example of how demands for Black empowerment centered on entrepreneurship and job training came to supplant more radical demands for economic justice. On this point, see Stephanie Dyer, "Progress Plaza: Leon Sullivan, Zion Investment Associates, and Black Power in a Philadelphia Shopping Center," in *The Economic Civil Rights Movement: African Americans and the Struggle for Economic Power*, ed. Michael Ezra (New York: Routledge, 2013); and especially Jessica Ann Levy, "Black Power, Inc.: Corporatizing Anti-Racist Struggles in the U.S. and Sub-Saharan Africa" (PhD diss., Johns Hopkins University, 2019).

40. Michael Harris to Edward J. Meade, Interoffice Memo, December 18, 1963, Ford Foundation—Gray Areas—1964 (January–June) folder, box 5, Paul N. Ylvisaker Papers; Edward J. Meade to Paul Ylvisaker, Interoffice Memo, December 19, 1963, Ford Foundation—Gray Areas—1964 (January–June) folder, box 5, Paul N. Ylvisaker Papers; Christopher F. Edley to Paul Ylvisaker, Interoffice Memo, January 2, 1964, Ford Foundation—Gray Areas—1964 (January–June) folder, box 5, Paul N. Ylvisaker Papers; Grant Payment to Philadelphia Council for Community Advancement, Ford Foundation—Gray Areas—1964 (January–June) folder, box 5, Paul N. Ylvisaker Papers.

41. Interview with Paul Ylvisaker by Charles T. Morrissey, 27 September 1973, pp. 49–50, folder 227, box 40, Oral History Project (FA618), Ford Foundation Records. See also Ferguson, *Top Down*, 62–63.

42. Interview with Paul Ylvisaker by Charles T. Morrissey, 27 September 1973, p. 50; Paul Ylvisaker to Norman W. MacLeod, February 28, 1964, Ford Foundation—Gray Areas—1964 (January–June) folder, box 5, Paul N. Ylvisaker Papers; "Ford Foundation Official Lauds City Poverty War, But Sees Changes Ahead," *New Haven Journal-Courier*, Thursday, March 17, 1966. On the accelerating pace of urban uprisings after 1965, see especially Peter B. Levy, *The Great Uprising: Race Riots in Urban America during the 1960s* (Cambridge: Cambridge University Press, 2018).

43. Allen J. Matusow, *The Unraveling of America: A History of Liberalism in the 1960s* (Athens: University of Georgia Press, 2009), 107–19.

44. Judith Russell, *Economics, Bureaucracy, and Race: How Keynesians Misguided the War on Poverty* (New York: Columbia University Press, 2004); Michael Gillette, *Launching the War on Poverty: An Oral History* (New York: Twayne, 1996), 89–103.

45. Immerwahr, *Thinking Small*, 148.

46. A discussion of policymakers' views of the relationship between community action agencies and local governments is found in Gillette, *Launching the War on Poverty*, 73–79.

47. On Ylvisaker's role in the task force, see Gillette, *Launching the War on Poverty*, 18–19, 62, 96; and Charles L. Schultze, Memorandum for Bill Moyers, January 30, 1964, Staff: White House Correspondence, 1963–1965 folder, box 41, R. Sargent Shriver Personal Papers, John F. Kennedy Presidential Library and Museum. For the text of the EOA, see Economic Opportunity Act of 1964, Pub. L. 88–452, 78 Stat. 508 (1964), 516. Shriver is quoted in Gillette, *Launching the War on Poverty*, 74.

48. Tersh Boasberg to Joseph A. Califano Jr., June 28, 1967, Staff: White House Correspondence, May–Dec 1967 folder, box 41, R. Sargent Shriver Personal Papers; Leon Sullivan to Henry Heald, June 25, 1965, Ford Foundation—Personal (1964–1965) folder, box 5, Paul N. Ylvisaker Papers. On the OIC's rapid growth, see Sullivan, *Build, Brother, Build*, 108–131. Historians who have uncovered the democratic and redistributive demands of groups that were funded through community action, including early welfare rights organizations, have rarely considered how much more financial support the War on Poverty provided to groups such as Sullivan's OIC. See, for example, Orleck and Hazirjian, eds., *War on Poverty*.

49. Reverend Leon H. Sullivan, Testimony before Senate Hearing on Urban Problems, December 12, 1966, pp. 7, 10, 22, box 53, R. Sargent Shriver Personal Papers. On the growing association between the War on Poverty and the urban uprisings, see Matusow, *Unraveling of America*, 269–73.

Chapter Seven

1. James Q. Wilson, *Negro Politics: The Search for Leadership* (Glencoe, IL: Free Press, 1960). On Gosnell and the place of Black politics in American political science before the Second World War, see Jessica Blatt, *Race and the Making of American Political Science* (Philadelphia: University of Pennsylvania Press, 2018), especially 134–35. On the tendency to understand Black politics in simplistic terms of racial representation, see especially Kevin K. Gaines, *Uplifting the Race: Black Leadership, Politics, and Culture in the Twentieth Century* (Chapel Hill: University of North Carolina Press, 1996); Manning Marable, *Black Leadership* (New York: Columbia University Press, 1998); Adolph Reed Jr., *Stirrings in the Jug: Black Politics in the Post-Segregation Era* (Minneapolis: University of Minnesota Press, 1999); and Erica R. Edwards, *Charisma and the Fictions of Black Leadership* (Minneapolis: University of Minnesota Press, 2012).

2. Lawrence Dunbar Reddick, *Crusader without Violence: A Biography of Martin Luther King, Jr.* (New York: Harper, 1959), 233; L. D. Reddick, "More about *Crusader without Violence*: Author's Rebuttal," *Phylon* 21, no. 2 (1960): 202–203; L. D. Reddick to St. Clair Drake, July 25, 1958, folder 31, box 8, St. Clair Drake Papers; Barbara Ransby, *Ella Baker and the Black Freedom Movement: A Radical Democratic Vision* (Chapel Hill: University of North Carolina Press, 2003), 170–208, 273–298.

3. Daniel Immerwahr sees the rise in incidence of discussions of the "Black community" in the mid- to late 1960s as a semantic and intellectual innovation that emerged because of efforts

to apply the techniques of overseas community development to the poor within the United States. Although there is a connection between the two, Immerwahr overstates his case when he writes that the phrase "Black community" was "hardly ever used before 1960 and in constant use thereafter." While Immerwahr cites the Google Ngram for the phrase "Black community" as evidence for the nonexistence of the concept before the 1960s and its rapid ascent thereafter, the trend he observes has much more to do with the increased use of the word "Black" as a racial identifier than with a truly novel understanding of the "Black community" as a collective subject. The Ngram for the phrase "Negro community" reveals that the formulation was in use beginning in the 1920s and was fairly widespread by the 1940s. See Immerwahr, *Thinking Small*, 159, 236n120. Prominent sociological studies that relied on an idea of a "Negro community" in the earlier era include Drake and Cayton, *Black Metropolis*; Hortense Powdermaker, *After Freedom: A Cultural Study in the Deep South* (New York: Viking Press, 1939); and Allison Davis, Burleigh B. Gardner, and Mary R. Gardner, *Deep South: A Social Anthropological Study of Caste and Class* (1941; repr., Columbia: University of South Carolina Press, 2009). A Google Ngram for the two phrases can be found at https://books.google.com/ngrams/graph?content=Negro+community%2Cblack+community&year_start=1800&year_end=2019&corpus=en-2019&smoothing=3.

4. Lloyd Ohlin and Richard Cloward, *Delinquency and Opportunity: A Theory of Delinquent Gangs* (1960; repr., Florence, KY: Routledge, 2000); Matusow, *Unraveling of America*, 109–111; Elizabeth Hinton, *From the War on Poverty to the War on Crime: The Making of Mass Incarceration in America* (Cambridge, MA: Harvard University Press, 2016), 20, 36–40.

5. Ben Keppel, *The Work of Democracy: Ralph Bunche, Kenneth B. Clark, Lorraine Hansberry, and the Cultural Politics of Race* (Cambridge, MA: Harvard University Press, 1995), 144–47; Daniel Matlin, *On the Corner: African American Intellectuals and the Urban Crisis* (Cambridge, MA: Harvard University Press, 2013), 44; Gabriel N. Mendes, *Under the Strain of Color: Harlem's Lafargue Clinic and the Promise of an Antiracist Psychiatry* (Ithaca, NY: Cornell University Press, 2015), 98.

6. "Psychiatric Unit to Watch Gangs," *New York Times*, May 15, 1961; "Who's Delinquent?" *Amsterdam News*, Editorial, May 20, 1961.

7. Letter to Commissioner Ralph W. Whelan, New York City Youth Board, May 23, 1961, folder 4, box 49, Kenneth Bancroft Clark Papers, Library of Congress; "Pastor Hits Youth Board's New Proposal," *New York Amsterdam News*, June 24, 1961.

8. Letter to Commissioner Ralph W. Whelan, May 23, 1961.

9. "After Mounting Protests, Youth Bd. Promises Study on Gang Study," *New York Amsterdam News*, July 1, 1961; "The Reminiscences of Kenneth B. Clark," April 7, 1976, pp. 150–53, Oral History Collection of Columbia University in the City of New York, http://www.columbia.edu/cu/lweb/digital/collections/nny/clarkk/transcripts/clarkk_1_4_150.html; "A New Agency Works in Harlem," *New York Amsterdam News*, October 13, 1962; Matlin, *On the Corner*, 45. On the discussions of HARYOU in the Johnson administration's Task Force on Poverty, see Arthur M. Schlesinger Jr., *Robert Kennedy and His Times* (New York: Houghton Mifflin, 1978), 409–12; and Gillette, *Launching the War on Poverty*, 18–19.

10. Charles E. Silberman, *Crisis in Black and White* (New York: Vintage Books, 1964), 196, 197–98.

11. Silberman, *Crisis in Black and White*, 354. On the funding of Silberman's research by the Ford Foundation, see Cazenave, *Impossible Democracy*, 198n23.

12. On Alinsky's relationship with Lewis, see Sanford Horwitt, *Let Them Call Me Rebel: Saul Alinsky—His Life and Legacy* (New York: Alfred A. Knopf, 1989), 99–101, 218–22. On Alinsky's hostility to leftist ideologies, see Saul Alinsky, *Rules for Radicals: A Practical Primer for Realistic Radicals* (1971; repr., New York: Vintage Books, 1989), 8–10.

13. Saul Alinsky, *Reveille for Radicals* (Chicago: University of Chicago Press, 1946), 87–98; Vijay Phulwani, "The Poor Man's Machiavelli: Saul Alinsky and the Morality of Power," *American Political Science Review* 110, no. 4 (November 2016): 863–75.

14. Famously, The Woodlawn Organization would go on to win a $1 million grant from the Office of Economic Opportunity in 1967 to organize young people connected to the Blackstone Rangers and East Side Disciples gangs, which drew the ire of conservative critics of the War on Poverty. See Hinton, *From the War*, 53.

15. Cazenave, *Impossible Democracy*, 198n23; Charles L. Schultze, Memorandum for Bill Moyers, January 30, 1964, Staff: White House Correspondence, 1963–1965 folder, box 41, R. Sargent Shriver Personal Papers.

16. "Best Seller List," *New York Times*, October 4, 1964, BR8.

17. Harlem Youth Opportunities Unlimited, *Youth in the Ghetto: A Study of the Consequences of Powerlessness and a Blueprint for Change* (New York: HARYOU, 1964), 97, 88–93.

18. Matlin, *On the Corner*, 89–93; Harlem Youth Opportunities Unlimited, *Youth in the Ghetto*, 580–81.

19. Harlem Youth Opportunities Unlimited, *Youth in the Ghetto*, 10, 76.

20. *Harlem Youth Report #5: Youth in the Ghetto and the Blueprint for Change*, pp. 2, 7, folder 9, box 50, Kenneth Bancroft Clark Papers.

21. *Harlem Youth Report #5*, 12.

22. Matlin, *On the Corner*, 104; Cazenave, *Impossible Democracy*, 109–114; Kenneth Clark to Arthur Logan, July 28, 1964, folder 6, box 49, Kenneth Bancroft Clark Papers.

23. Kenneth B. Clark, *Dark Ghetto: Dilemmas of Social Power* (New York: Harper & Row, 1965), xx. Daniel Matlin reports that the book "sold just under 38,000 copies in its hardback edition and a further 136,000 following a reissue as a paperback in 1967." It was also partially serialized in the *New York Post*. See Matlin, *On the Corner*, 43.

24. Bertrand Russell, "Statement on *Dark Ghetto*," folder 4, box 184, Kenneth Bancroft Clark Papers; Clark, *Dark Ghetto*, 29.

25. Clark, *Dark Ghetto*, 27, 213, 222.

26. Kenneth Clark and Jeannette Hopkins, *A Relevant War on Poverty: A Study of Community Action Programs and Observable Social Change* (New York: Harper & Row, 1969), 133–60.

27. Kenneth B. Clark, "Problems of the Ghetto," p. 12, folder 1, box 162, Kenneth Bancroft Clark Papers.

Chapter Eight

1. Peniel E. Joseph, "Introduction: Toward a Historiography of the Black Power Movement," in *The Black Power Movement: Rethinking the Civil Rights–Black Power Era*, ed. Peniel E. Joseph (New York: Routledge, 2006): 14–15. The protean nature of the Black Power slogan is rendered beautifully in Rhonda Y. Williams, *Concrete Demands: The Search for Black Power in the 20th Century* (New York: Routledge, 2015), especially 127–64.

2. Frantz Fanon, *The Wretched of the Earth*, trans. Constance Farrington (New York: Grove Press, 1963), 73. The importance of the idea of an "inferiority complex" to the Black Power movement is discussed in Matlin, *On the Corner*. For a competing view, which argues that Black Power activists rejected Fanon's notion of an "inferiority complex" as part of their broader rejection of "damage imagery" in social-scientific depictions of Black life, see Daryl Michael Scott, *Contempt and Pity: Social Policy and the Image of the Damaged Black Psyche, 1880–1996* (Chapel Hill: University of North Carolina Press, 1997), 172.

3. For examinations of diverse examples of this phenomenon, see especially Tanisha C. Ford, *Liberated Threads: Black Women, Style, and the Global Politics of Soul* (Chapel Hill: University of North Carolina Press, 2015); Russell Rickford, *We Are an African People: Independent Education, Black Power, and the Radical Imagination* (New York: Oxford University Press, 2016); and Martha Biondi, *The Black Revolution on Campus* (Oakland: University of California Press, 2012).

4. Malloy, *Out of Oakland*, 70–106. These links form the subject of Schrader, *Badges without Borders*.

5. Hannah Arendt, *On Violence* (New York: Harcourt, 1969). As historians of the Black Power movement have long noted, exploring the post-1965 history of the Black freedom struggle primarily through the lens of violence, whether deployed by the state or by insurgent groups, obscures critical issues. For one of many examples, see Peniel E. Joseph, "The Black Power Movement: A State of the Field," *Journal of American History* 96, no. 3 (December 2009): 751–76.

6. Plotting these coordinates of the reception of Fanon's thought in the United States serves a similar purpose for the Black Power movement in the mid-1960s as does Max Elbaum's discussion of how Third World Marxism influenced student radicals and the New Communist Movement between 1968 and 1973. See Max Elbaum, *Revolution in the Air: Sixties Radicals Turn to Lenin, Mao, and Che* (New York: Verso, 2002).

7. C. Wright Mills, "Letter to the New Left," *New Left Review* 1, no. 5 (September–October 1960): 22; Kevin Mattson, *Intellectuals in Action: The Origins of the New Left and Radical Liberalism, 1945–1970* (University Park: Pennsylvania State University Press, 2002); Howard Brick and Christopher Phelps, *Radicals in America: The U.S. Left Since the Second World War* (Cambridge: Cambridge University Press, 2015), especially 88–120.

8. Cruse, "Revolutionary Nationalism and the Afro-American," 74. For reactions to the Cuban Revolution on the US left, see Gosse, *Where the Boys Are*; and Rafael Rojas, *Fighting over Fidel: The New York Intellectuals and the Cuban Revolution*, trans. Carl Good (Princeton, NJ: Princeton University Press, 2016).

9. Cruse, "Revolutionary Nationalism and the Afro-American," 74, 75–76.

10. Cruse, "Revolutionary Nationalism and the Afro-American," 78, 86. On the relationship between Cruse and Haywood, see Johnson, "Between Revolution and the Racial Ghetto."

11. Cruse, "Revolutionary Nationalism and the Afro-American," 94.

12. Cruse, "Revolutionary Nationalism and the Afro-American," 82, 90.

13. Cruse, "Revolutionary Nationalism and the Afro-American," 91. On the weaknesses of Cruse's conception of a sharp division between integrationism and Black nationalism, see especially Singh, *Black Is a Country*, 185.

14. On James Boggs's intellectual development within the labor movement and the Black freedom movement, see Ward, *In Love and Struggle*, especially 37–59. On Grace Lee Boggs's

work with the Johnson-Forest Tendency, see Grace Lee Boggs, *Living for Change: An Autobiography* (1998; Minneapolis: University of Minnesota Press, 2016), 117–41.

15. This debate is explored in Ward, *In Love and Struggle*, 198–205. For an example of the political thought of the Correspondence group, see C. L. R. James, Grace Lee Boggs, and Cornelius Castoriadis, *Facing Reality* (Detroit: Correspondence Publishing Company, 1958).

16. Grace Lee Boggs quoted in Ward, *In Love and Struggle*, 321; James Boggs, *The American Revolution: Pages from a Negro Worker's Notebook* (New York: Monthly Review, 1963), 42.

17. Thomas J. Sugrue, *The Origins of the Urban Crisis: Race and Inequality in Postwar Detroit* (Princeton, NJ: Princeton University Press, 1996), 130–38; Heather Ann Thompson, *Whose Detroit?: Politics, Labor, and Race in a Modern American City* (Ithaca, NY: Cornell University Press, 2001), 36–37. As historian Jason Resnikoff argues, the idea of "automation" was regularly invoked to enhance the authority of management on the shop floor. See Jason Resnikoff, *Labor's End: How the Promise of Automation Degraded Work* (Urbana: University of Illinois Press, 2022).

18. Grace Lee Boggs, "Who Will Blow the Trumpet?," August 20, 1963, quoted in Ward, *In Love and Struggle*, 322; James Boggs, *American Revolution*, 33–41, 52.

19. Peniel Joseph, "Waiting till the Midnight Hour: Reconceptualizing the Heroic Period of the Civil Rights Movement, 1954–1965," *Souls* 2, no. 2 (2000): 6–17; Brandon M. Terry, "Requiem for a Dream: The Problem-Space of Black Power," in *To Shape a New World: Essays on the Political Philosophy of Martin Luther King, Jr.*, ed. Tommie Shelby and Brandon M. Terry (Cambridge, MA: Harvard University Press, 2018), 313–14.

20. "'A Statement to the South and Nation,' Issued by the Southern Negro Leaders Conference on Transportation and Nonviolent Integration," 10 January–11 January 1957," in *The Papers of Martin Luther King, Jr., Vol IV: Symbol of the Movement, January 1957–December 1958*, ed. Clayborne Carson, et al. (Oakland: University of California Press, 1992), 103. Available at https://kinginstitute.stanford.edu/king-papers/documents/statement-south-and-nation-issued-southern-negro-leaders-conference.

21. Gunnar Myrdal, *An American Dilemma: The Negro Problem and Modern Democracy*, Volume I and Volume II (New York: Harper, 1944); Roy Wilkins, "Desegregation North and South," *Current History* 32, no. 189 (May 1957): 283–87. On the "creedal narrative" of postwar racial liberalism, see Rana, *The Constitutional Bind*, 398–401.

22. Malcolm X, "The Ballot or the Bullet" (1964), in *Say It Loud!: Great Speeches on Civil Rights and African American Identity*, ed. Catherine Ellis and Stephen Drury Smith (New York: The New Press, 2010), 9.

23. Malcolm X, "Ballot or the Bullet," 12. On Malcolm X's shifting conceptions of revolution and their importance to the theoretical development of the Black Power movement, see Errol A. Henderson, *The Revolution Will Not Be Theorized: Cultural Revolution in the Black Power Era* (Albany: State University of New York Press, 2019), 1–94. On Black voters and the 1948 election, see Henry Lee Moon, *Balance of Power: The Negro Vote* (Garden City, NY: Doubleday, 1948). For more on African Americans' politics of petition at UN, see Anderson, *Eyes off the Prize*; MacKinnon, "Declaration as Disavowal"; and ch. 2 of this work.

24. Malcolm X, "Ballot or the Bullet," 13.

25. Malcolm X, "Ballot or the Bullet," 18.

26. Martin Luther King Jr., *Where Do We Go from Here: Chaos or Community?* (New York: Harper & Row, 1967), 4.

27. Fanon, *Wretched of the Earth*, 216.

28. Fanon, *Wretched of the Earth*, 94. Adam Shatz argues that the translation of "la violence désintoxique" as "violence is a cleansing force" is inapt, and that "disintoxicating" would be more accurate. See Adam Shatz, *The Rebel's Clinic: The Revolutionary Lives of Frantz Fanon* (New York: Farrar, Straus, and Giroux, 2024), 155.

29. On Farrington and her translation, see Kathryn Batchelor, "The Translation of *Les Damnés de la Terre* into English: Exploring Irish Connections," in *Translating Frantz Fanon Across Continents and Languages* (New York: Routledge, 2017); Kathryn Batchelor, "Fanon's *Les Damnés de la Terre*, De-Philosophization and the Intensification of Violence," *Nottingham French Studies* 54, no. 1 (2015): 7–22; and Ben Etherington, "An Answer to the Question: What Is Decolonization? Frantz Fanon's *The Wretched of the Earth* and Jean-Paul Sartre's *Critique of Dialectical Reason*," *Modern Intellectual History* 13, no. 1 (April 2016): 151–78. Despite the greater sensitivity to the philosophical nuance and referentiality in the later translation of *The Wretched of the Earth* by Richard Philcox, I rely on Farrington's translation, because it is the version that Fanon's first generation of English-language readers could access.

30. Aristide Zolberg and Vera Zolberg, "The Americanization of Frantz Fanon," *Public Interest* 9 (Fall 1967): 50; William L. Van Deburg, *New Day in Babylon: The Black Power Movement and American Culture, 1965–1975* (Chicago: University of Chicago Press, 1992), 60–61.

31. Loren Glass, *Counterculture Colophon: Grove Press, the Evergreen Review, and the Incorporation of the Avant-Garde* (Stanford, CA: Stanford University Press, 2013), 145–72; Batchelor, "Translation of *Les Damnés*," 52.

32. Jonathan Fenderson, *Building the Black Arts Movement: Hoyt Fuller and the Cultural Politics of the 1960s* (Urbana: University of Illinois Press, 2019), 6; "About Writers and Writing," *Negro Digest* 14, no. 9 (July 1965): 73; Roland Snellings, "Symposium: Negro Rights and the American Future," *Negro Digest* 15, no. 12 (October 1966): 66.

33. Ralph Gleason, "An Introduction to Frantz Fanon," *Ramparts* (March 1966), 36–7.

34. Frantz Fanon, "Racism and Culture," *Streets* 1, no. 2 (May–June 1965): 5–12; Frantz Fanon, *Toward the African Revolution*, trans. Haakon Chevalier (New York: Monthly Review, 1967), 29–44; Interview with Maro Riofrancos, January 28, 2022.

35. Fanon, *Toward the African Revolution*, 35, 36, 42, 44. On the rise of individualistic explanations of racism across the West, see Gordon, *From Power to Prejudice*; and Alice L. Conklin, *In the Museum of Man: Race, Anthropology, and Empire in France, 1850–1950* (Ithaca, NY: Cornell University Press, 2013). On the place of Négritude at the Congress, see especially Merve Fejzula, "Gendered Labor, Negritude, and the Black Public Sphere," *Historical Research* 95, no. 296 (August 2022): 423–46.

36. Maro Riofrancos to James Boggs, June 3, 1965, folder 2, box 2, James and Grace Lee Boggs Papers, Walter P. Reuther Library, Archives of Labor and Urban Affairs, Wayne State University; James Boggs to Maro Riofrancos, June 6, 1965, folder 2, box 2, James and Grace Lee Boggs Papers; James Boggs, Review of Frantz Fanon, *The Wretched of the Earth* (Grove Edition of *The Damned*), n.d., folder 9, box 1, James and Grace Lee Boggs Papers. Boggs's view that Fanon's writing involved a sense of totality is somewhat ironic because of the skepticism toward the concept of totality that pervaded the work of Sartre, one of Fanon's major influences. See Martin Jay, *Marxism and Totality: The Adventures of a Concept from Lukács to Habermas* (Oakland: University of California Press, 1984), 331–60.

37. James Boggs to Maro Riofrancos, June 6, 1965; James Boggs, Review of Frantz Fanon, *The Wretched of the Earth*; Fanon, *Wretched of the Earth*, 102.

38. Andre Gunder Frank, "The Development of Underdevelopment," *Monthly Review* 18, no. 4 (September 1966): 17–31; Samir Amin, *Accumulation on a World Scale: A Critique of the Theory of Underdevelopment* (New York: Monthly Review, 1974); Fanon, *Wretched of the Earth*, 101.

39. Forman briefly discussed his plans to write a Fanon biography in his autobiography. See James Forman, *The Making of Black Revolutionaries* (1972; Seattle: University of Washington Press, 1997), 531–32. Forman's intermittent efforts to establish a Frantz Fanon Institute have received almost no scholarly attention, but they occupied a significant amount of his time and attention between the summer of 1968 and the fall of 1970, eventually becoming part of his plans for the Black Economic Development Conference. See Diary Entry, August 26, 1968, folder 10, box 82, James Forman Papers, Library of Congress; James Forman to Josie Fanon, August 27, 1968, folder 10, box 82, James Forman Papers; James Forman to St. Clair Drake, January 28, 1969, folder 1, box 7, James Forman Papers; Articles of Incorporation of Franz Fanon Institute, October 1970, folder 8, box 82, James Forman Papers. For a brief discussion of Forman's "obsession" with Fanon, see Shatz, *Rebel's Clinic*, 365–67. On the decline of SNCC's organizing efforts, see Clayborne Carson, *In Struggle: SNCC and the Black Awakening of the 1960s* (Cambridge, MA: Harvard University Press, 1996), 229–43.

40. Forman, *Making of Black Revolutionaries*, 103. On Forman's studies with Drake, see Forman, *Making of Black Revolutionaries*, 83–84. On Forman's influence on SNCC's internationalism in the early 1960s, see Fanon Che Wilkins, "The Making of Black Internationalists: SNCC and Africa before the Launching of Black Power, 1960–1965," *Journal of African American History* 92, no. 4 (Autumn 2007): 467–490. A concise account of Cold War African Studies that focuses on the field's connections to major philanthropies can be found in Parmar, *Foundations of the American Century*, 149–79.

41. Wilkins, "Making of Black Internationalists," 477–87.

42. On the organizational and personal conflicts within SNCC in 1966–67, see Carson, *In Struggle*, 215–64. On Forman's trip to Lusaka, see Carson, *In Struggle*, 266; and Forman, *Making of Black Revolutionaries*, 483.

43. Student Nonviolent Coordinating Committee, "The Indivisible Struggle against Racism, Apartheid and Colonialism," pp. 6, 10–11, folder 2, box 21, James Forman Papers; Charles M. Payne, *I've Got the Light of Freedom: The Organizing Tradition and the Mississippi Freedom Struggle* (Oakland: University of California Press, 1995), 363–90.

44. John Munro, "Imperial Anticommunism and the African American Freedom Movement in the Early Cold War," *History Workshop Journal* 79, no. 1 (Spring 2015): 52–75.

45. O'Dell quoted in Nikhil Pal Singh, "'Learn Your Horn': Jack O'Dell and the Long Civil Rights Movement," in *Climbin' Jacob's Ladder: The Black Freedom Movement Writings of Jack O'Dell*, ed. Nikhil Pal Singh (Oakland: University of California Press, 2010), 30. For more on the importance of *Freedomways*, see Ian Rocksborough-Smith, "'Filling the Gap': Intergenerational Black Radicalism and the Popular Front Ideals of *Freedomways* Magazine's Early Years (1961–1965)," *Afro-Americans in New York Life and History* 31, no. 1 (January 2007): 7–42.

46. J. H. O'Dell, "Foundations of Racism in American Life," *Freedomways* 4, no. 4 (Fall 1964): 530, 532.

47. O'Dell, "Foundations of Racism," 532. On Goldwater's combination of these two strands of conservative politics, see Kim Phillips-Fein, *Invisible Hands: The Making of the Conservative Movement from the New Deal to Reagan* (New York: Norton, 2009), 115–49.

48. J. H. O'Dell, "Colonialism and the Negro American Experience," *Freedomways* 6, no. 4 (Fall 1966): 296, 297, 301, 303.

49. J. H. O'Dell, "A Special Variety of Colonialism," *Freedomways* 7, no. 1 (Winter 1967): 8, 9, 11-12.

Chapter Nine

1. On the policies that created and maintained the "second ghetto," and the ways that struggles against these policies drove much of the civil rights movement in the North, see especially Sugrue, *The Origins of the Urban Crisis*; Arnold Hirsch, *Making the Second Ghetto: Race and Housing in Chicago, 1940–1960* (Cambridge: Cambridge University Press, 1983); Martha Biondi, *To Stand and Fight: The Struggle for Civil Rights in Postwar New York City* (Cambridge, MA: Harvard University Press, 2003); Jeanne F. Theoharis and Komozi Woodard, eds., *Freedom North: Black Freedom Struggles Outside the South, 1940–1980* (New York: Palgrave Macmillan, 2003); Robert Self, *American Babylon: Race and the Struggle for Postwar Oakland* (Princeton, NJ: Princeton University Press, 2005); and Keeanga-Yamahtta Taylor, *Race for Profit: How Banks and the Real Estate Industry Undermined Black Homeownership* (Chapel Hill: University of North Carolina Press, 2019).

2. See especially Edward Purcell, *The Crisis of Democratic Theory: Scientific Naturalism and the Problem of Value* (Lexington: University Press of Kentucky, 1973); John G. Gunnell, *The Descent of Political Theory: The Genealogy of American Vocation* (Chicago: University of Chicago Press, 1993); Sheldon S. Wolin, *Politics and Vision: Continuity and Innovation in Western Political Thought*, Expanded Edition (Princeton, NJ: Princeton University Press, 2016); Kyong-Min Son, *The Eclipse of the Demos: The Cold War and the Crisis of Democracy before Neoliberalism* (Lawrence: University Press of Kansas, 2020); and Samuel Moyn, *Liberalism against Itself: Cold War Intellectuals and the Making of Our Times* (New Haven, CT: Yale University Press, 2023).

3. C. Wright Mills, *The Power Elite* (New York: Oxford University Press, 1956); Robert A. Dahl and Charles E. Lindblom, *Politics, Economics, and Welfare* (Chicago: University of Chicago Press, 1953), 283; Robert A. Dahl, *A Preface to Democratic Theory* (Chicago: University of Chicago Press, 1956), 63–89. On the "Yale school," see Richard M. Merelman, *Pluralism at Yale: The Culture of Political Science in America* (Madison: University of Wisconsin Press, 2003). The pluralists, in portraying Mills as an outsider to a social-scientific consensus, both ironically increased his popularity with the New Left and obscured his deep connections with mainstream currents in sociology. See Daniel Geary, *Radical Ambition: C. Wright Mills, the Left, and American Social Thought* (Oakland: University of California Press, 2009).

4. Robert Dahl, *Who Governs?: Democracy and Power in an American City* (New Haven, CT: Yale University Press, 1961), 54, 61–2, 163.

5. Nathan Glazer and Daniel Patrick Moynihan, *Beyond the Melting Pot: The Negroes, Puerto Ricans, Jews, Italians, and Irish of New York City* (Cambridge, MA: MIT Press, 1963), 13, 17. For more on these discussions across the social sciences and American political discourse, see especially Matthew Frye Jacobson, *Roots Too: White Ethnic Revival in Post-Civil Rights America* (Cambridge, MA: Harvard University Press, 2006); Wendy L. Wall, *Inventing the "American Way": The Politics of Consensus from the New Deal to the Civil Rights Movement* (New York: Oxford University Press, 2007); Daniel Geary, *Beyond Civil Rights: The Moynihan Report and Its Legacy* (Philadelphia: University of Pennsylvania Press, 2015).

6. Glazer and Moynihan, *Beyond the Melting Pot*, 33, 84. On the place of Glazer and Moynihan in neoconservatism, see Justin Vaïsse, *Neoconservatism: The Biography of a Movement*, trans. Arthur Goldhammer (Cambridge, MA: Harvard University Press, 2010), 50–81.

7. Charles V. Hamilton and Frederick C. Harris, "A Conversation with Charles V. Hamilton," *Annual Review of Political Science* 21 (2018): 24–25.

8. Peniel E. Joseph, *Stokely: A Life* (New York: Basic Books, 2014), 173. The high priority placed on surveilling Carmichael is discussed at length in Joseph, *Stokely*, especially 135–36, 155–56, 192–93, and 247–48. For an analysis of geographically dispersed "revolutionary hubs" in the age of decolonization, see Abdel Razzaq Takriti, *Monsoon Revolution: Republicans, Sultans, and Empires in Oman, 1965–1976* (New York: Oxford University Press, 2013).

9. Kwame Ture (Stokely Carmichael) and Charles V. Hamilton, *Black Power: The Politics of Liberation* (1967; New York: Vintage, 1992), 4, 5, 16–20. On Carmichael's political thought and the conceptual innovation of "institutional racism," see Brandon M. Terry, "Stokely Carmichael and the Longing for Black Liberation: Black Power and Beyond," in *African American Political Thought: A Collected History*, ed. Melvin Rogers and Jack Turner (Chicago: University of Chicago Press, 2021), 593–630.

10. Ture and Hamilton, *Black Power*, 5.

11. Ture and Hamilton, *Black Power*, 10. Of course, scholars of European colonial rule would dispute the characterization of colonial offices as monolithic. For one example, see Cooper, *Colonialism in Question*.

12. Ture and Hamilton, *Black Power*, 44, 45, 47. For Du Bois's essay, see W. E. B. Du Bois, "Close Ranks," *The Crisis* 16 (July 1918): 111. While Carmichael later disowned the passage about "closing ranks," Hamilton continued to defend it. On this point, see Stokely Carmichael, "Pan-Africanism—Land and Power," *The Black Scholar* 1, no. 1 (November 1969): 36–43; and Charles V. Hamilton, "An Advocate of Black Power Defines It," *New York Times Magazine*, April 14, 1968. On the incorporation of the Black Power movement into existing structures of politics, especially at the municipal level, see especially Robert C. Smith, "Black Power and the Transformation from Protest to Politics," *Political Science Quarterly* 93, no. 3 (Autumn 1981): 431–43; Johnson, *Revolutionaries to Race Leaders*; Devin Fergus, *Liberalism, Black Power, and the Making of American Politics, 1965–1980* (Athens: University of Georgia Press, 2009); Ferguson, *Top Down*; and Rickford, *We Are an African People*.

13. Cruse, "Revolutionary Nationalism and the Afro-American," 77.

14. On the relationship between *Crisis of the Negro Intellectual* and Cruse's earlier work, see Singh, "Negro Exceptionalism: The Antinomies of Harold Cruse." For a critical examination of *Crisis of the Negro Intellectual*, and Cruse's negative opinion of Caribbean immigrants in particular, see James, *Holding Aloft the Banner of Ethiopia*. Hortense Spillers offers an insightful retrospective on Cruse's work, paying particular attention to his arguments about economics and cultural labor, in Hortense Spillers, "The Crisis of the Negro Intellectual: A Post-Date," *boundary 2* 21, no. 3 (Autumn 1994): 65–116. For a variety of perspectives on *Crisis*, some of which explore Cruse's views on international affairs, see the essays in Watts, ed., *Harold Cruse's The Crisis*.

15. Harold Cruse, *The Crisis of the Negro Intellectual: A Historical Analysis of the Failure of Black Leadership* (1967; repr., New York: New York Review Books, 2005), 85, 86, 94, 320.

16. Cruse, *The Crisis of the Negro Intellectual*, 354, 391, 342, 344.

17. Cruse, *The Crisis of the Negro Intellectual*, 260.

18. Cruse, "Rebellion or Revolution?–I," in *Rebellion or Revolution?*, 110–111, 188.

19. Levy, *The Great Uprising*, 1. Elizabeth Hinton, *America on Fire: The Untold History of Police Violence and Black Rebellion Since the 1960s* (New York: Liveright, 2021).

20. National Advisory Commission on Civil Disorders, *Report of the National Advisory Commission on Civil Disorders, New York Times Edition* (New York: Alfred A. Knopf, 1968), 2.

21. Albert O. Hirschman, *The Passions and the Interests: Political Arguments for Capitalism before Its Triumph* (1977; Princeton, NJ: Princeton University Press, 2013), 40; Anton Jäger, "The Semantic Drift: Images of Populism in Post-War American Historiography and Their Relevance for (European) Political Science," *Constellations* 24 (2017): 310–23.

22. Roberta Wohlstetter, *Pearl Harbor: Warning and Decision* (Stanford, CA: Stanford University Press, 1962); Albert Wohlstetter, "The Delicate Balance of Terror," *Foreign Affairs* 37, no. 1 (1958): 211. On the Wohlstetters' influence on US foreign policy, see Andrew Bacevich, "Tailors to the Emperor," *New Left Review* 69 (May–June 2011): 101–124; and Ron Robin, *The Cold World They Made: The Strategic Legacy of Roberta and Albert Wohlstetter* (Cambridge, MA: Harvard University Press, 2016).

23. Schrader, *Badges without Borders*, 27–51.

24. Albert Wohlstetter and Roberta Wohlstetter, "Metaphors and Models: Inequalities and Disorder at Home and Abroad," RAND Corporation, D-17664-RC/ISA, August 27, 1968; Albert Wohlstetter and Roberta Wohlstetter, "'Third Worlds' Abroad and at Home," *The Public Interest* 14 (Winter 1969): 88–107. For a similar perspective on the influence of Fanon in particular, see Zolberg and Zolberg, "The Americanization of Frantz Fanon."

25. Wohlstetter and Wohlstetter, "Metaphors and Models;" Wohlstetter and Wohlstetter, "'Third Worlds' Abroad," 101.

26. Wohlstetter and Wohlstetter, "'Third Worlds' Abroad," 90; Gary S. Becker, *The Economics of Discrimination* (Chicago: University of Chicago Press, 1957), 6.

27. Raymond Price, *With Nixon* (New York: Viking Press, 1977). On the lasting impact of the 1968 presidential election on US politics, see Michael A. Cohen, *American Maelstrom: The 1968 Election and the Politics of Division* (New York: Oxford University Press, 2016).

28. Richard Nixon, "Address Accepting the Presidential Nomination at the Republican National Convention in Miami Beach, Florida," August 8, 1968, The American Presidency Project, https://www.presidency.ucsb.edu/documents/address-accepting-the-presidential-nomination-the-republican-national-convention-miami.

29. Touré Reed explores this longer history as it relates to the Urban League in the first half of the twentieth century. See Touré F. Reed, *Not Alms but Opportunity: The Urban League and the Politics of Racial Uplift, 1910–1950* (Chapel Hill: University of North Carolina Press, 2008).

30. Joshua D. Farrington, *Black Republicans and the Transformation of the GOP* (Philadelphia: University of Pennsylvania Press, 2016), 170–95; Leah Wright Rigueur, *The Loneliness of the Black Republican: Pragmatic Politics and the Pursuit of Power* (Princeton, NJ: Princeton University Press, 2015), 136–76.

31. "Liberals, Conservatives Combine on Self-Help Bill," *Newsday*, July 25, 1968. On the Community Self-Determination Act, see Van Deburg, 137–40; Nishani Frazier, *Harambee City: The Congress of Racial Equality and the Rise of Black Power Populism* (Fayetteville: University of Arkansas Press, 2017), 194–206; and Mehrsa Baradaran, *The Color of Money: Black Banks and the Racial Wealth Gap* (Cambridge, MA: Harvard University Press, 2017), 174–75. See also, more generally, Laura Warren Hill and Julia Rabig, eds., *The Business of Black Power: Community Development, Capitalism, and Corporate Responsibility in Postwar America* (Rochester, NY: University of Rochester Press, 2012).

32. Roy Innis, "Separatist Economics: A New Social Contract," in *Black Economic Development*, ed. William Haddad and C. Douglas Pugh (Englewood Hills, NJ: Prentice-Hall, 1969).

33. *Financial Institutions and the Urban Crisis: Hearings before the United States Senate Committee on Banking and Currency, Subcommittee on Financial Institutions*, 90th Cong. 3 (1968) (statement of Walter F. Mondale, US Senator from the State of Minnesota). See also Taylor, *Race for Profit*, 48–54.

Chapter Ten

1. Robert L. Allen, *Black Awakening in Capitalist America: An Analytic History* (1969; repr., Trenton, NJ: Africa World Press, 1992), 2; Cobb, *Native Activism in Cold War America*; Dan Berger and Roxanne Dunbar-Ortiz, "'The Struggle Is for Land!' Race, Territory, and National Liberation," in *The Hidden 1970s: Histories of Radicalism*, ed. Dan Berger (New Brunswick, NJ: Rutgers University Press, 2010), 57–76; Sonia Song-Ha Lee, *Building a Latino Civil Rights Movement: Puerto Ricans, African Americans, and the Pursuit of Racial Justice in New York City* (Chapel Hill: University of North Carolina Press, 2014). For the parallel story of the idea of internal colonialism in Chicano thought and activism, see Mario Barrera, *Race and Class in the Southwest: A Theory of Racial Inequality* (South Bend, IN: University of Notre Dame Press, 1979); Ramón A. Gutiérrez, "Internal Colonialism: An American Theory of Race," *Du Bois Review: Social Science Research on Race* 1, no. 2 (2004): 281–95.

2. Robert L. Allen, "Hanoi Readies for Final Attack," *National Guardian*, October 14, 1967, folder 61, carton 1, Dr. Robert L. Allen Papers, BANC MSS 2017/193, The Bancroft Library, University of California, Berkeley; "Notebook: Black Power Conference, Newark, New Jersey, and Core Press Conference, 1967," folder 53, carton 1, Dr. Robert L. Allen Papers; Allen, *Black Awakening*, 17.

3. Jane Berger, *A New Working Class: The Legacies of Public-Sector Employment in the Civil Rights Movement* (Philadelphia: University of Pennsylvania Press, 2021), 3; J. Phillip Thompson, III, *Double Trouble: Black Mayors, Black Communities, and the Call for a Deep Democracy* (New York: Oxford University Press, 2006).

4. Allen, *Black Awakening*, 11, 194, 262, 13.

5. Kwame Nkrumah, *Neocolonialism: The Last Stage of Imperialism* (London: Thomas, Nelson, and Sons, 1965).

6. Ture and Hamilton, *Black Power*, 10; Martin Kilson, *Political Change in a West African State: A Study of the Modernization Process in Sierra Leone* (New York: Atheneum, 1966).

7. Allen, *Black Awakening*, 14, 17. Historian Richard Rathbone has revised the view that the structures of authority of nationalist governance completely replaced chieftaincy in Ghana, arguing that, in many areas, the CPP worked to gain the favor of chiefs as it pursued its aims. See Richard Rathbone, *Nkrumah and the Chiefs: The Politics of Chieftaincy in Ghana, 1951–60* (Athens: Ohio University Press, 2000).

8. Allen, *Black Awakening*, 17, 19, 65.

9. Allen, *Black Awakening*, 50, 177, 178, 182; Cruse, *The Crisis of the Negro Intellectual*, quoted in Allen, *Black Awakening*, 179.

10. Allen, *Black Awakening*, 261–62, 268–73.

11. National Black Economic Development Conference Program, folder 9, box 4, Kenneth and Sheila Cockrel Papers, Walter P. Reuther Library, Archives of Labor and Urban Affairs, Wayne State University; Keith Dye, "The Debate on Reparations before the Debate on

Reparations at the National Black Economic Development Conference in Detroit, 1969," *Michigan Historical Review* 46, no. 2 (Fall 2020): 175–86.

12. Judy Tzu-Chun Wu, "An African-Vietnamese American: Robert S. Browne, the Antiwar Movement, and the Personal/Political Dimensions of Black Internationalism," *Journal of African American History* 92, no. 4 (Fall 2007): 491–515.

13. Robert S. Browne, Keynote Speech Delivered at National Black Economic Development Conference, Detroit, Michigan, April 25, 1969, folder 3, box 1, Dan Georgakas Papers, Walter P. Reuther Library, Archives of Labor and Urban Affairs, Wayne State University.

14. Robert S. Browne, Keynote Speech, National Black Economic Development Conference.

15. Boggs's speech was later printed in *Review of Black Political Economy*. See James Boggs, "The Myth and Irrationality of Black Capitalism," *Review of Black Political Economy* 1, no. 1 (Spring–Summer 1970): 28, 29–30, 35.

16. Boggs, "Myth and Irrationality," 32. On the dialectic between optimism and dystopian thinking that pervaded ideas of a "post-industrial society," see Howard Brick, "Optimism of the Mind: Imagining Postindustrial Society in the 1960s and 1970s," *American Quarterly* 44 (September 1994): 348–80.

17. James Forman, "The Black Manifesto," *Review of Black Political Economy* (Spring 1970), 40, 44.

18. National Black Economic Development Conference Program, folder 9, box 4, Kenneth and Sheila Cockrel Papers; Forman, "Black Manifesto," 40. On the takeover of the conference by Forman and his allies, see Dye, "Debate on Reparations," 176–77.

19. Forman, "Black Manifesto," 40–41; Murray Kempton, "The Black Manifesto," *New York Review of Books*, July 10, 1969, https://www.nybooks.com/articles/1969/07/10/the-black-manifesto/.

20. Kempton, "Black Manifesto;" Keith Dye, "The Black Manifesto for Reparations in Detroit: Challenge and Response, 1969," *Michigan Historical Review* 35, no. 2 (Fall 2009): 53–83.

21. Dye, "Black Manifesto for Reparations," 79. On Mae Mallory, see Ashley D. Farmer, "'All the Progress to Be Made Will Be Made by Maladjusted Negroes': Mae Mallory, Black Women's Activism, and the Making of the Black Radical Tradition," *Journal of Social History* 53, no. 2 (Winter 2019): 508–30.

22. Minutes, Steering Committee and Invited Guests, Black Economic Development Conference, August 15, 1969, folder 6, box 1, Dan Georgakas Papers; Minutes of the Executive Meeting, Black Economic Development Conference, Inc., December 14, 1970, folder 6, box 1, Dan Georgakas Papers; Dan Georgakas and Marvin Surkin, *Detroit, I Do Mind Dying: A Study in Urban Revolution* (1975; New York: South End, 1998), 80; Countryman, *Up South*, 270, 281.

23. Georgakas and Surkin, *Detroit, I Do Mind*, 107–130; "A Brief History of Black Economic Development Conference, April 1969–October 1972," folder 9, box 4, Kenneth and Sheila Cockrel Papers.

24. Kempton, "Black Manifesto;" Dye, "Black Manifesto for Reparations," 83.

25. For more on this point, and on the manifesto's place in the longer history of Black demands for reparations, see Walter Johnson, "Slavery, Reparations, and the Mythic March of Freedom, *Raritan* 27, no. 2 (Fall 2007): 41–67.

26. Johanna Fernández, *The Young Lords: A Radical History* (Chapel Hill: University of North Carolina Press, 2020); Paul Chaat Smith and Robert Allen Warrior, *Like a Hurricane: The Indian Movement from Alcatraz to Wounded Knee* (New York: New Press, 1996).

27. Jakobi Williams, *From the Bullet to the Ballot: The Illinois Chapter of the Black Panther Party and Racial Coalition Politics in Chicago* (Chapel Hill: University of North Carolina Press, 2013).

28. Kyle T. Mays, *An Afro-Indigenous History of the United States* (Boston: Beacon, 2021), 123–33.

29. Deloria, *Custer Died for Your Sins*, 2. On Deloria, see especially David Martínez, *Life of the Indigenous Mind: Vine Deloria Jr. and the Birth of the Red Power Movement* (Lincoln: University of Nebraska Press, 2019); and Temin, *Remapping Sovereignty*.

30. Deloria, *Custer Died for Your Sins*, 7–8, 170. For more analysis of the challenges Indigenous activists faced in formulating their political vision between the frameworks of civil rights and national liberation in this era, see Bruyneel, *The Third Space of Sovereignty*, 123–69. The persistent failures of frameworks of legal and cultural recognition for Indigenous nations is addressed further in Glen Coulthard, *Red Skin, White Masks: Rejecting the Colonial Politics of Recognition* (Minneapolis: University of Minnesota Press, 2014).

31. Deloria, *Custer Died for Your Sins*, 174, 179, 180.

32. Deloria, *Custer Died for Your Sins*, 181; Kyle Mays, "A Provocation of the Modes of Black Indigeneity: Culture, Language, Possibilities," *Ethnic Studies Review* 44, no. 2 (Summer 2021): 42. See also Robin D. G. Kelley, "The Rest of Us: Rethinking Settler and Native," *American Quarterly* 69, no. 2 (June 2017): 267–76.

33. Deloria, *Custer Died for Your Sins*, 26, 193. On development politics and American Indian activism, see especially Cobb, *Native Activism*; and Megan Black, *The Global Interior: Mineral Frontiers and American Power* (Cambridge, MA: Harvard University Press, 2018).

34. Rana, *The Constitutional Bind*, 590–96, quoted at 592.

35. Berger and Dunbar-Ortiz, "'The Struggle Is for Land!': Race, Territory, and National Liberation," in *The Hidden 1970s: Histories of Radicalism*, ed. Dan Berger (New Brunswick, NJ: Rutgers University Press, 2010), 57–76; Ward Churchill and Jim Vander Wall, *Agents of Repression: The FBI's Secret Wars against the Black Panther Party and the American Indian Movement* (Cambridge, MA: South End Press, 1988).

36. Joshua Bloom and Waldo E. Martin Jr., *Black against Empire: The History and Politics of the Black Panther Party* (Oakland: University of California Press, 2013), 66–73, 122–23; Malloy, *Out of Oakland*, 110–114; Nikhil Pal Singh, "The Black Panthers and the 'Undeveloped Country' of the Left," in *The Black Panther Party Reconsidered*, ed. Charles E. Jones (Baltimore: Black Classic Press, 1998), 57–105; Yohuru R. Williams, "American Exported Black Nationalism: The Student Nonviolent Coordinating Committee, the Black Panther Party, and the Worldwide Freedom Struggle, 1967–1972," *Negro History Bulletin* 60, no. 3 (July–September 1997): 13–20.

37. Malcolm X, "The Ballot or the Bullet," in *Malcolm X Speaks: Selected Speeches and Statements*, ed. George Breitman (New York: Grove, 1965), 35. On Cleaver's central role in elaborating the demand for a plebiscite, see Malloy, *Out of Oakland*, 112. For an analysis of the Republic of New Afrika's demand for a UN plebiscite, and the group's broader engagement with international legal arguments, see Sam Klug, "'What, Then, of the Land?': Territoriality, International Law, and the Republic of New Afrika," *Journal of the History of International Law* 23, no. 1 (February 2021): 184–205.

38. *Black Panther*, May 4, 1968, 7; Eldridge Cleaver, "The Land Question and Black Liberation," in *Eldridge Cleaver: Post-Prison Writings and Speeches*, ed. Robert Scheer (New York: Random House, 1969), 61, 67.

39. Cleaver, "Land Question," 67. The claim-making strategies of "states-in-waiting," or national minorities who asserted a right of self-determination *within* postcolonial states, are explored in Lydia Walker, *States-in-Waiting: A Counternarrative of Global Decolonization* (Cambridge: Cambridge University Press, 2024).

40. Malloy, *Out of Oakland*, 114.

41. Lydia Walker, "Decolonization in the 1960s: On Legitimate and Illegitimate Nationalist Claims-Making," *Past & Present* 242, no. 1 (February 2019): 233.

42. Bloom and Martin, *Black against Empire*, 354; Farmer, *Remaking Black Power*, 77–92; Alondra Nelson, *Body and Soul: The Black Panther Party and the Fight against Medical Discrimination* (Minneapolis: University of Minnesota Press, 2013), 61–64.

43. Huey P. Newton, "Speech Delivered at Boston College: November 18, 1970," and Huey P. Newton, "Intercommunalism: February 1971," in *The Huey P. Newton Reader*, ed. David Hilliard and Donald Weise (New York: Seven Stories, 2002), 160–75, 181–99. Judson L. Jeffries argues that Newton's philosophy of intercommunalism "grew out of the Panthers' fundamental ideological position on internationalism," but in fact it marked an important shift. See Judson L. Jeffries, *Huey P. Newton: The Radical Theorist* (Oxford: University Press of Mississippi, 2002), 79. More sensitive to the evolving nature of Newton's views on the international order are Cedric G. Johnson, "Huey P. Newton and the Last Days of the Black Colony," in *African American Political Thought: A Collected History*, ed. Melvin L. Rogers and Jack Turner (Chicago: University of Chicago Press, 2021), 631–59; John Narayan, "Huey P. Newton's Intercommunalism: An Unacknowledged Theory of Empire," *Theory, Culture & Society*, online only (2017): doi 10.1177/0263276417741348; and Malloy, *Out of Oakland*, 174–81. For an analysis of the shift to a "pointillist" version of US hegemony—one that relied on control of military bases, technologies of communication, and standardization of commercial objects and social practices, but only minimally on territorial sovereignty—see Immerwahr, *How to Hide an Empire*, 213–401.

44. Newton, "Speech Delivered at Boston," 169; Newton, "Intercommunalism," 187. On the "waning of territoriality," see Charles S. Maier, "Consigning the Twentieth Century to History: Alternative Narratives for the Modern Era," *American Historical Review* 105, no. 3 (June 2000): 807–31, quoted at 818. On the "Black spatial imaginary," see George Lipsitz, *How Racism Takes Place* (Philadelphia: Temple University Press, 2011).

45. Newton, "Intercommunalism," 188, 187.

46. James Boggs to unknown recipient, March 28, 1973, folder 10, box 2, James and Grace Lee Boggs Papers.

47. The Institute of the Black World in Atlanta represents one example. See Institute of the Black World, ed., *Education and Black Struggle: Notes from the Colonized World* (Cambridge, MA: Harvard Educational Review, 1974); Derrick E. White, *The Challenge of Blackness: The Institute of the Black World and Political Activism in the 1970s* (Gainesville: University Press of Florida, 2011).

48. Robert L. Allen became senior editor of *The Black Scholar* in 1971. For an examination of the social and intellectual history of Black Studies at San Francisco State University, see Biondi, *The Black Revolution on Campus*, 43–78. For more on Robert Browne's career, see Judy Tzu-Chun Wu, *Radicals on the Road: Internationalism, Orientalism, and Feminism during the Vietnam Era* (Ithaca, NY: Cornell University Press, 2013).

49. Robert Blauner, *Racial Oppression in America* (New York: Harper & Row, 1972); William K. Tabb, *The Political Economy of the Black Ghetto* (New York: W. W. Norton, 1970); Donald J.

Harris, "The Black Ghetto as Colony: A Theoretical Critique and Alternative Formulation," *Review of Black Political Economy* 2, no. 4 (Summer 1972): 3–33; William K. Tabb, "Marxian Exploitation and Domestic Colonialism: A Reply to Donald J. Harris," *Review of Black Political Economy* 4, no. 4 (December 1974): 69–87.

50. Drake and Cayton, *Black Metropolis*, 762, 767.

51. St. Clair Drake, "The 'Internal Colony': Mere Analogy or Scientific Concept?," pp. 1, 21–24, folder 8, box 23, St. Clair Drake Papers.

52. Drake, " 'Internal Colony,' " 9, 22.

53. Brenda Gayle Plummer, *In Search of Power: African Americans in the Era of Decolonization, 1956–1974* (Cambridge: Cambridge University Press, 2012), 193–99; Getachew, *Worldmaking after Empire*, 176–81.

54. UN General Assembly, *Resolution 3201*, "Declaration on the Establishment of a New International Economic Order," May 1, 1974, http://www.un-documents.net/s6r3201.htm. On the NIEO, see especially Getachew, *Worldmaking after Empire*, 142–75; Moyn, *Not Enough*, 89–118; Vanessa Ogle, "State Rights against Private Capital: The 'New International Economic Order' and the Struggle over Aid, Trade, and Foreign Investment, 1962–1981," *Humanity* 5, no. 2 (Summer 2014): 211–34; Johanna Bockman, "Socialist Globalization against Capitalist Neocolonialism: The Economic Ideas Behind the New International Economic Order," *Humanity* 6, no. 1 (Spring 2015): 109–28; and Umut Özsu, *Completing Humanity: The International Law of Decolonization, 1960–82* (Cambridge: Cambridge University Press, 2023), 104–55.

55. "Address by Secretary of State Kissinger: The Challenge of Interdependence," New York, April 15, 1974, *FRUS, 1969–1976*, vol. XXXVIII, doc. 32: https://history.state.gov/historicaldocuments/frus1969-76v38p1/d32; Daniel J. Sargent, *A Superpower Transformed: The Remaking of American Foreign Relations in the 1970s* (New York: Oxford University Press, 2015), 153, 165–97.

56. Michael Franczak, "Losing the Battle, Winning the War: Neoconservatives versus the New International Economic Order, 1974–82," *Diplomatic History* 43, no. 5 (2019): 867–89; Michael Franczak, *Global Inequality and American Foreign Policy in the 1970s* (Ithaca, NY: Cornell University Press, 2022), 63–94.

57. Daniel Patrick Moynihan, "The United States in Opposition," *Commentary* 59 (March 1975): https://www.commentarymagazine.com/articles/daniel-moynihan/the-united-states-in-opposition/. For more on Laski's influence on anticolonial thought, especially in India, see Karuna Mantena, "On Gandhi's Critique of the State: Sources, Contexts, Conjunctures," *Modern Intellectual History* 9, no. 3 (November 2012): 535–63; and Nazmul Sultan, "Between the Many and the One: Anticolonial Federalism and Popular Sovereignty," *Political Theory* 50, no. 2 (April 2022): 247–74.

58. Moynihan, "United States in Opposition;" Robert W. Tucker, "Oil: The Issue of American Intervention," *Commentary* 57 (January 1975): https://www.commentary.org/articles/tucker-robert-w/oil-the-issue-of-american-intervention/.

59. Franczak, "Losing the Battle," 878–79.

60. Office of Policy Planning and Research, United States Department of Labor, *The Negro Family: The Case for National Action* (Washington, DC: Government Printing Office, 1965); St. Clair Drake, "Moynihan and the Third World," *The Nation*, July 5, 1975, 8–13. On Moynihan's "benign neglect" memo, see Geary, *Beyond Civil Rights*, 199–205.

61. Drake, " 'Internal Colony,' " 22.

Epilogue

1. On cultural nationalist organizations' retreat from political organizing, see especially Rickford, *We Are an African People*, 219–52; and Scot Brown, *Fighting for US: Maulana Karenga, the US Organization, and Black Cultural Nationalism* (New York: New York University Press, 2003). On the Black Panther Party's electoral work in Oakland, see especially Murch, *Living for the City*, 191–228; and Robyn C. Spencer, *The Revolution Has Come: Black Power, Gender, and the Black Panther Party in Oakland* (Durham, NC: Duke University Press, 2016), 143–76. On the work of the TWWA into the late 1970s, see Farmer, *Remaking Black Power*, 159–92.

2. On the respective approaches of the Carter and Reagan administrations to the UN and the decolonizing world, see Sean T. Byrnes, *Disunited Nations: US Foreign Policy, Anti-Americanism, and the Rise of the New Right* (Baton Rouge: Louisiana State University Press, 2021), 153–89. On human rights in US foreign policy in the 1970s, see especially Samuel Moyn, *The Last Utopia: Human Rights in History* (Cambridge, MA: Harvard University Press, 2010); Sargent, *A Superpower Transformed*, especially 198–228; Barbara J. Keys, *Reclaiming American Virtue: The Human Rights Revolution of the 1970s* (Cambridge, MA: Harvard University Press, 2014); and Sarah B. Snyder, *From Selma to Moscow: How Human Rights Activists Transformed U.S. Foreign Policy* (New York: Columbia University Press, 2018). On the international economic consequences of the "Volcker shock," see Leo Panitch and Sam Gindin, *The Making of Global Capitalism: The Political Economy of American Empire* (New York: Verso, 2013), ch. 6.

3. On the pastoralist vision in Black nationalism, see Russell Rickford, "'We Can't Grow Food on All This Concrete': The Land Question, Agrarianism, and Black Nationalist Thought in the Late 1960s and 1970s," *Journal of American History* 103, no. 4 (March 2017): 956–80. For Wilson's views on the "underclass," see William Julius Wilson, *The Truly Disadvantaged: The Inner City, the Underclass, and Public Policy* (Chicago: University of Chicago Press, 1987). For a critical examination of the "underclass" idea, see especially Adolph Reed Jr., "The 'Underclass' as Myth and Symbol: The Poverty of Discourse about Poverty," in *Stirrings in the Jug: Black Politics in the Post-Segregation Era* (Minneapolis: University of Minnesota Press, 1999), 179–96.

4. Harold Cruse, citing historian Theodore Draper, refers to Black nationalism as the "rejected strain" in African American politics in *The Crisis of the Negro Intellectual*. See Cruse, *The Crisis of the Negro Intellectual*, 4. On TransAfrica, see Randall Robinson, *Defending the Spirit: A Black Life in America* (New York: Penguin, 1999). On the foreign policy of Mickey Leland and the Congressional Black Caucus, see Benjamin Talton, *In This Land of Plenty: Mickey Leland and Africa in American Politics* (Philadelphia: University of Pennsylvania Press, 2019). On Jesse Jackson's messages about South Africa and Palestine in his presidential campaigns, see especially Karin L. Stanford, *Beyond the Boundaries: Reverend Jesse Jackson in International Affairs* (Albany: State University of New York Press, 1997), 137–60; and Michael R. Fischbach, *Black Power and Palestine: Transnational Countries of Color* (Stanford, CA: Stanford University Press, 2018), ch. 10.

5. Aziz Rana, "Decolonizing Obama," *n+1 Magazine* 27 (Winter 2017), https://www.nplus onemag.com/issue-27/politics/decolonizing-obama/.

6. US Department of State, Bureau of Cultural and Educational Affairs, "Mandela Washington Fellowship for Young Leaders," https://www.mandelawashingtonfellowship.org/; Barack Obama, "Remarks by the President in Town Hall with the Washington Fellowship for Young African Leaders," July 28, 2014, Obama White House Archives, https://obamawhitehouse.archives .gov/the-press-office/2014/07/28/remarks-president-town-hall-washington-fellowship-young -african-leaders.

7. Obama, "Remarks by the President."

8. Destin Jenkins, *The Bonds of Inequality: Debt and the Making of the American City* (Chicago: University of Chicago Press, 2021), 15, 18.

9. Michelle Kaske and Jim Wyss, "Puerto Rico Is Out of Bankruptcy After a $22 Billion Debt Exchange," *Bloomberg*, March 14, 2022, https://www.bloomberg.com/news/articles/2022-03 -15/puerto-rico-bankruptcy-set-to-end-with-22-billion-debt-exchange#xj4y7vzkg; "World Bank Releases $100 Million for Zambia amid Substantial Delays in Debt Restructuring," World Bank Press Release, December 20, 2022, https://www.worldbank.org/en/news/press-release/2022/12/20 /world-bank-releases-100-million-for-zambia-amid-substantial-delays-in-debt-restructuring; Theophilus Acheampong, "Ghana's Debt Restructuring Has Stalled: Here's Why," *The Conversation*, January 25, 2023, https://theconversation.com/ghanas-domestic-debt-restructuring-has-stalled -four-reasons-why-198239.

10. Scott Kurashige, *The Fifty-Year Rebellion: How the U.S. Political Crisis Began in Detroit* (Oakland: University of California Press, 2017); Jerome Roos, *Why Not Default?: The Political Economy of Sovereign Debt* (Princeton, NJ: Princeton University Press, 2019).

Index